To Cai
from V

Happy Birthday!
2025

MINNIE PALLISTER

THE VOICE OF A REBEL

Alun Burge

PARTHIAN

Parthian, Cardigan SA43 1ED
www.parthianbooks.com
© Alun Burge 2023
ISBN 978-1-914595-79-0
Edited by Dai Smith
Typeset by Elaine Sharples
Printed by 4edge Limited
Published with the financial support of the Books Council of Wales.
The Modern Wales series receives support from the Rhys Davies Trust.

the RHYS DAVIES TRUST

British Library Cataloguing in Publication Data
A cataloguing record for this book is available from the British Library.
Every attempt has been made to secure the permission of copyright holders to reproduce archival and printed material.

To Hywel, my friend

*Minnie Pallister
1918*

CONTENTS

Abbreviations

Introduction 1

PART ONE – FEARLESS 7
1. A Pilgrim's Progress, 1885–1914 9
2. 'A New Star on the Horizon', 1914–1918 33
3. Organiser, 1918–1922 71
4. Propagandist, 1923–1926 119

PART TWO – DARING TO BE 159
5. Invalid, 1927–1932 161
6. Writer and Journalist, 1933–1937 201
7. A Pacifist in Total War, 1938–1945 237
8. Broadcaster, 1945–1960 297

Acknowledgements
Photos
Index

ABBREVIATIONS

AGM	Annual General Meeting
ASLEF	Associated Society of Locomotive Engineers and Firemen
BBC	British Broadcasting Corporation
BPP	British People's Party
BUF	British Union of Fascists
CO	Conscientious Objector
CND	Campaign for Nuclear Disarmament
CPGB	Communist Party of Great Britain
DLP	Divisional Labour Party
DORA	Defence of the Realm Act
ILP	Independent Labour Party
J.R.M	James Ramsay MacDonald
LPF	Labour Pacifist Fellowship/Labour Peace Fellowship
MFGB	Miners' Federation of Great Britain
MOI	Ministry of Information
NAC	National Administrative Council
NEC	National Executive Committee
NCAC	National Council Against Conscription
NCCL	National Council for Civil Liberties
NCF	No Conscription Fellowship
NFWT	National Federation of Women Teachers
NMWM	No More War Movement
NUDAW	National Union of Distributive and Allied Workers
NUR	National Union of Railwaymen
NUT	National Union of Teachers
PPU	Peace Pledge Union
RIO	Regional Information Officer

RKP	Routledge and Keegan Paul
SLP	Socialist Labour Party
SWMF	South Wales Miners' Federation
SWSS	South Wales Socialist Society
TUC	Trades Union Congress
UDC	Union of Democratic Control
WAC	Women's Advisory Committee
WFL	Women's Freedom League
WGC	Welwyn Garden City
WI	Women's Institute
WSF	Workers' Suffrage Federation

INTRODUCTION

'the real lives of people as we set them in biographies are often so glamorous and so romantic and so fantastic that nothing – not even the most extraordinary thriller – can come up to them.' (Minnie Pallister, 'Talking About Reading', *Woman's Hour*, 10 May 1951)

Even before she was identified by Keir Hardie in 1915 as a new star bursting over the political horizon, Minnie Pallister's life was exceptional. Later, whether she was making rousing speeches from halls and hillsides, under police surveillance and twice accused of sedition for her opposition to the Great War, rescuing Jews from Nazi Germany, being banned by the BBC for her politics or likely inspiring a character of Spike Milligan in his writing of *The Goon Show*, she was such a compelling figure that *Woman's Hour* serialised her 'Life Story' over five episodes in one week during her lifetime.

Minnie Pallister emerged from the male-dominated, heavily industrial South Wales valleys, where women had difficulty being accepted as public figures, to become one of the most important woman Labour politicians from Wales of the first half of the twentieth century. In the way she helped embed Labour as a political force and instil in people a belief that the future was in their own hands, she made an invaluable contribution to the shaping of modern Wales. Fearless, principled and always challenging, not least around gender, Minnie worked tirelessly for the causes to which she was committed: socialism, pacifism and, of course, feminism. As an outstanding woman to emerge from the Independent Labour Party, Minnie was to Wales what Jennie Lee was to Scotland and Ellen Wilkinson was to England. Perhaps the first person ever to make a political broadcast on radio, she was one of the first women to stand for Parliament and between the two world wars influenced the development of a woman's agenda within Labour both in Britain and abroad. Hailed as the best woman socialist orator in the country, her intellect, personality and platform presence helped propel her to the high echelons of Labour politics. Through all, her voice – *that* voice – defined her and set her apart. On the brink of an outstanding political career in which she could reasonably have reached high government office, Minnie suffered a catastrophic illness. Starting with a loss of her voice, it overwhelmed her body, removed her from public life and reduced her to the edge of penury. Required to find different ways of expressing herself and earning a living, after years of invalidity, she recovered to reinvent herself as a journalist on the *Daily Herald*. Almost by chance she became one of the first pioneering 'agony aunts' on what was the largest newspaper in the country. Then, after more than a decade of silence, she found voice sufficiently to become a lauded broadcaster for a new radio audience. Minnie's willingness to publicly share her infirmity and its consequences, in print and on-air, mark her out as one of the early originators of the 'illness memoir', a comparatively rare phenomenon at the time.

Always pushing the BBC to get her radical agenda accepted, twice she was taken off-air because of her outspoken politics or principles, including for her pacifism during the Second World War when again she came under the watchful eye of the authorities. A household name on the radio throughout the 1950s, Minnie was an outstanding presence on *Woman's Hour*, lending a cutting edge to the more housewifely fare of light entertainment and domestic assurance. Often difficult to handle, she helped change the ways women saw themselves and their life situations. All the while, Minnie worked with and through women's organisations, not least Women's Institutes, promoting radical change by gently forming the outlooks of 'ordinary' women. From the 1920s to 1950s, she was an exceptional advocate of women's rights, tackling issues of equality and gender relations in a way that makes her a forerunner of the Women's Liberation Movement, helping to lay the foundations for women's rights today. Previously unrecognised, she is an outstanding feminist of the twentieth century.

Minnie's character was paradoxical. Her gaiety of spirit masked a powerful intellect. Her inner strength was shot through with self-doubt. Combining fearlessness and insecurity, she was brave enough to take on police authorities in Nazi Germany, yet would not sleep in a house alone. Able to dominate audiences of thousands, she would be unable to enjoy the occasion as she fretted over the thickness of her ankles. Through it all, though, even when

INTRODUCTION

her voice was silenced by infirmity, one element was unshakable – Minnie Pallister was a rebel at heart.[1]

Minnie's life defies easy categorisation. For the first thirty-seven years, hers was primarily a story of Wales and its politics, albeit one that impinged heavily on the wider British agenda. Minnie's second thirty-seven years were lived in England and she operated at a British level, primarily in journalism, broadcasting and through women's organisations and issues. Her career did not have linear progression and circumstances made her existence a series of sharp lurches, including occupying different jobs at different times in different places, complicated by her regular moves within and between Wales and England. Her sometimes erratic and uneven life comprised a series of disjunctures that render her elusive and contribute to her erasure from both Welsh and British popular memory. The challenge in rescuing Minnie has been to strike a balance between locating her early importance in Wales with that more widely later.

Minnie Pallister has lain practically unnoticed, largely absent from history as it has been written (rather than as it happened). She is an almost unheard-of figure with just passing references, the occasional glimpse, sometimes inexplicable, in the stories of others. In an obscure Parliamentary debate about transport networks in May 1970, Michael Foot evoked the memory of four socialist symbols – the Chartists, the hunger marchers, Minnie Pallister and Aneurin Bevan.[2] Such was her importance that Foot claimed that after she spoke from a soapbox in Tredegar Circle, they carried it over the mountains to Merthyr as a sort of relic so that it could be seen there.

The playwright, Trevor Griffiths, in his 1997 BBC TV drama, *Food for Ravens*, has Aneurin Bevan, near to death, memorialising an episode from his youth:

> Once. When I was young and easy. Your age. I carried a stool across a mountain. For Minnie Pallister to sit on. I'd written her a poem. I had it in my pocket.[3]

What's more, it happened. One of Bevan's first political acts *was* to carry the stool for Minnie to speak on a mountain top.[4] Minnie died in March 1960, four months before Nye, and the story was repeated by Foot in his 1962 biography, adding Nye always remembered the event.[5] But still no one grasped the importance of Minnie Pallister.

*

Writing the biography of an almost unknown person is like completing a gigantic jigsaw puzzle without a picture on the box. Normally, when starting research, you have a sense of what you're looking for, based in an understanding of time and place built up over the years as well as using the work of others. Searching for Minnie Pallister, by contrast, requires initially contending with a paucity of material. No collections of her papers exist, and her diaries are long lost. Other avenues, too, remain closed. Without any surviving close relatives, personal information – the sort that exists in family lore – was not passed down the generations to provide insight.

Although Minnie was an inveterate letter writer, apart from online references to a handful that survived in the collections of Vera Brittain, Norman Angell and George Orwell, initially there were only two sources of her correspondence – an incomplete and partial clutch in the papers of Ramsay MacDonald and her personal files at the BBC covering the last twenty or so years of her life. The archival record is particularly scant in terms of her personal life, and specifically of her relationships with men. The fragments of evidence that remain from 1916 and 1919 offer tantalising glimpses that suggest that her personal life was as dramatic and colourful as her public persona. Salvation lays in Minnie's published writings. Over six hundred articles, mainly from labour papers from the 1920s and 1930s, over one hundred and fifty radio scripts between 1938 and 1960, and her books and pamphlets contain autobiographical material which provides essential clues.

This biography is mainly chronological, though it occasionally deviates, fast-forwarding across decades. Only in that way is it possible to create a sense of her *being*. Mirroring her experience of a life cleaved by illness, this book is divided in two parts, and is reflected in its feel. The more episodic account of her life until 1926 is built from the printed sources available and from Minnie's own accounts. After 1927, access to personal correspondence gives the narrative a different texture.

Minnie's life illuminates many aspects of British history in the

INTRODUCTION

twentieth century. She adds a personal nuance to the public events through which she lived and brings us insights into the lives of those around her. Avid watchers of Bertrand Russell will delight in the goings-on of the summer of 1916. By looking at Ramsay MacDonald through Minnie's life, he is seen less as a political outcast and viewed in a more human light. And yet she stands as a significant figure in her own right. Politician, orator, pamphleteer, organiser, Minnie Pallister contributed to the shaping of modern Wales and its politics. An outstanding feminist, she also helped define and redefine women's broadcasting. Her messages on gender still resonate. Minnie Pallister remained a rebel until her last breath. Her voice deserves to be heard once again.

Alun Burge
Swansea

---

[1] This last point is adapted from Stuart Morris, 'The Flowers That Minnie Pallister Planted', *Woman's Hour* (*WH*), transmitted 27 March 1961.

[2] Welsh Grand Committee, 13 May 1970, Debate on Local Government Reorganisation in Glamorgan and Monmouthshire, Columns 22–26.

[3] Quoted in Trevor Griffiths, *Food for Ravens*, Oberon Books, 1998, p. 48.

[4] Minnie Pallister to Miss Molony, 26 February 1946, BBC Written Archives Centre (BBC/WAC) RCONT1 Pallister, Minnie (Talks file 3b).

[5] Michael Foot, *Aneurin Bevan 1897–1945*, MacGibbon and Kee, 1962, p. 26.

PART ONE
FEARLESS

CHAPTER ONE
A Pilgrim's Progress

In 1899, Rev William Pallister and his family – wife Rose, eldest daughter Julia, youngest daughter Gladys, and fourteen-year-old Minnie – went to live in Haverfordwest in Pembrokeshire. For the next twenty-three years Minnie lived in Wales and forever afterwards considered it to be her spiritual home.[1] Before Haverfordwest, her life, though relatively comfortable, had been as rootless geographically as it was rooted spiritually.[2] Born in Cornwall in 1885, the family's itinerant lifestyle took Minnie around the Methodist church circuits of Lancashire, Lincolnshire, Cumbria and Leicestershire before she arrived in Wales. She later asserted that her life had been shaped by her father William's occupation as a Wesleyan Methodist minister and the regular family removals.[3]

William had started work as a Durham coal miner, following his own father down the pit, but something had stirred. He left the mine in 1875, at around 24 years of age, to become ordained.[4] He married Rose, the daughter of a Wiltshire farmer, who was also a preacher and a progressive, in 1880. Theirs was an accomplished household and Minnie had both music and drawing tutors who introduced her to tools that enriched her life enormously.[5] With a domestic servant, none of the three sisters were expected to prioritise domestic duties, though Minnie learned cookery skills from her mother while inheriting her father's love of gardening. The enlightened nature of the household was evidenced by Rose teaching a maid to play the piano, an act which Minnie considered revolutionary.[6] Parental influences were strong but, with her parents occupied with church functions, Minnie thought she and her sisters may have had less of a family life than other children.[7]

An infant prodigy, Minnie could recite lengthy poems aged 3. She claimed that at an early age she was an expert in theology and believed that she had been born into the world to be and do good, and wanted as a child to be a missionary.[8] Her sheltered upbringing revolved around school, where she excelled in the classroom, and the Methodist Church.[9] Saturdays were spent working for good causes with Sundays reserved for worship. In the Pallister household, doing *anything* on Sundays, including reading novels or going to concerts, art galleries and parks and museums, was prohibited: people who did such things were considered 'not quite nice to know'.[10] As she grew out of childhood such strictures began to chafe, attending church became a matter of habit, and Sundays were a ritual to be endured. Although she had a strong faith, she had not yet discovered the Bible as either 'a supremely fascinating historical document or as a living guide to life'.[11]

In Haverfordwest, Minnie attended Tasker's, an old established and elite girls' school, where she won scholarships and prizes for scholastic attainment. By her mid-teens, she was an accomplished performer and pianist, earning encores for her recitations and playing a concert duet with Julia.[12]

In retrospect, Minnie considered herself to have been an equalitarian by this time, reading the socialist William Morris, the Christian socialist Charles Kingsley and the reports of Seebohm Rowntree and General Booth on social conditions.[13] Minnie thought the writings of Bernard Shaw first taught her to think for herself and gave her life direction. She also read Mrs Humphrey Ward on girls and sweated labour in London slums.[14] There were hints of the 'New Woman'. In 1900, aged 15, she delivered two recitations to a large audience of mainly women on 'Women's Rights'. If the sisters' riding of bicycles to the coast was a symbol of a female vanguard,[15] it was a paradoxical freedom made only partially manageable by the sisters binding their long skirts to the foot by elastic.[16]

Teaching was one of the few professional opportunities open for women. At the time, recalled Minnie, students from middle-class homes were encouraged to become elementary teachers. When she told her mathematics teacher at Tasker's that she intended to teach in an industrial area, the teacher, horrified, replied, 'My dear child you'll have no social standing', illustrating the class expectations and snobbery that constrained women of Minnie's background.[17]

Then, in August 1902, at the same time as the Rev William Pallister became superintendent for the Brynmawr Methodist circuit that included Blaina and Nantyglo in the eastern part of the South Wales coalfield, Minnie transferred to Cardiff Higher Grade School to study for her school matriculation. It was the greatest excitement of her adolescent life for, without brothers, boys were a mystery and joining a mixed class of boys and girls felt wildly romantic.[18] For Minnie, however, Cardiff was a sordid, squalid city. She experienced little enough of it, though, for she lodged with an affluent but deeply religious, narrow-minded family.[19] Sundays in particular were deadly boring as, after three or four attendances at the Wesleyan Chapel during the day, they sang hymns until bedtime.[20]

After matriculating in the London examination's first division, in 1903 Minnie entered the University College of South Wales & Monmouthshire to take a two-year Normal teacher training course.[21] It was still uncommon for a girl to go to university, yet all three Pallister sisters received a good education. Julia became a music teacher and concert pianist, Minnie a schoolteacher and Gladys a dispensing chemist.[22] In the university, the inspirational Millicent Mackenzie, the first female professor in Wales, was responsible for the women's teacher training department. Active in political, social and cultural affairs, Mackenzie became associated with the women's suffrage movement and the Independent Labour Party (ILP), before becoming the first woman Labour Parliamentary candidate in Wales, standing for the University of Wales constituency.[23] However, neither university nor Mackenzie had much impact in broadening Minnie's outlook. She later acknowledged that she did little more than dutifully pass exams there and in 1905 took the Queen's Scholarship Examination and was awarded a double first.[24]

One reason Minnie offered as later explanation for her lack of involvement in public life was that she became engaged to be married.[25] In the image Minnie later projected of herself she said she became engaged only because of the flaw in her personality in doing whatever she was asked, so when a man asked her to marry him she agreed, but never got as far as actually marrying. On another occasion she wrote that from an early age she had an intense dislike of the idea of marriage.[26] Minnie later had different versions of her past for different audiences.

Minnie recognised that chance played an important part in moulding her life's direction. Had there been teaching vacancies in Cardiff when she qualified, she speculated, she would probably have continued lodging with the Methodist family, might have married, and would not have come into contact with politics.[27]

There was a second factor. In 1905 William Pallister and the family home moved from Brynmawr to Gower when he became Minister of Pitton Methodist Chapel, but there he suffered a stroke from which he never properly recovered.[28] Minnie returned to live in the new family home in the west, possibly to provide support. His faculties impaired, William was unable to fully carry out his duties. He was moved after only two years before becoming a supernumerary in 1910 and retired in Southampton in 1911, where Gladys, still living with her parents, studied at university.[29] In retirement William and Rose lived near other former members of the Methodist circuit who provided a friendship network.

It was probably her father's connections rather than mere coincidence that led to Minnie obtaining a teaching post in Brynmawr. Minnie was nearly 21 years old and the 'greenest thing ever' when she started as a Head Certificated Assistant at Brynmawr Elementary School on 26 February 1906, earning £70 a year.[30] Pitchforked into a school with a habitually drunken headmaster, her nerves were taken to breaking point by the mental and physical exhaustion of attempting to teach sixty six-year-olds all day long.[31] Twelve months later, in the head's absence, she was put in charge of the school.[32] Although the family had left the town, Julia still lived there, performing regularly, until her marriage to Bertram Higman in 1909, when she moved to India where Higman had been born and now served as the Chief Commercial Manager on the East India Railway based in Delhi.[33] It was, though, a reassurance in those first professional years of her life for Minnie to have her older sister Julia nearby.

Like the rest of an economically booming South Wales, Brynmawr was a magnet for workers seeking high wages for hard and dangerous work. Prosperous, cosmopolitan, and overwhelmingly working class, its population of seven thousand people was still growing. A centre for shopping and entertainment, it had a strong sense of itself through its own institutions including chapels, friendly societies, and trades unions. Situated at the head of a ribbon of coal communities which meandered down the Western Valley through Blaina and Nantyglo to Abertillery and Cwmtillery, the town marked the edge of the industrial world. To the north lay the Black Mountains and rural mid Wales, only a few miles distant, but a world away in lived experience.

Brynmawr had been established in the early nineteenth century as a new settlement to provide labour to nearby ironworks. As with the rest of the district, it grew rapidly in the following decades. Although it did not initially have either a chapel or a company shop, as transport links improved its accessible location made it a natural hub. Workers and families who settled from elsewhere in Wales and the west of England were joined after 1820 by immigrants from Ireland and it was estimated that in 1822 an estimated 50,000 ironworkers and coal miners lived on the hills between Merthyr and Abergavenny. There Welsh and English languages coexisted in the workplace and on the street and were only divided by chapel denominations.

Brynmawr sat at the edge of the north-west Monmouthshire valleys in an area that became known as 'The Black Domain'. There industrial workers met on isolated hills to organise resistance against the harsh conditions in the ironworks and coal mines and the monopoly position of company shops that kept workers in perpetual debt. Miners, plagued by poor working practices, methods of payment and job insecurity caused by irregular and short-time working and unemployment, were in regular conflict with coal owners.[34] They adopted early forms of collective action, resorting to campaigns of intimidation and violence that would provide a foundation for the deep sense of community, solidarity and social justice that developed in different forms over the next seventy years. Later, the working people of the area looked to Chartism, then friendly societies, co-operatives, trades unions and political parties for different forms and structures through which to collectively improve their lives and protect their interests.

Nothing Minnie had previously experienced prepared her for life in industrial South Wales. When she arrived in 1906 it was to enter an alien world. Her first sight of Brynmawr had been when she had visited her family from university in a blizzard, one Christmas, which she likened to arriving at the end of the world.[35] Now, travelling by train north along valley floors through colliery villages, grown economically strong by the insatiable demand for steam coal from 1860, but matched by a decline in iron and steel working, the sense of the foreign and unfamiliar went beyond the topography and built environment to be fashioned into the very fabric of the society. As she became immersed in the strange, self-contained life of the mining town, where everything pivoted round the colliery, and with all aspects of life 'subordinated to the central fact, the pit' and the needs of its three shifts, she, too, became shaped by its rhythms and routines.[36]

The harsh realities of a valley town, daily working-class life and the circumstances of the children in her classroom revealed aspects of people's existences that forced her to reappraise. Still primarily concerned with saving individuals from the sins of the world and raising money for good causes, Minnie felt depressed at the poverty and suffering as her futile efforts did not address the realities of people's lives and their housing conditions, with their back to back terraces and open street drains.[37] She admired and marvelled at miners' wives, later depicting their life as 'an epic of impossibilities achieved'.[38] Miners' hardships were well documented, she said, but newcomers were staggered by the domestic hardships endured by women and, over decades, Minnie catalogued their labours.[39] Her exposure to the brutal economic and social realities of coal society had a profound effect, posing questions to which her religious faith and hesitant, vaguely Liberal politics had inadequate answers.[40]

Outside school, Minnie's life in Brynmawr, at first, was dominated by the chapel, with its weeknight religious services, class meetings and choir practice, and where she played a dreadful harmonium. She visited neighbouring chapels to hear Welsh sermons just for the beauty of the language. Gradually Minnie became involved in the broader social life of the town, including conducting and accompanying winning juvenile and adult choirs.[41] Inspired by the discipline and unity of purpose of a choir, her love of performing was paralleled by her growing experience in handling and leading large groups of adults as well as children.[42]

After newly-wed Julia emigrated, Minnie lodged with Willie Davies, a colliery clerk in his mid-forties, in his bay-fronted terraced house in Alma Street. Davies was known as 'Willie Davies the blind' since diabetes had badly affected his sight. She probably found the accommodation through a fellow lodger, Lydia Atherall, who was an assistant mistress in the same school as Minnie. Here Minnie found freedom and support, and all three would remain lifelong friends.[43] A novelty was that Saturday nights were free and, with Davies and Atherall, she walked over the mountain to Ebbw Vale to see silent films, as there was no cinema in Brynmawr. Before walking back over the mountain they would buy chips, eating them in the street out of newspaper in 'little abbreviated bags which only grow in chip shops'.[44] An inverted snob about the ways of eating chips, she later used it to exemplify her closeness to working-class culture, contrasting it with the social superiority affected by some others.

Her cloistered existence, one that had sheltered her from worldly pleasures such as dancing, playing cards, going to the theatre or drinking alcohol, now eased as she took advantage of the opportunities available in a vibrant popular culture of the sort that existed locally right across South Wales. Her widening horizons brought her into contact with drama as she produced and acted with the 'Vagabonds' Amateur Dramatic Society and joined the committee of the new Operatic Society, once taking a minor part in a comic operetta, but she acknowledged she had a terrible singing voice. As Minnie's personal boundaries expanded, she even attended a Tennis Club Ball. However, she did not regret having been brought up a puritan, later commenting that she appreciated the values and sense of service it instilled.[45] Holidays were spent visiting her parents and her sister Gladys, when they would walk for miles in the New Forest.[46]

If the world of Brynmawr challenged Minnie, Minnie represented a challenge to Brynmawr. First-generation middle-class professional women such as Minnie, who had degrees of social and economic autonomy, did not fit within established structures of society and unsettled the status quo.[47] Minnie joined a group of single women teacher friends who were active in the town, one of whom was Margaret Judd. Minnie and Judd became joint secretaries of the Brynmawr Mutual Improvement Society where Minnie was also in charge of the musical part of the Society's bioscope, a form of cinema. She provided musical monologues and amusing recitations about contemporary politics, including a satire called 'The Social State'.[48] As with her schoolgirl recitations on women's rights, Minnie observed what was happening in society and commented, though initially she did not actively engage.

Minnie was being shaped both by conditions in Brynmawr and through her work. Tentatively involved in her trades union, when the Brynmawr and District National Union of Teachers (NUT) invited teachers from across the Monmouthshire valleys to a conference to hear Isabel Cleghorn of the National Federation of Women Teachers (NFWT) and Vice-President of the NUT, Minnie drew on her performing skills to provide conference entertainment.[49]

Throughout her later political life, she would use her performing ability as a useful complement to her activism. In contributing to the culture of the movement as well as its politics, she made a winning contribution and earned the admiration that offset some of the insecurities she unnecessarily felt over her appearance.[50]

If it was local conditions that moved Minnie to find new ways of achieving economic and social change, her inspiration for action came from national political figures. She was 'strangely warmed' by a functional talk on Parliament by Will Crooks, MP for Woolwich, probably under the auspices of the Mutual Improvement Society.[51] Then her life changed forever when she encountered socialism at a public meeting held by Victor Grayson, a colourful figure who had shot to prominence after winning a Parliamentary by-election as a socialist candidate in Colne Valley in Yorkshire. Typical of Grayson was his 'racy' speech in Abertillery, four miles down the valley from Brynmawr, when he addressed unemployment, poverty and ownership of the land and looked forward to the time when the House of Commons floor would have to be covered with matting to prevent its scratching with hob nails. The chair of the meeting, Ted Gill, who would become a political comrade of Minnie's, called for the industrial capital of the country to be in the hands of the people.[52] Minnie's fate was sealed when she chaired a meeting of Katharine Bruce Glasier speaking on education in a drab little hall in Ebbw Vale. A socialist propagandist and regular visitor to South Wales, Katharine Bruce Glasier was the first political figure Minnie ever met personally. She brought Minnie into politics, introducing her to a strand of ILP socialism that was not rooted in class conflict and that offered a political avenue to a form of collective salvation that Minnie could embrace wholeheartedly.[53]

The ILP had been established in 1893 and was the 'political heart' of, first, the Labour Representation Committee and, from 1906, the loose alliance of trades unions and socialist societies that made up the Labour Party. The ILP developed a strong base in Scotland and in the cotton and woollen mills of Lancashire and Yorkshire. In South Wales it was much weaker. Poor organisation, low union membership among the miners, and a strong Liberal political and cultural tradition closely linked to nonconformity, limited the ILP to only four branches prior to the 1898 miners' lockout. Merthyr, where a branch was formed in 1897, and where membership grew during the lockout to 278, was one area of strength.

In 1900, based on an alliance of radicals, socialists and trades unionists, Keir Hardie, the towering figure of the ILP, was elected to represent Merthyr in Parliament, so building on the town's distinctive radical history that stretched from the Rising of 1831 through the election of Henry Richard in 1868.[54] The Merthyr experience was not yet repeated elsewhere in South Wales, though by 1910 the Party was gaining ground, and in the Rhondda it was becoming an important part of the labour movement where it provided a 'propagandist fervour and an intellectual edge manifestly sharper than anything else being offered'.[55]

A number of prominent miners' leaders were members of the ILP, including Vernon Hartshorn in Maesteg, Noah Ablett in the Rhondda, C. B. Stanton in Aberdare and James Winstone in Monmouthshire.[56] A generation of younger miners attracted by independent Labour politics included Jim Griffiths in Ammanford and, a few years later, Aneurin Bevan in Tredegar.[57] However, the South Wales Miners' Federation (SWMF), the strong and well-organised union that was formed out of the 1898 lockout, was dominated by a Lib-Lab leadership that was antagonistic to socialism.[58] Only when labourism became a presence across the coalfield would an alliance between trades unionists and the ILP around a Labour platform become possible. That process was underway when, in the Rhondda, the Cambrian Combine dispute in 1910/11 ruptured industrial politics, destroying the South Wales coal industry's conciliatory approach, undermining Lib-Labism, and enabling the rise of socialism and industrial unionism, including the Unofficial Reform Committee with its revolutionary publication, *The Miners' Next Step*.[59]

*

Whatever the differences and divisions in the early twentieth-century South Wales labour movement, one feature was constant – it was an overwhelmingly male environment. The dominance of heavy industry and limited formal employment opportunities for women largely precluded their involvement in trades unions, particularly in comparison with their sisters in the textile areas of Yorkshire and Lancashire – teachers were an exception. Women's Co-operative Guild and Women's Labour League branches, which provided working-class women with means of engaging elsewhere, did not exist in the valleys before 1909/10. Minnie was one of the pioneering Labour women in Wales, like Rose Davies in Aberdare and Elizabeth Andrews in the Rhondda, both of whom were three years older, and also members of the ILP.[60] However, as a comparatively recent arrival to the area, without roots in the working class and with only shallow ones in the labour movement, Minnie's relationship with the wider tumult in South Wales following the convulsion of the Cambrian Combine strike was no more than tangential.

Focussing on party political proselytising rather than industrial issues rooted in class conflict, Minnie applied basic principles to address the most challenging of problems. Displaying an earnestness bordering on innocence, she leapfrogged the incremental gradualism of much of the labour movement, promulgating the notion that through political power and collective action, poverty and sickness might be abolished rather than just alleviated. Hitherto, in her faith-based work, she had been occupied 'rather hopelessly' as a type of social worker with individuals who were poor, drunken, non-believers, or the sick; the ILP's appeal lay in an alternative form of missionary work that offered collective salvation. While Minnie remained a firm abstainer and continued to oppose gambling, her view of sin shifted from being about personal behaviours to recognising that low wages, slums, and unemployment could be the result of social and economic forces beyond an individual's control.[61] She did not wrestle with her faith as much as transfer it from the Church to the ILP. Its radical socialism was, for her, as close as politics could get to Christianity, providing 'a bridge to cross the gaping chasm between the ideals of human brotherhood and the realities of daily life'.[62] While the chapel remained her place of worship, henceforth the Sermon on the Mount was a workable way of life and the ILP was the instrument to achieve it.[63] Jim Griffiths echoed Minnie almost exactly, seeing ILP socialism as a new religion, with the route for achieving its idealistic programme through parliamentary action reflecting the changing temperament of the South Wales coalfield.[64] Even her Sunday observance eased as she participated in ILP events often scheduled for Sunday evenings.

Under the influence of Katharine Bruce Glasier, for Minnie, as for many others, joining the ILP was a life-changing act that involved new ways of being, new friendship networks, and the reorganisation of her life. The Party's mystique, with its own value system based in ethical socialism, and asking moral questions of every issue, appealed to Minnie. The ILP went beyond having an economic analysis of how society should be changed and who owned the means of production to take on the ethical and spiritual aspects of building a new social order. Minnie caught the last phase of such 'New Life Socialism' before it was snuffed out by the deluge of the Great War, though its principles continued to underpin the ILP. For those adherents who looked for social transformation to include relationships, the emancipation of women and sexual liberation and vegetarianism (just as with feminism of the 1970s and 1980s) the personal and political were henceforth indivisible. Over time, Minnie embraced each aspect of her new creed as she built a personal code by which to live. As she later acknowledged to George Orwell, it took her many years to supplement such beliefs with the 'economic foundation of my faith'.[65]

Katharine Bruce Glasier and Minnie had a lot in common. Katharine Bruce Glasier's father was a Congregationalist minister, so both were morally earnest daughters of the Manse with sheltered upbringings. Each became a 'breathless idealist' for the ILP's brand of socialism and campaigned for a complete transformation of all aspects of society whether general economic and social conditions or the situation within one's own life and relationships.[66] Both were highly intelligent and skilled orators. Katharine Bruce Glasier's mentoring of Minnie grew into a lifelong friendship.

The ILP followed the principle that in a democracy nothing can be effectively done without the informed consent of the people. Before the Great War, at street corner meetings, in public halls, on open-air platforms, selling newspapers, writing pamphlets or publishing books, the skills of the ILP propagandist sought to create public opinion.[67] Minnie acted with the conviction of a true believer and accepted – embraced even – the hardships based in discipline and self-sacrifice that had her slogging in all weathers from place to place for years on end, as if a member of a religious sect. Minnie declared that only those who had endured the road of the early socialist evangelists knew how rough it was, as they travelled the length and breadth of Britain.[68] The most effective of proselytisers, she became the missionary she had imagined as a child, albeit a political one. She cast her nets widely.

MINNIE PALLISTER: THE VOICE OF A REBEL

*

A speech by Minnie in late 1911, or early 1912, to the New Era Union in Abertillery was sufficiently memorable for 19-year-old Christopher Grieve, later better known as the Scottish poet Hugh MacDiarmid, to recall it over fifty years later.[69] It is the first early sighting of that combination of voice, intellect and personality which was the essence of Minnie Pallister and that would shape her life's path for the next fifty years. Having arrived in South Wales in 1911, Grieve was a journalist for the *Monmouthshire Labour News* in Ebbw Vale, a newspaper sponsored by the Miners' Federation.[70] He immersed himself in the labour movement, and was actively involved in the ILP, claiming to be instrumental in setting up four branches.[71] That he remembered Minnie alongside other outstanding figures of the South Wales coalfield like Noah Ablett and Frank Hodges indicates a great deal about her personal impact.[72]

Grieve's account in 1911 of anti-Jewish disturbances reported on the events that erupted around Minnie locally. He described the 'pogroms' in Tredegar, Rhymney and Ebbw Vale, spreading to Brynmawr and elsewhere, as his first experience of 'war reporting'. Likening it to living on top of a volcano, he, perhaps implausibly, claimed to have witnessed seventeen baton charges and the Riot Act being read three times in different towns.[73] Yet in her numerous later accounts of her time in Brynmawr, Minnie never referred to these major events. Although they would have been on everyone's lips, perhaps they did not fit her narrative, one that emphasised the good character of the Welsh miners, their eisteddfodau, and dedication to the chapel. Not for the last time did Minnie only report what she wanted to see.

Grieve returned to Scotland in 1912 having fallen foul of the miners' leaders who served on the paper's editorial committee and who objected to the extreme nature of his articles (the contents of which are now lost), and for which he was unrepentant. He described himself as becoming 'shipwrecked on hidden rocks of implacable liberalism and nonconformity suddenly in bright seas of labourist activity'.[74] These too were the waters Minnie navigated.

Another avenue for Minnie to become involved in labour movement activities was through her musical ability. It is not known how her unorthodox contribution in accompanying 'the inimitable "Casey"' (Walter Hampson), came about. Casey was an itinerant ILP entertainer who travelled from town to town in Britain, giving lectures, telling stories and playing his violin, and was described as 'a vehicle for socialist propaganda'.[75] Seeing himself as a wandering minstrel, he was said to bring joy to his audiences with his quirky personality, infectious enthusiasm and musical prowess. An accomplished musician, he had played in Manchester's Hallé orchestra, before being victimised for his Musicians Union activities. He travelled everywhere in stout boots and wore a black velvet coat, with his fiddle slung over his shoulder in a case with leather strap, his only other luggage being a walking stick.[76]

Their first performance together was probably to Newport ILP on a Sunday evening in December 1911.[77] Then, during her school holidays, the pair toured the Monmouthshire valleys 'in the wettest week since the flood',[78] of which Casey wrote that only the pen of Edgar Allen Poe could do justice to the beauty of Blaina, Nantyglo and Ebbw Vale in a thunderstorm.[79] Addressing Minnie as 'My dear Oasis in a Desert of Unsympathetic Piano Smashers', Casey suggested they do a national tour together, with Minnie as pianist and elocutionist.[80] However, that arrangement did not materialise and by 1913 Casey had a permanent accompanist.[81] Minnie and Casey were part of the ILP's rich culture that existed in South Wales either side of the Great War as it sought in a unique way to weave culture, politics and life to build the labour movement and help lay the foundations for a new social order.[82] The adulation Minnie received from their performances provided her with the affirmation on which she thrived and which she would need throughout her life.

Minnie was, at this cusp time, one of a number of ILP teachers who played significant roles in promoting socialism and later opposing the Great War.[83] Teachers, who often came from working-class families, occupied a socially ambiguous position in South Wales.[84] This was reflected in the class-based criticism Minnie experienced when miners taunted her about long, paid holidays. She responded that they would be better off spending their time in the union to get paid holidays for themselves rather than scolding her for hers.[85] Their needs, though, were more basic. When one million British miners started a successful five-week strike for a minimum wage on 1 March 1912, Brynmawr miners picked coal from the tips and dug levels that pock-marked the coal outcrop near the town; Minnie's school stayed open through the Easter holidays to feed their necessitous children.[86]

A month after the strike ended, the 1912 ILP national conference was held in Merthyr. Although some in the Party saw it as an out-of-the-way place, its political, industrial and economic importance placed it at the centre of events.[87] Merthyr was the base of Keir Hardie, while the South Wales valleys had earned the reputation of being industrially and politically the most advanced part of Britain through the Cambrian Combine dispute in the Rhondda, the Tonypandy 'riots', and the victory of the national miners' strike.[88] Primary agents of socialism in South Wales, ILP members were key to the labour movement, even though they were only a minority in it.[89] Keir Hardie's words were harnessed in describing the socialism preached by the ILP as 'parliamentary in character but revolutionary in intention and radical in practice'.[90] With its distinctive socialist position, the ILP, rightly, saw itself as the political vanguard of the Labour Party.[91] Minnie was part of that comparatively small group who were committed to challenging Liberal and Lib-Lab domination, presenting an alternative vision of how society should be and then transforming it through taking over the leadership of their society. Perhaps equally importantly, they helped instil the belief that in doing things for themselves the people themselves could bring about necessary change.[92]

*

Minnie's first national ILP conference was a gateway to a new world. A delegate from Brynmawr, she rubbed shoulders with local and national figures in a political extravaganza. Before the conference started, a Saturday evening women's suffrage demonstration, organised by the Women's Social and Political Union (WSPU), attracted 1,500 people and the following afternoon the National Union of Women's Suffrage Societies (NUWSS) held an open-air demonstration.[93] With major NUWSS, Women's Freedom League (WFL) and WSPU presence at the conference, and pro-suffrage speeches by leading ILP figures Philip Snowden, Hardie and George Lansbury, the conference was dominated by the women's question.[94] More than 3,000 people attended the Party's Sunday evening demonstration that was chaired by Hardie. As speakers and members of the ILP National Administrative Council (NAC) mounted the platform, they were met by waves of cheering.[95]

Attracted by its glamour and excitement, at the same time as the ILP offered a means to change society, it also provided personal opportunities. While she was totally committed to the cause, for which she would gladly sacrifice herself, it also increasingly provided a route for her to pursue personal ambitions. After the national conference, Minnie became more involved in industrial politics when the ILP's 'Campaign for Socialism' directly challenged industrial unionism, which in South Wales was a competing conception of how to build a new society. The campaign argued for the need to achieve political power through Parliament to gain economic freedom, rather than rely on narrow industrial means to achieve change. Declaring that sectional strikes alone were inadequate, it reasoned that the industrial labour movement needed to adopt ILP political principles to address economic and social injustice. The campaign was launched nationally in Brynmawr by Jim Winstone, miners' agent for the Eastern Valleys who the previous month had become Vice-President of the South Wales Miners' Federation (SWMF).[96] He was one of the first socialist miners' leaders in South Wales, was a staunch member of the ILP and edited the *Monmouthshire Labour News*. He would become an ally of Minnie. As competing views within the labour movement contested what were the best means to achieve social transformation, Minnie chaired a Newport meeting on 'The Present and Future of the Labour Movement'.[97] For the next decade she would have to contend with those 'advanced men' who advocated 'direct action' but who saw no incompatibility between their industrial unionism and their membership of the ILP.[98]

*

Attitudes to women within the ILP varied in different parts of Britain, as did the way women's issues were addressed. While formally there was equal membership and no barriers to women's involvement, and it was nominally the political party most open to women and their participation, practice sometimes differed. Yorkshire apparently was more welcoming while Glasgow and London were more hostile. In South Wales, women had participated in the Party since its earliest days, but the ILP was not an empowering environment for them. Nationally it gave precedence to the male worker and his concerns, including the eight-hour day and the minimum wage.[99] Although the ILP might support women's suffrage, with its socialist politics defined by and for males, the ILP did not prioritise women-related issues before the Great War and women members were largely anonymous, assuming responsibility for activities such as the musical programme at events, providing teas and running children's choirs.[100] Minnie, however, was not confined by gendered constraints.

If it was challenging being a young, single, middle class, university-educated, woman, socialist operating within the structures of the male-dominated, industrial, working-class South Wales labour movement, where men's economic and social position dictated that their needs were prioritised, Minnie's intellect, oratory and personality made her difficult to dismiss. Although it would not have been easy for any woman to gain respect or be seen as an equal in such an environment, and many women would have been excluded, marginalised or intimidated, Minnie was able to create a space in which to operate. In the positions she came to hold and in the way she discharged her duties, Minnie shows there could be exceptions to received notions about women's marginalisation in the pre-war labour movement in South Wales.[101]

In September 1912, Minnie was appointed lecture secretary in the Monmouthshire ILP Federation, probably the first woman in South Wales to hold a secretary's post.[102] She immediately organised events, starting with a fortnight's tour of Monmouthshire by Harry Dubery, an ILP lecturer who went from village to village proclaiming the cause.[103] As her profile began to rise, her organisational involvement was both political and cultural. At the 1913 National Eisteddfod in Abergavenny, on the same day that Ted Gill and Jim Winstone spoke at the ILP rally, more than 12,000 people saw Minnie take part in a 'great national pageant', *The Coming of Cymru*, depicting the history of Wales, which she had also helped organise.[104]

One incongruous aspect of her early political activities is Minnie's lack of interest in, or involvement with, the suffrage movement. Even though she was surrounded by its presence, such as at the 1912 ILP Merthyr national conference, she did not participate. Minnie attended one or two suffrage meetings, probably of the Women's Freedom League, which was organised by her friend

Margaret Judd early in 1914, but later acknowledged that the suffragette campaign touched her very little.[105] If there was a part of the suffrage movement with which Minnie would have associated, it was the Women's Freedom League.[106] Militant but non-violent, the WFL used civil disobedience and passive resistance to pursue its ends. While the vote for women was central for the League, its wider agenda promoted women's equality and addressed issues including domestic service and other reforms affecting women.[107] Membership of the League was 'particularly strong' among members of the National Federation of Women Teachers and nationally the League had retained its ILP roots and socialist leanings and meetings were often held under ILP auspices and there was some overlap in membership. However, women's suffrage was outside her political frame of reference.

Instead, Minnie and Katharine Bruce Glasier were part of a significant strand that questioned whether suffrage was the key to achieving social changes. They believed that too much attention was given to the franchise at the cost of addressing economic and social conditions, and that the suffrage campaign drew women away from the more important struggle for socialism.[108] They considered that the structural causes of social ills, including the needs of women, were best addressed by a broader approach of building socialism through the ILP. That included attaining full adult suffrage rather than following the narrower focus on 'Votes for Women'. In the 1950s Minnie explained that her choice of social movements in which to become involved was determined 'consciously or unconsciously' by the extent to which they would help transform society. The election of the 1945–51 Labour governments confirmed her course as having been the right one.[109] By that time, though, Minnie had long admired the 'magnificent organisation and flawless strategy' of the suffrage movement, as well as the sacrifices of 'timid and retiring women' who took part, saying the 'whole thing was stupendous, a miracle of courage, skill, endurance, brilliance, teamwork!'[110] Indeed, she had reversed her earlier position of not operating through the separate women's sphere and, from the 1930s, worked primarily through the women's movement as the best means to achieve changes in women's lives.

However, there is no evidence that, before the Great War, Minnie specifically raised concerns related to the unequal position of women in capitalist society. Although she was conscious of the hardships of miners' wives, in her analysis of poverty and exploitation she did not highlight women's social, economic or political emancipation. She did not prioritise domestic issues, which were of most concern to the women in South Wales. Nor did she engage with the still-nascent women-only organisations of labour that highlighted them.[111] Although within a few years she would demonstrate a natural flair in working with and organising working-class women, before the Great War she operated in the mainstream of labour agitation, displaying a capacity to advance her views in meetings dominated by working-class men. She learned to navigate her way through the male-dominated structures of the ILP, working with, and within, male definitions of socialism, consciously building alliances and friendships that helped her meteoric rise through the mainstream of the Party. Possessing an abundance of charm that equalled her ability and commitment, she thrived in primarily male labour environments.

In June 1914, Minnie was elected President of the Monmouthshire ILP Federation, which had nineteen branches, and became an *ex oficio* member on the ILP's South Wales Divisional Council. She was in all likelihood the first woman to become president of an ILP Federation in Wales, which reflected her capacity and the regard in which others held her. *Common Cause*, 'the organ of the women's movement for reform', stated that hers was probably the highest position held by any Labour woman in Wales.[112] Possessing the skills and presence for others to entrust her with the post, Minnie was still in her twenties. Surrounded by older male figures of stature, she would have needed their support and patronage to become elected. The most likely key influential individuals were Jim Winstone and Ted Gill, who Minnie replaced as president upon his becoming president of the South Wales ILP Division. Gill, of Abertillery, was in his early thirties, a member of the SWMF Executive Committee, and an outstanding presence in Monmouthshire industrial politics.

To mark her presidency, in August 1914, *Llais Llafur* published a long interview with Minnie. She spoke of housing and local government, education, and opportunities for recreation and leisure. At a time when chapels could be hostile to socialists and refuse them use of their rooms, Minnie revealed how close she was to organised religion and the social gospel. Vernon Hartshorn had written that nonconformist leaders (in contrast to those of the Church of

England) were 'amongst his most cunning and unscrupulous enemies', who were 'bitterly opposed' to the socialist and labour movements.[113] ILP members could be expelled from their chapels for their politics, and the deacons of Nazareth Chapel in Mountain Ash forced out Rev George Neighbour, when he refused to agree not to preach socialism. But Minnie cautioned that no good was done to the cause of Labour by a wholesale condemnation of organised Christianity and warned it would be well for the Labour Party, especially in Wales, to remember this. At a time when the issue of women's political rights was to the fore, tellingly, Minnie made no reference to women or their social, economic or political situation.[114]

Her appointment as president coincided with a hard-hitting article by Ellen Wilkinson on women's exclusion from trades union organisations and political parties in 'man-made Socialism'. For Wilkinson, women had to work out for themselves what they wanted from a socialist state. Minnie and Wilkinson shared strikingly similar backgrounds. A Wesleyan Methodist and university-educated, Wilkinson, who was six years younger than Minnie, joined the ILP in 1912 and, like Minnie, was 'practically a vegetarian'. Both opposed gambling and drinking alcohol. Like Minnie, Wilkinson, who was from Manchester, was nurtured into the movement by Katharine Bruce Glasier.[115] But their politics differed over women's suffrage to which Wilkinson was committed and, unlike Wilkinson, Minnie was not yet vocal on the place of women within the labour movement. Over the coming years, as their often intersecting careers ran in parallel, personal and political differences would continue.

Minnie took on the presidency at a key moment. Three days after her interview appeared, Germany invaded Belgium and Britain declared war on Germany. Abruptly and unexpectedly, the country was at war. As the Great War cursed her generation, it transformed Minnie's life, as she fully came of political age.

---

[1] Pallister to Bradney, 7 November 1946, BBC WAC RCONT1 Pallister (Talks 3b).

[2] 'The Lettuce', *Auckland Star*, 18 May 1936.

[3] 'Flowers of My Life', *Woman's Hour* (*WH*), broadcast 6 January 1959.

[4] *An Alphabetical and Chronological Arrangement of the Wesleyan Methodist Ministers and Preachers on Trial in Connection with the British and Irish Conferences*, 1916, John Ryland Library, Manchester University.

[5] Pallister to Scott-Moncrieff, 2 March 1960, BBC WAC RCONT1 Pallister (Talks 10).

MINNIE PALLISTER: THE VOICE OF A REBEL

[6] 'A Puritan Takes Stock', *WH*, 5 April 1955.

[7] 'Flowers of My Life'.

[8] 'Looking Back', BBC, *The Book of Woman's Hour*, Ariel Productions, 1953, pp. 212–3.

[9] 'Memories 1900–1910', *WH*, 21 June 1954.

[10] 'A Puritan Takes Stock'; *Is Your Drinking Really Necessary? The Second Agnes E Slack Saunders lecture*, National British Women's Temperance Association, nd; *Man and Metal*, November 1940; 'Life Story (1)', *WH*, 23 June 1952; 'Looking Back', p. 212.

[11] 'Anniversaries', *WH*, 10 October 1952; 'A Puritan Takes Stock'; Pallister to Scott-Moncrieff, 15 June [1954], BBC WAC RCONT1 Pallister (Talks 6).

[12] Memories 1900–1910'; 'Looking Back', pp. 212–3; *Pembrokeshire Herald and General Advertiser*, 20 September 1901, 16 May & 19 December 1902; *Haverfordwest and Milford Haven Telegraph and General Weekly*, 1 November 1899 & 31 October 1900.

[13] Outline of Proposed Talk on Political Woman in 'Woman Takes a Look at the 20th Century', attached to Pallister to Quigley, 27 May 1954, BBC WAC RCONT1 Pallister (Talks 6).

[14] 'Ends and Beginnings', *WH*, 26 July 1956; Deleted sentence from script 'Memories 1900–1910'.

[15] Sheila Rowbotham, *Dreamers of a New Day*, Verso, 2010, p. 2.

[16] *Haverfordwest and Milford Haven Telegraph and General Weekly*, 19 December 1900; 'Minnie Pallister Talking', *WH*, 21 September 1954; 'Memories 1900–1910'.

[17] 'Memories 1900–1910'.

[18] *Pembrokeshire Herald and General Advertiser*, 22 August 1902; Memories 1900–1910'.

[19] Pallister to Scott-Moncrieff, 15 June [1954], BBC WAC RCONT1 Pallister (Talks 6)

[20] 'The Beauty of Cities', *WH*, 30 May 1958; 'Memories 1900–1910' including deleted section of script.

[21] *Cardiff Times*, 21 February 1903.

[22] 'The Miracle of the Movies', *People's Weekly*, 28 April 1930; 'Life Story (1)'; Gladys Pallister Obituary, *Bexhill Observer*, 11 March 1972.

[23] Beth Jenkins, 'Mackenzie [nee Hughes], (Hettie) Millicent', *Oxford Dictionary of National Biography* (*ODNB*), accessed 9 August 2018; 'In Search of Millicent Mackenzie' session, *To Build a Better World: Millicent Mackenzie 1918 and the Progressive Dream*, day school, Cardiff, 24 November 2018.

[24] *Cap and Gown*, November 1903, Vol 1 No 1, June 1904, Vol 1 No 5 to 1906/7, Vol II No 3, February [1905] & Vol II No 4, March, 1905; Pallister to Scott-Moncrieff, 15 June [1954], BBC WAC RCONT1 Pallister (Talks 6); General Register of Women Students No 1, Normal Department, University College of South Wales & Monmouthshire; *Pioneer*, 11 September 1915.

[25] Pallister to Scott-Moncrieff, 8 June [1954], BBC WAC RCONT1 Pallister (Talks 6)

[26] 'Life Story 1 & 2'; Minnie Pallister, *Cabbage for a Year*, Blackie, 1934, p. 8.

[27] Pallister to Scott-Moncrieff, 8 June [1954], BBC WAC RCONT1 Pallister (Talks 6).

[28] Minutes of the Methodist Conferences 1918, p. 102, University of Manchester Special Collection.

[29] *An Alphabetical and Chronological Arrangement...*, p. 186.

[30] Deleted lines from script 'Life Story (2)', *WH*, 24 June 1952; Brynmawr Infants School Log Book, 1893–1915, GEA285/02, Gwent Record Office; General Register of Women Students No 1.

[31] 'Memories 1900–1910'; Pallister to Miss Benzie, 16 January 1946, BBC/WAC/RCONT1 Pallister (Talks 3b); 'Where Does Mother Come In?', *Labour Woman*, June 1937; *New Leader*, 24 October 1930.

[32] Brynmawr School Log Book, 28 February 1907.

[33] *South Wales Gazette*, 28 February 1906, 1 February 1907 & 26 February 1909; 'Flowers of My Life'; I am grateful to Huw Bowen and Margaret Makepeace, Lead Curator for the East India Company Records at the British Library, for the information on Bertram Higman.

[34] Hilda Jennings, *Brynmawr*, Allenson, 1934; David J. V. Jones, 'The Scotch Cattle and the Black Domain', *Before Rebecca Popular Protests in Wales 1793–1835*, Allen Lane, 1973, pp. 86 113.

[35] 'Life Story (2)'.

[36] 'South Wales and The ILP', BBC Welsh Home Service, 12 April 1949; *Daily Herald*, 1 March 1935; Jennings, chapters 2–4; 'Life Story (2)'; 'Looking Back'.

[37] 'Life Story (2)'; 'South Wales and The ILP'.

[38] *Daily Herald*, 1 March 1934.

[39] 'Life Story (2)'.

[40] Jennings, p. 34; *Daily Herald*, 17 October 1935.

[41] *South Wales Gazette*, 24 April 1908.

[42] Pallister, *Cabbage...*, p. 163.

[43] Information provided by Davies's great niece, Vivienne Williams; 'I've Been Thinking...About Wales'; Pallister, *Cabbage...*, pp. 92–4; GEA285/08 Log Book 1915–1977.

[44] Pallister, *Cabbage...*, p. 94.

[45] *Man and Metal*, November 1940; *Is Your Drinking Really Necessary?*; 'I've Been Thinking...About Wales', *WH*, 2 March 1953; 'Reading Your Letters and Answering Your Questions', *WH*, 18 February 1958; *Abergavenny Chronicle*, 13 May & 2 December 1910; *South Wales Gazette*, 13 May & 25 November 1910.

[46] Deleted comment, 'Flowers of My Life', *WH*, 6 January 1959.

[47] Rowbotham, *Dreamers...*, p. 24.

[48] *Brecon & Radnor Express, Carmarthen and Swansea Valley Gazette, and Brynmawr District Advertiser*, 25 June 1914; *South Wales Gazette*, 29 October 1909; *Abergavenny Chronicle*, 25 March, 9 & 23 December 1910.

[49] *South Wales Gazette*, 1 July 1910.

[50] 'Minnie Pallister Speaking', *WH*, 21 April 1954; see also her thinly disguised autobiographical piece in the *Daily Mirror*, 23 November 1936.

[51] This was probably in January 1907. 'South Wales and The ILP'; *Evening Express*, 19 January 1907; *South Wales Gazette*, 25 January 1907.

[52] Raymond Challinor, *The Origins of British Bolshevism*, Croom Helm, 1977, p. 21; *Labour Leader*, 26 November 1909; *South Wales Gazette*, 3 December 1909.

[53] Pallister to Quigley, 11 July [1952], BBC WAC RCONT1 Pallister (Talks 5); *Bournemouth Times and Directory*, 14 July 1923; *South Wales Gazette*, 2 July 1909; 'I Knew Her: Katharine Bruce Glasier', *WH*, 31 March 1953.

[54] David Howell, *British Workers and the Independent Labour Party*, MUP, 1983, esp. pp. 26–7.

[55] Chris Williams, *Democratic Rhondda Politics and Society, 1885–1951*, UWP, 1996, p. 81.

[56] Vernon Hartshorn was miners' agent for Maesteg in 1906, then President of the

SWMF from 1922. Elected MP for Ogmore in 1922, he served as Postmaster General in the 1924 Labour Government and Lord Privy Seal in 1930-1. Noah Ablett was an industrial unionist and founder member of the Unofficial Reform Committee and a coauthor of the pamphlet, *The Miners' Next Step*. Committed to independent working-class education, he was involved in establishing the Plebs League and the Central Labour College. He became miners' agent for Merthyr in 1918. Charles Butt Stanton was miners' agent for Aberdare. In 1915, on the death of Keir Hardie, he was elected to Parliament as a pro-war MP, before being defeated in 1922. Jim Winstone, miners' agent for the Eastern Valleys, became President of the SWMF in 1915.

[57] Jim Griffiths became miners' agent for the Anthracite District in 1925, MP for Llanelli, 1936-1970 and served as Minister for National Insurance in the 1945 Labour Cabinet. Aneurin Bevan, MP for Ebbw Vale, 1929-1960, was Minister of Health and Housing in the same government. Between them, they established the Welfare State.

[58] Howell, pp. 28 & 245-251; Peter Stead, 'Vernon Hartshorn: Miners' Leader and Cabinet Minister', *Glamorgan Historian*, Vol VI, 1969, p. 89.

[59] See Williams, Chapter 2.

[60] Rose Davies was the first woman chair of Aberdare Trades and Labour Council by 1918 and in 1925 was the first woman elected to Glamorgan County Council, later becoming its chair. She contested the Honiton Parliamentary seat in 1929. Elizabeth Andrews became a Labour Party women's organiser in 1919, a post she held until 1947. She gave evidence to the Sankey Commission on the coal industry in 1919.

[61] *Man and Metal*, November 1940.

[62] *New Leader*, 14 February 1930.

[63] 'Life Story (3)', *WH*, 25 June 1952; *Is Your Drinking Really Necessary?*; 'Looking Back', p. 213; 'A Puritan Takes Stock'.

[64] James Griffiths, *Pages from Memory*, J. M. Dent, 1969, p. 14.

[65] Sheila Rowbotham, *The Friends of Alice Wheeldon*, Pluto, 1986, pp. 8-9; Stephen Yeo, 'A New Life: The Religion of Socialism in Britain 1883-1896', *History Workshop Journal*, Issue 4, Autumn 1977, pp.10-14; Pallister to Orwell, 16 January 1938, ORWELL/H/2, UCL Special Collection.

[66] Laurence Thompson, *The Enthusiasts*, Gollancz, 1971, pp. 65-67 & 75; see Krista Cowman, '"Giving them Something to Do": How the Early ILP Appealed to Women', in ed. Margaret Walsh, *Perspectives from Labour History*, Ashgate, 1999, pp. 120-1.

[67] Point made by Challinor about the Socialist Labour Party, pp. 28-9.

[68] 'I Knew Her: Katharine Bruce Glasier'.

[69] Established in 1909, the New Era Union's social gospel sought 'a reformed social and economic order free from the evils of poverty and deprivation'. It had a 'lively culture of debate and discussion' and a unique form of combining 'education, social work and some spiritual guidance.' (See Richard Lewis, *Leaders and Teachers, Adult Education and the Challenge of Labour in South Wales, 1906-1940*, UWP, 1993, pp. 94-6).

[70] Grieve to Ogilvy [sic], nd, ed. Catherine Kerrigan, *The Hugh MacDiarmid-George Ogilvie Letters*, Aberdeen, 1988, p. 3.

[71] Grieve to Ogilvie, 24 October 1911, ed. Alan Bold, *The Letters of Hugh MacDiarmid*, Hamish Hamilton, 1984.

[72] Memorandum of meeting between C. M. Grieve and R. Page Arnot, 20.8.65, Ronald Frankenberg papers, folder 16, South Wales Coalfield Collection, Swansea University. A miner in Abertillery, Hodges went to Ruskin College in 1909 before becoming miners' agent for the Garw Valley. In 1918 he became Secretary of the Miners' Federation of Great Britain then Labour MP for Lichfield in 1923.

[73] Quoted in Kerrigan, letter of 24 October 1911; W. Dale Nelson questions the reliability of parts of Grieve's account, *Gin Before Breakfast*, Syracuse, 2007, p. 140.

[74] Grieve to Ogilvie, 20 August 1916, quoted in ed. Bold. It is to be lamented that no copies of the *Monmouthshire Labour News* are extant, so we do not have Grieve's articles or his accounts of Minnie's meetings.

[75] John Paton, *Proletarian Pilgrimage*, Routledge, 1935, pp. 300–1.

[76] Sylvia Pankhurst described him as the 'caustic Irish fiddler…striding the platform like a quizzical satyr, lean and fit for leaping as a goat; his hard legs tightly cased in knee breeches; his goat's face, handsome in its odd way, more than half covered by a short, stubbly black beard. All the wild things of the woods seemed to gambol around him when his fiddle sounded…' quoted in E. Sylvia Pankhurst, *The Home Front*, 1932, republished Century Hutchinson, 1987, p. 318.

[77] *Labour Leader*, 8 December 1911.

[78] 'The Beloved Vagabond', *New Leader*, 25 July 1930.

[79] *Labour Leader*, 29 December 1911.

[80] Elocution was a skilled form of public speaking involving voice production, gesture and delivery at which Minnie excelled.

[81] *Labour Leader*, 17 December 1914; *Pioneer*, 5 July 1913 & 11 September 1915. Casey's visits to Wales, associated writings and propagandising deserve their own study.

[82] 'The Beloved Vagabond'; Naomi Reid, 'Hampson, Walter ('Casey'), *Dictionary of Labour Biography (DLB)*, Vol VI. See also June Hannam, '"In the Comradeship of the Sexes Lies the Hope of Progress and Social Regeneration": Women in the West Riding ILP, c.1890–1914', ed. June Rendall, *Equal or Different, Women's Politics 1800–1914*, Basil Blackwell, 1987, p 220.

[83] June Hannam and Karen Hunt, *Socialist Women*, Routledge, 2002, p. 35.

[84] Eddie May, 'The Mosaic of Labour Politics, 1900–1918', in eds. Duncan Tanner, Chris Williams and Deian Hopkin, *The Labour Party in Wales 1900–2000*, UWP, 2000, p 63; A. J. B. Marwick, *The Independent Labour Party (1918–32)*, unpublished BLitt, Balliol; Oxford, June 1960, p. 53.

[85] *Man and Metal*, August 1937.

[86] *Weekly Argus*, 23 March 1912; Brynmawr School Log Book, 9 April 1912.

[87] Comments reported by Keir Hardie, *Labour Leader*, 16 February & 17 May 1912.

[88] Independent Labour Party, *Report of the 20th Annual Conference, Merthyr*, held at the Olympia Rink on 27 and 28 May 1912.

[89] Claim by Mardy Jones in June 1909, quoted in Martin Wright, *Wales and Socialism*, UWP, 2016, p. 207 & p. 85.

[90] Gwyn A. Williams, *When Was Wales?*, Penguin, 1985, p. 265, paraphrases Hardie from *Labour Leader*, 31 May 1912.

[91] Wright, p. 1; *Labour Leader*, 17 May 1912; Raymond Postgate, *The Life of George Lansbury*, Longmans, 1951, p. 94.

[92] Wright, Chapter 3; Thompson, p. 92.

[93] *Labour Leader*, 24 & 31 May 1912.

[94] Ryland Wallace, *The Women's Suffrage Movement in Wales*, UWP, 2009, pp. 166 & 173–4.

[95] *Labour Leader*, 31 May 1912.

[96] *Labour Leader*, 27 June 1912.

[97] *Labour Leader*, 1 August 1912.

[98] See also Vernon Hartshorn, 'Liberalism and Labour in Wales', *Labour Leader*, 12 January 1912.

[99] Hannam, '"In the Comradeship…"', pp. 214 & 225; June Hannam and Karen Hunt,

'Gendering the Stories of Socialism: An Essay in Historical Criticism', ed. Margaret Walsh, *Working Out Gender*, Routledge, 1999, esp. pp. 106–7 & 112–3; Hannam & Hunt, *Socialist Women*, p. 6; Wright, pp. 124–5; Stephen Brooke, *Sexual Politics Sexuality, Family Planning and the British Left from the 1880s to the Present Day*, Oxford, 2013, paperback edition, p. 27.

[100] Hannam and Hunt, *Socialist Women*, p. 3; *Labour Leader*, 19 January 1912; May, 'Mosaic' p. 63.

[101] Women's exclusion from labour movement politics has been referred to by, for example Chris Williams, *Capitalism, Community, and Conflict*, UWP, 1998, pp. 111–3; Lowri Newman, *A Distinctive Brand of Politics: Women in the South Wales Labour Party*, University of Glamorgan, M Phil, 2003, p. 16 and Ursula Masson, 'Introduction', Elizabeth Andrews, *A Woman's Work Is Never Done*, Honno Classics, 2006, p. xx.

[102] *Labour Leader*, 19 September 1912; *South Wales Daily News (SWDN)*, 9 September 1912.

[103] *Labour Leader*, 8 May, 5 June, 17 July, 2 October, 13 November & 11 December 1913, 28 May & 4 June 1914.

[104] *Labour Leader*, 12 June & 17 July 1913; *Pageant of Gwent Given at Maindiff, Near Abergavenny, on Occasion of the Royal National Eisteddfod of Wales, August 4th, 1913*; *Llais Llafur*, 13 June 1914; Pallister to Quigley, 21 January 1943, BBC/WAC/RCONTI Pallister (Talks 3a); 'Life Story (2)'.

[105] 'Memories 1900–1910'; *The Vote*, 16 January 1914; information provided by Ryland Wallace.

[106] Wallace, pp. 102 & 119; Claire Eustance, *'Daring To Be Free'; The Evolution of Women's Political Identities in the Women's Freedom League 1907–1930*, PhD, York, 1993, p. 61; Wallace email to author, 11 March 2016.

[107] Wallace, pp. 115, 119, 127 & 181.

[108] Chris Waters, 'New Women and Socialist-Feminist Fiction: The Novels of Isabella Ford and Katharine Bruce Glasier', eds. Angela Ingram & Daphne Patai, *Rediscovering Forgotten Radicals: British Women Writers, 1889–1939*, University North Carolina Press, 1993, p. 32; Hannam & Hunt, *Socialist Women*, pp. 37 & 51.

[109] *Is Your Drinking Really Necessary?*.

[110] *Daily Herald*, 22 February 1934.

[111] Hannam & Hunt, *Socialist Women*, pp. 22 & 59/60; Laura Ugolini, 'It Is Only Justice to Grant Women's Suffrage: Independent Labour Party Men and Women's Suffrage, 1893–1905', eds. Claire Eustance, Joan Ryan, Laura Ugolini, *A Suffrage Reader*, Leicester, 2000, pp. 128–9.

[112] *Abergavenny Chronicle*, 12 June 1914; *Labour Leader*, 11 September 1913 & 2 February 1912; Lewis, p. 66; *Common Cause*, 26 June 1914.

[113] Wright, p. 215; *Labour Leader*, 27 October 1911.

[114] *Llais Llafur*, 1 August 1914.

[115] *Labour Leader*, 2 July 1914; *Llais Llafur*, 13 June 1914; Paula Bartley, *Ellen Wilkinson From Red Suffragist to Government Minister*, Pluto, 2014, pp. 4–5; *Dundee Courier*, 1 December 1926, Ellen Wilkinson Scrapbook, Labour Party papers. Microfilm Reel No 30, held in Cardiff University Special Collections; Betty D. Vernon, *Ellen Wilkinson*, Croom Helm, 1982, Chapter 1; Paula Bartley, *Labour Women in Power*, 2019, Palgrave online version 384.8

CHAPTER TWO
'A New Star on the Horizon'

When the First World War started, Minnie was holidaying with her parents in Southampton, so she was absent from the ILP's anti-war demonstrations that immediately took place in Brynmawr and elsewhere in South Wales. By the time she returned home, the world she had left only a week before had gone for ever. The declaration of war was greeted enthusiastically by most of the population, including in South Wales and, within eight weeks, over three-quarters of a million men rushed to enlist. Labour unrest, which had been prevalent up to the outbreak of war, temporarily subsided. Most – though not all – women involved with suffrage suspended their campaigns in order to aid the war effort. In a country mainly united behind the war, and against a national wave of pro-war fever, the ILP was largely isolated in opposing the conflict. With war the defining issue, the ambition of achieving any kind of socialist transformation had to be put on hold. As a prominent local leader in an unpopular anti-war party that was generally considered unpatriotic, Minnie would be tested as never before.

Unlike the ILP, the Labour Party supported the war, resulting in Ramsay MacDonald resigning as Labour Party chair. Although MacDonald was not a pacifist and his position was not 'Stop the War' but 'Peace by Negotiation', he became identified as the leader of the anti-war movement. His stand invigorated the ILP and he won admiration among the pacifist community, but his pro-war friends became estranged and Minnie, who had become close to him since her involvement in the ILP, would have seen the personal toll it took.[1] Over time, the organisational relationship between the ILP and the Labour Party suffered a breakdown due to their opposing positions on the war, which led to the ILP becoming 'little more than a sect, cut off from the main stream of British politics'.[2] Although the two parties would be reconciled after the war, tensions around their divergent political cultures continued until the ILP disaffiliated from the Labour Party in 1932.

There were a range of anti-war positions within the ILP. Some, including Fenner Brockway, were pacifists, others opposed the war as anti-imperialists, while the Clydesiders in Glasgow concentrated on class-based opposition to rent increases, profiteering and working conditions. Minnie shared George Lansbury's and Philip Snowden's Christian opposition to taking life, while also holding Clifford Allen's view that the war was an extension of the political and economic system of capitalism and that both sides were equally to blame.[3] Although the ILP had been badly divided before the war, in the face of hostility internal factionalism was put aside and the differing anti-war positions coexisted.[4]

For Minnie the first challenge was the churches. Her belief in the commandment 'Thou Shalt Not Kill', and her view that war was inconsistent with Christianity, put her at odds with pro-war church leaders. Increasingly outspoken, in January 1915, she addressed Newport ILP on 'Has the Church always been the Enemy of Progress?'[5] She retained her personal faith and remained an attending member of chapel, but now disregarded the church as an instrument capable of facilitating societal change.

In April 1915, Minnie was one of twenty-one delegates from Wales who attended the ILP Annual Conference in Norwich. The Party's first national conference since the outbreak of war, it took place in a hostile atmosphere and delegates were abused in the streets. When planned venues were withdrawn, the conference was only able to proceed when a Primitive Methodist chapel was made available by the congregation and where the minister was a pacifist.[6] Keir Hardie, in his last major ILP appearance, made a resolutely anti-war speech.[7] It was Minnie's second national conference and she was the only other speaker from Wales. Given less than two minutes to prepare, she caused a sensation in moving the vote of thanks to the chair, Fred Jowett. Describing herself as 'a grave object of suspicion', she said the church was suspicious of her because she was a member of the ILP and the ILP was suspicious of her because she was a member of the church. Before the war, she added, she had urged religious ministers to speak out on social questions, but they had replied they had to concentrate on spiritual not materialistic matters. During the war they preached sermons using their pulpits as recruiting platforms for the armed forces. Turning on its head the interview she had given to the *Labour Leader* eight months earlier, when she had defended organised religion and criticised Labour's condemnation of the churches, she now condemned words in the religious press that were 'breathing the spirit of hatred' while those in the ILP paper *Labour Leader* were 'breathing the spirit of Christ Himself'.[8]

Hardie wrote on the front page of the *Pioneer* that Minnie's eloquence held the conference in awe, saying that with her maiden conference speech she 'burst like a new star on the horizon' and declared hers to be the speech of the conference.[9] W. C. Anderson MP, former chair of the Labour Party National Executive Committee (NEC), predicted that Minnie was a young woman who was destined to play an important part in the future of the ILP.[10] The Norwich conference transformed Minnie's life, catapulting her to prominence across the South Wales labour movement and affording her a national ILP profile.

Minnie's conference appearance, and Hardie's praise, led to new opportunities that Minnie had to fit in alongside her teaching responsibilities. In June, Merthyr's *Pioneer*, the most significant of the localised ILP papers in Britain, named her as a welcome addition to the paper's writers. The first article in her 'Pinpricks of Poverty' series argued that, as South Wales prospered, absolute poverty was becoming rarer for most. However her biting assessment, based on visiting a collier friend, his wife and eight children, declared that there now existed a 'well-to-do poverty' where people's basic needs were met but where they could not afford to fall ill or be injured for, although they contributed to the wealth of the country, they were vulnerable as they had no wider claim on the community.[11] Another article, on religion and politics, earned from Hardie the comment: 'If those are your views go ahead, and God speed.'[12]

Minnie's first newspaper articles displayed a flair for writing that, in the interwar years, would find full expression. It was, though, the spoken not the written word that proved her main inspiration at this time. Following Hardie's praise, speaking invitations poured in and, such was the curiosity to hear Minnie speak, that when she addressed Merthyr ILP for the first time, giving two lectures in one day, comrades travelled from neighbouring valleys to hear her.[13] Although she reported being filled with trepidation in speaking to such a renowned branch, one attendee, who afterwards walked home eight miles across mountain tops, reported it would have been worth walking twice that distance to hear her.[14] Still a novice at the art of 'semi-educational, semi-propaganda' fee-paying work of part-time ILP lecturers,[15] wherever Minnie now spoke, she left a lasting impression.

However, although a fluent and effective public speaker, during the first two years of hostilities, while she was opposed to the war, she was not entirely outspoken in her criticisms. While she chaired meetings for ILP, No Conscription Fellowship (NCF) and Union of Democratic Control (UDC), where speakers opposed the war, she had not yet turned her own eloquence fully against it. Her publicly reported talks on The Social Ideal, William Morris, and the realities of classroom teaching were not connected with the war, much less opposed to it.[16] Even when, in early 1916, she finally started addressing the conflict, her arguments were limited to the government's wartime economy campaign and the resulting hardship and poverty, rather than condemning the war itself.[17]

The circumstances of war and military losses radicalised the situation and radicalised Minnie. As *the* anti-war party, the ILP became the target for hostility causing it to be isolated further, with halls closed to it and its meetings disrupted.[18] Attitudes hardened and ILP offices and homes in South Wales, as elsewhere in Britain, were raided by the police, and its newspapers and leaflets were seized. Under pressure, ILP branch numbers in South Wales fell from 75 in February 1915 to 58 in February 1916.[19] As the Party increased its anti-war propaganda, the opprobrium intensified. As a prominent member, Minnie suffered abuse.

Although now marginal within the labour movement, the ILP was at the centre of the anti-war movement and was closely linked to both the NCF and the National Council Against Conscription, (NCAC), known after mid-1916 as the National Council for Civil Liberties (NCCL), which sought to protect all citizens against the 'overzealous' enforcement of wartime military service and Defence of the Realm Act legislation (DORA). In Wales, Ivor Thomas, of Briton Ferry, as the NCAC/NCCL organiser and also the Wales representative on the ILP's National Advisory Council, was in the 'engine room' of opposition to the war.[20] His leadership provided a bridge between the anti-war movement and the trades unions, as he knitted together the wider labour movement including most districts of the SWMF with chapels and women's organisations.[21] Morgan Jones, who had replaced Ted Gill as the South Wales ILP President, after Gill had recanted his opposition to the war and enlisted, was chair of the South Wales Division of the NCF.[22] By the end of the year, Minnie joined them as the most prominent anti-war woman in the labour movement in Wales.

Minnie first encountered the idea of an individual's refusal to fight when she heard the case for conscientious objection expounded by Clifford Allen at an ILP meeting she chaired in his home town of Newport.[23] Allen, the son of a draper, was former chair of the Cambridge University Fabian Society. One of the founders of the socialist-pacifist NCF in late 1914, he soon became its chair and was at the heart of the organisation. The NCF consisted of young men of military age pledged to decline to serve, whatever the penalty for refusing. It gave voice to conscientious objectors (COs) and supported them practically and morally.[24] Although membership was only open initially to men of military age, 'associate members', comprising women and men not of military age, were allowed to join from May 1915. The following month, a South Wales Division was established.

Allen was a regular speaker in South East Wales in the autumn of 1915, including addressing a meeting in Brynmawr with Minnie presiding.[25] At this distance it is not possible to know the extent to which his frequent visits were motivated by his personal interest in Minnie. Allen was described as having 'the face of a saint and a martyr (which was how he liked to look his enemies would hint), a frail body, stooping shoulders, a will of iron and a fairly shrewd mind'.[26] Beatrice Webb noted his 'spiritual countenance, fine gentle voice and quiet manner' though Allen's halo was observed as being of the 'militant Jesuit type'. Bertrand Russell so admired Allen, he described him as 'a man of genius'.[27] There was no doubting Allen's absolute commitment to the cause or the physical and mental suffering he endured. Allen's principled stand, genuine sense of sacrifice, and intelligence, added to his already saintly allure, made him attractive to women. Minnie's winning combination of intellect, commitment, personality and good looks also made her alluring. Sharing the intensity of supporting an unpopular cause, by the summer of 1916 there was talk of their marrying.

The first national NCF Convention, in November, brought together a disparate group of pacifists, socialists, religious believers and others that Allen formed into a coherent and very well-organised group.[28] The historian of the NCF said:

> With relatively little money and almost no popular support, the fellowship attracted a remarkably able band of social activists and political organizers [who] shaped an organisation that caused the government more grief than any other body of dissenters against the war.[29]

It was timely. In January 1916 the Government introduced conscription for single men that in May was extended to all men aged between 18 and 41. A wave of anti-conscription events occurred across South Wales, which involved miners' lodges, trades councils, ILP and NCF branches. The ILP also provided a platform for the radical-pacifist UDC, which opposed secret diplomacy and alliances and sought Parliamentary control over foreign policy. When its speakers came to Wales and spoke against the war, Minnie regularly chaired their meetings, broadening her network to include UDC Liberals including Arthur Ponsonby and E. D. Morel, who later joined the ILP, as well as Norman Angell. By now Minnie had moved to Ar y Bryn in Greenland Road, Brynmawr. When the UDC's Charles Trevelyan MP came to Brynmawr, Minnie invited him to stay, asking him to bring a photo as 'I am making a collection of all the celebrities who sleep in my Prophet's Chamber', hung in a row on the wall.[30] A main organiser of anti-war activity, Minnie developed links with a wide range of individuals across the political spectrum that would serve her well. Throughout her life, Minnie was an assiduous networker who excelled in maintaining her contacts, knowing how to use them both for the cause and, at times, for her personal advantage.

On Friday 7 April, Ramsay MacDonald took the 3.30 pm train from Paddington to travel to Brynmawr where he would speak that evening, staying for the weekend at Minnie's. That journey marks the beginning of a period of five months when we have privileged access to Minnie's private life and have some idea of, or at least can make reasonable assumptions about, the relationships she had with men. They remind us that against the sombre backdrops of the battles of Verdun and the Somme, personal lives still existed alongside and sometimes intertwined with war and the struggle for peace.

Minnie chaired MacDonald's Market Hall meeting of 1,500 people, an occasion which was threatened with violence.[31] A MacDonald biographer wrote of that period: 'Every meeting a possible riot, at every meeting the booing, the jeers and the shouted insult.'[32] In Brynmawr, MacDonald spelled out the mission of international socialists and justified the ILP's stand arguing there was no party more entitled to claim that it stood for the soul of the country than the ILP. He won loud applause for saying the churches were reneging on their Christian mission, adding that for twenty months the people of the country had been deceived and the war was still no closer to ending. He dismissed the call for 'a fight to the finish' because of its cost in terms of lives lost and the misery entailed for widows and orphans, presciently adding it would only sow seeds for further conflict, as peace could not be imposed by force.[33] On Sunday he met Minnie and her friends, Willie Davies and Lydia Atherall, before speaking in Blaina and Ebbw Vale. His diary for Saturday 8 April is blank,[34] but it is possible to surmise what he did, for he wrote to Minnie:

> I do not know if you still entertain projects of Llanthony. It is an out-of-the-way place where only dreams can reach it – and not feet.[35]

Although MacDonald was a prodigious walker and would have had no difficulty covering the twenty-mile round trip from Abergavenny to Llanthony, they travelled partly by bicycle, starting with a four-mile freewheel downhill ride from Brynmawr.[36] It was a trip that would have later significance.

Minnie and MacDonald had probably first met in 1911.[37] They formed a trio with Ivor Thomas, who was devoted to MacDonald and became a lifelong friend of Minnie. In June 1916, Minnie proposed changing the schedule for MacDonald's visit to South Wales that she was coordinating. He retorted:

> Good Heavens! Three score and ten meetings in South Wales that weekend! I am engaged to Pontypool. It wears my ring on its finger, and you want me to desert it for a hobble skirt and a Paris hat called Cardiff. I expect that of Ivor who has no religion. But of you! What is Wesleyan Methodism and Sunday School teaching coming to? Do I behold the deterioration of futurism? Or is it the innate evil of Eve?... Work out more details. Check my topography as I have no map here. Propose times and redraw plans with explanation of how the impossible can be done.[38]

They show that even in addressing mundane meeting arrangements MacDonald could create something irresistibly playful. When Minnie congratulated MacDonald on his 50th birthday, he responded:

> From the wickedness of your heart you have congratulated me on my increasing age. Youth, like you, puts its mile-stones on the middle of the road so that it may keep its eyes on them; age, like me, puts them amongst the shading weeds at the side so that it may forget them. Wait till you are fifty, bald and bent and then tell me what your feelings are when some young colt of a creature comes up hilariously, smacks you on the back and shouts: 'Hulloo, old woman, glad to see you getting on in years.'[39]

These extracts, provided by Minnie for publication in a sympathetic biography of MacDonald, are engaged and engaging. They border on the flirtatious and demonstrate a relaxed familiarity. However, it is reasonable to conclude that a deeper relationship existed between them around that period, and that it was sexual. MacDonald got on better with women than men, enjoyed their company and gossiping with them. Since the death of his wife in 1911 he was at times desperately lonely, and was known to be close to several women, including having an intimate relationship with Lady Londonderry and Molly Hamilton, whom MacDonald's children thought he might marry, though none could replace Margaret.[40] Minnie has previously been considered as no more than a friend of MacDonald's, but strong circumstantial evidence and the depth of personal bond that Minnie and MacDonald demonstrated to one another in the decade to MacDonald's death in 1937 could only have been the product of years of prior mutual commitment, and reinforce the view that Minnie's name should be added to those women to whom MacDonald was 'very close'.[41]

Two weeks after his April stay in Brynmawr, MacDonald and Minnie attended the Easter ILP national conference where the Party declared itself pacifist. The following weekend, Minnie and Allen were scheduled to speak in Newport, but Allen was unable to attend as, having been called up, he was working his way through the Appeals Tribunals in London.[42] As men were conscripted, brought before military tribunals and gaoled, women stepped in to assume their roles in the NCF and the ILP. Minnie had stood down as President of the Monmouthshire ILP Federation at its 1916 AGM. There she had spoken feelingly for Hardie, their lost leader who had died the previous September, broken by the war and the enthusiastic working-class support for it. Now, months later, with Reg Ley, the Monmouthshire Federation's Secretary serving six months' hard labour at Wormwood Scrubs[43] and Edward James, the Federation's lecture secretary in Walton Gaol 'for conscience's sake', Minnie assumed a secretary's role.[44]

As spring turned to summer, Minnie stepped up her overt opposition to the war and sought to galvanise resistance, though the daily distraction of sixty infants confined her anti-war involvement to evenings, weekends and holidays. Minnie's association with the leading opponents of the war, and the positions she took, marked her out unfavourably in the eyes of many of the people of Brynmawr, including the parents of the children she taught. Although she was shunned, including by family and friends, it did not stop her. At a major NCAC peace conference of labour, co-operative and religious organisations in Brynmawr on 24 June, she spoke, alongside Philip and Ethel Snowden, of the terrible state into which the country had fallen and of the need for united action for peace.[45] When the Snowdens subsequently addressed a series of huge meetings in the valleys of Monmouthshire and East Glamorgan, Minnie saw it as proof that 'the common people of the country' did not want war. She was overstating the case, but it did show that in some communities, where the ILP was strong, or where there was particular faith-based opposition, there were pockets or even centres of anti-war resistance.[46]

A distinct political consciousness existed in the struggle of mining communities that ran from Brynmawr down to Abertillery. There, in addition to support for the ILP and the NCF, opposition to the war was manifested in a cluster of NCCL branches[47] as well as in the strongest concentration of support for the Workers' Suffrage Federation (WSF) in Britain outside its London East End base. While other women's suffrage societies were overwhelmingly middle class, the WSF, led by the socialist anti-war agitator Sylvia Pankhurst, had working-class appeal. Its call for adult suffrage and an end to the war, its campaigns to alleviate local suffering, especially food shortages and the plight of young children, and its condemnation of 'profiteers who exploited the miseries of the people', resonated locally.[48] A strong relationship developed between women of the upper Western Valley and the women of London's East End, following Pankhurst's tour of late May/early June 1916. Minnie, active in her support of the WSF, recalled Pankhurst as 'wan and pale after much forcible feeding', and weighed down as she was by lugging with her copies of the WSF's newspaper the *Dreadnought*.[49]

The war's intensification propelled Minnie hither and thither, speaking and organising. Against the backdrop of the carnage of the Battle of the Somme, when Mrs Melvina Walker of the Poplar Branch of the WSF toured in early July, Minnie supported her Blaina event and chaired her open-air meeting in Abertillery.[50] Minnie now was openly and loudly against the war. July culminated with the Monmouthshire leg of Bertrand Russell's month-long anti-war speaking tour of South Wales where Minnie moved the peace negotiation resolution at his Abertillery meeting before supporting the last meeting of his tour in Brynmawr on Monday 24 July.[51]

Born into an aristocrat family, with a grandfather who had been a prime minister, Russell was an already renowned Cambridge philosopher. However, the Great War had a profound impact on him and on the South Wales tour he found his political voice.[52] Too old to be conscripted (and therefore ineligible for full membership of the NCF), he had thrown himself into NCF activities, writing for its journal *Tribunal*, which the authorities repeatedly attempted to shut down.[53] Now, in late July 1916 he met Minnie Pallister, who was equally emboldened in her opposition to the war. Although she had been told Russell preferred to stay in a hotel, Minnie had written to him declaring 'I want you to stay here.' She advised he might not care for the hotels in Brynmawr and promised '1. Unlimited baths 2. Plenty to eat 3. An enormous welcome. Will this do?' before adding 'I put the baths first because socialist and Peace People seem to prefer bathing to eating.' Her quirky letter, with the entreaty to *'please'* bring a picture of himself as 'every celebrity who sleeps in my "Prophet's Chamber" has to be hung on the wall in a black frame as a warning to evildoers', was sufficiently enticing for Russell to stay two nights.[54]

Before his arrival, Russell received a 'private' letter from Catherine Marshall, the NCF national secretary, priming him to sound out Minnie about coming to work in the NCF's London headquarters. Minnie's organisational skills may not have been the only factor at play, for Marshall added that Minnie sounded 'just the kind of person he [Allen] ought to marry, as well as just the kind of person we want – [for his personal work]'[55] Perhaps Minnie had prompted Marshall, for a handwritten note read: 'Miss Pallister: imploring for work BR to [word unclear] her on Monday.'[56] If Minnie did take the initiative, was she acting for the cause, to be near the centre of events, attracted by the prospect of working in London, or to have time with Allen? As, unlike MacDonald, Allen offered a realistic prospect of a long-term relationship, including the possibility of marriage, it was probably a combination of these factors that led her to start work on 31 July in the NCF London office for the duration of her school summer holidays.

The summer of 1916 was one of turmoil for the NCF and Minnie arrived at a critical time. Although she would have known something of the situation in advance, little could have prepared her for what she encountered. On her first day, with male leaders being gaoled, Allen, accompanied by supporters, surrendered himself to the authorities at Lavender Hill police station. He was taken back into custody on 11 August before being handed over to the military authorities. Court-martialled on 23 August, he was given one year's hard labour.[57]

Minnie joined a close team with a shared commitment and strong bonds of trust. Tremendous stresses were placed on members of the National Committee by the authorities and there were heavy workloads and pressures on staff.[58] Their 'exciting and risky work' was at times semi-clandestine, with secret meetings and coded messages due to official harassment.[59] During Minnie's first week, the office was raided by police. Joan Beauchamp, who worked in the Press and Publication Department that summer, described the NCF as being, in effect, an illegal organisation, defying both military and civil authorities. A more judicious observation is that, while the NCF was never illegal, it was seen as subversive, so its premises were raided, publications seized and members repeatedly court-martialled or prosecuted.[60]

Within the intensity of the NCF London office, Marshall was central, bringing her organising and lobbying skills previously used in the suffrage movement. However, with the all-consuming nature of the cause, she was working too hard and driving herself towards a nervous breakdown. Russell worked under the direction of Marshall and Allen and the three of them, with Brockway, had a form of executive status in the organisation.[61] Minnie worked closely with Russell and Allen in a privileged position close to the centres of authority.[62] In an environment where these leading characters called one another 'comrade',[63] Minnie's cheery countenance and intelligent enthusiasm complemented Russell's irrepressible drive, Marshall's efficiency and Allen's organisational brilliance. After only a week, Minnie was considered to replace Runham Brown in maintaining contact between headquarters and the NCF organisation across the country, should he be detained by the military. Marshall had wanted Minnie to understudy Runham Brown for a month and become the person 'who would visit branches & stir them up & help them where they are weak'. This would have entailed her giving up her teaching profession and moving to London to become a full-time anti-war activist and would have been ideally suited to Minnie's skills. However, the risk of Runham Brown being picked up any day under the Military Services Act meant they needed someone who could replace him immediately and Minnie did not, as yet, have sufficient experience.[64] Even so, the experience in the NCF office affirmed for Minnie the importance of dedicating her working life to a cause in which she believed. Henceforth it would be a matter of when and under what circumstances it occurred, rather than if.

*

This was an exhilarating time for Minnie. Far removed from Brynmawr and the routines of the classroom, she adjusted readily to London life and meeting people normally only encountered when they visited South Wales. She stayed in Upper George Street off Bryanston Square, Marylebone, where MPs and government ministers lived in ornate houses surrounding private, tree-lined gardens. Outside the office, Minnie was soon entangled in a bewildering web of messy interpersonal relations with other NCF workers, a situation which operated in parallel with the intense formal functioning of daily work at headquarters. Those involved in this web included Allen, Marshall, Russell and Lady Constance Malleson, a married actor daughter of Earl Annesley who preferred her stage name 'Colette O'Niel', and of course Minnie herself.

Before Minnie had moved to London, Marshall had contacted Russell on the dynamics of the relationship between Minnie and Clifford Allen. Allen, said Marshall, was opposed to Minnie working in London as he thought she wanted to marry him and he was not sure whether or not he wanted to marry her. Marshall added:

> It would be wrong to throw any distractions in his way just now when he is so over wrought & needs all possible strength & poise; but he is not the person to show himself to be distracted I doubt, and she is no babe to prick her fingers and cry...[65]

The extent to which Minnie had been aware of these machinations is unclear, but she was apparently well enough known to those in the London office for such judgements to be made. However, Allen's impression that Minnie wanted to marry him was not necessarily an accurate depiction. If Minnie's interest in Allen had been a reason to go to London, it may well have cooled by the time she arrived. Certainly, after Minnie started working in London, Russell wrote to his lover, Ottoline Morrell, about Minnie and Allen. On Allen's view that 'Miss P.' wanted to marry Allen but that Allen wasn't sure whether or not he wanted to marry her, Russell interpreted things differently. Describing Allen and Minnie as old friends, Russell thought Allen was wrong. 'She is competent & agreeable, & likes him; but I don't think she likes him as much as he deserves.' In fact, Allen and Minnie's relationship had almost certainly been sexual.[66] Minnie had confided in Russell, 'he & I made love to each other, & got quite hurt'.[67] While there is ambiguity as to which of them was hurt, in view of Russell's comment that Minnie wanted Allen less than he deserved, the likelihood seems that it was Allen who was hurt. If Russell's views accurately reflected Minnie's feelings, she may have changed her mind; or possibly Allen was exaggerating her interest in marrying.[68] This situation cannot have been easy for Marshall because that summer Marshall was falling in love with Allen, so may have been jealous of Minnie who was five years younger.[69]

Russell, though, was perhaps being deliberately coy with Morrell about his own relationship with Minnie. His brief neutral description of Minnie disguised an association that was more intimate than he may have wanted Morrell to realise. Russell was 44, Morrell 43 and Minnie 31. Although Russell's affair with Morrell was winding down, he knew she could display possessiveness when he formed associations with other women.[70] Russell was fascinating to women readily attracted by his intellect and his personality, even if not physically. O'Niel conveyed something of Russell's charisma when she wrote nearly fifty years later: 'Russell, to some of us who were young in 1916, was the sun which lit our world.'[71] Minnie, it appears, shared that view and Russell had reason for thinking Minnie may have been keener on him than on Allen.

A letter from Minnie to Russell sometime in August 1916 leaves no doubt as to her interest in him. Displaying an easy familiarity, the letter was challengingly playful. Flattering while mock-admonishing, it was flirtatiously submissive and shot through with intimacy. Exchanging ideas, she duelled with him on the nature of impulse and Christianity; she accused him of being out of touch with ordinary people and perhaps alluded to the possibility of them living together.[72] For a letter of only 370 words it packs a punch.

The first section of the letter mock-scolded Russell for having sent an exaggerated note about Allen's condition in military detention: 'How naughty of you to send that dreadful letter & give us such a fright,' before updating Russell on Allen's situation and adding 'Just like you to get worried over C A in a minute – but I like you awfully for it somehow.' Next Minnie made clear her envy of Miss Kyle to whom at that time Russell was dictating his last lecture on 'Political Ideals' and who he described as 'the most perfect secretary who ever existed'.[73] Reporting that Miss Kyle was 'awfully anxious to type your lectures', Minnie submissively commented:

> She appears to think it a great privilege to take down your thoughts. So it is. I wish I could type. When I learn may I type your things?

If Russell had returned from South Wales with a 'deeper knowledge of how people lived and a renewed faith in their judgement',[74] it was suggested that Russell was unable to make contact with other people so did not derive authentic sensations from his own life but lived his life vicariously through other people.[75] Russell acknowledged to Morrell that he found it difficult to talk to ordinary people.[76] Perhaps Minnie detected this, as her letter quickly changed from compliance to challenge.

> I have thought of heaps of things I don't agree with you. I think your knowledge of *ordinary people* is limited [emphasis in origi-

nal]. You have mixed with clever people – & rich people – & governing sort of people a lot but I don't believe you really know the common people like me. Have you ever eaten chips out of a newspaper in the street? If not you are not really a democrat!

Minnie's next single sentence chose to differ with Russell on his most solid ground – ideas. For Russell, sharing and testing his ideas with the women and men with whom he closely engaged was important. When staying with Minnie in Brynmawr and now in London, Russell was finalising *Principles of Social Reconstruction* which considered why war was fought and how to prevent it. Described as 'one of Russell's most original and enduring contributions to social and political thought' it was published in the United States under the title *Why Men Fight*.[77] Analysing the social order and looking at the state, education, marriage, religion, law and property among others, he concluded that impulses in people's behaviour have 'more effect than conscious purpose in moulding men's lives'.[78] Or as a biographer puts it 'people are moved to act as often by blind and unconscious impulses as by conscious and directed desires'.[79]

One chapter of Russell's book related to Religion and the Churches, where he recognised the existence of 'some form of religion, so firmly and sincerely believed as to dominate even the life of instinct'.[80] Indeed it was a feature of his life, for Morrell's faith was a central, yet sometimes divisive, part of her relationship with Russell.[81] Now he encountered a similar faith in Minnie. Evidently Minnie and Russell were discussing his ideas as she took issue with part of his argument, saying: 'With regard to impulse the case for Christianity is that it substitutes a new motive power instead of natural impulses,' although this one sentence is the only hint we have of their deliberations.

On her comments on his relations with ordinary people and on Christianity she added provocatively: 'Bear these in mind so that we can fight next time we meet.' While we do not know what Russell thought of Minnie's intellect, the way they dialogued over some areas and duelled over others shows intellectually and socially Minnie was no passive woman who sat meekly in awe of him.

Minnie's final point is the most intriguing.

> Re marriage question[:] 2 men collaborate to write a book and share a flat[;] a man and a woman coll.[aborate] to write a book and share a flat. Why not? In what way is 'Career' of one sacrificed?

At first, this appears to be a comment on Russell's book chapter 'Marriage and the Population Question'. Written at a time when Russell's own marriage to his wife Alys had foundered, the chapter's early pages were about the breakdown of marriage, or divorce. He noted there existed a 'widespread but flimsy hypocrisy' around marriage and a narrow code of marriage conventions which could not be broken, one of which was: 'A man may not live openly with a woman who is not his wife.' While he believed the law ought to be indifferent to the 'morality' of the issue, and hoped that a new form would be developed, 'based upon liberty, justice, and love, not upon authority and law' in practice, to be seen to be breaking the code, could ruin a career.[82] The intricate lengths to which he had gone to sustain, yet hide, the relationship with Morrell shows that while he might write about the need for a new morality, in practice he was deeply bound by societal convention.[83] Minnie took issue.

Deeper consideration suggests that Minnie was not only commenting on Russell's chapter but also wanting a relationship with Russell ('not necessarily marriage'), rather than with Allen.[84] Perhaps the conclusive argument that Minnie suggests living together is in the way she ends this section: 'If I worry you[,] write and tell me to shut up.' Had this been merely neutral feedback as part of a scholarly discussion, rather than being a practical consideration of their personal circumstances, Russell would have had no grounds to be worried. Minnie ended her letter with the heavily suggestive 'Yours gratefully (for physical & mental food etc. etc.)'. It is hard not to conclude that they were lovers.

If women often felt exploited by Russell,[85] this letter suggests Minnie gave as good as she got. While recognising Russell's special qualities, she was also prepared to point out his deficiencies. She respected his intellect and was ready to defer to him in support of his work, but she was not daunted by his mind, status, social position or fame and would seem to have considered herself his equal in some ways – and possibly an appropriate partner. It shows Minnie operated as an independent, confident and assertive woman in her personal as well as her political life. The impact of Russell on Minnie is difficult to quantify although their paths regularly crossed in pacifist circles until the 1950s. Russell's autobiography lacks detail saying only 'I sought about for some other woman to relieve my unhappiness, but without success until I met Colette.'[86] During August, while Minnie made her pitch for Russell, Russell noticed the young, beautiful, pacifist O'Niel. Ten years younger than Minnie, she had an open marriage with her husband, actor Miles Malleson (alongside whom Minnie would work as a pacifist decades later). Six weeks later, on 23 September, Russell and O'Niel began their affair.[87]

The private life journey taken by the innocent 21-year-old who arrived in Brynmawr in 1906 to the 31-year-old woman working in the NCF office is not known. By the summer of 1916 Minnie was an open and independent woman, who had aspirations for her future and looked to shape her personal and professional life on her own terms, unconstrained by the expectations and judgements of others in ways that would limit most young women teachers from Brynmawr. Able to articulate her wants and desires, she realised the power she held in being personally, physically and intellectually attractive to some of Britain's progressive anti-war leaders. The three with whom she can be linked, MacDonald, Allen and Russell, and with whom she probably had sexual relationships, were all prominent men, with finely honed intellects and each was pilloried for his beliefs. Whether they were representative of her life more generally is unknown for, apart from a few moments in 1919, those months are the only time in Minnie's life that her relationships with men can be viewed, but it feels unlikely to have been exceptional.

Had Minnie continued to live and work within London's radical social circles, doubtless she would have appeared in further written accounts and would have acquired a prominent public profile. However, after making a brief guest appearance in the lives of others who considered themselves of sufficient importance, or with the historical consciousness, to keep their papers, Minnie returned to South Wales where, in different social and cultural circumstances, people did not. The momentary glimpse of Minnie's personal life ends and those with whom she briefly spent time in London largely disappear from primary view.

*

After the glamour of London, back in the 'dismal shabbiness' of the valleys, Minnie became part-time secretary of the NCF in Wales.[88] On top of her full-time work as a teacher, she took on what was initially intended as an organisational role that saw her immersed in correspondence during the evenings and conducting visits on weekends. The demanding position involved coordinating support to the approximately 900 COs across Wales, monitoring where they were being held, visiting them in barracks, prison and military camps, acting as a friend of the defendant and a witness in military tribunals and courts martial, and providing intelligence on COs' movements around the army and prison system to the NCF's Information Bureau. Minnie also coordinated support to COs' dependents.[89] This work had been part of Morgan Jones responsibilities as the Welsh NCF chair, until his arrest.[90] Now, with Jones in gaol, Minnie divided his work with Henry Davies who, as a male of conscription age, adopted the public responsibilities including chairing events as well as assuming the duties of Welsh representative on the NCF National Committee.

From a pacifist perspective, things were very gloomy. The NCF was harassed by the authorities and treated with hostility by the public. Arrests were so frequent that, by September, the situation was acute.[91] Women associate members became essential in maintaining the organisation, replacing the COs who had to relinquish organisational responsibilities when imprisoned. Emrys Hughes was in Devizes prison, and would spend the next three years in detention, while Agnes, his sister, was secretary of Aberdare NCF.[92] Three brothers of the future novelist, Lily Tobias, were gaoled as COs and a fourth was imprisoned for avoiding military service. Tobias, as NCF activist from Ystalyfera, attended courts martials, undertook prison visits and advised relatives.[93] Her novel *Eunice Fleet* portrayed the cruelties, injustices and anguish suffered by COs in prison as well as the psychological importance of NCF prisoner visits. A central character was the NCF organiser, a schoolteacher named Laura Fenwick, who was equally distrusted for her support of COs as for advocating peace. It is unknown whether Tobias based any of Fenwick's character on Minnie. Unlike the fictional Fenwick (but like the real-life Morgan Jones) Minnie did not lose her teaching job for her activities, but she and her comrades would have felt the same levels of social ostracism as Fenwick experienced in the novel's portrayal.[94]

Emrys Hughes, Morgan Jones and Minnie were three of the many ILP teachers in Wales who provided an important strand of opposition to the war. They were part of what Ness Edwards, an Abertillery CO, graphically described as a 'jigsaw puzzle of anti-war ideas' held by 'a collection of religionists, humanists, ethicists, and cranks ... [and] all other types of anti-warites — the socialists, anarchists, and syndicalists' in the NCF.[95] Minnie had to navigate this uneasy alliance. Also, for all the theoretical equality in the Fellowship, with increasing numbers of women assuming organisational roles, it was difficult for a woman operating in a man's organisation. Just like Marshall, the national secretary, Minnie needed the use of guile to get the men to do what she wanted, and drew on her years of experience in the ILP.[96]

NCF headquarters highlighted the importance of keeping in touch with female relatives and suggested bringing together wives, mothers and sweethearts, perhaps even weekly as a good means for the NCF to gather information and also allow women to be cheered by one another's company.[97] This is the first known experience of Minnie working with women collectively and individually on their needs; it would find full expression in coming decades.

Although it was not initially part of her brief, Minnie's articulate advocacy of the COs' case became just as important to the cause as her organising. The power of her voice in meetings and on the platform, arguing the case for COs, and generating a wide range of support, made her a prominent advocate in South Wales. Minnie was proud of her NCF allegiance and her photographic portrait bore the prison arrow symbol of the NCF in solidarity with those in prison who were 'winning the order of the broad arrow'.[98]

Minnie was to the fore as an organiser.[99] In October she arranged part of a South Wales tour for Helena Swanwick of the Women's International League, a feminist suffrage organisation that campaigned for peace. A member of the UDC executive on the outbreak of war, Swanwick was twenty years older than Minnie. Swanwick recalled being met at Brynmawr railway station by Minnie, with whom she was staying, before addressing an ILP meeting. The highly demanding Swanwick was, however, unimpressed by Minnie and Ivor Thomas lamenting 'They are the most haphazard organizers here!' adding: 'The people are so good and intelligent and the organizing so rotten.'[100] Swanwick's assessment was harsh, particularly of Thomas, of whom she complained 'I begin to doubt whether he knows what he's doing at all.' In contrast, Marshall considered Thomas to be 'an extremely effective organiser'.[101] Later experience would show Marshall's to be the accurate assessment. Minnie too had shown herself to be a competent organiser.

Minnie's profile was now high and her voice became a powerful instrument against the war. She presided over the NCF Welsh Divisional Convention public meeting of Brockway, who was acting NCF Chair in place of the gaoled Allen, though he too would be gaoled and in turn replaced by Russell.[102] On Friday 10 November, Minnie and Fred Jowett MP spoke at an ILP public meeting in Blaenavon. Jowett, a pioneer socialist who had started working in Yorkshire factories as a boy, was a founder member of the ILP. Chair of the Party following the death of Keir Hardie, he had great integrity, was faithful to his principles, and was greatly respected.[103] The following morning, Minnie accompanied Jowett to Cardiff, an hour away by train, where both were to speak at the 900 strong NCCL conference in the Cory Hall.[104] Other speakers on a strong platform were J. H. Thomas MP, the railwaymen's leader, MacDonald, Swanwick and Ivor Thomas, the conference organiser, with Winstone in the chair. They were greeted by a remarkable ovation from delegates of trades union branches; trades councils; socialist and peace societies; religious organisations; co-operative societies and women's organisations.

However, the conference did not proceed, as a mob, led by among others the jingoistic C. B. Stanton, a rogue ILP miners' leader, smashed up the event in what became known as 'The Battle of Cory Hall'. The disruption that prevented the meeting from proceeding illustrated the conflict between pro and anti-war elements in South Wales. The 'sober assessment' of the intelligence services was that the event 'highlighted the strength and potential of the anti-war movement' rather than success on the part of the mob.[105] The disrupted conference was reconvened in Merthyr on 9 December under the auspices of the Peace Council, with Minnie, W. H. Mainwaring of Clydach Vale and Ivor Thomas among its organisers. Attended by over 2,500 people, and again chaired by the 'notorious' Jim Winstone, MacDonald expressed alarm at the reduction in civil liberties, while Swanwick called for a negotiated peace.[106] Minnie admired Winstone's bravery in consistently placing himself alongside those opposed to the war for he was not a pacifist, but as the person with the highest public profile in Wales perceived to be against the war, he was the target for the greatest bile.[107]

By late 1916, Minnie's pacifist activities made her subject to monitoring by the police and security services. In December she was listed among those who the authorities considered to be potentially prejudicial to war ambitions.[108] Regular surveillance of and reporting on activists reflected the government's nervousness over the anti-war movement. It also recognised the importance of ILP strongholds in influencing workers' attitudes in the rail and coal industries.[109] Initially the authorities misjudged Minnie. Perhaps it was her comparatively recent assumption of the Welsh NCF secretary's role, or the poor quality of their intelligence, that led them to incorrectly identify her as from Merthyr district, and their record merely read 'Clever. Attended Merthyr Peace Meeting. Presided at Meeting of Miss Pankhurst, Cardiff. Not extreme.'[110]

However, the police quickly revised their view and became increasingly concerned at her activities. Three times, in January, March and apparently December 1917, she was recommended for prosecution under DORA, on two occasions for sedition. The first was a 'disloyal' speech at Aberaman, on 11 January 1917. Then on Sunday 4 March, Minnie addressed the Rhondda Socialist Society, which was being revived by A. J. Cook, with Arthur Horner as secretary.[111] Minnie was conscious that she was talking to the pre-war militants of the Unofficial Reform Committee (URC) in their old haunt, the Aberystwyth Restaurant, Tonypandy, where they had drafted *The Miners' Next Step* pamphlet. Now, as they regrouped, Minnie told them that NCF headquarters was mindful of the significance of the Rhondda as an epicentre of industrial struggle.[112]

It was this issue that perhaps made the authorities most worried. For the significance of Minnie's presence lay not just in the content of her speech, but also in what the authorities regarded as a potentially subversive alliance forming between the primarily middle-class opponents of the war and working-class opponents of conscription.[113] According to the verbatim police report, Minnie outspokenly criticised the Government's economy campaign as 'a manoeuvre', lambasted the wealthy for telling workers to be economical, and contrasted their lives with the experience of the rich, describing the difference as a catalogue of injustice and inequality.[114] Perhaps another sin in the eyes of the authorities was her even-handedness towards British and Germans, saying they were not all beasts or brutes on either side. She stressed that although the militarists had captured the imagination of the young, and the term pacifist had become a reproach, 5,000–6,000 COs were determined to resist. As a highly articulate anti-war advocate making common cause with the miners, she highlighted that, as there was not yet conscription of miners for the army, many in the Rhondda were still untouched by the military machine so had not yet had to make sacrifices and she therefore called on them to support the dependents of COs who were. She was backed by W. H. Mainwaring, the secretary of the URC before the war, and now local branch secretary of the NCF, who moved a resolution for a levy for COs.[115]

As the situation became more critical, increasingly large anti-conscription meetings took place, with the NCF growing from a 'small propaganda body' into a 'substantial movement'.[116] By the end of 1916, Minnie had stepped from the margins of the labour movement to a central position in the anti-war movement in Wales, and her name ranked high among those seen by the authorities to pose a threat to the prosecution of the war. Minnie was one of forty-two people, including MacDonald, Tom Mann and Pankhurst, as well as Horner, W. H. Mainwaring and Winstone, who were recommended by Capt. Lionel Lindsay, the Chief Constable of Glamorgan, for prosecution in 1917. She was the only woman from Wales who was listed. Although decisions on who to prosecute under DORA were now taken by MI5 and Special Branch, rather than the local constabulary, Lindsay had no doubt. He considered Minnie's Tonypandy speech to be seditious, and called on the Competent Military Authorities to prosecute her but, much to Lindsay's frustration, they did not do so.[117]

*

Events beyond Britain catapulted Minnie to greater prominence, not only as the outstanding woman in Wales against the war, but also as a clarion voice advocating revolutionary social and political change. When news of the February Russian Revolution which overthrew the Tsarist regime reached Britain in mid-March 1917, it changed the way pacifists related to the war, marking a shift towards finding political ways forward. It also impacted profoundly

'A NEW STAR ON THE HORIZON'

on the labour movement that was now considered a potential source of anti-war opposition and even revolutionary change, including on the newly formed trades and labour councils whose numbers were rapidly expanding across South Wales. A fortnight after the news broke, Minnie chaired MacDonald's meeting in Bargoed where he declared that the Russia revolution meant a new life for the world; that revolution, like war, was contagious and that none could tell how far it would spread, or who would next join in.[118] MacDonald saw the Russian Government as the 'spiritual cousin' of the ILP and in the programme of the Petrograd Soviet 'the ILP finds a new justification and expression of its policy'.[119] As a wave of 'Russia Free' May Day rallies took place across Britain, Minnie topped the bill at Bargoed's first annual Labour Day demonstration, which was used to welcome the Russian Revolution. Despite being denied the New Hall at the last moment, a huge crowd filled the Workmen's Institute, in what was reportedly a highly successful meeting.

RUSSIA FREE RUSSIA FREE
NEW HALL, BARGOED.
A GREAT DEMONSTRATION
will be held at above Hall
ON SUNDAY, MAY 6th, 1917,
TO WELCOME THE ADVENT OF THE RUSSIAN REVOLUTION.
Speakers:
MISS MINNIE PALLISTER (Brynmawr).
ARTHUR PONSONBY, Esq., M.P.
Chairman: Jas. Winstone, Esq., J.P., S.W.M.F.
Admission 6d. Doors open 2.25 p.m.
Meeting Commences 2.45 p.m.
ALL DEMOCRATS RALLY ROUND!

Minnie ironically said 'being a woman and therefore having no brains and no understanding', she could not understand the contradiction in their being able to celebrate freedom of speech and of the press in Russia, along with the liberation of all political prisoners, while the British Government did the very opposite; so she settled for offering the Russian revolutionaries envious congratulations in the cause of justice, brotherhood, and peace. Her demand for the release of all British COs and political prisoners was greeted by a 'storm of applause', made all the more poignant by the reading of a letter from Morgan Jones, who was still in gaol. The meeting unanimously supported the resolution calling on every government to follow the Russian example by re-establishing industrial, civil, and religious liberty, freedom of speech and of the press; releasing all political and religious offenders, abolishing all privileges of class, race, or sex, and renouncing all claims to annexations or indemnities. The meeting ended with the singing of the Red Flag and three cheers for international socialism.[120]

The Russian Revolution energised the NCF, something much needed after the tough times endured in 1916 and early 1917. The NCF now added support for Russia to its other work, and the position taken by the Russian Provisional Government, including an amnesty for political offences and an extension of political liberties and adult suffrage, providing British pacifists with an important point of reference.[121] Throughout the spring, summer and autumn of 1917, Minnie criss-crossed South Wales speaking to countless NCF and ILP branches, as well as Trades and Labour Councils and Socialist Societies to support the Russian Revolution, oppose the war, and promote socialism. One regular talk was the 'Fascination of War', when she spoke on 'the horrors of peace' with its inequitable and cruel system of competition and capitalism.[122]

After three years of terrible warfare, for those experiencing both the threats and the exhilaration associated with resistance, developments in Russia were electrifying. Infused by a revolutionary spirit, the Council of Workers and Soldiers Delegates, commonly known as 'The Leeds Convention', held on Sunday 3 June, suggested that similar change might be possible in Britain. The convention called for a peace without annexations or indemnities, and the rights of peoples to self-determination, full civil liberties as well as the establishing of workers' and soldiers' councils across the country. Attended by over 3,000 anti-war socialists and pacifists and dominated by the ILP, the speakers and supporters read like a *Who's Who* of Minnie's address book.[123] A week later Minnie reported back to an Ynyshir meeting intended as preparation for the resultant South Wales Workers and Soldiers Council conference, scheduled for Swansea in July, on the effect of the Russian

Revolution upon the Great War. This meeting, organised by Horner for the Rhondda Socialist Society, with Arthur Cook and Ablett as Minnie's supporting speakers, was the first of three planned meetings, to be followed by Tom Mann and Sylvia Pankhurst.[124] Minnie, by now a prominent propagandist, whose presence, power of oratory and popularity saw her cheered on taking the platform, was becoming a force to be reckoned with.[125]

Sylvia Pankhurst and Minnie's shared socialist beliefs and their opposition to the war brought them together regularly. Minnie organised several tours for her almost exact contemporary, chaired a number of her meetings, spoke alongside her on several occasions and, when Pankhurst appeared in Brynmawr on various occasions between June 1916 and July 1918, she no doubt stayed with Minnie.[126] The only remaining branch of Pankhurst's WSF in Wales, Brynmawr and Nantyglo, was intelligently active in adapting the WSF's East End strategy and policies to the circumstances of the coalfield.[127] It applied for representation on the local Food Control Committee, but was refused permission. Even so, it planned to send a deputation to schools to investigate underfeeding amongst the children, as many colliers in the district were under-employed.[128]

Food shortages and prices increasingly became a key issue, particularly as a result of submarine warfare. In May dissatisfaction with the Government's food-control policy was expressed during a conference of Trades Unions, Labour and Co-operative organisations of East Glamorgan and Monmouthshire, where Minnie moved a resolution calling for local authorities to have powers to set up special Food Control Committees, so that consumers could be registered and guaranteed an equitable distribution of food. This was complemented by her call for representatives of Labour, Co-operative, and Industrial Women's Organisations to be co-opted to these municipal food-services. Furthermore, she added, if Government failed to take prompt measures to address the growing difficulties of food supply and exploitation of consumers by food profiteers, a national deputation, drawn from all parts of the country, should be organised to appeal directly to Parliament.[129]

In early July, Minnie was summoned to the family home due to her father's illness and he died on 18 August, aged 66. Minnie's family were her bedrock. Now, with the death of her father and Julia living in India, although she had extended family networks through her parents, her immediate family, in practice, became reduced to her mother, Rose, and sister Gladys. During Minnie's absence, the South Wales Workers and Soldiers Council conference in Swansea, in which she would otherwise have played a prominent role, was smashed up by discharged soldiers, sailors and women munitions workers as the confrontations between the anti-war minority and pro-war majority continued.[130] Undeterred, after another visit by Pankhurst to Brynmawr, Minnie was the main speaker at the second anniversary memorial meeting of Keir Hardie's death.[131]

As the main pillars of war resistance were provided by radical nonconformity, the local ILP and the NCF, addressing chapels became an increasing feature of Minnie's anti-war activity. She delivered an 'inspiring' hour-long talk at Bryn Seion Chapel, Craigcefnparc, a known haven for anti-war activists, and one of a number of chapels in the Swansea Valley where the congregations included ILP members and supported the anti-war movement.[132] In December when she addressed a peace meeting at the Jerusalem English Baptist Church in Briton Ferry, nicknamed the 'Kaiser's Temple' for its enthusiastic support of the anti-war movement, three police officers and a police reporter were in attendance. Minnie paid tribute to the approximately 100 conscientious objectors in Aberavon and Briton Ferry. It was proportionately by far the heaviest concentration of COs in Britain, reflecting the strength of ILP presence there.[133] Saying 'The world owes everything to the conscientious objector' she added of Jesus 'We could not meet in this chapel to-night were it not for him.'[134] It was too much for the Chief Constable of Glamorgan who a few days later submitted another unsuccessful recommendation that Minnie be prosecuted for a disloyal and seditious speech.[135]

Unlike in the Second World War, when war impacted indiscriminately and equally on everyone military or civilian, during the Great War those in the army bore the brunt of direct suffering while, for those at home, life continued in many ways unaffected. However, because of the path she chose, her visits to detained COs, her support to their families, and her experience of the hostility to her NCF and ILP work, Minnie was as engaged with the war as it was possible for a non-war worker to be. She was close to those involved in the informal 'shadowy' networks, including ILP and NCF members in Abertillery and Wattsville that helped COs who were on the run evade the authorities.[136] Encountering the might of the state arraigned against them was profound as 'the war-time experiences of the ILP members in the NCF burned deep into their political souls'.[137] In 1924 Minnie wrote: 'It was hard to face the bitter attacks of countless enemies. It was hard to stand with one's back against the wall fighting for very existence.'[138] In the mid-1950s she recalled:

> It all seems like a dream now: my friends in prison; the vast peace meetings in Wales where we would collect thirty or forty pounds for the fund for their families...the peace conferences broken up by hooligans; the times we had to be rescued from the mob; the making Germany pay; the bitter disillusion...and always the exhilaration of being in a small minority fighting with our backs to the wall, hated by the public, ostracised by family and friends, but with a burning conviction that we were right.
>
> Have we kept anything out of this struggle? Was it worthwhile?
>
> It's always worthwhile to be on the side of the angels. It may be all we got out of those strenuous years, but it's enough.[139]

Those bonds formed during the war endured. Minnie would later be sustained in times of greatest need by 'the friendship of those who fight a lone cause [that] is like no other friendship'.[140]

Despite referring to being hated by the public and ostracised by family and friends, Minnie was not completely shunned. She continued teaching and throughout the war remained an adjudicator at the Brynmawr eisteddfod. She also performed with Margaret Judd in the Cafe Chantant, Gilwern for the Red Cross Society and appeared at fundraising concerts for Brookfield Red Cross War Hospital in Walthamstow, the Mayor's Local War Fund, and the Borough's Overseas Soldiers & Sailors Reception Fund. Indeed, while the war was still on, Minnie was co-opted onto the Breconshire County Education Committee even though the *Brecon County Times* had clamoured for action against the NCF, describing it as 'an enemy within the gates' and the military authorities in Brecon had taken action against those distributing NCF pamphlets.[141] Perhaps her preparedness to help wounded and other soldiers saved her from the worst opprobrium.[142]

MINNIE PALLISTER: THE VOICE OF A REBEL

*

From the autumn of 1917, shifts occurred in Minnie's priorities. Having been one of the most prominent voices in South Wales in support of the February Russian Revolution, she was unenamoured with the October Revolution, reflecting a shift in opinion of many on the left in Britain. When the Bolshevik Revolution transformed the political landscape, Minnie continued to respect Russia's right to choose its own path to self-determination but very quickly saw Russia as no longer a beacon for liberty or an example to Britain, so it became less a focus of her work. In contrast, Pankhurst became a strong supporter of the Bolsheviks, and then of British communism as Minnie and Pankhurst's views diverged. There is no evidence of their being in contact beyond 1918.

Also Minnie gave up her position as NCF secretary in Wales, while continuing to support COs as part of her political work.[143] Her resignation paralleled those of Allen, Marshall and Russell from the national leadership of the NCF, all of whom were demoralised by internal divisions. Allen and Brockway now felt the socialist movement, rather than the NCF, had 'first claim' on them, as did Minnie, who was sufficiently prominent in the ILP to be listed in the 1918 Party diary.[144] Indeed her prioritising of the NCF had never been to the exclusion of the ILP. In 1917 she stood to be the Wales member of the ILP NAC. As the only woman, and a comparatively inexperienced one at that, standing against experienced comrades including Ivor Thomas and George Neighbour, Minnie showed she lacked neither ambition nor political self-confidence.[145]

A third decisive shift occurred in autumn 1917 when Minnie started to focus more on women, both in relation to policy and organisation. It is likely that the influence of pacifist feminists with whom Minnie worked during the Great War, including Marshall, Swanwick, Ethel Snowden and Pankhurst, who had earlier campaigned for women's suffrage, contributed to this change. Although Minnie had associated with the WSF in 1916, she had not otherwise demonstrated a specific commitment to women's issues. Now, sometimes addressing three meetings a day, she argued for women's involvement in the labour and peace movements, declaring that they belonged to women as much as men. Embarking on a course that she would sustain for the rest of her life, through topics such as 'Unity of Man, Man and Woman & Nations' and 'Women and

War', she made earnest appeals to a range of audiences that included increasing numbers of women.[146] By late 1917, Minnie was involved in the Women's Peace Crusade. Started in June 1916 in Glasgow, by mid-1917 the ILP was supporting the Crusade, largely at the behest of Margaret Bondfield and Katharine Bruce Glasier. Anti-militarist and socialistic rather than just pacifist, it was aimed at working-class women in their own communities. Fuelled by anger against conscription and military tribunals, the slaughter of the trenches, food shortages and price increases, the Crusade 'captured the war-weary, dissident spirit', as the *Labour Leader* called on ILP women to prevent another winter of war.[147] After four branches were established in Wales, a new Bargoed branch decided to meet chapel congregations as they came out of Sunday service and to canvas all women in the district door to door to call for peace. It invited Ethel Snowden, who had lead responsibility for the Crusade within the ILP, and Minnie, to address them. In October a branch was established in Brynmawr, with Minnie as secretary. When Mrs Snowden spoke there, with Minnie presiding, sixty children held peace flags, sang and did recitations, as part of what has been described as an energetic and innovative woman-focussed, single-issue campaign.[148]

Now Minnie fused socialism, pacifism and the rights of women in her campaigning. In Abertillery she talked about 'The Women's Franchise and The Food Question', and to the Abergavenny Free Church Girls' Guild on 'The place of women in the social and political life of the future'.[149] Minnie's advocacy of family allowances made her an early adopter of the cause propagated by the social reformer Eleanor Rathbone, who published her proposals in spring 1918.[150] Within months Minnie was making the case in South Wales, addressing the structural causes of the gendered inequalities that South Wales's industrial society imposed upon women. Her years working in the valleys had made their mark and Minnie understood that women's economic dependence on men's earnings, their tendency to marry early, and the often unpaid and unrecognised nature of their work made this a fundamental issue. Minnie also made far-reaching proposals for the provision of suitable work for women thrown out of employment after the war, including establishing baby clinics, which could employ women doctors and where mothers could learn about feeding and hygiene. She called for swimming baths and gymnasia where women would work as instructors, and advocated co-education to help create better quality relationships between the sexes. While she could speak equally to men and women on issues that concerned them, her socialist politics were now infused with a gender-based analysis that challenged the male domination of society.[151]

Minnie increasingly addressed workers' meetings, as well as party political, pacifist and church events, and her regular invitations from Rhondda miners' groups indicated her standing with them. In yet another Ynyshir meeting, Horner, in the chair, called for men in South Wales to stand by those on the Clyde and 'stop the bloody audacious war'. A. J. Cook said he would prefer to be shot before being taken to the army and hoped that if they tried to take men for the military, that not a ton of coal would be available for the navy. For once Minnie's contribution did not alarm those undertaking police surveillance, who instead saved their ire for the company she kept.[152]

The pace that Minnie sustained during the second half of the war was relentless. The physical demands of undertaking political work every night after school and at weekends were enormous. Having to rely on inter-valley train journeys that sometimes required multiple changes, she would arrive home late on Sunday evening, physically exhausted, after speaking in remote places, prior to her return to the classroom on the Monday morning.

With war weariness setting into the population, the ILP's anti-war position won new adherents. Branch numbers in Wales rose markedly as persecution and repression now added to its membership.[153] While the majority of people continued to support the men at the front, the inequality of sacrifice and war profiteering was increasingly questioned.[154] It was still, though, a hostile time for the ILP. Minnie's appearance with MacDonald in Mountain Ash had to be moved when the venue was withdrawn and their next meeting in Ebbw Vale was also difficult with an ugly scene outside and the crowd in a 'dangerous mood'.[155]

Party political issues came to the fore in early 1918. At the Welsh ILP conference, where a general election programme and activities were prepared for the reorganised South Wales constituencies, Minnie moved the resolution calling for land nationalisation, which was approved. The Party also agreed to the election of the first permanent ILP organiser for Wales, which later would have significance for Minnie.[156] However, the role occupied by the ILP within the Labour

Party was threatened shortly afterwards by the Labour Party's adoption of a new, nominally socialist, constitution. Drafted by Arthur Henderson, it introduced individual membership for the first time, providing an alternative route for joining other than through the ILP, so challenging much of the ILP's *raison d'etre*.[157] The constitution transformed the Labour Party, replacing a looser federation with a more structured organisation of branches and constituency parties and set up a new organisation for women.

Although the majority of trades unionists were portrayed as being suspicious of the ILP because of its opposition to the war, the bitter differences that existed nationally between the unions and ILP were not reflected locally.[158] Embracing the changes, Minnie helped build the new Labour Party. In Brecon and Radnor constituency, where she was the only woman elected to its executive committee, Minnie was involved in establishing the Party's machinery, and was a speaker at Labour's first demonstration there. Perhaps recognising that the needs of most women were different from her own, while focussing her own involvement on the Party's male-dominated mainstream, she urged the ten newly formed local branches to help organise women into sections.[159] When the trades unions in Abergavenny formed the new local Labour Party, they invited Minnie, the solidly anti-war ILPer, as its inaugural speaker. Taking the ideals of the labour movement and the part that women should play as her themes, Minnie argued that women coming into the labour movement would help define its aim. One of the first demands, she said, was that mothers should have pensions, so that their children would not be seen as a burden but a joy, and allowing women to gain a degree of independence from their husbands.[160]

The Great War transformed Minnie and her politics. Her outlook on the role of women, as well as the church, had undergone profound changes. The experiences she endured and the challenges she faced in the four years of war made her into a much tougher operator. Her growing political maturity, with her capacity to apply what she had learned from the society around her, allowed her to create a vision of what it meant to be a socialist woman in Wales. In the summer of 1918, at 33 years of age, she obtained the platform to promote it.

MINNIE PALLISTER: THE VOICE OF A REBEL

[1] Mary Agnes Hamilton, *Remembering My Good Friends*, Jonathan Cape, 1944, p. 79; Marquand, pp. 170 & 203; Paton, *Proletarian Pilgrimage*, pp. 248–250 & 291–2; Lord Elton, *The Life of James Ramsay MacDonald*, Collins, 1939, p. 297.

[2] David Marquand, *Ramsay MacDonald*, Jonathan Cape, 1977, pp.169–174, esp. p. 171.

[3] See Thomas C. Kennedy, *The Hound of Conscience*, Arkansas, 1981, p. 50 & Aled Eirug, *The Opposition to the Great War in Wales, 1914–1918*, UWP, 2018, p. 50; Fenner Brockway, *Inside the Left*, George Allen & Unwin, 1942, pp. 51–2.

[4] R. E. Dowse, *Left in the Centre: The Independent Labour Party, 1893–1940*, Longmans, 1966, p. 21. The war united the ILP but divided Minnie, Jim Winstone and Ted Gill, who until then had been closely politically aligned. Gill, the President of the South Wales ILP, was initially against the war but changed his position and enlisted. An outstanding miners' leader, he was equally a natural leader of men in the army. The military recognised his qualities and he was commissioned – rare for someone of the working class – and sent back to Abertillery as a recruiter. There, he and Minnie, former comrades, would be in opposition. It is interesting how the army identified able, prominent, local ILP leaders and returned them to their own communities to turn opponents of the war into 'patriots'. Another was Bill Collins, a journalist with *Llais Llafur*. A prominent ILPer and friend of Minnie, after enlisting he was sent back to recruit among his former ILP comrades in the Swansea Valley. (See William Collins, Autobiography, unpublished manuscript, nd, p. 124, Glam RO, DX356/1.)

[5] *Labour Leader*, 7 January 1915.

[6] Letter from Chief Constable, Norwich, 1 April 1915, HO 45/10741/263275; Brockway, *Inside the Left*, p. 63; Pankhurst, *Home Front*, p. 225; Frank Meeres, *Dorothy Jewson*, Poppyland Publishing, 2014, p. 37.

[7] *Pioneer*, 10 April 1915.

[8] *Pioneer*, 11 September 1915; Pallister, *Cabbage...*, p. 3; Report of ILP Norwich conference, April 1915, p. 48.

[9] *Pioneer*, 17 April 1915.

[10] *Pioneer*, 12 June 1915.

[11] *Pioneer*, 12 June & 20 November 1915; sketch referred to on 11 September 1915.

[12] *Peace News*, 28 September 1956.

[13] *Pioneer*, 12 June & 25 September 1915.

[14] *Pioneer*, 25 September 1915.

[15] Thompson, p. 92.

[16] *Labour Leader*, 25 February, 22 April, 6 May & 28 October 1915; *Pioneer*, 27 March & 29 May 1915.

[17] *Labour Leader*, 17 December 1914, 10 & 17 February & 23 March 1916; *Pioneer*, 15 January & 27 May 1916.

[18] Marquand, p. 188.

[19] Eirug, *The Opposition...*, p. 57.

[20] Ivor Thomas worked in the tinplate works from 15 years of age, initially as an office boy before becoming a tinplate finisher. A trades union activist, he became a member of the National Executive of the Dockers' Union in 1914. He was secretary of Briton Ferry ILP and a member of the ILP NAC. He was founding secretary of Aberavon Labour Party, a post he held until 1922 when he resigned through pressure of work, having become a full-time trades union organiser in Newport in 1921.

[21] Eirug, *The Opposition...*, pp. 125–6, 133 & 135; David Egan, 'The Swansea

'A NEW STAR ON THE HORIZON'

Conference of the British Council of Soldiers' and Workers' Delegates, July 1917: Reactions To The Russian Revolution of February 1917, and the Anti-War Movement in South Wales', *Llafur*, Vol 1 No 4, Summer 1975, pp. 19 & 22–3, quoted in Eirug, *The Opposition...*, p. 50.

[22] Morgan Jones was a teacher who was imprisoned for his conscientious objection. Elected MP for Caerphilly in 1921, he held junior ministerial posts in the 1924 and 1929–31 Labour Governments. *Labour Leader*, 17 June 1915; *Pioneer*, 19 June 1915; Eirug, *The Opposition...*, pp. 48–9 & 137–8; Kennedy, p. 81; Cyril Pearce, review of *Writing About Britain's 1914–18 War Resisters – Literature Review*, (review no. 1779) DOI: 10.14296/RiH/2014/1779 Accessed 28 March 2016.

[23] *Peace News*, 3 March 1956.

[24] Eirug, *The Opposition...*, p. 123.

[25] *Pioneer*, 9 October 1915; *Labour Leader*, 11 November & 2 December 1915.

[26] Quoted in Constance Malleson, *After Ten Years*, Jonathan Cape, 1931, p. 100.

[27] Beatrice Webb Diary, 8 April 1916; Hamilton, *Friends*, p. 116; Jo Vellacott, *Bertrand Russell and the Pacifists in the First World War*, St Martin's Press, 1980, p. 47.

[28] Arthur Marwick, *Clifford Allen: The Open Conspirator*, Oliver & Boyd, 1964, pp. 24–26.

[29] Kennedy, p. 56.

[30] *UDC* [The Journal], Feb 1916, p. 40, & June 1916, p. 87; Pallister to Trevelyan, nd, Sir Charles Phillips Trevelyan papers, Extra Series, 1986, Newcastle University Archive, CPT/1/7/51.

[31] 'South Wales and the ILP'.

[32] Elton, p. 290.

[33] *Pioneer*, 15 April 1916.

[34] Diary 1916, Ramsay MacDonald Papers, RMD/2/15, University of Manchester Special Collection; *Pioneer*, 1 April 1916; *Labour Leader*, 6 April 1916.

[35] MacDonald to Pallister, 3 April 1916, reproduced in Elton, p. 301.

[36] Elton, p. 300; 'I've Been Thinking...About Wales'.

[37] Minnie stated she met Macdonald at her first conference. Her first known conference was Merthyr in May 1912, though, as MacDonald was not present, they must have met earlier. Minnie later recalled MacDonald's daughter, Shelagh, who was born in December 1910, as 'a wee baby', which would suggest Minnie knew the MacDonald family at least around the time of the death of MacDonald's wife Margaret in September 1911. Pallister to Scott-Moncrieff, 2 March 1960, BBC WAC RCONT1 Pallister (Talks 10); Pallister to MacDonald, nd but post 27 April 1927, MacDonald papers, PRO 30/69/1172 Pt II.

[38] MacDonald to Pallister, 12 June 1916, reproduced in Elton p. 301–2.

[39] MacDonald to Pallister, 13 October 1916, reproduced in Elton p. 302.

[40] No personal correspondence between Minnie and MacDonald exists before 1927 in the MacDonald archive, although two beautiful photographs of Minnie, dated 1917 and 1919, are there. Minnie would have written regularly to MacDonald prior to 1926 but the letters are missing. There are no letters relating to his 1916 Brynmawr stay, although the equivalent 1916 letters for Bertrand Russell and Charles Trevelyan are in their respective collections. In 1937 Minnie recalled receiving MacDonald's 1916 reply saying he would come to Brynmawr. (Pallister to MacDonald, 30 April 1937, MacDonald collection, PRO 30/69/759.) Nor is there correspondence relating to his Porthcawl visit in 1922, where Minnie then lived, when he stayed for days. Their absence highlights an unfillable gap in writing of Minnie and MacDonald's relationship. MacDonald's archive is enormous, lifelong, is systematically preserved and could be assumed to be representative, if not complete. In the context of an extensive, highly organised, well-maintained collection, the absence of Minnie's personal letters strongly

indicates a conscious weeding of correspondence. There is a parallel: no correspondence exists in MacDonald's papers relating to Molly Hamilton, although portrait photos of Hamilton are also held in his collection. (Marquand, pp. 406–7.) A direct descendant of MacDonald acknowledged to me that the family was protective of his reputation and was 'odd' in relation to matters such as weeding of his correspondence. Moreover, Merryl Caleb, who later taught in the same school, was told by Miss Doubleday, a former teacher who had worked with Minnie, that in the staff room Minnie described herself as MacDonald's mistress. (Statements, 1 & 16 March 2024.)

[41] Marquand, pp. 135, 406–7 & 686. MacDonald's love letters to Londonderry were addressed 'My Dear Ladye', reminiscent of his addressing Minnie as 'Your Laidieship' a decade earlier and as 'My dear old Ladye' in 1929.

[42] *Labour Leader*, 27 April & 4 May 1916.

[43] Information provided by Eirug.

[44] *Labour Leader*, 22 June 1916.

[45] *South Wales Argus*, 26 June 1916; *Labour Leader*, 29 June 1916. Philip Snowden, a nonconformist product of working-class Yorkshire and a pacifist, was 'the NCF's real voice in Parliament'. (Kennedy, p 110.) Ethel Snowden was a middle-class schoolteacher and Christian Socialist who was active in the ILP and the suffrage movement before the Great War.

[46] *Labour Leader*, 29 June 1916. For places of high anti-war resistance see Cyril Pearce, *Communities of Resistance, Conscience and Dissent in Britain during the First World War*, Francis Boutle, 2020.

[47] Eirug, *The Opposition*, p. 129, fn 18, based on undated security service paper KV 2/665

[48] Ryland Wallace, email to author, 11 March 2016.

[49] *Labour Leader*, 25 May & 1 June 1916; *Pioneer*, 3 June 1916; *Woman's Dreadnought*, 3 June & 20 July 1918; 'Memories...'. I am grateful for information received from Ryland Wallace about Pankhurst in South Wales.

[50] *Pioneer*, 15 July 1916; *South Wales Gazette*, 14 July 1916; *Woman's Dreadnought*, 15 & 22 July 1916.

[51] Russell to Morrell, undated, Russell papers, Bracers reference, 18582, .001403 2.67 RA3 69, McMaster University Archive, transcript provided by Kenneth Blackwell; *Pioneer*, 29 July 1916.

[52] Ronald W. Clark, *The Life of Bertrand Russell*, Cape, Weidenfeld & Nicolson, 1975, pp. 294–6; Vellacott, *Bertrand Russell...*, pp. 18 & 91.

[53] See Ray Monk, *Bertrand Russell*, Jonathan Cape, 1996, pp. 382–3; Joan Beauchamp 'What Women Have Done: War Resistance 1914–1918', *Peace News*, 9 April 1938; Alan Ryan, *Bertrand Russell: A Political Life*, Allen Lane, 1988, pp. 55 & 60.

[54] Pallister to Russell, undated, 2502.054152 5.36 RA1 710.

[55] Marshall to Russell, 21 July 1916, 78198 .052665 5.30 RA 710, although her bracketed phrase was scored through.

[56] NCF related Papers and Correspondence, July 1916, D/MAR/4/8, Marshall collection, Cumbria Record Office.

[57] Marwick, *Clifford Allen*, pp. 33 & 35.

[58] Vellacott, *Bertrand Russell...*, pp. 107 & 122.

[59] Vellacott, *Bertrand Russell...*, p. 241; Clark, p. 293.

[60] Beauchamp, 'What Women Have Done...'; Jo Vellacott, *Pacifists, Patriots and the Vote*, Palgrave, 2007, p. 147.

[61] Vellacott, *Bertrand Russell...*, pp. 34–5 & 42; Vellacott to author 13 April 2016.

[62] Russell to Morrell, nd, but early August 1916. 18356.001193 2.65 RA3 69 transcription provided by Kenneth Blackwell, McMaster University.

[63] Vellacott to author, 13 April, 2016; Clark, p. 294.

[64] Marshall to Pallister, 9 August [1916], D/MAR/4/9, NCF Papers August 1916.

[65] Marshall to Russell, 21 July 1916, 78198 .052665 5.30 RA1 710 copy provided by Bridget Whittle, McMaster University.

[66] This assessment is based on my reading of Allen's unpublished diary for 1918–19.

[67] Russell to Morrell, undated, but thought to be on 8 August 1916, 18356.001193 2.65 RA3 69 transcription provided by Kenneth Blackwell.

[68] It may be that, in Minnie, Allen met his match. As well as Russell's reservations about Minnie's feelings for Allen, Allen indicated that Minnie may have commented that he would never attract a wife unless he got his teeth fixed. See Martin Gilbert, *Plough My Own Furrow*, Longmans Green, 1965, p. 109.

[69] Jo Vellacott, 'Marshall, Catherine Elizabeth', *Oxford Dictionary of National Biography*, https://doi.org/10.1093/ref:odnb/38527.

[70] Vellocott, *Russell...*, p. 123.

[71] Quoted in John G. Slater, 'Lady Constance Malleson, "Colette O'Niel"', 1975, from *Into the Tenth Decade: Tribute to Bertrand Russell*, 1962, p. 31; message reprinted in Constance Malleson, 'Fifty Years: 1916–1966', in R. Schoenman, ed., *Bertrand Russell: Philosopher of the Century*, Allen & Unwin, 1967, p. 24 https://mulpress.mcmaster.ca/russelljournal/article/download/1435/1462 accessed 29 May 2019.

[72] Pallister to Russell, undated but mid-August 1916, 79556 .054154 5.36 RA1 710, McMaster University.

[73] Russell to Morrell, 10 August 1916, 18606 .001424 2.67 RA3 69, McMaster University.

[74] Vellacott, *Bertrand Russell...*, p. 91.

[75] D. H. Lawrence, referred to in Monk, pp. 427/8.

[76] Monk, p. 436.

[77] Monk, pp. 401 & 446.

[78] Bertrand Russell, Preface, *Principles of Social Reconstruction*, Allen & Unwin, April 1923 edition, p. 5.

[79] Monk, p. 446.

[80] Russell, *Principles*, p. 191.

[81] See, for example, Monk pp. 235–6, 241–245.

[82] Russell, *Principles*, pp. 173–4, 185 & 190.

[83] See, for example, Monk, chapters 7 & 8.

[84] Email exchanges with Vellacott, April 2016.

[85] Ryan, p. 87.

[86] *The Autobiography of Bertrand Russell 1914–1944*, George Allen and Unwin, 1968, pp. 25–6.

[87] Malleson, *After Ten Years*, p. 106; Russell, *Autobiography*, p. 25.

[88] Term used by Emrys Hughes to Russell in 1917, quoted in Kennedy, p. 293; Vellacott, *Bertrand Russell...*, p. 152. Before leaving London, Minnie apparently suggested that the NCF create a full-time organiser post, but a part-time role was agreed with Minnie's expenses covered by a special fund raised in South Wales. (Draft letter with deletions, Marshall to Pallister, 29 August 1916, D/MAR/4/9.)

[89] 'Suggestions and Instructions to Visitors', D/MAR/4/10 September 1916, NCF papers, Marshall collection; Eirug, *The Opposition...*, pp. 19, 136, 144/5 & 170.

[90] Morgan Jones to Clifford Allen, 29 May 1916, quoted in Keith Robins, 'Morgan Jones in 1916', *Llafur*, Vol 1 No 4, 1975, p. 39.

[91] Organisation Department to Dear Comrade, 21 September 1916, Misc Communications from NCF & FSC 1915–1919, MS Vol 149 File 1, Friends House.

[92] *Aberdare Leader*, 20 May 1916; *Pioneer*, 17 June 1916; Phillip Adams, *Not in Our Name*, Phillip Adams, 2016, p. 117.

[93] Jasmine Donahaye, 'Introduction', Lily Tobias, *Eunice Fleet*, Honno, 2004 edition, pp. xi–xii.

[94] Tobias, pp. 114 & 141.

[95] Ness Edwards, *A Rebel's Testament*, unpublished manuscript, pp. 1–2, 1994/17, Swansea University Coalfield Collection. A miner, Edwards attended the Central Labour College, later becoming a Miners' Agent. He was Wales's first labour historian, writing books on working-class organisation. He was MP for Caerphilly from 1939 to 1968 and Postmaster General in the Attlee Government.

[96] Vellacott, *Bertrand Russell...*, p. 142.

[97] Kennedy, p. 185; Eirug, *The Opposition...*, pp. 144–5; Letter, 21 September 1916, Misc Communications from NCF & FSC 1915–1919, MS Vol 149 File 1, Friends House.

[98] *Labour Leader*, 5 August 1920.

[99] On consecutive weekends, Mr & Mrs Snowden, Dick Wallhead and Bob Smillie spoke in Brynmawr. Minnie admired Smillie, the leader of the British miners, for his incorruptibility and for remaining faithful to his own people and their needs. Smillie would lead national opposition to conscription. He too stayed at Minnie's home. (*Labour Leader*, 21 & 28 September & 5 October 1916; *Man and Metal*, March 1940.)

[100] Letter of 14 October 1916, reproduced in H. M. Swanwick, *I Have Been Young*, Gollancz, 1935, pp. 294–5.

[101] Eirug, *The Opposition...*, p. 125.

[102] *Tribunal*, 2 November 1916.

[103] *Labour Leader*, 16 November 1916; Paton, *Proletarian Pilgrimage*, p. 291.

[104] *Pioneer*, 18 November 1916.

[105] Eirug, *The Opposition*, pp. 130–1. The following day a private conference of 200 delegates from South Wales ILP branches addressed by MacDonald, in the same venue, proceeded uneventfully. (Aled Eirug, 'The Security Services in South Wales During the First World war', *WHR*, 28/4, 2017, p. 767.)

[106] *Labour Leader*, 30 November 1916; Eirug, 'The Security Services...', pp. 771; Eirug, *The Opposition...*, p. 131. The description of Winstone is in Chief Constable, Glamorgan to Competent Military Authority, 5 & 9 March 1917, HO 45/10742/263275, see Eirug, 'The Security Services...', p. 776.

[107] Eirug, *The Opposition...*, pp. 54 & 132; Pallister to John E. Morgan, 14 December 1950, Morgan Collection, Swansea University South Wales Coalfield Collection, uncatalogued.

[108] Milner Papers, Dep 377, Leaves 168–178, Bodleian Library, provided by Eirug; see also Aled Eirug, 'Spies and Troublemakers: How British Intelligence Targeted Peace and Labour Activists in South Wales at the Height of the Great War', *Llafur*, 2016, pp. 103–115, esp. 112.

[109] Eirug, 'The Security Services...', pp. 754, 762 & 768.

[110] Milner papers.

[111] Chief Constable, Glamorgan to Competent Military Authority, 5 March 1917, HO

45/10742/263275. Thanks to Eirug for this reference. *Pioneer*, 10 March 1917; Nina Fishman, *Arthur Horner, 1894–1944*, Lawrence & Wishart, 2010, p. 53. Both Cook and Horner would go on to become outstanding leaders of the South Wales and British miners.

[112] Hywel Francis and David Smith, *The Fed*, Lawrence & Wishart, 1980, p. 24; Gwyn A. Williams, *When Was Wales*, 1985, p. 240; Dai Smith, *Wales! Wales?*, George Allen & Unwin, 1984, pp. 64 & 96.

[113] Eirug, 'The Security Services...', p. 754.

[114] In particular Minnie identified Violet, daughter of Asquith, the former Prime Minister, who became Lady Bonham Carter. Their paths would cross forty years later. Mark Hayman points out that Minnie's was one of the 'isolated voices' in the country making these points. ('The Labour Party and the Monarchy', Ph.D, Warwick, 1999, p. 136.)

[115] Police notes of a speech by M. Pallister, March 4, 1917, HO 45/10742/263275. A miner in Cambrian Colliery, Mainwaring was part author of *The Miners' Next Step*. After the war he was a lecturer in the Central Labour College, then miners' agent in the Rhondda from 1924 to 1934, when he became MP for Rhondda East.

[116] Eirug, *The Opposition...*, p. 154; Martin Ceadel, *Pacifism in Britain 1914–1945*, Clarendon, 1980, p. 33.

[117] Eirug, 'The Security Services...', p. 776; Eirug, *The Opposition...*, p. 69; letters and reports Chief Constable, Glamorgan to Competent Military Authority, 5 & 9 March 1917 HO 45/10742/263275.

[118] Ceadel, *Pacifism...*, p. 52; *Labour Leader*, 7 April 1917.

[119] Marquand, pp. 207 & 208.

[120] *Pioneer*, 5 & 19 May 1917; *Labour Leader*, 10 May 1917; *The UDC*, Vol 2 No 8, June 1917, pp. 95–6.

[121] Vellacott, *Bertrand Russell*, pp. 154–7.

[122] *Labour Leader*, 5, 12 April & 14 June 1917; *Pioneer*, 21 April 1917.

[123] Walter Kendall, *The Revolutionary Movement in Britain 1900–1921*, Weidenfeld & Nicholson, 1969, p. 175; https://www.marxists.org/history/international/social-democracy/1917/leeds.htm accessed 26 March 2017. They included Allen and Anderson, Jowett, Lansbury, MacDonald, Sylvia Pankhurst, Russell, Phillip Snowden and Dick Wallhead.

[124] *Pioneer*, 16 June 1917; Fishman, *Horner*, p. 55.

[125] Probably through Minnie's contact with Horner, her sister Gladys worked as a dispenser for Mardy Miners' Medical Aid scheme. (Arthur Horner, *Incorrigible Rebel*, McGibbon & Kee, 1960, p. 62.)

[126] 'Memories...'

[127] Wallace, pp. 235–6.

[128] *Woman's Dreadnought*, 9 December 1916 & 31 March 1917; *Workers' Dreadnought*, 8 December 1917.

[129] *Pioneer*, 19 May 1917.

[130] Brynmawr School Log Book, 13 July 1917; Minutes of the Methodist Conferences 1918, p. 102, University of Manchester Special Collection; *Labour Leader*, 2 August 1917; Egan, pp. 19 & 22–3.

[131] *Labour Leader*, 6 September 1917; *Pioneer*, 15 September & 6 October 1917.

[132] Eirug, *The Opposition*, pp. 18–9.

[133] Pearce, *Communities of Resistance*, pp. 218 & 224–5; Eirug, *The Opposition*, p. 75.

[134] *Pioneer*, 6 October & 29 December 1917; *Labour Leader*, 19 August 1920.

[135] Letter of 27 December 1917 referred to in Chief Constable to Colonel Kell, 15 March 1918.

[136] See Rowbotham, *Friends...*, p. 38 for these networks; also author interview with Neil Fisher and Harold Jones, 12 June 1982.

[137] Dowse, p. 27.

[138] *New Leader*, 25 April 1924.

[139] *Peace News*, 3 March 1956.

[140] *New Leader*, 25 April 1924.

[141] *Brecon County Times*, 13 April & 11 May 1916, 2 October 1918.

[142] *Abergavenny Chronicle*, 7 May 1915, 6 April, 7 September, 5 October, 30 November 1917, 29 March & 26 April 1918; *Brecon Radnor Express*, 13 May 1915 & 4 July 1918; *Brecon County Times*, 22 June 1916.

[143] *Labour Leader*, 29 November 1917; Eirug, *The Opposition*, p. 144.

[144] Ceadel, *Pacifism...*, p. 53; Vellacott, *Bertrand Russell...*, pp. 218–9; Kennedy, *Hound...*, p. 243.

[145] Annual conference programme of the ILP, 8–10 April 1917, Marshall papers, D/MAR/5/6.

[146] List of A. J. Cook meetings monitored by the police, HO 45/263275; *Pioneer*, 10 November & 29 December 1917; *Labour Leader*, 1 November 1917.

[147] Jill Liddington, *The Long Road to Greenham*, Syracuse, 1991 edition, pp. 109–110. See also Hamman & Hunt, *Socialist Women*, p. 186. Four of the thirty-three branches of the Crusade were in Wales – Briton Ferry, Port Talbot, Merthyr and Newport, locations that largely reflected ILP areas of strength.

[148] *Labour Leader*, 21 June, 5 July, 27 September, 11 October & 3 November & 13 December 1917; Hannam & Hunt, *Socialist Women*, p. 186.

[149] *Labour Leader*, 14 March 1918; *Abergavenny Chronicle*, 19 April 1918.

[150] Susan Pedersen, *Eleanor Rathbone and the Politics of Conscience*, Yale, 2004, p. 151; Harold Smith, 'Sex vs. Class: British Feminists and the Labour Movement, 1919–1929', *The Historian*, 1 Nov 1984, 47, 1, p. 27. Family allowances were also described as mother's pensions, endowment of motherhood or children's allowances.

[151] *Abergavenny Chronicle*, 7 June 1918 & 30 August 1918.

[152] Deputy Chief Constable to Chief Constable Glamorgan Constabulary, 22 January 1918, HO 45/10743/263275.

[153] Eirug, *The Opposition...*, p. 57; Dowse, pp. 28 & 30; *Labour Leader*, 11 April 1918.

[154] Richard Lewis, 'Political Culture and Ideology, 1900–1918', in eds. Duncan Tanner, Chris Williams and Deian Hopkin, *The Labour Party in Wales 1900–2000*, UWP, 2000, p. 68.

[155] MacDonald's diary, 14 April 1918, PRO 30/69/1753/1; 'South Wales and the ILP'.

[156] *Pioneer*, 19 January 1918; John Saville, 'Richard Wallhead', *DLB*, Vol III.

[157] Dowse, p. 32; May p. 82.

[158] Marquand pp. 228/9; May p. 82; Dowse pp. 31 & 33; David Howell, *MacDonald's Party: Labour Identities and Crisis 1922–1931*, Oxford, 2002, p. 238.

[159] *Brecon & Radnor Express*, 21 February 1918; *Brecon County Times*, 16 May 1918 & 7 August 1919; *Daily Herald*, 8 August 1919.

[160] *Abergavenny Chronicle*, 7 June 1918.

CHAPTER THREE
Organiser

Divisional Organiser

At the Welsh ILP Conference, in June 1918, it was announced that Minnie had been appointed the Party's Welsh Division's organiser. Finally, she was employed full time for 'the cause', and no longer were her efforts confined to evenings, weekends and school holidays. In welcoming her appointment, the conference chair, George Neighbour, pointed out that Minnie's success depended on branch secretaries implementing her organisational recommendations. He cautioned that she had been appointed as an organiser rather than as a propagandist and that they should use her less as a speaker so she could focus on organising, even if it was 'less artistic or noisy'. Perhaps recognising that Minnie was a more natural propagandist than organiser, the *Pioneer* interpreted Neighbour's comments as a warning to Minnie as well as to branch officials.[1] However, the style of work she developed – organisational building through propagandising – sidestepped the paper's concerns.

The ILP within Wales had strong roots in the coalfield and the coastal ports of Cardiff, Newport and Swansea.[2] It was a working-class party of largely miners, dockers and metalworkers and many of its leaders were from the iron and steel industries.[3] Some prominent miners' leaders including George Barker and Jim Winstone were members, and at lodge level individuals had considerable influence.[4] However, while it had a good presence in valleys' towns including Aberdare and Merthyr where there was a range of employment, it was less strong in colliery villages. There the nature of the SWMF and the role of its miners' lodges as the principal labour organisation in the valleys meant it occupied the political space elsewhere taken by the ILP, all of which had an impact on how Minnie could do her job.[5] The ILP had little presence beyond South Wales. The ILP worked with the local Trades and Labour Councils, now numbering around fifty, that had grown rapidly during the war, and provided backbone, and sometimes a radical edge, to the strengthening labour movement. As an organisation affiliated to the Labour Party, the ILP operated alongside the trades and labour councils, trades union branches, and women's sections and guilds in a complex constitutional arrangement which allowed it to function simultaneously as an independent Party yet also as a component part of the Labour Party. Practicable locally, nationally it would, in time, become a source of conflict.

When she started her new job at the beginning of September, Minnie was the first full-time female labour organiser in Wales. As Divisional Organiser, she pursued a broad socialist programme and made women's rights and gender relationships an integral part of mainstream ILP activity and central to the wider social and economic struggle. Her importance in projecting this vision of a society, one that crucially included more equal gender relations, has been previously unnoticed.

On assuming her post, Minnie immediately implemented a strategy of spending concentrated periods on developing particular geographical areas to convert latent support there into active engagement. It was so successful that it set the pattern for structured visits over the coming two years. During that first week, Minnie trudged the length of the Aberdare valley, walking from community to community, through pouring rain, to visit sympathisers in their homes during the day, who she then invited to special branch meetings in the evening with the intention of converting them into members. Combining house calls, meetings and platform speaking, she advocated socialism, pacifism and women's rights in equal measure. The *Pioneer* attributed her success to the way in which she engaged women members to undertake localised organisation, and it urged other branches to copy the Aberdare model. Having experienced the organising capacity that women could bring, henceforth, in whatever context, Minnie would draw upon it. Inspired by Minnie's clarion call, women and men were attracted to the ILP in equal measure, with fifty women and fifty-three men joining in Aberdare.[6]

Minnie's next visit, to the Merthyr area, coincided with John Bruce Glasier's last speaking tour of South Wales.[7] He was already terminally ill when they jointly addressed the Keir Hardie memorial meeting. There, under the theme 'Women and the War', Minnie claimed that men had made such a mess of the world they should stand aside to let women do it. She deplored the argument that the protection of women and children legitimised war and hoped the coming of women into politics would mean the death of that lie. Deploying the idiosyncratic argument that being linked to the pacifist minority over the past four years had brought the comradeship of belonging to a despised minority, she appealed to women to join the ILP, not for an easy time – the future after the cessation of hostilities would present greater challenges than faced hitherto – but as the only fight worth fighting.[8]

The labour movement in Wales had not previously encountered a phenomenon like Minnie Pallister. Her tours became such a sensation that the *Pioneer* ran a series called 'Round About with Minnie'. Described in the *Llanelli Star* as 'Wales' Great Woman Orator',[9] over thirty months new branches were started, others resurrected and 'North Wales opened...like a flower under her ministrations'. Her propaganda work was done on street corners and 'over the washing tubs of our wives', as well as in branch committee rooms and on the platform.[10] Newspapers related how she held her audiences 'spellbound'. One report read, 'If to invoke feelings in others, experienced by oneself, is art, then the compliment can honestly be paid Miss Pallister that she's an artist.'[11] Another sympathetic account provided a sense of her powers:

> I am running the risk of being charged with writing in superlatives, but I must place it on record that this was the most remarkable address of the whole campaign. Touches of pathos and poetry, flashes of humour, apposite illustrations, stories told with the skill of an accomplished raconteuse, and sound economics all these were embodied in a torrent of eloquence that simply carried the audience off its feet.[12]

As well as organising locally, Minnie pushed the Divisional Council to create the machinery to improve Divisional structures and bring organisational sustainability, and she identified the necessary posts and their duties. To overcome precarious finances, she elaborated plans to fund the running of the Divisional Council and, although stone-walled, overcame objections to establish the nucleus of a Divisional Fund to allow central control over the work in Wales. Moreover, she all but covered her wage costs through charges for her appearances on platforms in England. The ever-admiring *Pioneer* was sufficiently impressed to suggest her 'shrewd attention to the business and detail side of affairs...would serve to make her a dangerous rival for some of the magnates of the business world'.[13]

In Wales and beyond, Minnie addressed gender issues head on. Although potentially highly divisive, it became an important part of Minnie's work. In Brynmawr, using what was described as the most robust language, Minnie spoke on 'Woman, the Slave of Man'.[14] From now on, Minnie would argue that the transformation in gender relationships was as important in achieving structural social and economic transformations as the nationalisation of industries and the provision of social services. A talk on the 'Ethics of Freedom' traced the history of woman 'from master's slave to merely household drudge'. In Gloucester she spoke on 'Woman: Slave, Rival, Comrade – Which?' calling for equality of the sexes to be recognised in practice as well as in theory, for example in equal pay for equal work.[15] During the war, women had been seen as men's economic rival, doing what had hitherto been regarded as men's work. She accepted that when soldiers returned they should get their old jobs back but, she contended, women must not be thrown 'on the industrial scrap heap, and placed at the mercy of men'. Instead, she stated 'Woman is, and must be, man's comrade' as she was 'not a creature to be petted, but must go hand-in-hand with man, and attain that fullness of life which such a relationship would make possible'.[16]

In the way she tackled sex-based inequalities and challenged traditional patterns of how men and women related, Minnie did not accept a labour culture that prioritised class over gender, but brought gender and class into a single perspective. While she recognised the demands of working men within labour's cause, she could speak to both sexes equally on the separate issues that concerned them. Minnie's socialist politics were infused by a gender-based analysis that identified where women's needs and interests differed from those of men, discussed how the two interacted, explored where men's and women's interests might be in conflict and proposed where men should concede ground. In seeking to further women's interests, Minnie argued for a combination of economic, employment, political and educational equalities. As well as the principle of women using their vote, she highlighted the changes that could be achieved by doing so, including family allowances, health care, quality housing, good schools and communal kitchens to reduce the burden of work on women in the home. It was for women to ensure that there were laundries 'at every street corner' where washing and ironing was done, pithead baths to keep dirt out of the homes and nursery schools as a preparation for elementary and secondary schools, as all would reduce women's burdens.[17] Declaring that the future of the political world depended upon women, she said it required women becoming active politically to participate in the broad agenda of changing society and overturning the political system that prevailed. To overcome women's lack of influence, Minnie advocated their standing for public office and robustly argued that as man-made laws had made women's life drudgery, the time had come for women to start taking their places in Council Chambers and the House of Commons to change them. Calling on women to join the ILP, she declared it was 'the only party which had a programme placing women on the same basis as men' and called on women to join so that each could be a woman in her own right and not merely somebody's wife or sister or mother. Taken together, it was a revolutionary package. In the way she developed and articulated her vision, rooted in and shaped by her experiences, Minnie demonstrated she was one of the major thinkers on women and gender relationships in Wales in the first half of the twentieth century. While not all of her proposals found purchase, a century later Minnie would have been cautiously pleased at the progress that had been made.

Through her practice of politics Minnie created her own vision of what it meant to be a socialist woman in Wales. At its heart was the reshaping of relationships between men and women. In town and village, without antagonism or seeking conflict, she used argument and humour to promote her vision. Although it has been suggested that women in the Labour Party did not challenge the separate gender roles in interwar South Wales, Minnie, through the ILP (which provided a major political component of the Labour Party) was forthright. Women responded to the gendered content of her firm messages by forming 'quite a respectable part' of those attending meetings. There, Minnie would not accept that women were relegated to the margin of meetings or should defer to men. She proudly joked that one husband said that ever since he had brought his wife to hear her speak, he had had to wash the dishes and clean the house himself. A reporter noted 'One woman...told me she was glad her husband was [there] to hear the straight talk from Miss Pallister.'[18]

Minnie also put words into action. In Neath, she walked into a laundry one dinner hour and the encounter led her to take up the issue of wages and conditions in the industry.[19] At the Lady Windsor colliery miners' lodge, the men had been considering for eighteen months whether to support the installation of pithead baths. While it was women who had to wash the miners' filthy work clothes, and therefore stood to benefit most from the installation of pithead baths, only men were entitled to vote on the issue. Minnie addressed the men in the colliery but they voted by 486 to 261 to reject installing baths.[20] As the lodge leadership in Lady Windsor was amongst the most progressive in the coalfield, the scale of resistance confronting Minnie and other advocates of pithead baths, such as Elizabeth Andrews, was clear.[21] Minnie repeated her message more formally to the South Wales Regional Survey Committee of the Ministry of Health where she described a typical day for a miner's wife, setting out the standards the ILP wanted for new housing.[22] However, it was not until the industry was nationalised nearly thirty years later, when a Labour general election victory brought about structural change, that a comprehensive programme to install pithead baths was introduced.[23]

The dominance of heavy industry meant there were comparatively few formal employment opportunities available locally for women. In spite of their hard work, women's essential activities in the home went unrecognised and unpaid. Drawing on what she had observed of women's lives in the valleys from 1906 and learning from the writings of others, Minnie identified the structural bias operating against women. At the Merthyr Rink she explicitly challenged the male-dominated culture of the South Wales valleys and its relegation of women to inferior positions. The *Pioneer* explained 'Her theme on Sunday was the old, old one of the common people, and more especially of the common everyday wife of the common everyday man, but it was treated different.' It is worth quoting:

> Full of revolutionary fervour – not the anarchic, chaotic, bloodletting that is the common view of revolution, but the crystalline pure translation that Socialism stands for an economic and intellectual revolution, and [with] the high moral tone that has always characterised her rebel speeches, she moved her audience deeply...

It continued:

she had something to say of the selfishness of the superiority of the everyday husband...And the women, women who since the day of the passing of the matriarchy have been ground down to the level of the domestic animals, by their common owner, lordly man, the private property right established and holder [sic], she, too, was taught a lesson of emancipation, not a sex emancipation, but a broader and more glorious human emancipation in which the woman would complement the man, and as comrade and colleague work out with him her own emancipation and his...

The task seemed hard, and mayhap to the individual consciousness not worthwhile, but playing around the feet of such... were the children, and in shadowy outline beside them were the children of the generations unborn. There was the prize.

Minnie's arguments and aspirations challenged the existing world and projected a vision for future generations. The paper concluded: 'It is that absorbidness [sic] in our movement that marked Miss Pallister out as the one organiser we have produced in our area, it is that which has made her organising work so successful...'[24]

However, while they were well received in Merthyr, not everywhere was open to the ILP's pacifist or feminist messages and the response could be hostile. In Kenfig Hill, Minnie and a fellow speaker received rough receptions. While the audience would listen to ILP proposals for economic transformation and the need for independent Labour Parliamentary representation, once it turned to the war and the prospects for peace, the speaker was heckled. When Minnie told the men to treat women more as comrades, rather than house-drudges, 'So frequent became the interruptions... that the chairman said he would have to close the meeting if better order could not be kept.'[25] The Rhondda, with its particular brand of socialist politics, remained largely impervious to ILP wooing.[26]

On 11 November the war ended with an Armistice with Germany. Three days later, the Government called a snap general election. Minnie's planned activity was set aside and election campaigning was prioritised. She loved elections. Without organisational responsibilities, she became fully occupied as a speaker, addressing several meetings each evening.[27] After supporting the Labour candidates in Neath and Aberavon, Minnie transferred to Aberdare to support Rev T. E. Nicholas, ('Niclas y Glais') who was opposed by the jingo C. B. Stanton.[28] Nicholas was a Congregationalist Minister who sought to bridge the gap between nonconformity and ILP socialism and was a staunch opponent of the war. In a fraught contest in which Nicholas's pacifism was on trial, Minnie sought to depersonalise the situation. The principle was bigger than personalities, she argued, for in voting against the Labour Party people would be voting against themselves.[29]

On Saturday 7 December, at the large, set-piece, Labour election campaign event in Wales, Arthur Henderson and Minnie addressed a crowded Cory Hall in Cardiff to promote Labour's programme.[30] Although they had been on different sides over the war, Henderson and Minnie's presence on the same platform, less than a month after the war ended, symbolically presented the image of Labour Party and ILP reunited in Wales to face the post-war world. Henderson, a trades unionist, Wesleyan Methodist, and MP since 1903, had supported both the war and conscription and earned the opprobrium of some in the ILP, including Snowden.[31] A key figure in the Labour Party and its chair, he had been the most prominent Labour member in the wartime coalition Cabinet. However, he was concerned that the division in the Labour Party over the war should not become irrevocable and he had worked with MacDonald to prevent it. Minnie's address focussed on women. The fate of the coming election depended on them, she declared. While her speech was not reported in detail, Minnie's thinking at the time was expounded in a major article in the *Pioneer*. Taking her cue from the lives of ordinary women and children, she explained that a wife's daily struggle and the drudgery of housework were not 'ordained from on high' but the result of a political system where politicians were not interested in improving workers' lives. That could be changed by the election of a government that put people above property and again encouraged women to participate in politics. As most women over thirty now had the vote under the 1918 Franchise Act, she reasoned that they would be to blame for the conditions they allowed, and she urged them to actively work for the ILP.[32]

It appears, though, that Minnie was not among those women eligible to vote as her name is not listed in the Electoral Register for Brynmawr for 1918. As a single woman over thirty who was not a house owner, or married to a man who owned a house, nor strictly the holder of a degree although she held a university qualification, Minnie's eligibility to vote depended on whether or not she provided her own furniture for her rented accommodation.[33] It appears she did not.

The election took place on 14 December but because of the need to transport troops' ballot papers, the count was delayed until 28 December. With the outcome unknown, two days after the vote, Minnie was involved in a remarkable concert in Ystradgynlais, to support the Estonian violinist, Eduard Soermus. Soermus was a Bolshevik who had fled Russia after being sought by police for participating in the 1905 revolution. Having attended the St Petersburg Conservatoire, where Tchaikovsky, Prokofiev and Shostakovich had also studied, he built an international reputation in exile, touring Europe by giving recitals.[34] From 1916 Soermus lived in Merthyr with his wife and two children, and from his South Wales base he supported the October 1917 revolution and the Hands Off Russia Campaign.[35] Seeing art as the 'most perfect expression of the liberated soul and spirit of humanity', he considered music as having a direct link in helping emancipate the working class and establishing socialism.[36] The South Wales ILP strongly supported Soermus and organised his 1918–19 tour. Likening Soermus to the great democrat artists Shelley, Walt Whitman and William Morris, the *Pioneer* labelled his concert at the Olympia Rink in Merthyr as the musical event of the year, where over a thousand people 'sat in ecstatic rapture'.[37] In Ystradgynlais, as his English was limited, Minnie addressed the meeting on Soermus's behalf and accompanied him on piano.[38] When travelling to Merthyr, in mid-tour, Soermus was arrested and deported to Finland where he was gaoled. By late 1919 he and his family were in Petrograd (later Leningrad, now St Petersburg).[39] Displaying the constancy she demonstrated towards her friends, Minnie stayed in touch. Even after Soermus died in Moscow in 1940, Minnie maintained contact with his wife; in 1956 her scribbled note asked 'Did you hear from a Virginia Soermus? Tell me when I see you.'[40]

With war fever at its height, all anti-war MPs, including Jowett, Snowden, MacDonald and Anderson, lost their seats in the election.[41] Even Henderson, whose support for the war was unquestionable, was defeated. In South Wales all three ILP candidates were beaten, as was Jim Winstone in Merthyr, although fighting on a straight Labour Party ticket. Elsewhere in the valleys Labour representation increased dramatically as 'patriotic' miners' union representatives won seats in an enlarged Parliamentary Labour Party.[42]

It has been argued that the Great War helped remove the ILP from the centre stage of Welsh labour politics.[43] However, while the ILP was unpopular immediately after the war, winning no Parliamentary seats in Wales, by 1921 it had staged a comeback and remained a significant presence in Wales at least until 1926. All the evidence is that Minnie shared the view that the period from 1918 was one of 'high hopes and confident assurance' for the ILP.[44] Although it had a mountain to climb to regain its former position, it rallied to help shape the overall politics of South Wales.

*

An important influence in Minnie's personal as well as political development was the writings of Edward Carpenter. Carpenter was a philosopher, poet, prison reformer and gay rights activist. His works were widely read in left-wing circles, had a status among socialists, feminists and progressives, and left an incalculable impact on individuals. A socialist, pacifist and humanitarian, he was an advocate of the 'simple life', including a healthy diet. Minnie adopted some of the lifestyle approaches he espoused that included simple living, vegetarianism and dress reform, including wearing sandals.[45] Carpenter explored the relationship between personal emancipation, sexual politics and social emancipation. His three works published by the Labour Press Society, *Woman and Her Place in a Free Society*; *Sex-Love and Its Place in a Free Society*, and *Marriage in a Free Society*, examined the fate of women over centuries. They described how women had been reduced to a life of household drudgery and often isolation, and had become mere chattels or property of men. He advocated 'permanent and life-long union' based in the 'sweet comradeship of love' and an open, sincere and equal relationship between the sexes, free of dependency, which could only be achieved by women having economic independence.[46] The essence of Carpenter's arguments ran through Minnie's gendered reasoning for decades after the Great War and her crystalline revolutionary Merthyr speech was Carpenter's philosophy applied to South Wales family life.

Carpenter's impact on Minnie though went further than her public pronouncements. When considering the nature of personal and emotional relationships between the sexes, Carpenter argued that, within a balanced relationship, sex was a natural and beautiful thing, which found full expression in the bond between sex and love, when desire was matched by dedication to another person.[47] Carpenter was willing to separate sex from procreation, to acknowledge its pleasurable nature for women and to give birth control 'central importance' as a basis for freeing love 'from darkness and shame'. These were all in conflict with the established views of wider society, which regarded them as 'unclean'.[48] If Carpenter's influence was at its peak in the years before the Great War, transformed sexual relationships associated with Carpenter's 'ethical socialism' still prevailed in some currents of the left in the 1930s.[49] Jenny Cuthbert, an ILP member in interwar South Wales, was aware of ILP women who were considered 'advanced sexually'.[50] It is not known whether Minnie's ILP comrades considered her to be one of them. As an independent woman, both economically and intellectually, Minnie's morality would have been under scrutiny in the society she inhabited.[51] An incident occurred probably between 1917 and 1919

> where a bloke trying to take the rise out of Minnie Pallister in the meeting in Brynmawr shouted out, "What's your attitude to, do you believe in free love[?]". And Minnie Pallister got up and said, "Is there any other sort[?]. Do you know of any other kind[?]". And she didn't enter into any further debate and everybody that was on her side, cheered.[52]

While Minnie could deftly deflect jibes, this anecdote would suggest that in some minds Minnie was associated with 'free love', a phrase used as a slur that carried the connotation of promiscuity and that was used against those on the left.[53]

Women wishing to be sexually active outside marriage were at risk from huge social pressures that repressed sexual instincts and distorted relations with men as well as other women.[54] Even strong independent socialist feminist women expressed caution. Stella Browne, the feminist and birth control campaigner, said in 1917 that women who did not want marriage but who wanted a sexual relationship were confronted by the 'whole social order'. In 1925 Dora Russell commented that fear of scandal meant women were compelled to outwardly conform to societal norms and that their private activity could not be matched by public declarations.[55] What impact this may have had on Minnie's life is unknown. For many activists in the labour movement with a background in nonconformity, their notions of respectability made them uneasy with 'lifestyle' issues.[56] Minnie had already experienced hostility over opposing the war. If her lifestyle and relationships with men were known, they would have provided further cause for comment and been frowned upon by many. All the more important that the space offered by the ILP and NCF provided Minnie with a sense of belonging, affirmation and solidarity in her personal as well as political life.

By the end of the war Minnie was a mature woman who led a single, varied, rewarding life. She had economic independence, was sexually active and chose sex for pleasure with, one assumes, the risks of pregnancy reduced by birth control. This combination allowed a freedom rare for women at the time. While Minnie never talked about sex publicly, or about birth control until later in the 1920s, by the middle of the Great War she had sufficiently shrugged off nineteenth-century nonconformist inhibitions to talk openly about sex in private.

Minnie appears in the diaries of Clifford Allen in an entry of October 1918:

> Strangely enough on Sunday came a letter from Minnie Pallister which I think I must call a love letter. It moved us [Bertrand Russell and Allen] both intensely: we thought it one of the most pathetic and lonely letters we have read for a very long time. She seems to have deceived herself into believing that sex played no part in what she thought and had written but surely the letter denied this. She is in an agony of loneliness with a ten-year love tragedy and now a life of politics. BR so anxious that [unclear] make her see the intense interest of [illegible word] of service' in the world; he dreaded lest she should suffer self-humiliation after writing such words.[57]

Allen noted: 'A difficult business.'

For New Year 1919, Allen joined Russell and O'Niel and for days the three talked about sex and love.[58] On 3 January he noted 'Wrote Pallister in a.m.'. The content of the letter is unknown. Two days later Allen recorded:

> Went for a short walk alone and...[t]hought much about Minnie Pallister. I have no love for her – if by that I mean I wish to share everything in life with her – but I have an affection for her freshness and vitality and beauty and sincerity, and I realise she is lonely and starved. To spend bits of one's life in comradeship and sex intercourse would help me I believe and equally give her life, colour and warmth. But I do not know whether she might not become lonely and even more unhappy if such an experience had to be temporary. What ought I do? Ought I to be over-careful in deciding what is best for other people?

However, it was not in Allen's nature to give consideration to what was best for women in his life. That same day he and Russell argued furiously. 'BR plunges out at me for my brusque treatment of women' and 'argued quite viciously that I thought women dirt.' As Russell's treatment of women could be appalling, this was condemnation indeed.[59] Did Minnie sense this in Allen? She later reflected that 'great men did not make good husbands' and that 'excellent men' were not always the easiest to live with.[60] In early September 1919 Minnie rang Allen, wanting to see him. They met, but the confident, experienced woman now held no appeal for Allen who considered her 'less innocent & insisted in talking much of sex. But she is now unattractive & without taste'. This statement though says more about the man whose diary is a litany of his devouring of innocents before discarding them than it does about the woman who had outgrown him.[61]

Aside from sex, Allen described Minnie as being in a 'strange transition stage' having left teaching and being full of enthusiasm for her new job as an ILP organiser. He considered her 'clearly a good propagandist' who still maintained her romantic sincerity but was 'afraid she will become typically ILP doctrinaire'. He added 'she doesn't seem given to understand how to adapt her propaganda to the opponent's state of mind: she believes so much in her principles [&] formulae that she thinks they must ultimately convince if repeated often enough or persistently enough.'[62] This was valid criticism that she later recognised in herself.[63] After a decade in politics, Minnie was becoming hardened, but was still learning. Allen also observed: 'She is clearly developing political ambition & wants to be 1st woman MP.'[64] Such ambitions were not fanciful. During early 1919, Minnie was a frequent visitor to South West Wales and such was her impact that the *Labour Leader* raised the prospect of her being the next Llanelli Labour Parliamentary candidate.[65]

*

Minnie was operating in a society in flux. After the war, South Wales was at its most febrile industrially and politically. The miners' union demanded nationalisation of the coal industry, while industrial unionists proposed the use of direct action as a way to achieve workers' control. Russia was a galvanising issue for many on the left. As soldiers returned from the trenches, those women who had been employed during the war were required to return to the home. During the local elections, Minnie spent a week in Mountain Ash where Noah Tromans, the Unofficial Reform Committee miners' leader, and George Neighbour, stood as ILP candidates. Neighbour topped the poll and Tromans was also elected. The *Pioneer* reminded readers how, during the war, the ILP had been subject to abuse 'from all quarters', but said a shift was taking place and that a process of acceptance had started.[66] The release of conscientious objectors became social occasions. However, Morgan Jones was still held in gaol where incarceration was taking a heavy toll on his mental health. In a Bargoed meeting, Minnie and Emrys Hughes demanded his release. When someone tried to disrupt it, he was floored by a blow from another member of the audience who then said 'Go on with your speech, lady'.[67]

The Labour Party conference in Southport in late June was the first since the end of the war where pro-war majority and anti-war minority met. Minnie shared the sense of 'otherness' the ILPers felt from the rest of the conference, whether from their caucusing beforehand or their social on the first evening. There was a 'tightness' felt by the ILP members towards one another that resulted from what its members had endured together during the war, with a spirit of comradeship felt by those 'people who know what it is to stand together with their backs against the wall, fighting against tremendous odds'.[68] Minnie was attending the Labour Party conference for the first time as the Welsh representative in an ILP delegation that included Philip Snowden, David Kirkwood, MacDonald and Dick Wallhead.[69] Describing the conference as 'stormy', she observed that rank and file workers were unsympathetic to a cautious political approach, were anxious for action, and were taking a wider view of world events including on Russia. Some delegates attacked the ILP for its rejection by the electorate and for its disproportionate influence within the Labour Party. Philip Snowden had addressed the ILP's fundamental differences with the Labour Party at the earlier ILP annual conference when his hard-hitting speech spelled out the limitations of the Labour Party's economic policy, civil liberties and international policy, as well as defending the ILP's opposition to the War.[70] Now he insisted that the increased electoral influence was due to the work ILP members did within the Labour Party. By the end of the conference, though, Minnie felt that, after 'the long years of misunderstanding and struggle', delegates were to a great extent supportive of the ILP.[71] Minnie concluded she had never enjoyed anything half as much in her life as the conference and was glad to be a member of the socialist section of the Labour Party. The ILP's influence was out of all proportion to its size, morale was high, and its anti-war position allowed it to be seen as the soul of the Labour Party.[72] One question was unresolved. Against a backdrop of the 'three most momentous years' for the miners between 1919 and 1921,[73] the Sankey Coal Commission considered the future of the mines. In the heavily conflictual industry, which was still under government control, Minnie pointedly asked 'Where do industrial questions [e]nd and political questions begin?'[74] It was a question that would be contested repeatedly, by miners, owners and government alike, with much pain, until 1926.

On her return from the conference, Minnie became immersed in the Swansea East by-election, where David Williams was the ILP candidate. Although he was defeated, he reduced the Liberal majority from 4,730 to 1,092, a considerable improvement on his general election performance of eight months earlier.[75] The campaign brought Minnie together again with Elizabeth Andrews. The previous month each had given evidence to a Ministry of Health Inquiry on housing.[76] Now they spoke together from the same platform, possibly for the first time. It was Andrews' first by-election campaign after taking up a post in March 1919 as the Labour Party's women's organiser for Wales.[77] From that spring, therefore, a complex situation existed, with two Labour political organisers, both women, operating in Wales, working for different political organisations, with different but overlapping roles and agenda. Andrews represented the institutional strength of the newly reorganised Labour Party, but held the narrower remit of being its woman organiser, which largely confined her to the marginalised and subordinated Party structures that were designated for women and their causes. Her primary role was the steady building of the Party's women's organisation, which she then maintained for nearly three decades. Andrews' notes on Wales in *Labour Woman* convey an institutional formality, a sense of Party machinery functioning, of labourism at work, rather than the evangelical striving for a socialist cause.[78] The ILP was affiliated to the Labour Party and was part of it, but retained its separate identity and organisation. Minnie's job as ILP Divisional Organiser for Wales covered the full range of political issues, including those related to gender, which she promoted from within the mainstream of the ILP and from the perspective of the most socialist component within the Labour Party. With the extension of the franchise to women, far from their being marginalised, Minnie made women integral to a broader socialist programme.

Had Minnie and Andrews developed a collaborative and productive relationship, they could have formed a powerful and possibly transformative alliance, bringing together Labour and the ILP on women's issues, but they did not. Instead of cooperating, they vied to occupy political space and an opportunity was lost. Without an amicable coexistence, it cannot have been easy for either Andrews or Minnie, with Minnie having to deal with Andrews who had the institutional weight of the Labour Party behind her and Andrews having to contend with the well-established, brilliantly articulate and charismatic ILP organiser who had already built a formidable reputation and outshone her from the platform.

In content, style and tone, Minnie's approach as ILP organiser was in marked contrast to that of Andrews and the Labour Party. This was due to the nature of the Parties each represented, their respective political programmes, the attitude that each of the two women adopted in engaging with women and men, and their different characters and personalities. Andrews and Minnie both joined the ILP before the Great War, and both had the wherewithal to break into the male-dominated structures of the labour movement, with Andrews joining the executive of the Rhondda Labour Party in 1916. Andrews and Minnie appear to have held markedly different positions on the Great War as it appears that Andrews supported the war which, as a member of the ILP, would have been problematic. In her autobiography Andrews was sketchy on her position on the conflict, which was the most tumultuous issue of the day, but elsewhere she commented that women were called upon to play their part and were given the opportunity to serve on committees and in wartime industries. She herself served on the War Pensions Committee and the Disablement Training Committee.[79] Did Andrews align herself less with the ILP during the Great War because of its pacifism and become more a 'Labour Woman'?

Although they overlapped and interconnected and could belong to the same organisations in the labour movement, 'Labour Women' in the Labour Party and 'Socialist Women' of the ILP were not the same thing and differed particularly over the 'gendering of politics'. Whereas 'Socialist Women', including Minnie, consciously sought to challenge male-dominated left politics,[80] 'Labour Women', including Andrews, when addressing any conflict of loyalties between gender and class, accepted the deferential position of women. Any deviation from this by Labour Party women organisers was actively discouraged.[81] This could extend to working lives. If, like the vast majority of men and women in South Wales valleys society, Andrews accepted the gendered division of industrial and domestic work, Minnie, in contrast, saw the resulting economic dependency experienced by some women as a form of drudgery little removed from slavery. Such differences in perspective could be evident in the way that Minnie and Andrews related to men and women in the organising of meetings. Whereas when Andrews addressed meetings she hoped that the men would 'invite their wives to take part in such gatherings', Minnie would not accept deference of a woman to a man or having women relegated to the margin.[82]

At the time of the Swansea by-election, Andrews was at the beginning of a long, single-job career during which she came to show that she was a good organiser within a strong Party bureaucracy, and she became a woman of substance.[83] Minnie's political work life consisted of bursts, typically of two to three years, in increasingly challenging environments over less than two decades. Minnie and Andrews were cut from different cloths, and operated in such contrasting ways that trying to rate their respective contributions is difficult. However, each in her separate way made an outstanding contribution to the cause of labour.

*

Although the war was over, hostility towards the ILP over its pacifism always threatened, though it could be averted. At one meeting Minnie tackled head-on potential troublemakers who warned they would break up the meeting if the Red Flag was sung. She successfully defused a difficult situation and the socialist anthem was sung without disruption.[84] However, when David Kirkwood spoke in Brynmawr, the meeting turned into a riot. During the war he had been arrested under DORA, then court-martialled with other members of the Clyde Workers' Committee and deported from Glasgow to Edinburgh. Now he explained the events on 'Red Clydeside' including the effectiveness of mass picketing and his arrest as a leader during Glasgow's 'Battle of George Square' in January 1919. Thirty years later Minnie recalled how one slighting reference to Lloyd George quickly changed the mood of the meeting. The following day Minnie and Kirkwood were refused the car booked to take them to Merthyr and had to walk two miles to Beaufort, so arrived late for the Merthyr event. When Minnie spoke at the next public meeting in Brynmawr, trouble was anticipated, but order was maintained.[85]

In Russia, the Bolsheviks were 'fighting for their lives'[86] against White Russian forces supported by the British and other armies of intervention. Minnie strongly supported the 'Hands Off Russia' campaign and in late July she addressed a series of meetings in the Aberdare valley. At one, convened by the SWMF and branches of the rail unions NUR and ASLEF, she protested against intervention and linked it to the abolition of conscription in Britain, as well as the release of political prisoners and better treatment for discharged and demobilised men.[87] At the Divisional Conference in January 1920, the Welsh ILP followed Scotland in demanding the ILP's withdrawal from what it saw as the failed Second International of social democratic parties and decided by 91 votes to 62 to affiliate to the Moscow-aligned Communist Third International, putting it at odds with Labour Party policy.[88] In what was described as a fighting speech, Minnie reported that the valleys were 'absolutely ripe' for the ILP, but she pointed out that while many comrades admired Russia she doubted that many were prepared to emulate the Russian levels of hard work to achieve a social revolution in Britain.[89] Following the positions taken in Wales and Scotland, the national ILP conference voted overwhelmingly to disaffiliate from the Second International, though it did not commit to affiliating to the Communist International, a view with which Minnie concurred.

The post-war ILP leadership in Wales were those who had opposed the war and led the struggle for conscientious objection. When Emrys Hughes was elected as the Divisional President, he put it down to the notoriety he had obtained during his three years in gaol as a CO.[90] He analysed that just over a year before, owing to its unpopularity over the war, the ILP had been almost annihilated as a political force. Now he identified a marked change to be taking place, and the ILP's condemnation of the Versailles peace treaty to be shown as justified.[91] Morgan Jones, who had been a cause célèbre as a CO, became the second ILP organiser and secretary for Wales alongside Minnie, after his release from gaol.[92]

A unique insight into the left landscape in South Wales in mid-1920 is given by organisers' questionnaires, completed by Minnie and Morgan Jones.[93] Their insights and complex analyses of the pressures felt by the ILP at the time are at odds with those traditionally portrayed. Usually the ILP is presented as coming under pressure from the Labour Party following adoption of its revised constitution in 1918, drafted by Henderson after his resignation from Lloyd George's government, and the foundation of the Communist Party. However, Jones considered the Labour Party would not succeed where the ILP already had a propaganda base. As the ILP provided 'much of the vigour' in the local labour movement, its role remained significant.[94] Jones judged the Labour Party would, however, appeal as a 'milder (and more respectable!)' alternative in areas where there was no ILP activity.[95] For Minnie the threat did not come from outside attack but internally. The main obstacle to ILP progress, Minnie concluded, was 'a scarcity of people willing to dedicate the whole of their spare time to socialism'. She concluded the risk lay in the ILP losing its identity because intelligent working-class male members were diverted from socialist activities by being overburdened by non-ILP demands in local government, the trades unions and the church. Displaying her lifelong inclination to regard her own cause as the only one of importance, she criticised work undertaken in labourist and other activities (in spite of any consequent pragmatic achievements) as time lost to socialist organising, even considering Parliamentary work and running local elections as dissipating effort. If Minnie's perception of the best way to build socialism reflected the ILP's priorities, it markedly differed in approach from the incrementalism of the Labour Party. Industrial crises had also kept ILP men very busy, whether on the railways or with coal nationalisation campaigns. An exception was the successful miners' propaganda committees, mainly because they utilised ILP speakers coming into Wales, and she cited the Rhondda district's large Sunday meetings that were addressed by many prominent ILP speakers. Probably drawing on her NCF experience, Minnie identified the remedy as enlisting women officers who were not diverted by trades union and local government activities.[96]

From the left the challenge came from two sources. One with which Minnie and Jones had to deal was the infiltration of the ILP by the Socialist Labour Party (SLP), around which 'a terrific storm raged' from late 1919. The SLP was the nearest thing to a Bolshevik party in Britain. It employed tactics later called 'entryism' and worked to take over and crush the ILP in South Wales from within. In Abertillery, for example, the SLP adopted the guise of an ILP branch and sent delegates to a meeting in Aberdare to establish an unofficial ILP Federation in South Wales.[97] While it looked as if the ILP might lose some of its best branches to the SLP, the challenge was seen off and nowhere did the SLP permanently displace the ILP.[98]

Another challenge that Minnie and Jones considered 'particularly difficult' came with the formation of the South Wales Socialist Society (SWSS). Its strategy was based in direct industrial action and rejection of the core ILP belief of political activity. It was organised by the 'advanced men' whom Minnie had addressed in the Rhondda, including Arthur Cook and Arthur Horner.[99] As the ILP did not have an industrial organisation, when a significant number of activists, including some ILP members, used industrial means to achieve political ends, the ILP was put at a disadvantage and left exposed.[100] Described by the ILP organisers with concern as being 'a great movement', the SWSS succeeded in infiltrating some ILP branches, and a few were taken over or smashed. Only with the 1921 and 1926 miners' lockouts was the inadequacy of a reliance on industrial unionism and direct action finally exposed. In contrast, even though individual communists could also be members of the Labour Party, the embryonic Communist Party of Great Britain did not merit being mentioned in the questionnaires. However, when parts of the SLP and the SWSS joined the Communist Party, it developed an industrial leadership in the mining industry but was of comparatively little import before 1927. Therefore the notion that in the early 1920s the ILP was outflanked either by the reorganised Labour Party or the newly founded CPGB is somewhat ill-founded.[101]

The challenge from the right came from unexpected quarters. With little significant competition from the Tories or Liberals, the more effective and reactionary opposition was of a 'camouflaged "non-political" organisation', the RAOB (The Buffaloes). It had a considerable hold and 'again & again...successfully thwarted the ILP'. However, in spite of pressures from left and right, the questionnaires show Minnie and Jones brimming with confidence. The ILP in South Wales was thriving and the growth in the Party and electoral results would show their optimism was justified.[102]

Minnie loved the political life she was living. At the delayed open-air May Day meeting in Briton Ferry she and Tom Mann spoke from a platform comprising two planks across trestles, so that when Mann stamped up and down and banged the frail table she was grateful to still be there when it was her turn to speak.[103] In late June, her appearance in Merthyr was described as having 'no peer even in the story of those thousands strong meetings... in the Rink'. She applauded London's East India dockers for having refused to load munitions on the *Jolly George* destined to undermine the Bolshevik regime, describing it as 'the finest thing that had happened for several years'. The refusal, she said, signalled that workers were losing the fear of their bosses and a slavery mentality. Minnie saw a change in labour, shifting attention from hours and wages towards what she described as 'freedom'. Having played its part in awakening the slaves, the ILP's job was now to lead them. Minnie ended her speech with a manifesto for how a new type of woman with backbone 'would demand for men the same moral and mental standard that they set up for themselves'. Women would no longer be divorced from life but would regain their rightful position in the world doing creative work including spending more time in the council chamber.[104]

This was Minnie's last contribution as the ILP's Wales Divisional Organiser. In May, an advert appeared for a woman full-time organiser-agent for Aberavon Labour Party with the appointment to be made in conjunction with Labour Party headquarters and carrying a salary of £250 pa.[105] Minnie was apparently approached to apply but long hesitated before accepting because while she broadly supported the Labour Party, her heart was with the ILP. Although her employment with the ILP formally ended, she justified leaving (perhaps to herself) by arguing that in a sense she was still working for the Divisional Council stating 'I couldn't do anything better for the ILP in Wales than help to return Mr Ramsay MacDonald for the Aberavon constituency.'[106]

On 3 July, the *Pioneer* announced her appointment with the headline 'Minnie Pallister: Severe Loss to ILP Movement in Wales'. The paper paid a fulsome tribute to the Party's first full-time organiser. Her significant contribution included an organisational restructuring that provided the ILP across Wales with the solid platform that allowed it to regain its position as the primary force for promoting socialism in Wales during the early 1920s. Her organising capacity 'on the stomp' saw the Party gain a presence in North Wales and branches opened or revived elsewhere. However, it was the power of her oratory as a rallying point in the cause of progressive change that stood out. Through it she had highlighted the issue of gender relations as central within the household and broader society and created her own vision of what it meant to be a socialist woman in Wales. In coming years, she would take those messages to the rest of Britain.

*

Agent

When Ramsay MacDonald was selected as Aberavon's candidate in February, his nomination was unopposed. Ivor Thomas's role had been key. He was Secretary of the 1,000-member strong Briton Ferry ILP branch, and also Secretary of Aberavon Divisional Labour Party, which he had been central in establishing. It was to Thomas that Minnie had to send her job application. Thomas, MacDonald and Minnie formed a powerful troika which sought to catapult

MacDonald to Parliament, so resurrecting a political career that had been stymied by his opposition to the war.

Minnie's brief was to organise the large, scattered, constituency with its markedly increased 35,000 electorate that had miners and metalworkers in almost equal measure, as well as those women over 30 who had been enfranchised in 1918.[107] The task was daunting. In the 1918 general election, the Liberal candidate had secured 62 per cent of the vote and a near-6,000 majority that MacDonald would have to overturn, even without the added burden of his war record. Contemporary commentators suggested MacDonald's chances of victory were not promising. Indeed, a 1923 biography of MacDonald, suggested Aberavon had been considered 'hopeless'.[108] Having been out of Parliament for four years, Minnie later recorded that it was thought MacDonald would never get back.[109] The publication *Foreign Affairs*, which branded itself as a 'Journal of International Understanding', highlighted the importance of returning him for Aberavon, loftily proclaiming the 'battleground is not a group of small industrial towns in South Wales, it is the world'.[110]

On her appointment, Minnie moved to 89 Suffolk Place, Porthcawl. She had lived in Brynmawr for fourteen years, the longest duration of her life in one place to date. Now her new home was a comfortable seaside resort that was a politically challenging part of the Aberavon constituency. If her task to organise the Aberavon constituency was large, her challenge to reach and convert the groups who were antagonistic to MacDonald's wartime record was larger still. Previous experience had taught MacDonald the impact of newly enfranchised women. When he contested Leicester West in December 1918, opponents made his character central to the campaign and women in particular were hostile. Badly beaten, MacDonald's 'haunting memory' was 'of the women – bloodthirsty, cursing their hate...'.[111] They would be a key group for Minnie to win over. Another disaffected group was discharged servicemen, and in his first speech as Labour candidate in Briton Ferry, MacDonald had sought to build a bridge towards them, stating 'your cause is my cause'.[112] However, a Labour Party meeting in Porthcawl had been broken up by a group who complained about MacDonald's war record and who tried to occupy the platform. The fighting, booing and noise lasted about an hour until MacDonald was forced to withdraw.[113] Aberavon would be no easy contest.[114]

MacDonald visited the constituency for a few days every few months, moving from village to village, holding meetings in chapels, with trades unions and women's groups. Visits by 'the Chief', as Minnie and others close to him in Party circles addressed him, were preceded by extensive preparatory work by Thomas and Minnie, involving detailed itineraries and meticulously planned events.[115] In November, MacDonald made an uncompromising speech at an Aberavon Labour Party conference on the ILP's unpopular position on the war, and the consequences of imposing the peace of the victor.[116] Unbending in his views on the conflict, while his arguments on the moral imperative of nationalising the mining industry could be well received, his unwillingness to dilute his messages on the war did not help win over doubters.

Although Minnie excelled at propagandising and had acquitted herself well as an ILP regional organiser, she was less experienced in the detail of constituency organisation, lacked some of the necessary skills and had much to learn. She felt 'crushing responsibility' in carrying 'the life and career of a man in my hands', as well as the future of part of the labour movement.[117] Ivor Thomas recognised she needed mentoring and closely supervised her work, encouraging her to understand the troubles she was encountering and identify if someone was obstructing her.

The constituency apparatus could have been bolstered by the involvement of Elizabeth Andrews, but there is no sign of her appearing in Aberavon during the nearly three years of the campaign. Indeed, there is a strong suggestion that Andrews was kept out. An intriguing indication of the rivalry that existed almost certainly between Minnie and Andrews was referred to by Thomas who wrote that 'the little one' was…:

> not kindly disposed towards you, you should know that, and the reason is obvious. We have no room for her in our division, and she knows that. Leave her to me and I will do very well with her. The job we are engaged in is a "boss job".[118]

Minnie was generally seen as a warm, friendly, person by most men and women. However, at various stages in her political life she could have difficulties with some women, resulting in competitive or even antagonistic relations. One such person with whom an uneasy relationship existed seems to have been Elizabeth

Andrews. On this occasion the internal Party battle was resolved by Thomas playing the trump card of the authority of MacDonald, the Party leader, in Minnie's favour. Any rivalry that existed between them beforehand was exacerbated by Aberavon. The enmity endured. When, in the 1950s, Andrews published her autobiography, of which it was said she generously named and praised the efforts of other women in the movement, there was no mention of Minnie.[119] At that time Minnie had a national profile, so would have been hard to overlook. If history is made by those who write it, the omission of Minnie from Andrews's account contributed to her subsequent absence from the received history of labour in South Wales.

Ivor Thomas was aware of the significance of the chapels and they were prioritised. He counselled Minnie to take soundings with the ministers wherever she went as 'if we can prevent them coming out openly against us it will be something.' Although MacDonald came to believe that nonconformity in industrial South Wales was becoming politically divided and that many were coming over to Labour, Thomas was more cautious.[120] Only one minister of religion would appear on a public platform for Labour during the election.[121] While things were proceeding well in some parts of the constituency, in the mining villages of the Afan Valley, traditional strongholds of nonconformity and Liberalism, Labour had made little headway.[122]

Even so, a first-hand account in *Foreign Affairs* in early 1921 observed that some who had previously been 'indifferent or hostile' to MacDonald were becoming his staunch defenders. MacDonald's meetings with women had 'worked a miracle' and concluded the women of the constituency had come together 'and work as I have rarely seen even women work'.[123] This was down to Minnie who was described as 'a mixture of whirlwind and June roses. She is irresistible!' The Party, it said, had been wise to choose her as the election organiser. The intoxicating description in such a heavyweight publication of Minnie and Ivor having the 'easy, confident buoyancy of accomplished fighters' conveys something of the mood in Aberavon at the beginning of 1921.

During the campaign, local and international politics fused. Minnie spoke at a 'tremendous' protest meeting against British military forces intervening against the Bolsheviks, and she chaired a meeting on Russia addressed by Jessie Stephen, another remarkable, young ILP woman.[124] However, as implacably as Minnie supported Russia's right to be Communist, and opposed any British intervention that sought to undermine it, she just as strongly opposed communism making headway in Britain or to the ILP being co-opted to the Communist cause. In January 1921 the Welsh Divisional ILP conference rebuffed its communistic element by reversing the decision to affiliate to the Third International. It also 'decisively' rejected the proposal that declared the ILP to be a Communist organisation.[125] A small number of ILP branches in South Wales, where communist sympathisers were in the majority, broke away, taking property and funds with them.[126] Decades later the issue still rankled and Minnie resented how 'the CP stole our ILP premises in Wales...killing some of our people with anxiety'.[127] Though the ILP was simultaneously criticised for being both too left wing or for not being left wing enough, it succeeded in occupying the important political space that existed between the empiricism of the Labour Party and the dogmatism of the Communist Party.[128]

By the time the *Foreign Affairs* article was published in February 1921, Aberavon expectations had been given a severe jolt. MacDonald had nursed the Aberavon constituency for nearly a year when Arthur Henderson suggested that, rather than wait for the general election, MacDonald should instead fight the Woolwich by-election on 2 March. Will Crooks, who had been Labour MP for eighteen years, was resigning through ill health. So strong was Labour's hold there that Crooks had been unopposed in 1918, the local council and Board of Guardians were overwhelmingly Labour, and the Party was strongly organised. MacDonald's reported reluctance to leave Aberavon may have related to how his anti-war stance would be received in Woolwich, where the largest employer was the arsenal. That month, the Aberavon constituency regrettably agreed to MacDonald fighting Woolwich. The *Pioneer*, with a certainty that invites a fall, declared the outcome of the by-election assured.[129]

Within a week Minnie was drafted to Woolwich as organiser, campaigner and propagandist. Ivor Thomas was sure she would be a tremendous success but cautioned her not to overdo it. Jessie Stephen was brought from Bermondsey to help mobilise the women's vote.[130] Also working for the campaign was Molly Hamilton, who Minnie met for the first time. A self-proclaimed devotee of MacDonald, Hamilton travelled to Woolwich each evening after work in central London, undertaking routine tasks like addressing envelopes and canvassing door to door. Hamilton had travelled a parallel path to Minnie. Both were in university in Cardiff around the same time, when Minnie was a student and Hamilton, three years older, was on the staff. Hamilton had joined the ILP in 1914 and was also active in the anti-war movement. In the way that Minnie's personal and political lives often intersected, Hamilton was MacDonald's admirer and lover, having apparently succeeded Minnie in MacDonald's affections. If there was a period when Minnie and Molly were rivals for MacDonald, it would have been 1919–20. By 1921, Minnie was an essential person in MacDonald's political life, and Hamilton was in a personal relationship with him and shortly to be his biographer.[131]

Two days before the poll, Minnie and Margaret Bondfield addressed a special meeting for women voters at Plumstead Baths. Twelve years older than Minnie, Bondfield was an enormously experienced socialist, feminist and pacifist.[132] So huge was the attendance that they had to requisition a larger hall, and even that was packed to bursting.[133] The huge eve of poll march and rally was said to have attracted 20,000 people.[134] The result confounded expectations. MacDonald lost to the Conservative Unionist, Capt Robert Gee VC, by 13,724 votes to 13,041, with the defection of women voters seen as key to MacDonald's defeat.[135] The *Pioneer* concluded that while Gee was not a significant political figure, his win was in part due to his war record, winning the Victoria Cross, and clever tactics.[136] Was the quality of Minnie's organising inadequate? Was she less attuned to working-class life in Woolwich than in South Wales? With over 100,000 civilian and military workers employed in the arsenal during the war, Woolwich was the wrong constituency to be contested by the leader of the anti-war movement. Moreover, unlike Aberavon Minnie had not had a long period to work with the women of the constituency to shape their outlook. Intended as a comeback for the ILP, and having put its all into the election, with the defeat at Woolwich the ILP was still a political outcast and MacDonald's war record was 'an insuperable barrier'.[137]

Back in Porthcawl, Minnie immediately wrote to MacDonald saying she 'lived through Hell the last hour of the Count' with the result in doubt until the last minute. She recognised they had been strategically outmanoeuvred.

What a fool I was not to grasp the game. They knew the mans[']
[*sic*] vote was gone, & they just stirred up the quiet home
women with Zeppelins and the wounded V.C..[138]

Minnie continued: 'I just keep on torturing myself by wondering if it *would* have made any difference if I had got out a strong bill for women only.' Her self-flagellation was unrelenting: '*Why* did I address those silly evening meetings? I should have had nothing but women's demonstrations.' She felt she had failed MacDonald completely asking, 'Can you ever forgive me?' and wondered whether the remorse she felt would send her 'quite mad'. However, in the same letter Minnie acknowledged that at times she believed that once the opposition had played the wounded VC card nothing could have made any difference. Minnie pleaded with MacDonald 'If only you will come back [to Aberavon] I will give the whole summer to intensive work among the women.' Recognising that the strain on him must have been 'fearful' she concluded: 'I shall never forget your white face on that awful night. I just loathe myself.'[139] On Sunday 6 March, Minnie gave an account of the Woolwich election to Briton Ferry ILP and a month later she was still 'awfully distressed'.[140] Perhaps responding to Minnie's plight, MacDonald visited Porthcawl where he stayed for a few days.[141] Some compensation would be found in the lessons she learned in Woolwich were applied to good effect in Aberavon.

On 5 March the Aberavon Labour Party affirmed its continued support for MacDonald's candidacy, should he wish to stay. MacDonald replied that Woolwich demonstrated he was still a 'very vulnerable candidate' due to the 'clouds of poison gas' in which he had been enveloped during the war and he offered to stand down as his personal reputation was so low he did not wish to be an impediment to winning the Aberavon seat.[142] Thomas sought to convince MacDonald that Aberavon was winnable, arguing that Minnie had done excellent work and her influence was being seen in parts of the constituency that were previously hostile.[143] One who disagreed was the Secretary of Woolwich Constituency Labour Party who, after visiting Aberavon, informed MacDonald that he was pessimistic and did not share Aberavon's confidence that MacDonald would win. In a comment that may have carried an implicit criticism of Minnie, he contended its organisation was not being properly attended to and insisted that 'a good man is at once placed in Port Talbot'. On 18 May MacDonald wrote privately to Thomas saying he was going to write to 'MP' about the constituency.[144]

Engaged by the prospect of an election, and perhaps doubting Minnie's capacity, MacDonald wrote a detailed three-page letter on electoral preparations, including establishing committee rooms and skeleton election committees, and compiled canvassing registers, even down to the number of envelopes needed. He analysed the electoral registers for each village, and identified Aberavon and Port Talbot as places in the constituency where his Woolwich experience might be repeated and where the election could be decided.[145] While recognising Minnie had been doing good work in those two areas, he was concerned that meetings would not be enough and that different tactics should be employed. The election would be about his character and track record, so his biography should be well circulated, discussed and defended, he advised.[146] The second half of 1921 saw close and detailed planning by MacDonald and Thomas that provided strategic direction for the election campaign. Minnie carried out the operational plan, but she did not devise it. In November, Thomas and MacDonald still considered Aberavon and Port Talbot as discouraging. Egerton Wake, the Labour Party's National Agent added pressure by informing Thomas that 'all eyes will be upon you' to make up for Woolwich.[147] Minnie later realised how inexperienced she had been for the tasks required and how Thomas's support enabled her to do the job; she was embarrassed that he had done the hard work while allowing her to take the credit and limelight.[148]

In March 1921, Minnie was the Briton Ferry delegate to the Southport ILP national conference, where MacDonald topped the NAC poll, confirming his centrality to the Party. However, Allen, although still physically ailing, was wresting the Party away from the traditional leaders, MacDonald and Snowden, whom Allen thought able and sincere but 'terribly reactionary'[149], and Wallhead had succeeded Snowden as ILP chair.[150] Conference delegates voted overwhelmingly against affiliation to the Third International and against the communist position, ratifying the position taken in Wales in January. Minnie, as was becoming customary, moved the vote of thanks to Wallhead, saying his worth and that of their other leaders could be measured by the value their enemies put on them.[151]

Three days after the conference ended, on 1 April, a three-month lockout in the coal industry started. The pits had returned from government to private control. 4,000 men were out of work in the Afan Valley, 3,000 on short time, with only 2-3,000 in full-time work.[152] When the owners sought wage cuts, the miners resisted. Locally and nationally the ILP did everything it could to support the miners practically and called for the socialisation of the mines to replace private ownership. On 24 April, Minnie spoke in Trafalgar Square for the Save the Miners' Children Committee where Margaret Bondfield, George Lansbury, and Lady Lutyens also spoke.[153] MacDonald addressed the Afan Valley miners' May Day rally and a speaker from the Rhondda NUR addressed an open-air meeting in Cwmavon on 'The ILP and the Miners' Crisis' where he linked the miners' plight to the impact of the Versailles Peace treaty, which the ILP had strongly opposed.[154]

The lockout was a disaster for the miners. The national wage agreement was abolished, and wages were heavily cut. However, the ILP's support of the miners resulted in a bond that lasted a decade. As the protracted pain of the lockout displaced something of the enduring memories of the war, the image of the ILP at the centre of the miners' struggle offset that of a Party which had opposed the war and support grew in the previously lukewarm colliery villages of the Afan valley. While economic hardship led to formal ILP membership declining in South Wales mining villages, the ILP's sway within the SWMF increased and a year later Minnie referred to the *Western Mail* complaining about the disproportionate influence of ILP members in the miners' union.[155]

In salving the position of the ILP, the 1921 miners' lockout transformed MacDonald's fortunes and his chances of winning Aberavon. This process was further aided when the limitations of relying solely on industrial action was exposed after the Triple Alliance called off its proposed national transport and rail workers' strike of solidarity with the miners. It would take the 1926 miners' lockout to complete the process, but the balance between the industrial and political in the South Wales labour movement was shifting away from industrial unionism towards party political action. Although it would take five more years and great suffering to reach the denouement, direct action, which had caused such difficulty for the ILP before the lockout, was seen to have failed.

As the lockout ended, Alf Onions, the Labour MP and former

leader of the SWMF died, and a by-election was called in Caerphilly. Morgan Jones, Minnie's erstwhile fellow Party organiser, gained the support of the miners' lodges and won the nomination to stand as the candidate. The Caerphilly electorate was well aware that this local teacher was an ILP stalwart, prominent anti-war activist and a leader among conscientious objectors, who had suffered in gaol. The ILP and Labour Party poured organisers and propagandists into the constituency. Minnie transferred to Caerphilly to support the campaign and when Katharine Bruce Glasier arrived at Porthcawl on Thursday 18 August, partly for holiday and partly to campaign in Aberavon, Minnie met her, turned her around, and sent her to Caerphilly to work on the by-election.[156] Elizabeth Andrews was there and the women of the Women's Co-operative Guild were also active. Emrys Hughes described the campaign as a crusade. He noted: 'Miss Pallister and Mrs Andrews, with their band of women workers, have never tired, and one realises what a factor the working women's votes will be when the Labour Party starts to work in real earnest.'[157] Hughes detected a change in attitude as years of antagonism towards the ILP over the war died away. Hughes's report said although the opposition used ex-servicemen, including Captain Gee MP VC, who only six months earlier had beaten MacDonald in Woolwich, attempts to play the 'conchie' card failed and there was now no fear of disturbance. The war days were over.[158]

The by-election saw the first appearance of a Communist Party candidate advocating change by force, allowing its appeal in a working-class constituency to be judged. Minnie shared the *Labour Leader*'s view that the Communist Party did not grasp the psychology of the British working class and that 'The workers do not understand why the ultra-revolutionary has appeared'. She agreed with its telling phrase that what was progressive in Russia was retrogressive in Britain, for the building of a socialist commonwealth could be achieved without the use of a single bullet through organising and mobilising working people and gaining control of the institutions of government.[159] The election of minority Labour administrations in 1923 and 1929 pointed towards what might be possible with the final vindication happening with the election of a majority Labour Government in 1945. At the August by-election, Morgan Jones received 13,699 votes against 8,958 for the Liberal and 2,592 for the Communist. His victory showed that, within the Labour fold, the ILP's indigenous form of socialism was more rooted in the South Wales working class than the Communist Party's alien version. Significantly it was the first Parliament victory for a conscientious objector since the war. The 'huge victory' in Caerphilly boded well for Aberavon.[160]

After Caerphilly, Katharine Bruce Glasier stayed in Porthcawl of which she enigmatically noted: 'Miss Pallister & Lydia Hatherall (of Brynmawr) & Gladys – a very interesting but complex home circle.' Undertaking meetings across the constituency, Bruce Glasier registered 'J.R.M needs a lot of bolsterings'.[161] Such misgivings were surprising after the Caerphilly result, but MacDonald's doubts were based in his misreading of the situation. Shifts were taking place across the constituency and support was becoming unified around him. Even some of his most bitter former opponents now backed him. MacDonald's pessimism was slow to abate. In late November, after five good meetings, he conceded that all change was in his direction but that the change needed to be big as 'My folks suffer from too much optimism.'[162]

When he was absent, Minnie kept MacDonald's profile to the fore, speaking on his late wife, Margaret, who had been chair of the Women's Labour League and the following month Malcolm MacDonald, Ramsay's son, spoke to Briton Ferry ILP.[163] By the time MacDonald returned to Aberavon the following year, the tide had turned decisively. He was overwhelmed by his reception in 'Bolshevik Briton Ferry'. There a procession of hundreds of children marched through the streets headed by a body of National Union of Ex-Servicemen, organised by W. H. Vaughan, an active local leader who wanted an alternative to the British Legion. At MacDonald's meeting they formed a guard of honour. Minnie reported the young people of the town had been captured for labour.[164]

The decisive shift was helped in some small part by the launch in late 1921 of the *Afan Sentinel*, a local monthly journal by Aberavon DLP. Chatty and accessible, much of the content was written by Minnie or influenced by her, including 'Our Women's Page'. Analysing contemporary social issues from a Christian perspective, the *Sentinel* located poverty and war as products of capitalism, with religious figures providing articles on industrial, labour and religious themes. The *Sentinel* ranged from local issues to international affairs, MacDonald provided a regular article and each month an ex-soldier wrote an 'ex-servicemen's page' that dealt with problems they were encountering. Even the normally sedate co-operative movement got caught up in the moment. The two local co-operative societies placed a joint advert appealing to 'Workers – Women and Wives' to 'Come and Join us and assist in the overthrow of the capitalist system which callously and mercilessly drags and keeps you down'. As Co-operative adverts usually promoted Wheatsheaf boots or offered a savings club for future purchases, such language was unusual and reflected the prevailing highly politicised local atmosphere.[165]

While she had written locally for the *Pioneer* and the *Sentinel*, from March 1922 Minnie's articles appeared in the national *Labour Leader*. Minnie's first major piece 'Today's Price – One Shilling' looked at the treatment of young girls including their rape and murder and the prostitution of one by her mother. Minnie argued that offences against girls were minimised or the blame was put on them. She criticised male judges and magistrates who judged women that way, and advocated larger numbers of women in those positions to help protect young girls.[166] She contended that men should be educated to respect women and women should be educated to have a higher self-worth. Minnie identified the overwhelmingly unbalanced nature of the messages in women's magazines as causing women to unconsciously lose their self-respect. She noted 'the enormous increase of literature of a pernicious type' in 'little magazines of an apparently harmless nature, with their little paper patterns and beauty hints, etc.' that incessantly repeated that the only thing women should do was make themselves attractive to men. Her critiques of the role and content of women's magazines would be repeated over the next forty years, before being echoed by feminists in the 1970s and 1980s. Minnie was a woman way ahead of her time.

Paradoxically, in the same article Minnie stated, 'I have never been a feminist', adding she did 'not recognise sex antagonism'. Before 1918, socialist women did not use the term 'feminist' and most were still reluctant to use it in the 1920s, as it was 'equated with antagonism to men'.[167] Women labour organisers 'were at times hostile to the label and all it implied'.[168] Minnie might have chosen to not describe herself as one, but in arguing for the extension of social and economic rights to women, and challenging traditional gender roles, she was one. Three features of feminism have been identified in the 1910s and 1920s: an opposition to the control by one sex of the rights and opportunities of the other; the belief that women's subordinate position was socially constructed, rather than grounded in any natural order; and finally the belief that women were not only linked by biological sameness, but also by 'some level of identification with the group called women'.[169] By these measures and in the way she sought to bring women together to achieve sexual equality while recognising sexual difference, Minnie Pallister was a convinced feminist.

At the time, the Labour Party was keeping feminist organisations at a distance because it considered them 'reactionary'.[170] Rather than working through feminist outlets, Minnie chose to explore gender issues with a labour audience by using the structures and publications of the mainstream labour movement. In the *Labour Leader* Minnie tackled an issue central to the women's movement and its debates on the nature of feminism. She wrote, 'Very often women who talk most of equality of the sexes do most to delay the establishment of that equality.' She argued that to be equal with something did not necessarily mean being like it. Although some 'so-called feminists' did not realise it, 'Equality is far from being synonymous with sameness', adding: 'Personally, if this were true, I should consider the price to be too high – equality would be very dear at the price.'[171] Around this time Minnie speculatively submitted an article to the *Daily News* that argued women had been blamed for everything since Adam and Eve. She was on the cliffs near Porthcawl one sunny bank holiday, when a friend dashed towards her carrying the newspaper. Minnie was stunned, later describing the 'intoxicating experience' of seeing herself in print in a national daily.[172] It opened a new avenue of activity that promoted her cause while also providing the affirmation she needed to fend off her ever-present underlying insecurity.

Her appeals to women were on a different basis from men. Rather than talking the language of political economy or the workplace, Minnie identified women's separate needs and used a different language to relate to them. She recognised the limitations placed on women, such as their attendance at meetings, and demonstrated how to prioritise women over men. A supporter of MacDonald, Joan Littlefield, visited Aberavon in March 1922 and observed Minnie in action. Littlefield was scheduled to speak with MacDonald on Labour's foreign policy in the largest cinema in

Port Talbot at an afternoon meeting specially convened for women, as they found it more difficult to attend evening meetings. Although not advertised widely, half an hour before the start every seat was filled and some people were accommodated on the platform, in the aisles, on the stairs and many stood. Littlefield recalled how, before the meeting started, Minnie addressed the audience saying: 'This meeting has been arranged primarily to meet the convenience of the women voters. Perhaps this is not entirely clear, since I see more than three hundred men present. As women are waiting outside, I will ask the gentlemen to be so kind as to vacate their seats and let the women in,' and they did. Littlefield said the incident illustrated how women's enfranchisement had changed their status as citizens, as until then any seat occupied by a non-voting woman at a political meeting was seen as wasted. Indicating the profound shift that had taken place, Littlefield said to MacDonald, 'Now I feel that I have not lived in vain'.[173] In the tight female social networks then existing in South Wales, news of what she had done would quickly have spread around the constituency. However, Minnie's actions would have been exceptional and few would have acted similarly in male-dominated South Wales.

Minnie drew on Aberavon when addressing a mass meeting at the April annual ILP conference in Nottingham, alongside Morgan Jones and Bob Smillie, who had stood down as President of the MFGB after the lockout.[174] In her speech Minnie said South Wales miners' wives had given her new hope in the way they had gone to the polls, so finding ways towards freedom.[175] The *Labour Leader* assessed the speech as 'witty, racy and, in parts, even rollicking' with nearly every sentence contained 'a neat point, and often a rattling good joke'. It suggested that her performance needed 'to add a little of the art of the actress to that of the reciter' before contrasting her with Morgan Jones, caustically pointing out he had too much of what Minnie lacked.[176] In Edinburgh, where Minnie was the only woman in the thirty-strong ILP delegation to the Labour Party conference, she intervened in the unemployment debate to present unemployment as primarily a woman's question as it affected married women probably more than anyone else 'although she had never had the misfortune to be either unemployed or married', before she railed against attempts to divide the employed from the unemployed.[177]

In preparation for the country-wide No More War demonstrations that were held to mark the anniversary of the outbreak of the Great War, Minnie was central to organising them across the Aberavon constituency. Set up in early 1921, the socialist-pacifist No More War Movement (NMWM) promoted personal resistance to war and to building effective opposition inside the labour movement to war. Emerging from the remains of the No Conscription Fellowship, its leaders were ILPers and Brockway was its chair.[178] On the day, Minnie spoke to a Bournemouth NMWM demonstration and the 'wonderful impression' she made would have lasting implications.[179]

As the range of her *Labour Leader* subjects expanded, her confidence grew. After the death of Lord Northcliffe, Minnie launched a tirade against his methods, excoriating the press baron for serving to 'the would-be patriot a dish of nationalism with a sauce of hatred, seasoned with selfishness' that was swallowed greedily. To 'the great god, Circulation' he offered readers a range of fare but never anything that would make them think. Saying he had built his power on his knowledge of the crowd, she pinpointed how he had played to their weaknesses. 'All his life he evaded realities, until at last he faced the one Reality which not even a newspaper proprietor peer can evade.' Casey described it as 'the finest, most terse and truthful' and splendidly woven indictment that showed Minnie as an original thinker not a 'dealer in second-hand thought hash'. He called for her criticisms to be elaborated into a pamphlet.[180]

As her impact increased, Minnie was given the *Labour Leader*'s full front page for an article headed 'US', which was written to inspire the ILP's upcoming autumn campaign on overthrowing economic imperialism. As capitalism could not be altered or mended, she argued, this was not a moment to be ashamed of ILP policy on international socialism, but 'to preach it unceasingly'. She proclaimed the ILP had a vital role in educating thousands of people who were thinking about politics for the first time. Her powerful piece concluded:

> We were right on the War. We were right on the Peace. We were right on Reparations. We were right on Russia. We were right on Ireland.[181]

To accompany her article the paper profiled Minnie in 'Our Portrait Gallery', declaring there was no more gifted younger person in the ILP. Named as one of the national campaign speakers, she was allocated to Scotland, London, Midlands and Yorkshire. After she launched its autumn campaign to 2,000 people, Gorton ILP lauded Minnie saying 'Aberavon, we envy you!'[182] However, a general election called in mid-October 1922 derailed the campaign.

MacDonald's election was seen as vital for the labour movement. He travelled to Aberavon and spent three weeks holding meetings across the constituency, considering the fight in Aberavon to be harder than in most places. The Tory Party, he said, debased the campaign with 'misquotation, prevarication, and misrepresentation' which Labour countered with serious argument.[183] Emrys Hughes starkly presented Aberavon as being more than an election campaign; it was a battle for the ILP.[184]

Minnie composed a campaign 'battle song' to the tune 'Men of Harlech':

> Voters all of Aberavon
> Wisdom Show and Vote for RAMSAY
> Don't be bluffed they think it's easy,
> Vote for THE RIGHT MAN
>
> Ramsay, Ramsay. Shout it.
> Don't be shy about it.
> Labour's day is bound to come,
> We cannot do without it.
> On then Labour, on to glory
> 'Twill be told in song and story,
> How we fought at Aberafan
> On election day.[185]

As election date approached increasing numbers of people offered their services. Ernest Hunter, the national organiser, transferred to Aberavon. Maude Royden, who would play a later role in Minnie's life, visited for a week.[186] Nine years older than Minnie, Royden was a prominent Anglican, feminist, opponent of the Great War, strong supporter of the ILP and the NCF and, with Marshall and Swanwick, was one of the founding members of the Women's International League that sought to align feminism and pacifism.

As election fever built, MacDonald likened the Labour campaign to a religious revival.[187] At times it more resembled a military parade. On Monday 13 November, 48 hours before polling day, a night procession of nearly 2,000 ex-soldiers wearing medals and carrying torches marched in the constituency in support of MacDonald.[188] By the evening of the count Minnie said, that after years tramping 'so many weary miles' followed by three weeks of 'frenetic activity', despite the unbearable suspense 'she was almost too far gone to care'.[189]

MacDonald polled 14,318 votes, nearly double Labour's vote in 1918, and 3,204 more than his Unionist rival. Of the five ILP candidates in Wales only Jimmy Edmunds in Cardiff Central lost, Wallhead was returned in Merthyr, David Williams in Swansea and Morgan Jones in Caerphilly.[190] MacDonald returned to the House of Commons as the leader of the ILP and became the Labour Party's Parliamentary leader with 142 MPs including Snowden, Jowett, Lansbury, Ponsonby and Sir Charles Trevelyan. The duality in MacDonald's roles would prove a challenge, for while the ILP was an integral part of the Labour Party, it also had a distinctive, independent, existence within it. As the leader of both, MacDonald had to contend with, and was irritated by, ILP MPs who struggled within the Parliamentary Labour Party, often against him, to get their radical policies adopted.[191]

On his Aberavon success, MacDonald wrote immediately to Ivor Thomas: 'to you I owe it all. It has been a great victory and you are the master of it.'[192] Minnie came to recognise that, at a time when MacDonald 'had come within an ace of leaving public life forever' it was Thomas's work that created the machine that made victory possible.[193] A perceptive assessment by Emrys Hughes identified that victory lay in the effective pairing of Ivor Thomas, with his capacity for detail and routine work, with Minnie's 'good humour and energy...quick wit and human touch'.[194] Minnie's contribution was recognised by MacDonald who acknowledged 'Nothing in the election was more remarkable than the women's vote' with many women prepared to vote differently from their husbands. Their level of political sophistication he put down in part to the education which had been directed towards them over the previous three years. Thirty years later, W. H. Vaughan, the ex-servicemen's leader who by then was General Secretary of Aberavon Labour Party, said it was the catalytic effect of Minnie's organising women that 'helped more than anything else to put Ramsay MacDonald into Parliament'.[195]

Learning the lessons of Woolwich and converting it into victory in Aberavon allowed Minnie to put the trauma of MacDonald's earlier defeat behind her. Two years later she drew on her experiences in her book *Orange Box: Thoughts of a Socialist Propagandist*, where she explored how the approaches required to organise women who had only recently gained the vote differed from those used with men and trades unions members.[196] It was important learning shared.

As well as her work in Aberavon, Minnie had become President of the South Wales Division of the ILP following the 1921 lockout. On the Divisional Council were Emrys Hughes, Henry Davies, Vice President, Ivor Thomas, Treasurer and Morgan Jones, representing the Division on the NAC. The strong Divisional leadership confronted two major challenges – the aftermath of the miners' lockout, with depressed trade, short-time working and unemployment in the coal industry, and addressing the changing national imperatives of the ILP. Branch numbers and membership had initially dipped after the lockout, but changes in attitudes towards the ILP saw new branches established, membership increase and affiliation fees more than double in South Wales.[197] Continuing the work she had undertaken as full-time organiser, Minnie oversaw the reconstituting of the Division to cover the whole of Wales and led the campaign of reorganising branches and federations and opening new branches, particularly in West Wales. Bringing discipline and efficiency to the loosely organised and highly decentralised Party was a challenge. The Welsh ILP reflected the national position of enthusiasm and growth, combined with financial problems so, to address the debt of £100 incurred by the Welsh Division in rebuilding the branch and federation network, Minnie launched a financial appeal.[198] Minnie was now more than an inspirational platform speaker as she developed the analytical and organisational skills and breadth of experiences needed in a rounded politician.

Minnie's Presidency coincided with Allen's election as ILP national treasurer in early 1922, from which began his domination of the Party. Brockway, who went back to work in the national ILP office as Organising Secretary and then General Secretary, noted that Allen was exceptionally able. Showing 'organising genius' in transforming the ILP, Allen combined political principle with business acumen as he used his connections with wealthy donors formed through the NCF to finance his vision of the Party and its expansion.[199] Allen's impact led to the launch of the 'Now for Socialism' campaign in January 1923. Aimed at educating people that socialism was not a bureaucratic system but one that encouraged workers towards responsible service to the community, which broadly chimed with Minnie's own views, in what was described as a period of frantic activity, the campaign organised nearly 600 conferences and demonstrations in the first months of the year.[200]

To launch the campaign in Wales, Minnie presided over a conference in Cardiff where she identified a great change in the political mentality of Wales, which she said now had a greater proportion of Labour members than any other part of Britain.[201] Three weeks later, Minnie addressed the ILP Welsh Divisional Council's 'Great Trade Union and Labour Conference' in support of a 'Bold Socialist Policy' including ending poverty, economic justice including control of industry in a Socialist Commonwealth, and the repudiation of war and immediate universal disarmament. After addressing a demonstration the following evening, she undertook a speaking tour of the valleys in support of the campaign.[202] Such events were well-attended but they may have achieved little as ILP influence over trades unions was small as their main allegiance was to the Labour Party. Nor did union leaders support the ILP policy of guild socialism of which Minnie too was critical. Even so, the ILP was prominent in the early 1920s and politically overshadowed the fledgling Communist Party in South Wales. Worryingly, however, an erosion of support was starting to occur, with some members beginning to put their 'moral and spiritual' and financial efforts, that would previously have gone into the ILP, towards the Labour Party.[203] The last action of Minnie's Presidency of the Welsh Division of the ILP was an 'Urgent & Important' call for mobilisation to oppose breaking trading relations with Russia.[204] Then, at the Division's May annual conference, she stood down as President because she had already taken up a new position of National ILP Propagandist.

Minnie left behind a remarkable record in Welsh frontline politics. She had been President of the Monmouthshire ILP Federation from 1914 to 1916 and secretary of the NCF in Wales from 1916 to 1917. In the five years between June 1918 to May 1923, she had been South Wales ILP Divisional Organiser (1918 to 1920); MacDonald's organiser-agent in Aberavon (1920 to 1922) and

President of the South Wales, and then the Wales Division of the ILP (1921 to 1923). In the decade from 1912, during a critical period in its political and social formation, she helped shape the way that the people of Wales saw themselves and helped channel that expression into a party-political form. Minnie had shown herself to be a supreme propagandist, making a unique contribution in the promotion of socialism in South Wales and, less successfully, seeking to give that socialism a gendered perspective. As one of the organisers whose efforts resulted in a century of domination by the Labour Party, she helped make early twenty-first century Wales what it is today.

By the time she left Wales, Minnie was its outstanding woman Labour politician, its best woman orator and a prominent and influential figure in the labour movement generally. Not that she ever really left South Wales. For although she left it physically, she later wrote that no one who had lived there left it spiritually. Minnie recognised and loved the solidarity integral to valleys' life and its distinctive spirit.[205] Throughout her life she would return, back to her home in Wales.

---

[1] *Pioneer*, 19 January & 8 June 1918.

[2] The ILP's role, campaigns and growth in South Wales during the period after the war have hitherto been overlooked. While it has been acknowledged that pre-war ILP culture was imported into the Labour Party as it expanded dramatically in parts of the coalfield after 1918, the ILP's post-war role, its resources, the activities of its full and part-time organisers, its work with women, and how it continued to directly influence the Labour Party, deserve greater recognition.

[3] Prominent were Ivor Thomas and D. L. Mort of Briton Ferry, and David Williams, a Swansea boilermaker.

[4] George Barker was miners' agent for the Monmouthshire Western Valleys. He was MP for Abertillery from 1920 to 1929.

[5] Table, Number of ILP branches, ILP 6/9/5, LSE archive; Marwick, *ILP* thesis, pp. 17 & 50.

[6] *Aberdare Leader*, 28 September 1918; *Pioneer*, 14 & 28 September, 12 & 26 October 1918.

[7] Thompson, p. 227.

[8] *Pioneer*, 12 & 19 October 1918.

[9] *Llanelli Star*, 22 March 1919.

[10] *Pioneer*, 3 July 1920.

[11] *Pioneer*, 25 October 1919.

[12] *Pioneer*, 13 September 1919.

[13] *Pioneer*, 29 May & 3 July 1920.

[14] *Labour Leader*, 14 November 1918.

[15] *Gloucester Journal*, 27 December 1919.

[16] *Glamorgan Gazette*, 13 September 1918.

[17] *Labour Leader*, 1 April 1920; *Merthyr Pioneer*, 3 April 1920.

[18] *Cambria Daily Leader*, 1 & 7 July 1919; *Labour Leader*, 17 July 1919; *Pioneer*, 5 July 1919.

[19] *Pioneer*, 8 March & 12 April 1919; *Labour Leader*, 6 March 1919.

[20] Opposition was based in a combination of reasons including on health grounds while others ranged from the moral to the practical, including the impropriety of large numbers of men seeing one another naked, cost, or the risk of losing clothes. (Neil Evans and Dot Jones, 'A Blessing for the Miner's Wife: The Campaign for Pithead Baths in the South Wales Coalfield, 1908-1950', *Llafur*, 1994, p. 12.)

[21] Michael Lieven, 'A Fractured Working-Class Consciousness? The Case of the Lady Windsor Colliery Lodge, 1921', *WHR*, December 2003, pp. 749-751; J. E. Morgan, *A Village Workers' Council*, Celtic Press, nd, p. 63.

[22] Evidence of Minnie Pallister, 21 June 1920, Ministry of Health, *Report of the South Wales Regional Survey Committee*, held by Neil Evans.

[23] Evans and Jones, pp. 20-1.

[24] *Pioneer*, 15 March 1919.

[25] *Pioneer*, 2 November 1918.

[26] A local political dynamic existed in the Rhondda. Chris Williams has referred to a melange of groups there that included the South Wales Socialist Society, the Rhondda Socialist Society and the Unofficial Reform Committee. (*Democratic Rhondda*, pp.152-3) W. H. Mainwaring, presiding over one of Minnie's meetings, appealed for unity amongst the socialist elements in the Rhondda. He judged that while the local movement may have been theoretically sound, it was utterly helpless and ineffective without organisational unity. (*Pioneer*, 12 October 1918; *Labour Leader*, 3 October 1918).

[27] 'Life Story (3)'.

[28] *Cambria Daily Leader*, 26 November & 2 December 1918; *Llais Llafur*, 7 December 1918; *Pioneer*, 7 December 1918.

[29] Marquand, p. 233; *Labour Leader*, 28 November 1918; *Aberdare Leader*, 7 & 14 December 1918.

[30] *Western Mail*, 9 December 1918.

[31] Chris Wrigley, *Arthur Henderson*, GPC, 1990, p. 90.

[32] *Pioneer*, 30 November 1918.

[33] Lydia Hatherall, a former fellow lodger of Minnie, is listed in the Electoral Register.

[34] Known as the Red Violinist, he was painted as The Blue Violinist by Marc Chagall.

[35] Harri Kõrvits, *Eduard Soermus – Der Rote Geiger*, VEB Deutscher Verlag für Musik, Leipzig, 1978, pp. 111-2; 114-5 & 118. I am grateful to Johann Sienz for translation. Rachel Holmes, *Sylvia Pankhurst*, Bloomsbury, 2020, p. 528.

[36] *Pioneer*, 20 & 27 April 1918; *Programme, Ewvard Soermus, Olympia Rink, Merthyr, 23 April, 1918*, CPT/1/6/1, Newcastle University Special Collection.

[37] Kõrvits, pp. 113-4, 118; *Labour Leader*, 12 September 1918.

[38] *Llais Llafur*, 21 December 1918; Kõrvits, pp. 113-4.

[39] *Pioneer*, 8 March 1919; Kõrvits, pp. 140 & 192; *Soermus The Russian Violinist*, Agenda Press, 1924, pp. 4-5.

[40] Pallister to Derville, 2 November [1956], BBC WAC RCONT1 Pallister (Talks 8).

[41] Marwick, ILP thesis, p. 57.

[42] Duncan Tanner, 'The Pattern in Labour Politics in Wales, 1918–1939', in eds. Duncan Tanner, Chris Williams and Deian Hopkin, *The Labour Party in Wales 1900–2000*, UWP, 2000, p. 113; Howell, p. 23.

[43] May 'Mosaic...', p. 82.

[44] Quote taken from Hamilton, *Friends*, p. 107.

[45] Lesley A. Hall, *Sex, Gender and Social Change in Britain Since 1880*, Macmillan, 2000, p. 76; Lesley Hall 'Arrows of Desire', *British Sexual Utopians of the Late Nineteenth and Early Twentieth Century and the Politics of Health, Socialism and Sexuality Workshop*, International Institute of Social History, Amsterdam, 2000 p. 3; Sheila Rowbotham, 'In Search of Carpenter', *History Workshop*, Issue 3, 1977, p. 126.

[46] Edward Carpenter, *Marriage in a Free Society*, Labour Press Society, 1894, pp. 12, 18, 27–8 & 35; Edward Carpenter, *Woman and Her Place in a Free Society*, Labour Press Society, 1894.

[47] Edward Carpenter, *Sex-Love, and Its Place in a Free Society*, Labour Press Society, 1894, p. 19.

[48] Jeffrey Weeks, *Sex, Politics and Society*, Routledge, Second Edition, 1989, pp. 172–3.

[49] Rowbotham, *Carpenter*, p. 129; Lesley Hall '"No Sex Please, We're Socialists": The British Labour Party Closes Its Eyes and Thinks of the Electorate' in Jesse Battan, Thomas Bouchet and Tania Regin, *Meetings and Alcoves: The Left and Sexuality in Europe and the United States since 1850*, L'Institut d'histoire contemporain, 2004, pp. 65–6.

[50] Jenny Cuthbert, interviewed Sue Hamill, 15 May 2008, DWAW29, Glamorgan Record Office.

[51] See Karen Hunt, *Equivocal Feminists, The Social Democratic Federation and the Woman Question 1884–1911*, Cambridge, 1996, pp. 86–8.

[52] Len Jeffreys, transcript of interview by Hywel Francis and David Egan, 20 September 1972, South Wales Miners Library.

[53] Hunt, *Equivocal...*, pp. 86–8.

[54] See comments of Stella Browne quoted in Lesley A. Hall, *What A Lot There Is Still To Do: Stella Browne (1880–1955) – Carrying the Struggle Ever Onward*, eds., Claire Eustance, Joan Ryan and Laura Ugolini, *A Suffrage Reader*, Leicester, 2000, p. 196.

[55] Hall, *Sex...*, pp. 100–1.

[56] Hall, 'No Sex...', pp. 65–6.

[57] Allen unpublished diary, Tuesday, October 22nd to Monday, Oct. 28th 1918. I have been unable to discover more about the 'ten-year love tragedy'.

[58] Allen unpublished diary, January 1st, 1919.

[59] Allen diary, 1st to 5th January 1919; see, for example, Monk on Russell's treatment of Helen Dudley, pp. 355–9 & 375–81.

[60] *New Leader*, 15 February & 12 April 1929.

[61] In contrast to his 'saintly' public persona, viewed through twenty-first century eyes, it is difficult to interpret Allen's detailed diary entries as anything other than those of a sexual predator preying on young vulnerable women.

[62] Allen diary, 5 September 1919.

[63] 'A Puritan Takes Stock', *WH*, 5 April 1955 & 'Minnie Pallister Talking', *WH*, 3 October 1955.

[64] Tellingly Allen had initially written she wished to be the first woman ILP MP, but deleted 'ILP'.

[65] *Labour Leader*, 6 February & 3 April 1919; *Pioneer*, 15 January, 8 & 15 February 1919; *Amman Valley Chronicle and East Carmarthen News*, 6 March 1919; *Llais Llafur*, 8 March 1919; *Llanelli Star*, 1 & 22 March 1919. In 1926, this became the theme of her pamphlet *Mrs Smith of Wigan*, a denunciation of the way Britain operated. (Minnie Pallister, *Mrs Smith of Wigan*, ILP, pp. 11 & 12.)

[66] *Pioneer*, 12 April & 10 May 1919.

[67] *Pioneer*, 14 June 1919; Dylan Rees, 'Morgan Jones' *DLB*, Vol IX, pp. 145–50; Robins, 'Morgan Jones...'; *Labour Leader*, 22 May 1919.

[68] Dowse, p. 34.

[69] *Labour Leader*, 12 June 1919.

[70] Chairman's Address, *Report of the ILP Conference*, April 1919, pp. 33–42.

[71] Conference Report, pp. 58–9; *Labour Leader*, 24 April 1919.

[72] Marquand, p. 255; Dowse, p. 34; *Pioneer*, 5 July 1919.

[73] Ness Edwards, *History of the South Wales Miners' Federation*, Lawrence & Wishart, 1938, p. 111.

[74] *Pioneer*, 5 July 1919.

[75] *Labour Leader*, 22 June, 10 & 17 July 1919; *Cambria Daily Leader*, 7 July 1919; *Pioneer*, 5 July 1919.

[76] Evidence, 21 June 1920, Ministry of Health, *Report of the South Wales Regional Survey Committee*.

[77] In March 1919 she was one of four women's organisers and her post covered Wales and parts of England, before she formally became the Labour Party's women's organiser for Wales in 1920.

[78] See, for example, 'Women in the Labour Party: The Work in Districts, Advisory Councils & Sections', *Labour Woman*, for 1922.

[79] Elizabeth Andrews, 'Wales –Then and Now: 1919–1947', *Labour Woman*, February 1948, reprinted Honno, 2006; Andrews, *A Woman's Work...*, p. 113 of Honno edition; Masson, Introduction,..., p. xi.

[80] For differences between 'Socialist Women' and 'Labour Women' see Hannam and Hunt, pp. 8–12.

[81] Ursula Masson & Lowri Newman, 'Andrews, Elizabeth', *DLB*, Vol XI, pp. 1–11; Pamela M. Graves, *Labour Women*, Cambridge, 1994, Chapter 1.

[82] See, for example, *Cambria Daily Leader*, 1 & 7 July 1919.

[83] Andrews was awarded an OBE for her service to women in the Labour Party in Wales.

[84] Focussing on ILP attitudes towards the soldier and how the Party fought for soldiers' wives and dependents and discharged and disabled men, Minnie reminded the soldiers that upon discharge they had to organise their own union to fight the very same government which the ILP had been fighting throughout the war. *Pioneer*, 27 September & 25 October 1919.

[85] 'South Wales and The ILP'; *Pioneer*, 16 August 1919; *Labour Leader*, 16 October 1919.

[86] Marquand, p. 254.

[87] *Aberdare Leader*, 26 & 29 July 1919.

[88] Ian Bullock, *Romancing the Revolution*, AU Press, 2011, p. 193.

[89] *Pioneer*, 7 February 1920.

[90] *Pioneer*, 24 May & 7 & 14 June 1919; Rees, 'Morgan Jones'; Robins, 'Morgan Jones...'

[91] *Pioneer*, 7 February 1920; Marwick, ILP thesis, p. 14.

[92] *Pioneer*, 16 August 1919.

[93] Questionnaires completed by Morgan Jones and Minnie Pallister, ILP 6/9/5, LSE.

[94] Howell, p. 238.

[95] Jones questionnaire.

[96] Minnie Pallister questionnaire.

[97] *New Era Union: Men's Sunday School Class Minute Book 1916*, Bert Pearce Collection, WD 1/24, NLW; Alun Burge, *From Abertillery to the Kremlin Wall: The New Era Union Men's Sunday School Class and the Impact of the Russian Revolution*, unpublished talk, Llafur Day School: The Anti-War Movement in Wales, 10 December 2016.

[98] Jones questionnaire.

[99] Jones questionnaire; see also Paul Davies, *A. J. Cook*, Manchester, 1987, p. 35.

[100] See, for example, Minnie talked at length about the causes of the recent railway strike. (*Aberdare Leader*, 18 October 1919.)

[101] Bullock, *Under Siege*, pp. 3–7.

[102] Jones and Pallister questionnaires.

[103] *Pioneer*, 22 May 1920; *Man and Metal*, April 1941.

[104] *Pioneer*, 3 July 1920.

[105] *Labour Leader*, 6 May 1920; *Pioneer*, 17 July 1920.

[106] *Pioneer*, 3 & 17 July 1920.

[107] Marquand, p. 280; J. Ramsay MacDonald, 'Aberavon', *Wanderings and Excursions*, Jonathan Cape, 1925, p. 111.

[108] H. Hessell Tiltman, *James Ramsay MacDonald*, Jarrolds, 1929, p. 138; Iconoclast [Mary Agnes Hamilton], *The Man of Tomorrow J. Ramsay MacDonald*, ILP, 1923, p. 88.

[109] Pallister to Quigley, 12 November [1937], BBC WAC RCONT1 Pallister (Talks 1).

[110] *Foreign Affairs*, February 1921.

[111] Marquand, p. 235; Elton, p. 345.

[112] *Pioneer*, 28 February & 6 March 1920; *Labour Leader*, 5 February & 4 March 1920; *Glamorgan Gazette*, 5 March 1920.

[113] *Everybody's Weekly*, 7 August 1948; *Glamorgan Gazette*, 5 & 26 March 1920 & 28 January 1921.

[114] I disagree with Howard's interpretation that MacDonald's victory was 'virtually inevitable'. (Chris Howard, 'The Focus of the Mute Hopes of a Whole Class' – Ramsay MacDonald and Aberavon, 1922–1929', *Llafur*, 1996, pp. 69 & 71.)

[115] Thomas to Pallister, 25 August 1920, PRO 30/69/1737.

[116] Tiltman, Appendix E.

[117] 'Life Story (3)'.

[118] Thomas to Pallister, 1 September 1920, PRO 30/69/1737.

[119] Masson, Introduction, p. xxiv.

[120] Thomas to Pallister, 25 August 1920, PRO 30/69/1737; MacDonald, 'Aberavon', p. 114.

[121] *New Leader*, 8 December 1922.

[122] *Labour Leader*, 5 February 1920; Thomas to Pallister, 25 & 29 August 1920, PRO 30/69/1737.

[123] *Foreign Affairs*, February 1921, pp. 130–1.

[124] *Labour Leader*, 19 August 1920; *Pioneer*, 21 August & 23 October 1920. Eight years younger than Minnie, Stephen had won a scholarship to train as a pupil-teacher, but family circumstances required her to become a domestic servant in Glasgow, where she organised her colleagues. Active in the WSPU before starting work with Pankhurst's WSF, Stephen became an ILP woman's organiser in Bermondsey in 1917, from which she was seconded to the National Federation of Women Workers where she had responsibility for domestic workers.

[125] *Pioneer*, 22 January, 5 February 1921; Marwick, ILP thesis, p. 115.

[126] Dowse, p. 58; Marwick, ILP thesis, p. 116.

[127] Minnie to Katharine Bruce Glasier, 11 October 1948, Glasier Papers, GP/1/2/ 347 (ii), Liverpool University Special Collection.

[128] Dowse, pp. 74–5.

[129] 29 & 30 January 1921, MacDonald's journal diary, PRO 30/69/1753/1; *Pioneer*, 12 February & 5 March 1921; *Glamorgan Gazette*, 18 February 1921; Stephen R. Ward, *Low Born Among The High Brows*, Peter Lang, 1990, p. 108.

[130] Thomas to Pallister, 26 February 1921, PRO 30/69/1737; Jessie Stephen, *When I Became a Parliamentary candidate*, unpublished, WCML PP/BIOGA/1/943.

[131] The nature of Minnie and Hamilton's relationship remains elusive. In the late 1930s, Hamilton played a key role in Minnie's life, helping her find employment. In 1944, Hamilton's *Remembering My Good Friends* provided a detailed dissection of MacDonald's complex character and exposed his strengths and failings, though she avoided mentioning she had been in a personal relationship with him. Nor did she refer to Minnie, although Minnie was woven through the experiences of which she wrote. Minnie's admiring review of Hamilton's book also revealed little. (Hamilton, *Friends*, pp. 145–6, though she incorrectly dates the by-election as 1920. Pallister, 'How to Make Friends', *John O'London*, 29 December 1944.)

[132] Bondfield had worked with the Shop Assistants Union, had been Secretary of the Women's Labour League, Chair of the Adult Suffrage Society, an officer of the National Union of General and Municipal Workers' Union and member of the TUC General Council.

[133] *The Pioneer and Labour Journal Special Election Supplement*, 26 February & 1 March 1921, PRO 30/69/1738.

[134] Marquand, p. 275.

[135] Stephen R. Ward, *Low Born...*, p. 109.

[136] *Pioneer*, 5 March 1921.

[137] Brockway, *Inside the Left*, p. 141; Marquand, p. 275.

[138] Pallister to MacDonald, nd, PRO 30/69/1738; 'Election Experiences', *Woman's Page*, 22 June 1945.

[139] Pallister to MacDonald, nd, PRO 30/69/1738.

[140] *Pioneer*, 12 March 1921; Thomas to MacDonald, 5 April 1921, PRO 30/69/1737.

[141] MacDonald's journal diary, 9 May 1921, PRO 30/69/1753/1.

[142] Thomas to MacDonald, 7 March 1921; MacDonald to Thomas, 8 March 1921, PRO 30/69/1737; Stephen R. Ward, *Low Born*, p. 111.

[143] Thomas to MacDonald, 5 April 1921, PRO 30/69/1737.

[144] Barefoot to MacDonald, 13 May 1921, MacDonald to Thomas, 18 May 1921, PRO 30/69/1737.

[145] MacDonald to Thomas, 19 July 1921, PRO 30/69/1737.

[146] MacDonald to Thomas, 12 & 19 July 1921, PRO 30/69/1737.

[147] MacDonald to Thomas, 8 November 1921, PRO 30/69/1737; Egerton Wake to Thomas, 22 July 1921, PRO 30/69/1737.

[148] Longhand addition to 'Life Story (3)' script; 'Minnie Pallister's Day', *WH*, 25 January 1956.

[149] *Labour Leader*, 25 March & 1 April 1920; Marwick, ILP thesis, p. 96; Allen diary, 9 Sept 1919, quoted Marwick, *Clifford Allen*, p. 53; Brockway, *Inside the Left*, p. 138.

[150] Ian Bullock, *Under Siege: The Independent Labour Party in Interwar Britain*, AU Press, 2017, pp. 32–4.

[151] Marquand, p. 275; *Pioneer*, 2 April 1921; *Report of 29th Annual ILP Conference*, p. 146.

[152] *Pioneer*, 12 February 1921.

[153] *Pioneer*, 16 April 1921; *Daily Herald*, 20 April 1921.

[154] Thomas to MacDonald, 7 March 1921, PRO 30/69/1737; *Labour Leader*, 10 June 1921.

[155] Marwick, ILP thesis, pp. 51 & 130; *Labour Leader*, 6 April 1922.

[156] Katharine Bruce Glasier, (KBG) Diary, 18 August 1921, GP 2/2/11.

[157] *Labour Leader*, 25 August & 1 September 1921.

[158] *Labour Leader*, 18 August 1921.

[159] *Labour Leader*, 18 August 1921.

[160] KBG, Diary, 18–31 August 1921, GP 2/2/9; *Labour Leader*, 25 August 1921.

[161] KBG, Diary, 18–31 August 1921.

[162] MacDonald's journal diary, 20 Oct & 2 Dec 1921, PRO 30/69/1753/1.

[163] *Labour Leader*, 15 December 1921 & 12 January 1922.

[164] *Glamorgan Gazette*, 21 July 1922; *Labour Leader*, 11 May 1922; *Afan Sentinel*, June 1922; *Port Talbot Guardian*, 12 August 1938.

[165] *Afan Sentinel*, December 1921, No 2 – July 1922, No 9.

[166] *Labour Leader*, 23 March 1922.

[167] Hamman & Hunt, *Socialist Women*, p. 10.

[168] June Hamman, 'Women as Paid Organisers and Propagandists for the British Labour Party Between the Wars', *International Labor and Working-Class History*, No 77, Spring 2010, p. 71.

[169] Claire Eustance, *Daring...*, pp. 20–2, using Nancy Cott, *The Grounding of Modern Feminism*, Yale, 1987.

[170] Martin Pugh, *Women and the Women's Movement in Britain 1914–1959*, Macmillan, 1992, pp. 134–5.

[171] *Labour Leader*, 18 May 1922. See Pedersen, *Rathbone*, Chapter 10.

[172] *Methodist Recorder*, 28 February 1957; 'Request Week', *WH*, 17 July 1951; Minnie Pallister Speaking, *WH*, 8 February 1954.

[173] Joan Littlefield, 'A Quarter Century of Women's Rights', quoted in *Britain*, British Information Service, New York, March 1943, pp. 55–56. Thanks to Pallavi Podapati for helping access this source; *Labour Leader*, 30 March 1922.

[174] *Nottingham Journal*, 17 April 1922.

[175] *Labour Leader*, 20 April 1922.

[176] *Labour Leader*, 6 & 20 April 1922; ILP Annual Conference report, 1922, p. 38.

[177] Labour Party conference report, 1922, pp. 207–11.

MINNIE PALLISTER: THE VOICE OF A REBEL

[178] *Labour Leader*, 27 July 1922; Ceadel, *Pacifism...* , pp. 70, 73 & 225–6.

[179] *No More War*, January 1923; *Labour Leader*, 18 May & 27 July 1922; *Afan Sentinel*, July 1922; *New Leader*, 9 March 1923; Brockway, *Inside the Left*, pp. 130 & 137.

[180] *Labour Leader*, 17 & 31 August 1922.

[181] *Labour Leader*, 31 August 1922.

[182] *Labour Leader*, 17 August 1922.

[183] Diary 1922, MacDonald papers, RMD/2/19; MacDonald, 'Aberavon', *Wanderings...*, p. 113.

[184] *New Leader*, 3 November 1922.

[185] J. Ivor Hanson, *Profile of A Welsh Town*, 2nd ed., 1969, p. 116; this full version of the song is in MacDonald papers, PRO.

[186] *New Leader*, 27 October 1922.

[187] MacDonald, 'Aberavon', *Wanderings...*, p. 113.

[188] *New Leader*, 17 November 1922.

[189] 'Life Story (3).

[190] Marquand pp. 283–4; *New Leader*, 24 November 1922; Dowse, p. 90.

[191] See Bullock, *Under Siege*, Chapter 6.

[192] MacDonald to Thomas, nd, No 44, PRO 30/69/1737.

[193] *John O'London*, 29 December 1944.

[194] *New Leader*, 3 November 1922.

[195] MacDonald, 'Aberavon', *Wanderings...*, p. 116; *SWDN*, 6 May 1923; W. H. Vaughan, *The Story of The Battles and History of the Aberavon Divisional Labour Party*, 1950, esp. pp. 2 & 12.

[196] Minnie Pallister, *The Orange Box: Thoughts of a Socialist Propagandist*, Leonard Parsons, 1924, pp. 48–51.

[197] *New Leader*, 14 & 21 September 1923; Marwick, ILP thesis, p. 234.

[198] *Labour Leader*, 31 August, 7 & 21 September 1922; *New Leader*, 24 November 1922; *Daily Herald*, 28 August 1922; *South Wales News*, 28 August 1922; Dowse, p. 71; 1922 ILP Conference Report, Nottingham, April 1922, p. 102.

[199] Marquand, pp. 269 & 276/7; Dowse, pp. 71, 76–7, 88–90, 98 & 141; Brockway, *Inside the Left*, p. 145; Marwick, ILP thesis, pp. 31–4; 'B' in the *New Leader*, 6 April 1923.

[200] *New Leader*, 12 January 1923; Dowse, p. 8.

[201] Welsh ILP Circulars, Small Collections Microfilm Reel No 2 Coll.Misc.371/2, LSE; *South Wales News*, 5 February 1923.

[202] *South Wales News*, 26 February 1923; *New Leader*, 2 March 1923; poster & letter, ILP 371/1 & 371/2.

[203] Dowse, pp. 86/7 & 100; *New Leader*, 15 November 1929. The available papers do not permit as assessment of the Wales ILP beyond 1923.

[204] Circular Letter, 5 May 1923, 371/2.

[205] *Daily Herald*, 1 March 1934; 'South Wales and The ILP'.

CHAPTER FOUR
Propagandist

In January 1923, Minnie began work as National Propagandist on the 'Now for Socialism' campaign. The *ILP Chronicle* said her appointment was greeted with 'A universal shout of welcome'.[1] After years in one place, Minnie's existence now became one of crisscrossing Britain promoting the cause of socialism in what she described as a 'queer and lonely life'.[2] Week after week, month after month, in a punishing schedule, she tore up and down the country, travelling on 'the great expresses' to Scotland or 'crawling along the valleys in little local puffers'. Speaking tours of Lancashire in January; London and the South East, South Wales, and the Midlands in February; and Yorkshire in March were followed by campaigning for an ILP candidate in the Ludlow by-election, then touring Derbyshire and Lincolnshire in April. Relying on the generosity and hospitality of local people who accommodated her, sometimes in unspeakable conditions, she would see new faces every night – comrades, but not friends.[3]

During those months she proclaimed the ILP's growing success was not because the Party had changed its views but because it had been true to them, and it was the country that was changing. She defended Russia from the new trade attack by the British Government and advocated diplomatic recognition for the Bolshevik Government. By May, speaking engagements were booked until the end of the year.[4] After such herculean efforts she was named 'one of the heroes of the campaign', as she 'completely overwhelmed' audiences.[5]

Minnie was probably the most impressive woman speaker in the labour movement. On the platform she had a unique style. She spoke very fast – twice as fast as most people – drawing on a 'wealth of material and metaphor' but 'no one ever tired of listening to her'. Jessie Stephen said Minnie spoke at a tremendous rate and often her remarks did not register immediately 'but after a few seconds there would be a burst of laughter'.[6] 'Her spontaneous infectious humour had her audiences rolling with laughter.'[7] Brockway wrote, 'She is one of the most brilliant speakers our movement has ever had.'[8] MacDonald was reported as saying Minnie was the 'finest woman speaker in the country'.[9] The most analytical consideration of her oratory came from Lucy Cox, who first met Minnie in 1922 when Cox was ILP Divisional Secretary for the South West, before she became General Secretary of the No More War Movement, then MP for Plymouth in 1945. Cox said that she heard all the great socialist women orators of that time – 'the power and eloquence' of Margaret Bondfield, the 'magnificent style' of Ethel Snowden, and the 'great emotional appeal' of Katharine Bruce Glasier. But for 'sheer delight and charm, Minnie surpassed them all'.[10] As Stuart Morris later observed, Minnie's secret lay in a gaiety of spirit that was coupled to a powerful intellect, fuelled by a rebel heart.[11]

Minnie now formally held the same position as Katharine Bruce Glasier, whose independent propagandist work had been brought under the NAC in October 1922. Their positions as propagandists were not without controversy. At the 1923 ILP conference, Jessie Stephen asked how the appointments had been made as she had seen no adverts for the posts, so had been prevented from being able to apply. Stephen, who considered herself one of the top three ILP women evangelists, along with Bruce Glasier and Minnie, was not satisfied with Brockway's explanation, for while extolling Bruce Glasier's and Minnie's qualities, he did not address the question.[12] Stephen had a valid point as her own track record equalled Minnie's. It may be that Minnie, appointed without advert or interview, enjoyed favoured status.[13] Although eminently equipped for the job, her path may have been smoothed by her relationships with Allen and MacDonald, the dominant people in the Party. However, in the ILP at that time, such appointments, without advert or interview, were common.[14]

Another controversy dogged Minnie's ambition. At the national conference, when she stood for election to the ILP NAC, Paton, the Scottish Divisional Organiser, objected to full-time paid officials, such as him and Minnie, standing for elected office. Even if it were not a breach of the constitution, he stated, it was undesirable. Wallhead, the retiring chair, and close friend of Minnie, declined to act as the constitution was silent on the matter.[15] Minnie was not elected, securing twelfth place among forty candidates.

However, it was significant that she was not content with being a paid official but had ambitions to positions of political leadership. Minnie was now in her mid-thirties and thrived on the rough and tumble of political life. Jim Middleton, the Assistant General Secretary of the Labour Party, might think her appearance 'peaches and cream', but the *New Leader* described her as hard-headed. Although considered very attractive 'with glowing cheeks and flaxen hair', she described herself as a hardened politician.[16] It was a beguiling combination.

When Allen replaced Wallhead as chair of the ILP, he consolidated his hold and sought to transform the Party from a primarily propagandist body into a policymaking one. There was 'tremendous élan' in Allen's Party and the years of Minnie's employment as national propagandist coincided with 'the pinnacle of its success'.[17] Allen emphasised the difference between being Labour and being a socialist and argued that the revolutionary role of the ILP within Labour lay in its selection of ideas and then in presenting a fearless programme to be followed without compromise.[18]

The ILP, though, was a Party divided. Every change Allen introduced was contested and every innovation resisted. While Allen's organisational reforms gave the ILP greater coherence, some on the NAC, including Wallhead and Jowett, opposed Allen's innovations.[19] At one level there was a 'hidden but real' conflict within the NAC between the regions and the London intellectuals, attracted to Allen's ILP, who began to dominate the Party. The strongly autonomous regions, over which the NAC's writ never fully extended, resented what they saw as centralising tendencies.[20] Brockway summarised the division as between the working-class membership outside London against the middle-class intellectuals and alleged careerists dominating Head Office. The division along class lines saw the Clydesiders pitted against Allen on almost every subject. As a part of his overhaul, Allen had already overseen the transformation of the *Labour Leader* into a more intellectual paper renamed the *New Leader*. Katharine Bruce Glasier, editor since 1917, was replaced by Brailsford under whose editorship it was seen by many as being too intellectual.[21] MacDonald was hostile to it, preferring the more amateur, organisational, democratic *Labour Leader* that he believed was more appealing to ordinary people. Possibly at MacDonald's insistence, Hamilton, who described the paper as being seen to represent a 'literary clique', was appointed assistant editor to counter Brailsford, a move he took as an insult.[22]

It is not easy to follow the shifting divisions and alliances facing Minnie, or her responses to them. Her written and spoken contributions were almost all externally directed, so how she aligned herself in relation to the organisational and political cross-currents and eddies in the ILP is difficult to glean. Did her years working at grassroots level in the community and her close associations with Allen and MacDonald allow Minnie to straddle both camps, rise above the fray, or be involved in the thick of political battle as allegiances shifted within the ILP? Her extended periods in the regions kept her grounded in the realities of the Party's base, and gave her credibility with them. Was she equally comfortable as a member of Soho's 1917 Club, where she mingled with the London set? Founded after the February revolution that overthrew the Tsar and located in a 'shabby little premises' that its founder, Leonard Woolf, described as 'the zenith of disreputability', the Club provided 'a meeting place for the interchange of opinion and information relating to Democracy and Internationalism', where there was no ceremony and everyone mixed freely.[23] Members included Anderson, Royden, Ethel Snowden and Hamilton. Around 4 pm each day, Virginia Woolf and the Stracheys arrived to join the labourites.[24] Although her work meant she was not a regular, when she met MacDonald at 'the Club' it would have been 'the 1917'.[25]

To support her job, Minnie moved from Porthcawl to 3 Palmerston Close, Welwyn Garden City (WGC), twenty-five miles north of London. There she became an urban pioneer in a new town that was 'very new and crumpled and unsteady, and temporary, very, very temporary'. Its first houses had been occupied from late 1920 and public buildings were still rudimentary; the bank was located in a log hut, and the cinema was made of corrugated sheets. There were no paved roads and wellington boots were essential footwear for the muddy lanes.[26]

The prospect of WGC would have enticed Minnie. The vision of its founder, Ebenezer Howard, was to establish a socialistic society imbued with Christian values based on cooperation. The prospectus promised that all land would be held in public ownership or in trust for the community.[27] The town was planned with wide streets, open spaces and gardens to house both working and middle-class residents and to address 'the condition of women in society', especially domestic drudgery.[28] The humane ideals, cooperation and community spirit of the town were actively promoted to readers of labour journals. *Labour Woman* described it as the sort of place the Labour Party wanted as part of a national housing scheme, with trees and fields as well as factories, shops and schools. A promotional *New Leader* article invited readers to visit and experience its 'Charm...Purpose and Healthful Surroundings'.[29] Although not all of its ambitions were fully realised, the physical attractiveness of the area is still evident today.

WGC had a radical atmosphere. Those who came to live there were considered public spirited – 'decent, well-meaning, liberal-minded, socialist-leaning, earnestly creative and outward looking'.[30] The people involved in establishing the garden city were generally Labourite, anti-war and chose to reside in the town. Almost exact contemporaries of Minnie, they promoted voluntary educational, health, social, cultural and sporting activities in the town.[31] Minnie would have been aware that MacDonald had been approached to join the Board but declined, arguing that his appointment would be controversial due to his opposition to the War.[32]

A popular image of WGC was 'a town of 200 people made up of socialists, idealists, utopians, vegetarians and cranks of all varieties'.[33] For sections of the national press they presented an easy target to be painted as eccentrics who wore rational clothes, including open sandals, no hats, and knickerbockers for men and flowing robes for women.[34] The town was described by one 1923 resident as 'a place where everybody belonged to a dozen societies, and was secretary of at least one'. It was claimed that the proportion of politicians, musicians, artists, professors and doctors was far higher than any equivalent town in the country.[35] The concentration of prominent ILPers, party, trades union and pacifist organisers, left-wing lawyers, publishers, journalists and writers who lived within strolling distance of Minnie is testimony to that. Seven Labour MPs and two Parliamentary candidates lived in the network of adjacent streets, with Dick Wallhead around the corner at 15 Valley Road, W. G. 'Bill' Cove at 30 Valley Road and Bernard Langdon-Davies, a publisher and fellow member of the 1917 Club, who would prove important to Minnie, later moving to 61 Valley Road.[36] If the town was 'cliquey',[37] it was based in the shared formative experiences of socialist pioneers before 1914, who suffered trauma and ostracism through their opposition to the Great War.

Out of step with mainstream British society, Minnie enjoyed the sanctuary of living among like-minded souls and of being part of networks that were at the heart of left-wing political developments in Britain.[38]

By the time Minnie arrived there was an array of groups with which she would have had an affinity. They included the Women's International League branch that heard Helena Swanwick speak on Moral Disarmament and the Vegetarian Society chaired by the left-wing cycling journalist and author 'Kuklos' (Fitzwater Wray). At Labour Party socials Flora Robson (who, when starting out in the theatre, worked in the town's Shredded Wheat factory) gave monologues.[39] However, Minnie's work largely prevented her from participating in the town's activities. Constant absences meant she was unavailable for musical or theatre practice or to assume roles in associations. She was not named in local newspapers as an officer of any organisation or as attending meetings or socials. Only once was she mentioned, speaking on the late Margaret MacDonald to the Labour Party's Women's Section.[40]

In May 1923, Minnie was profiled as 'Today's Cameo' in the *South Wales Daily News*. She was described as 'One of the most brilliant woman politicians that Wales has produced', though the article argued that, as Wales was 'backward' in giving women a chance to get to Parliament, Minnie would have to look elsewhere to be selected.[41] In fact moves were already underway. Following her appearance at the No More War demonstration in Bournemouth the previous year, Minnie spent a week there in March 1923 as part of the 'Now for Socialism' campaign. Such was her impact that Bournemouth ILP immediately sought to persuade her to stand as their candidate in the next Parliamentary election.[42] She was selected unanimously and local members said they were conscious of a great responsibility 'as the custodians of the political future of so brilliant an exponent of the principles of the ILP'.[43]

It is easy to see why Minnie was an attractive candidate for Labour in Bournemouth. Her political skills and personality made her an asset. Her love of people allowed her to make and retain friendships. She had natural vivacity, warmth, openness and generosity of spirit. She was cultured, loved books, theatre and the opera and was articulate, erudite and intelligent, while not narrowly intellectual. It was a winning combination. It is less easy to see why Bournemouth might have been attractive to Minnie. It was an unwinnable seat, which Labour had not even contested in 1922. Stephen, who fought South Portsmouth three times in the 1920s, noted that there was no great enthusiasm to select women candidates, so they tended to be confined to unwinnable seats. Decades later Stephen observed that while all wings of the labour movement had paid lip service to the principle of equality, women's experience gave lie to those pretensions.[44] Women needed to be brave to stand for Parliament at that time, and very few had the confidence and commitment to challenge conventional expectations. Labour men could be hostile to women in parliament.[45] Having for years endured being at times the only woman in male labour environments, and often presiding over them, Minnie had strategies to cope.

However, an intended summer of campaigning did not go well. The *New Leader* expressed 'extreme regret' that Minnie had suffered a health breakdown and that Captain Brennan, who had been appointed as third national propagandist, would fulfil her national speaking engagements until the autumn.[46] When she visited Bournemouth in July, for what had been intended as a fortnight's intensive campaigning with Katharine Bruce Glasier, all meetings had to be transferred indoors and addressed by Bruce Glasier with Minnie 'part of the scenery'. With symptoms that may well have been a portent of her future poor health, she was incapacitated for the duration of the summer campaign, including fifteen consecutive Sunday evening meetings.[47] In later meetings, although Minnie received a rousing reception, she had to rely on supporting speakers and was confined to fifteen minutes at the end of each one. It was misery for her to sit 'like a wax model', at meetings while others spoke for her.

While the nature of her illness is unknown, it prevented her contributing to the ILP's Hoddeson summer school. Under Allen, ILP summer schools became compelling social and educational occasions, attracting the famous who regarded contributing as a privilege.[48] At Hoddeson, participants were told that the ILP was moving fast and that the ethical conception of Socialism, which had hitherto been the basis of ILP thinking, needed to become sharper. Allen said that more emphasis must be placed on the failure of capitalism and its waste, inefficiency and stupidity, as well as on the struggle for power.[49]

Minnie's return to action was planned for the ILP fringe event at the Plymouth Trades Union Congress on 3 September. Two days later she debated 'Socialism Versus Capitalism' with the South Dorset Conservative Association agent in Weymouth. However, she had not properly recovered and engagements were cancelled for a further fortnight, although she made a 'brilliantly witty' impromptu appearance at a Gloucester ILP Federation rally where she emphasised the importance of capturing the imagination of young married women voters.[50]

By October, Minnie felt revived, describing herself as a war horse that scented battle. In Bournemouth, with evangelical belief, she said that ILP activity exemplified a new spirit that was going to awaken the country, with professionals as well as workers attracted to its ranks.[51] After a meeting where she spoke on industrial conditions and unemployment, she went to the local court to hear cases of people suffering hardship through rent payments. Seeking broad appeal and recognising that Liberals and former Liberals were essential for Labour, Minnie constructed arguments to appeal to them, without compromising her socialism. Echoing the evolutionary approach of MacDonald and Sidney Webb, she denied Labour's principles were 'something new and strange', adding that Labour was not 'a dangerous experiment' but simply the latest manifestation of the progress made over the centuries. The *Bournemouth Times* considered the campaign 'a great personal triumph' and the *New Leader* reported a south of England citadel being attacked as never before.[52] Minnie galvanised the local party, inspiring them to construct a labour hall.[53] Her legacy would be an active Labour political movement in Bournemouth.[54]

Minnie already had the backing of the Women's Freedom League (WFL), which leaned towards supporting women Labour candidates. In Poole, in a well-attended meeting on 'Why We Need More Women MPs', Minnie argued that 'woman is not simply an adjunct' to man' and had a better way of looking at issues than men, so needed to involve themselves in politics and international affairs.[55] In her front page article called 'When I Am MP', for the WFL publication *The Vote*, Minnie laid out her personal manifesto on gender relationships. She insisted on equal opportunities for women with men in every sphere of life and the 'absolute right of every woman to freedom of choice regarding her work in the community'.[56] She was unapologetic about being a woman, saying she had as good a grasp of politics as anyone else. Finally Minnie said she was not a feminist and fully approved of marriage, before adding to loud laughter 'for other people'.[57] Because of Minnie, a link developed between Labour in Bournemouth and the WFL nationally.[58] Although there is no firm evidence of Minnie having a relationship with the WFL before Bournemouth, afterwards she retained an association.

At a time when the internal *ILP Chronicle* revealed an organisation that believed the future was theirs,[59] as national propagandist, Minnie prepared for a national ILP autumn campaign that highlighted aspects of 'What a Socialist Government Would Do'. Starting with municipal elections in October, Minnie campaigned across the country on unemployment, housing, rates and taxes and education. A political propagandist at the top of her game, she talked for two hours on local government finance, holding her audience 'absolutely spellbound'. In November the campaign switched to international issues, including a socialist policy for addressing the condition of Europe, when Minnie spoke on providing security for common people in a chaotic continent where civilisations had been torn apart. The campaign closed with 400 'Never Again' demonstrations held on Armistice Day, with Minnie addressing 100 ex-servicemen in Fraserburgh, in northern Scotland.[60] She ended her strenuous Scottish tour at a social in Dundee on the evening of Saturday 17 November, where she learned that the Government had called a snap general election. Taking the midnight train, she travelled through the night to reach 'my own people' in Bournemouth.

On arrival, Minnie described local activists as resembling ants after their nest has been disturbed because, however carefully a constituency had been tended, the rhythm increased once an election was called. However, although it claimed to be well-organised and funded, Bournemouth Labour Party was ill-prepared. Minnie was experienced enough to know that an election was generally won long before a campaign started and with no central committee room or agent in place, enthusiasm alone was insufficient against well-organised Conservative or Liberal party machines.[61] In her formal adoption meeting, she called for a 'new social order' based on peace and cooperation at home and abroad.[62] Having experienced elections as a speaker and an organiser, Minnie now lived it as a candidate, recalling, 'I was carried about like a registered parcel, never had to make any arrangements or do anything for myself.'[63]

The novelty of a woman Parliamentary candidate brought national attention, with a photo series in the *Illustrated London News* catching her standing by a fisherman's boat at the crack of dawn. As she was the first woman candidate of any party to contest Bournemouth, her meetings attracted larger audiences than her male opponents as halls overflowed. Knowing there was no chance of winning, Minnie fought 'a propaganda fight', which included going to see Bournemouth play football. When she left, the crowd surged around her car, so she made an impromptu speech. Describing herself as a pacifist who dearly loved a fight, she said she used ideas, reason and argument rather than weapons. Although she was careful to acknowledge the contribution of 'the old Liberal Party', the Tories, through the Primrose League, sought to present her as supporting class war and the ILP as favouring those who supported violent revolution. The last meeting of the campaign was described as a great gathering, with the Town Hall packed, an adjoining lounge used as an overspill, and hundreds of people on the road outside. Loudspeakers were rigged for all sites and Minnie spoke for an hour. The local paper said that such scenes had not previously been seen in Bournemouth. Alan Wilton who wrote the 'Local Labour Notes' in the *Bournemouth Times* where he engaged in weekly combat with the anti-socialist arguments of the National Citizen's Union, reported the meeting as perhaps the most remarkable ever held in the town, particularly for the hundreds of young people attracted to it.[64]

Receiving nearly 6,000 votes and 20 per cent of the poll, Minnie discovered the limits of trying to overcome bedrock Conservative and Liberal support in an affluent, non-industrial, seaside town. The local paper considered her a 'formidable rival to any candidate of whatever cause', that not many men and few women could withstand a platform debate with her and she had 'commanded, received and deserved' the admiration and respect of all. Its assessment was that in speaking to the population and trying to inspire them, rather than point scoring, she had captured the town's imagination.[65] It concluded 'Miss Pallister is a politician to the finger tips. She is no blue stocking. She is a womanly woman', before adding 'she is a woman who will go far in political life'.[66]

Minnie did not succeed in her ambition of becoming the first woman [Labour] MP as Allen had registered four years earlier. Of fourteen women Labour candidates, three were elected: Susan

Lawrence in East Ham, Dorothy Jewson in Norwich and Margaret Bondfield in Northampton. At a social to thank her helpers, the 500 people present greeted Minnie with 'loud and prolonged cheering'. She said although she would not be joining the three Labour women in Parliament, she remained committed to standing again in Bournemouth, but until then she would return to platform work.[67] As in South Wales, Minnie had developed an enduring affinity and loyalty to Bournemouth and its comrades.

January 1924 provided a signal moment for the labour movement. MacDonald, with 191 MPs, formed the first Labour minority government. Of the ILPers, Snowden became Chancellor, Wheatley, who would be considered the most successful Labour Minister, became Minister of Health, and Jowett Commissioner for Works. As the Government was being formed, a rare sighting of Minnie as a political operator occurred. She protested, with others, to Allen, the Party Chair, about the failure to appoint Morel as Foreign Secretary, contrary to general expectations and her own hopes. Radical pacifist and critic of the Versailles peace treaty, Morel was the 'organising genius' of the UDC and led dissent against orthodoxy on British foreign policy and instead advocated a 'New Diplomacy'.[68] Allen explained why MacDonald had assumed the foreign affairs portfolio as well as the Premiership. In the event, MacDonald's handling of foreign affairs came to be considered one of the successful aspects of his administration.[69]

Less than three weeks after the Government came to office, Minnie was at the centre of an awkward incident that confirmed being a Parliamentary candidate was 'a weird experience' for an ordinary person. She later reflected that: 'From being nobody in particular, suddenly your lightest word is recorded, everything you do is news.'[70] Speaking at the 'usual Sunday Socialist meeting' in the magnificent three-tiered 3,500-seater St George's Hall in Bradford, Minnie made some throwaway comments on the Royal Family. Voicing 'grave doubt whether the Prince of Wales would ever ascend to the Throne...', she added it was 'not because of the country's objection to the personality of the King or the Prince' but 'because as citizens became more mature, old institutions would naturally fall away'. She added, 'If a woman cared to stand in the rain to see the Duke of York's wedding, it was not for anybody to take away her toys' but 'The woman must be helped to grow'. The account gained only two paragraphs in the inside pages of the *Yorkshire Evening Argus*, hardly warranting its dramatic headline 'Communism Coming?'.[71] However, the combination of negative comments about the Royal Family, her status as a Parliamentary candidate, and her proximity to the new Prime Minister gave the story unimagined newsworthiness. That same day it was picked up by newspapers as distant (yet as prominent) as the *Washington Post* and the *New York Times*. The *Atlanta Constitution* added the observation that Minnie 'may be said to interpret the feelings of the labour party on the subject, which naturally is republican'.[72] While there was no doubting Minnie's politics, it was amiss to attach the label 'republican' to either the Labour Party or the Labour Government. MacDonald was a firm royalist who had kept George Lansbury out of his Cabinet because of his attack on the monarchy.[73] Her Bradford comments would have made uncomfortable reading for MacDonald before his next weekly audience with the King.

Minnie was a robust defender of the Government, saying opponents were becoming alarmed at the competence it was showing.[74] She contributed to a *What is Socialism* symposium that had been initially convened as a follow up to 'the great "Socialism *versus* Capitalism" debate' in the House of Commons of a year earlier. Then Snowden had proposed a motion, heavily defeated, which referred to the failure of capitalism rooted in private ownership and called for its replacement by public ownership and democratic control. Now, with Labour in government, the context was transformed. Part of a line-up of contributors that reads as a virtual *Who's Who of Labour* from Attlee to Sidney Webb, Minnie's position was clear: The ILP, she said, 'did not appeal to the workers to overthrow capitalism because it was uncomfortable, but because it was wrong.'[75] In March, she saw an opportunity to make her case in the heart of the establishment. On the death of John Nicholson, the Unionist MP for Westminster, Minnie sought the Labour nomination to fight the seat, though she was still candidate for Bournemouth. The opponents were the Unionist candidate, Otto Nicholson and the Constitutionalist, Winston Churchill.[76] Although she had no chance of winning the election, her candidacy was intended as a challenge. In the event, she came second to Brockway in the selection, who came third in the by-election, but it indicated her preparedness to take the fight to all corners, whatever the odds.[77]

When campaigning with Minnie in Birmingham, Katharine Bruce Glasier recorded: 'A spate of words – but a dear lass.'[78] She added: 'Too much work!', referring to the incessant schedule of ILP propagandists. For Minnie a fortnight in Lincolnshire followed eight public meetings in Norwich in five days. Even the casual observer could see work was taking its toll. After Minnie had spoken for ten days in the towns and villages in Lancashire, the positive report of her visit ended with the ominous comment: 'That Miss Pallister's health may hold out to carry on the good work is the sincerest wish of the Oldham Federation.'[79]

As well as full-time propagandist and Parliamentary candidate, Minnie was a prolific writer. Her articles in the *Labour Leader* and *New Leader* covered a range of topics, including party organisation and women's issues. Her work also appeared in the *Daily Herald*, the radical *Daily News* owned by the Quaker Cadbury family, *The Star*, *London Opinion*, and even the *Sunday School Chronicle*, although her aspiration to be published in the *Manchester Guardian* apparently remained unfulfilled.[80]

Minnie's pamphlet *Socialism for Women* is an important tract. Published in March 1924, it formalised arguments she had been making since 1918. Part of an ILP series for women's study circles and discussion groups, it was a powerful work that sold well. Minnie observed that a woman had always been seen as a wife, mother or daughter 'never just as herself...it is this idea of belonging to someone, which is slavery'. Identifying women's dependency as key, for Minnie socialism bestowed personal freedom upon women 'by thinking of them as individuals quite apart from their relationship to men.'[81] The pamphlet examined issues including The Alleged Inferiority of Women; Sex Antagonism; Equality; Marriage; Prostitution; Women, Salaries and Equal Pay for Equal Work, and Women and Political Power. In looking beyond material improvements to profound changes in status and gender relationships, it was a significant contribution to what a woman-focussed socialism could look like. It was later used in syllabuses across the ILP and, because its use was not confined to women's groups, it presented cogent arguments on women's equality to men in the Party.[82] In Bournemouth, she suggested to a women's meeting that they should study *Socialism for Women* to help recruit and prepare other women for canvassing at the next election.[83]

In March, Minnie made her first public appearances in

Bournemouth since the election, speaking with P. C. Hoffman of the shop workers' union. Women in retail, the distributive trades and hotels were an important group in the town, comprising the bulk of women workers, and Minnie argued that they should be seen at the same professional level as lady doctors or lawyers. Minnie's relationship with the union's officials was close and it was helpful for aspiring Labour politicians to have the support of a trades union.[84] The shop workers already supported Ellen Wilkinson, who reportedly increased her political clout through their financial backing.[85] The following year Minnie appeared with J. R. Leslie, the union's General Secretary, in an effort to better organise Bournemouth shop workers.[86] For as long as she was politically active, Minnie would retain her connection with the shop workers' union. This was not the first group of undervalued workers Minnie had highlighted as deserving greater credit and reward. Previously she had promoted the case of domestic servants and urged a new outlook towards them.[87] In future she would similarly promote the cause of food producers.[88]

In York, the 1924 national ILP conference was addressed, for the first time, by its leaders as Labour Prime Minister and government ministers. Minnie recognised their new responsibilities made it hard to sustain 'the sweetness of the comradeship' and intimacy there had existed previously in the ILP and that relationships would change.[89] However, her comments masked the difficulties the Government was already experiencing. Paton wrote that while the ILP's public attitude towards the first Labour government was 'sympathetic and mildly critical', private opinions were more negative, with disappointment at its domestic performance, except for Wheatley's housing legislation. Many in the ILP saw capitalism collapsing and, in line with Allen's call at the 1923 summer school, felt more urgent action was needed than MacDonald's evolutionary approach.[90] If Labour was the mass party of the British working class which provided the best hope for achieving socialism in Britain, it was to the ILP that Minnie's primary political loyalty lay and she considered it to be the means for keeping the Labour Party on track or, in Paton's words, to 'goad the Labour Party into effectiveness'.[91]

Minnie's growing importance within the ILP was confirmed in the NAC election. Receiving more votes than prominent national figures, in a year she rose from twelfth to fifth place. In the final round, when four out of five were elected, Minnie was beaten only by four male MPs, two of whom were government ministers.[92] At the traditional Sunday evening conference event, she was the sole woman speaker alongside the four who had beaten her: Wheatley, Jowett, Maxton and Wallhead.[93] The following month, at the National Conference of Labour Women, she delivered what was described as one of the conference's best speeches in a debate that considered the position of the housewife.[94]

Minnie became one of the first – and possibly the first – person to give a political broadcast in Britain, in June, five months before the first Party political broadcast occurred during the 1924 general election. The BBC had only begun daily broadcasting in November 1922, and its early 'instinctive aversion' to covering politics was somehow overcome when her fifteen-minute talk on 'Changing Ideals' was transmitted on BBC Bournemouth.[95]

That summer Minnie took her first trip abroad that lasted six weeks. The *New Leader* reported that Minnie was wise to take things more easily as 'we do not want her to repeat last year's breakdown'. Her choice of Germany reflected her sympathy over the burden of war reparations and responded to adverts in *No More War* advertising holidays there as building 'Friendship with Germany'.[96] Staying in Aachen, a town on the Rhine still occupied by French troops, Minnie witnessed the impact of what she considered the injustice of the Versailles treaty. In spite of the dire economic situation, with the hyper-inflationary one trillion mark notes in circulation, resulting in considerable suffering, the German people were unfailingly kind and polite.[97] That holiday helped shape her attitude to Germany and its people and informed the foreign policy positions she adopted in the 1930s.

The holiday was not solely a political and economic study tour. Aachen was a spa and Minnie made a daily pilgrimage to take the waters at the Elisenbrunnen fountain, the symbol of the town. In the Opera House, opened in 1825, she heard Wagner's *Die Meistersingers* for the first time. Intent on experiencing the seedier side of Weimar life, she was disappointed that a disreputable-looking cabaret failed to live down to the anticipated level of wickedness. As an ex-shining light of the Band of Hope 'who had recited with gusto so many times "The Lips That Touch Liquor Shall Never Touch Mine"' she considered herself 'pretty shameless' for drinking lager in a bier-haus in a pine forest.[98]

Perhaps as a result of *Socialism for Women*, Maurice Marston (who was connected to the publisher Leonard Parsons, as well as being secretary of both the Society of Bookmen and the National Books Council) proposed 'out of the blue' that Minnie write a book.[99] *The Orange Box: Thoughts of a Socialist Propagandist* showed how to undertake effective propaganda from the platform to help offset the power of a critical press, which Minnie considered essential in helping a Labour government introduce policies to build a new society. Her book argued that in shaking off the yoke of its oppressor, a nation, class or sex did not end its problems, but for the first time began to face them.[100] One insightful section covered the lessons she had learned about organising women. Weaving class and gender, Minnie addressed what she described as the oppression of women. Having portrayed aspects of women's oppression for years, she now gave it detailed consideration. Tellingly, her author's note read, 'For the sake of brevity the word "man" is often used to include women. In no case does the word "woman" include man.'[101] Minnie's awareness of gendered language was not universal amongst early feminists and prefigured its importance to the modern women's movement.[102] Minnie would return to the issue of women's oppression regularly until her dying day.

Minnie believed the 'changed status and outlook' of women would alter the life of the country both for men and women. Elsewhere, she emphasised how recent were reforms that favoured women, including owning property and rights over children. In future, the status of women would depend on the status of married women, she opined, adding that women had been blamed for everything, ever since the Garden of Eden, and now blame fell on 'the modern woman'.[103] For Minnie, even small organisational issues had gender implications. Writing on whether there should be a joint subscription for married couples, she objected to those ILP women who 'vehemently opposed' lower levels as implying inequality. Pointing out that the relationship between the Party and single or married women consisted of much more than the level of 'subs' they paid, she explained that their other contributions far outweighed the financial and argued that until married woman had economic freedom and equality, equal subs might be a barrier for some. Minnie cheekily ended, 'Anyhow, need we add to the woman who has the disability of being married any other disability?'[104] The *Daily Herald's* review of *The Orange Box* said that Minnie had a 'keen eye' for unexplored opportunities for socialist propaganda and the reviewer was quite certain that Minnie would become a Labour MP. *The Bookman* highlighted her comment that 'Hatred is such a waste of time' and that it was 'the height of folly' to attempt to solve social problems by blaming others.[105] The book sold well and a year after publication was in its fourth impression.

*

In October 1924, the minority Labour Government was defeated in a no-confidence vote and a general election was called. Whereas the Bournemouth Party had been caught off-guard by the snap election of the previous year, and had been without funds, this campaign was better prepared. Hundreds of people were paying a penny a week to the election fund and one poor widow had saved a farthing a day since the last election, handing Minnie the 6s 10d she had accumulated.[106] The Liberal Party did not enter the contest and Minnie went head-to-head against the incumbent Conservative MP, Henry Croft, who was contesting the constituency for the sixth time. Throughout the campaign both candidates showed goodwill, fighting on principles not personalities.[107]

Minnie formally launched her campaign with the slogan 'Make Minnie Pallister Member of Parliament' or 'Make MP MP', although she argued that she did not want voters to vote for her, but to vote for socialism as she wanted 'to make Socialists'.[108] The *New Leader* reported Minnie putting up a magnificent fight in which she defended the Labour Government's foreign policies and MacDonald's drive for disarmament. Uncompromising when the issue of patriotism was raised, Minnie said that nothing was achieved by singing the national anthem. Criticising the raising of stone monuments to the fallen of the Great War while their widows and orphans were neglected, she argued the heroism of the dead was being used to perpetuate war, not to create peace. She later stated that housing, unemployment 'or a 'hundred and one other problems' should not be talked about until the peace problem and the women problem' were addressed. While people were interested in food prices and economics, 'the telling point is the Prime Minister's record for peacemaking'.[109] Enthusiasm for her campaign resulted in halls being too small to accommodate her audiences. Unrealistically, the *New Leader* suggested her prospects of winning the seat were rosy.[110]

Publication of the 'red-scare' Zinoviev letter, later shown to be a forgery, derailed Labour's national campaign.[111] All fight dissipated and at the eve of poll rally Minnie acknowledged its impact. On election day, Minnie travelled through the town wearing a bunch of yellow chrysanthemums. Confronted by a 'formidable' Tory machine with 160 cars available compared with 'three or four' for Labour, she encouraged her supporters to walk to polling stations. In the two-horse race, Minnie's vote increased by from 5,986 to 7,735 and her share of the poll from 19.5 per cent to 27.3 per cent. Even though she did not reach the 10,000 she had targeted, the campaign was buoyed by organisational advances. Once more the local paper acknowledged Minnie as an 'able champion' of the labour cause who would 'unquestionably' have won elsewhere.[112] Labour was defeated nationally and its number of seats declined from 191 to 151. Lawrence, Bondfield and Jewson lost, leaving newly elected Ellen Wilkinson as the single Labour woman MP, representing Middlesbrough.

The pages of the *New Leader* now prioritised tasks required to win the next election. Initiatives were unveiled to double membership, open new branches and undertake activity in backward and rural areas. Leading lights, including Minnie, launched 'A Personal Appeal' for people to join the ILP.[113] In practice, much of the campaigning fell to the three national propagandists. Minnie spent a week in the towns and villages of Northamptonshire, where Bill Cove had been elected in 1923 and there was not one ILP branch. In contrast, the following week, in well-organised Birkenhead, she sold 250 copies of her book.[114]

On 30 November, Minnie, with Herbert Morrison, Bob Smillie and George Lansbury, spoke at a 10,000-person rally for the *Daily Herald* at the Royal Albert Hall. Opening to the 'crashing strains of the "Marseillaise"', it was the culmination of a two-month campaign to gain new readers for the paper.[115] Referring to the Zinoviev letter, Minnie said the more workers who read the *Herald*, the more they would become 'plot and stunt' proof. Lansbury was a key figure at the *Daily Herald* after he had helped set it up during a printers' dispute in 1911 and had gained national prominence supporting women's suffrage as well as when along with other

Poplar councillors, he was gaoled in a revolt over the rates levels. At different times between 1913 and 1925, he was the proprietor, editor and director of the *Daily Herald*, under whose radical leadership the paper opposed the Great War and conscription, supported COs and welcomed both Russian Revolutions.[116] In 1922, with the circulation of the paper very low, it was taken over by the TUC and from 1926 Lansbury was its general manager.[117] His long association with the *Daily Herald* would later prove critical for Minnie.

Minnie returned to Bournemouth over Christmas. Then it was back on the road, week after week, month after month, meeting after meeting, tour after tour in a relentless schedule. London and Kent in January, Nottingham and Derby in February, followed by two 'strenuous and successful' weeks in Scotland in March.[118] With her diary full, bookings were already being taken for a year ahead. When she spoke to an estimated 3,000 people at Bournemouth ILP's May Day demonstration, she was among friends, then a week in Aberavon revealed an 'utterly amazing' spirit where, despite high unemployment in the mining villages, 'great audiences gather to hear the Socialist message'.[119] MacDonald's victory of two years earlier was now firmly consolidated.

From 1924 there was a concerted push to increase the prominence of women in the ILP. After Minnie and other leading women complaining about the absence of women on the NAC and the sparsity of women at other levels of the Party, partly in response, the ILP called on its branches to establish separate women's groups. Women were more prominent at the 1925 annual conference and a Women's Advisory Committee (WAC) was established to coordinate activity. Minnie was among its members. Although Minnie was unsuccessful in her bid for one of the four national seats on the NAC, for the first time two women, Margaret Bondfield and Dorothy Jewson, joined the NAC.[120]

Minnie was part of a thirty-strong delegation of ILP women who attended the National Labour Women's Conference in Birmingham. Although they played a leading part and influenced debates, Minnie was unhappy in the way the conference tended to consider uncontentious resolutions and, mindful that the previous year the Labour Party bureaucracy had insisted the conference reject the principle of family allowances, she suggested that, in future, the Labour Party women's conference should discuss controversial subjects.

Little progress was made within the labour movement for the family allowances campaign, until Eleanor Rathbone gave a talk at the 1924 ILP Summer School. There 'corporate enthusiasm' for the issue was gained, and Minnie and other leading ILP women took up the cause.[121]

Minnie was provided with an opportunity to shape the debates, as well as the organisation, when she was given temporary responsibility for establishing and editing the ILP's new monthly *Bulletin for Women Socialists*. It was an ideal role that used her understanding of women's issues, her writing and editing skills, and her experience in knowing how to build women's organisations locally. Intended as a forum for the exchange of ideas and experiences, the *Bulletin* was sent to the Party's women's groups throughout the country, where it was hoped it would have a strong coordinating influence. In the first issue Minnie outlined the purpose of the movement and advised group secretaries how to organise locally, with educational activity in study circles and discussion groups to consider equal pay, family allowances and birth control.[122] She steered the *Bulletin* to straddle 'old' and 'new' feminisms, supporting measures to improve women's conditions as well as strengthening their rights. For Minnie there was no incompatibility in promoting family allowances alongside measures advocating equality. The educational and organisational activities had a clear intention. Although family allowances and birth control were 'two of the most controversial issues relating to gender politics in the labour movement in the 1920s',[123] Minnie emphasised that afterwards a policy on these questions 'can be pressed in the wider Labour movement'.[124]

The first issue of the *Bulletin* was well received with letters arriving from all over the country. The August edition suggested every ILP branch should allocate a public meeting over the winter for increasing women's membership and strong, well-established groups should 'act as missionaries' in areas where no women's groups existed. Finally it proposed holding a conference of women members from all branches in each area.[125] That autumn, the *Women's Bulletin* came under the responsibility of the WAC, and its editorship transferred to Dorothy Jewson, who also became the Committee's National Organising Secretary. The *New Leader* attributed much of the rapid growth in the ILP's women's organisation to Minnie's early work with the *Bulletin*.[126]

On the morning of Sunday 9 August, Minnie and Oswald Mosley, rising stars in the ILP, jointly ran a session on communism at the national summer school in Easton Lodge, Dunmow. Mosley at 28 was nearly twelve years younger than Minnie and had only joined Labour the previous year, having been an Independent MP and before that a Conservative. The Labour Party rule, that a candidate had to be a Party member for a year before being allowed to contest a Parliamentary seat, was waived especially for him and he had unsuccessfully contested Birmingham Ladywood in 1924.[127] Such actions fuelled the 'suspicion and resentment' some felt at the privileged access he and his wife Lady Cynthia, 'Cimmie', had in the ILP and Labour Party.[128]

Minnie, Katharine Bruce Glasier and Dorothy Jewson left the summer school early to go as the ILP delegation to the Women's Socialist International Conference in Marseille. Bruce Glasier recorded 'a never to be forgotten journey'.[129] Minnie wrote of every small corner of French fields having its crop, with the battlefields of northern France having 'the heaviest crop of all – a crop of wooden crosses so closely set that from the train it seemed that one could not put a wedge between them'.[130] Their arrival in Marseille was met by a general strike with shops closed, no taxis or trams running and 'an apparently endless procession of workers demonstrating in the streets'. Eventually the Transport Workers Union gave permission to use the hotel bus to reach the Château des Fleurs where the conference was to be held in high, bare, shuttered rooms. Following two days later, Allen, Brockway, Bondfield and others arrived to attend the parallel Second Congress of the Labour and Socialist International, where delegates from over thirty countries were present.[131] Having been warned to expect 'a dirty, smelly port' which would be 'intolerably hot' the delegations found a beautiful bay and mountains providing the backdrop to the city, with cool breezes off the sea. Thursday was glorious and Minnie, Bruce Glasier and Pat Dollan, the chair of the Scottish ILP, walked around the town and explored the coast.[132]

The women's conference held on Friday 21 August, the day before the Congress opened, dealt with the state of organisation amongst socialist women in each country. Seventy delegates from twenty countries discussed sex equality, motherhood, marriage laws and legislation for illegitimate children. Minnie served on the War and Food Commission, representing the British labour women's organisations and gave the report back from the Commission to the conference.[133] On Saturday, Minnie journeyed back with Bruce Glasier along the Rhone Valley and on Sunday explored Paris. They visited the classic sights, including the Louvre and Montmartre, but overall Minnie considered the city 'tawdry', before returning to Britain. The trip left Minnie's head 'awhirl with impressions' of the landscape, the cafes, 'endless talk in diverse tongues'. In her report, Minnie hoped that with the machinery, constitution and powers now delineated, the Marseille conference meant 'a new phase of the great Women's movement has begun' with the Women's Socialist International becoming a 'definite' part of the international movement.[134]

How did Minnie stand in relation to her female peers? Minnie, Margaret Bondfield, Marion Phillips, Susan Lawrence and Ellen Wilkinson were all single, economically independent women, and Dorothy Jewson did not get married until she was in her early fifties. Phillips, Bondfield and Lawrence's loyalty to the Labour Party saw them prepared to subordinate women's priorities to those of the (male-dominated) working-class movement. The feminists Dorothy Jewson, Helena Swanwick and Dora Russell straddled the boundary between the labour movement and women's organisations, whereas Minnie succeeded in advocating women's issues by working through the labour movement and without alienating the Party leadership, as did Wilkinson.[135]

Minnie was closest to Wilkinson in terms of background. They shared many causes and both pursued socialism and feminism simultaneously (though Wilkinson's fellow travelling with the Communist Party was a difference), but there were tensions between them.[136] If Wilkinson 'employed a conventional femininity as a political resource'[137], Minnie, (like Hamilton and Swanwick) had an aversion to using lipstick and cosmetics to make herself attractive to men.[138] An 'instinctive self-publicist'[139] who wanted to be the centre of attention (as arguably did Minnie), as a young woman MP Wilkinson attracted press attention with her frequent fashion changes in hair, dresses and hats.[140] Also Stephen said Minnie disliked Wilkinson's 'bad habit of walking down the centre of the hall on arrival, expecting the applause which she always received, but completely disrupting the speech being delivered'. Minnie had experienced this more than once, but disappointingly Stephen did not repeat the 'suitable epithet' she said Minnie used to describe her behaviour.[141] In turn Wilkinson consciously distanced herself from the women who were close to MacDonald, whom she loathed. These presumably included Minnie and Hamilton.[142] Differences between Minnie and Wilkinson became manifested as competitiveness or rivalry, and later perhaps jealousy on Minnie's part.

At a time when pamphlets were central to the ILP's strategy of bringing Britain to socialism,[143] Minnie published three more in 1925 and 1926. *Socialism, Equality and Happiness* was aimed at young people as an introduction to the socialist case. After the experience of the Zinoviev letter, *The Candle In The Pumpkin: Why Be Afraid Of Bogies?*, based on a chapter in *The Orange Box*, was apposite. Minnie argued that people should not be frightened by scare stories against Labour and socialism, though she acknowledged that some people's 'treasured beliefs and prejudices' had to be tackled.[144] *Mrs Smith of Wigan* drew on her knowledge of ordinary people's lives in a powerful yet deliberately understated depiction. Seen through the everyday worries and hardships of a woman in the backstreets over two decades, Mrs Smith struggled to bring up her son, only to have him claimed by the army for the war. Its style of writing made it accessible to the general reader as much as to ILP activists. Minnie portrayed Mrs Smith's struggles to understand and deal with the world around her, including tensions in gender relations in the home. The most powerful line used is that when Mrs Smith mentioned economic or political concerns, her husband told her she was ignorant and 'did not know what she was talking about. She said no more.' The pamphlet was seen as a novelty among socialist pamphlets in mentioning neither socialism nor capitalism and simply concentrating on Mrs Smith and her family.[145] It was all the more powerful for doing so. A decade later, Minnie would return to the subject of Wigan in tackling George Orwell about his *Road to Wigan Pier*.

Minnie's intellectual contributions, including her book, four pamphlets and countless articles, were all built upon her organising roles and experiences and her work with women from 1918. From them she drew the conclusions that informed her writings. Added to her skills as a supreme propagandist, they carved out a distinct and prominent position for her, still a difficult achievement for women within the political movement.[146] One indication of Minnie's standing in radical circles was an invitation by Maude

Royden to speak at the Guildhouse in Eccleston Square, London.[147] Founded in 1921, the Guildhouse hosted lectures on major themes by 'some of the most distinguished and controversial figures of the day'.[148] As a Guildhouse speaker, Minnie joined an exalted group. The Visitors Book, which covers 1921 to 1936, provides an exclusive list of mainly progressive and cultural speakers including Mahatma Gandhi, Mrs Pandit, Albert Schweitzer, Krishna Menon, Hilaire Belloc, Walter de la Mare and John Masefield, as well as people who would become familiar in Minnie's later life including Sybil Thorndike and Vera Brittain. Only 109 people had lectured in the five years from 1921 to 1925, including Bondfield in 1922 and Annie Besant and MacDonald in 1924, before Minnie spoke on New Year's Day 1926. Eleanor Rathbone spoke three weeks later. Wilkinson was not invited until January 1932, even though from 1926 over fifty people a year were asked to speak.[149] Aptly, Minnie later described herself at this time as 'having had a lot of fame in a small way'.[150]

In October 1925, after internal wrangling, Allen resigned as ILP chair and Jowett became temporary chair. Minnie complained to Brailsford about the excesses and waste that had occurred at head office under Allen.[151] Later her criticisms became stronger. Although they were not aware of it at the time, she claimed, his becoming chair was the beginning of the end for the ILP. Whereas previously people had not joined for personal reward, under Allen's leadership large salaries were given to 'eminent men' who came into the ILP and wealthy careerists anxious to become Parliamentary candidates attached themselves to the Party.[152] It was under Allen's leadership that the Party she loved began to lose its soul.

However, before his departure Allen left an important legacy as architect of the 'Socialism in Our Time' strategy of which Brailsford was the main populariser. An economically expansionist policy for addressing unemployment and tackling poverty, its key features were a living wage and family allowances paid by the state.[153] For the left, 'Socialism in Our Time' was both a good programme and a symbol of resistance against Labour leadership orthodoxy.[154] MacDonald opposed 'Socialism in Our Time' because of its association with Brailsford and to him it 'mattered less as a programme than as a weapon in a struggle for power'.[155] Although Minnie did not agree with all of it, considering its guild socialist strand 'idiotic', she was deeply involved in the promotion of 'Socialism in Our

Time', and became one of the leading figures in promoting one of its central features, family allowances.[156]

Family allowances became a main theme of her long-term work as Minnie's speeches emphasised their importance in building 'real equality in the home'. At a conference of nine women's groups in North St Pancras, Minnie referred to their contribution to the economic independence of women.[157] She extended the argument by saying that the ILP supported an allowance for each child because they believed wages should be based on the economic needs of the family rather than the market value of wages; the bigger the family the greater the need. Funding, she argued, should be by direct taxation of unearned income, increased death duties and increased income tax. Minnie was also one of the prominent speakers for the ILP women's weekend, when all ILP groups were asked to convene special events for women from all sections of the labour movement in their area to consider family allowances; food prices and profiteering, and women's unemployment. A concerted push on family allowances saw Dorothy Jewson's *Socialists and the Family* appear, followed by Brailsford's 'Family and Wages' that argued that family allowances could be 'the beginning of the biggest change in the whole of the relationship of the citizen to the community, the status of woman, the relationship of the sexes, [and] the place of parenthood and family life generally...'. In June, Minnie made their case in an extended essay in the ILP journal, *The Socialist Review*.[158] Her radical ILP programme also identified the need for a communal food service, a national housing scheme and a communal boot supply.[159]

At the 1926 ILP conference in Whitley Bay, between 2 to 6 April, which Minnie attended as a delegate from Briton Ferry, the mood was optimistic. Party membership was at an all-time high and a *New Leader* editorial anticipated a Labour Government in power, confronted by the challenges provided by industry, banks and finance, food and agriculture and ending poverty through the redistribution of the nation's income. The ILP was shifting to the left, with Maxton, Brockway and the Clydesiders now in control of the NAC. Minnie's growing status was confirmed when she was elected to the NAC, replacing Margaret Bondfield. Three years criss-crossing Britain had allowed members to get to know her abilities, commitment, and personality and she had built a strong grassroots support base. Aptly she was made a member of the

NAC's Publications Committee. At a time when increased women's activity was seen as one of the most striking features of the ILP, it was Minnie who spoke to the conference on behalf of the Women's Advisory Committee.[160]

The key conference proposal was 'Socialism in Our Time'. Historians have subsequently and variously described it as 'magnificent' and 'the one constructive economic policy produced by British Labour before the crisis of 1931'. Although 'Socialism in Our Time' did not gain contemporary support across the wider movement, it confirmed the ILP's status as 'the guardian of British Socialism in the 1920s', and many of its policies were indeed adopted by the 1945 Labour Government. A precursor of post-1945 managed welfare capitalism, it showed the ILP to be the intellectual repository for democratic socialist ideas at this time, in contrast to the cautious and conventional orthodoxy of the Labour Party machine and the revolutionary dogmatism of the Communist Party.[161] By mid-April the organisational machinery was put in place to deliver the campaign through conferences, pamphlets and leaflets, to promote family allowances and a living wage.[162]

Minnie had planned to spend early May speaking alongside Henry Nevinson, the war correspondent and champion of causes, for Animals' Welfare Week, whose President was John Galsworthy and on whose National Council she served, (a position she apparently still held in 1940).[163] However, it did not take place as the country was overwhelmed by immediate events.

On 1 May 1926, a seven-month lockout of one million miners began, after the coal owners demanded reduced wages and longer hours. The labour movement rallied to the miners' cause and the TUC called a General Strike that lasted nine days. The struggle was titanic. Rail and transport workers, dockers, printers, and iron and steel workers were among the more than one million workers who went on strike in support of the miners. With the response overwhelming, large areas of industrial activity stopped. The ILP offered its considerable propaganda machine, its press and full-time workers, including Minnie. However, the TUC's determination to handle the strike as a narrow industrial dispute, rather than a political one saw the ILP and the Labour Party both marginalised, and Minnie therefore played no significant role.

After the TUC capitulated to the Government and called off the

General Strike, the miners stood alone. As the prospect of a long industrial struggle beckoned, the ILP immediately offered the Party's own resources, including its staff, to the miners. The 'Socialism in Our Time' campaign was postponed and instead a national propaganda campaign for the Miners' Relief Fund was launched. A levy on ILP members raised £50,000.[164]

In late May, Minnie's life changed completely. In the last stages of exhaustion and feeling very ill after forcing herself to keep speaking, she attended a consultant specialist's clinic. Suffering from a 'very tired' throat, something that had also incapacitated her in 1923, she anticipated a proposed cure. Her medical situation, however, was far more serious than she realised. The specialist told her that the muscles on her face and throat were becoming paralysed. He added that she would have to give up her political life and never speak again in public. 'Quite casually – like that'. Moreover, she was warned that if she did not stop she was 'in grave danger of slowly becoming completely paralysed' and of losing her power of speech altogether.[165] Minnie described her illness as nervous exhaustion or an 'obscure nervous malady'.[166] Whatever the precise diagnosis, an inability to swallow and jaw and facial pain and paralysis were not signs of an 'exhausted hysterical woman'.[167]

Minnie stumbled out of the clinic with her life in pieces having been told to abandon everything she cared most about in the world. To someone whose first love was politics and for whom public speaking was her lifeblood, this was devastating. Just at the point that her career was on a strong upward trajectory, Minnie was stricken. She told only those closest to her. Katharine Bruce Glasier's diary for Saturday 29 May 1926 read simply '"Minnie" – Alas' and she wrote to her son Glen to give him the news. Nine years later it was revealed that Minnie had been given only two years to live, a situation Minnie did not herself confirm until 1958.[168]

With such a catastrophic diagnosis, at any other time, perhaps Minnie would have eased off or stopped completely. However, with the miners locked out, she determined to keep working and drove herself until her illness completely overwhelmed her.[169] On Saturday 12 June Minnie attended the ILP Welsh Division annual conference, held in the heart of the South Wales coalfield. During the General Strike, the Pontypridd Central Strike Committee had controlled the town. Now, with the trades union movement defeated, the ILP Welsh Division was determined to keep supporting the miners. The following week Minnie addressed two meetings in support of the Women's Committee for the Relief of Miners' Wives and Children. At the Alexandra Palace she and Arthur Henderson addressed 2,000 women, before she spoke to 1,000 Hampshire women who marched through Petersfield with banners flying. Minnie's article 'In the Miners' Homes' provided a defence of the miners and their wives that drew on her intimate understanding of circumstances below and above ground, gained from seventeen years of working in the valleys. Though at times it lapsed into sentimentality, the article bitterly denounced the conditions the men suffered in the pit and those endured by women in the home, highlighting the plight of young single men who were not entitled to relief.[170]

On 31 July, Minnie welcomed the students to the ILP Summer School on behalf of the NAC, where the programme formally focussed on 'Socialism in Our Time'. John Wheatley provided the opening address, Minnie spoke on family allowances, Keynes on industry, and Hugh Dalton and Oswald Mosley on 'What the Next Labour Government Should Do'. However, the event was overshadowed by the miners' lockout. A. J. Cook spoke on the miners' struggle and Ellen Wilkinson on lessons of the General Strike. Minnie chaired the final week of the school, 'alert and humorous as ever'.[171]

After the summer school, delegates returned to the primary task of supporting the miners. Weaknesses in support within the Midlands miners' unions led the MFGB to request ILP help. Following a call for volunteers on 27 August, within 48 hours fifteen ILP speakers, including Minnie and Katharine Bruce Glasier, were mobilised. Under MFGB direction, they each addressed three meetings a day, supported by 35,000 copies of *The Miner* produced by the ILP.[172] Appealing to miners and their wives was difficult as they were in dire circumstances, so urges to resist any longer were initially met by extreme diffidence. Ten years later, Paton recalled 'the depressing effect of almost constant meetings'; in 'stricken villages' where they addressed 'men and women... grimly continuing an almost impossible fight'.[173] An assessment that the ILP's role in the lockout was 'marginal but not futile' underplays its significance.[174] Trying to stem the return to work as union solidarity crumbled, especially in Nottinghamshire where Minnie went, was a strategic intervention. It may not have been successful, but it was essential to try and shore up union resistance.

The toll of supporting the miners led to Minnie's health failing completely. The *New Leader* attributed her breakdown to 'her unstinted service in the ILP miners' campaign in the Midlands' while it was reported that Minnie became stricken after addressing sixteen open-air meetings in one week.[175] Struggling to keep going, Minnie returned to Bournemouth during early September for the TUC Congress, where, as Parliamentary candidate, she was featured in its souvenir brochure. She also attended the Women's Trade Union conference held there one evening. While she welcomed the initiative to hold a special women's conference for the first time, Minnie observed that although its role was to discuss the position of the woman worker, it was not strictly a women's conference as male delegates were there too. Ellen Wilkinson also objected because the subjects for discussion had been selected by the TUC General Council and addressed 'policy and family affairs' rather than the position of women working in industry. Also most of the speakers were men who, they felt, were lecturing them.[176] Jessie Stephen even referred to male members of union executives accompanying women delegates 'to ensure the women do exactly as they are told'.[177] The discussion on family allowances, which Minnie described as 'eagerly awaited' did not take place for 'organisational reasons'. Such manoeuvres were not uncommon. The *Bulletin* highlighted how the Labour Party had contrived to remove birth control from its conference agenda despite the decisions of successive Annual Conferences of Labour Women. The *Bulletin* urged ILP women to find out who was to be their delegate to the upcoming Labour Party conference and 'put "the fear of God" into him'.[178]

The focus on the miners' struggle had a marked negative impact on the work of ILP women. The annual conference of Labour women was postponed from May then cancelled. Although Minnie's *Socialism for Women* was republished as a pamphlet for the Party's autumn and winter study classes, the *Bulletin* to ILP Women's groups was not issued for months. While Minnie spoke on behalf of the NAC urging the setting up of women's groups in June, there was a hiatus until the WAC met in September.[179] When the WAC finally met, questions were asked as to why the committee had not been consulted on Minnie's nomination as the ILP's Women's Representative on the Labour Party Executive. While the pause between meetings might have contributed to the irregular method of Minnie's nomination, Minnie may have taken advantage of the situation, with her political ambition matched by her organisational guile. As a result, a rule change was proposed to determine how future elections of women delegates would take place that was agreed.[180] However, Minnie's nomination stood.

Meanwhile, Minnie was distressed to learn that Brailsford, one of the original architects of 'Socialism in our Time', was to leave his post as editor of the *New Leader*. Apparently forced out by the behind the scenes manoeuvring that Paton described as the 'hidden powers that controlled the National Council', Minnie commented to Brailsford that at the last NAC meeting 'we were all unanimous in desiring to retain the *Leader* and you'. She added, 'Whatever has happened since has been done obviously without the consent of the NAC as such, as we have not met.'[181] This time, the bypassing of the rules worked the other way.

Minnie was part of the ILP delegation to the Labour Party's Margate annual conference that took place in mid-October, during the latter stages of the miners' lockout. The mood of optimism that had existed at the time of the ILP's April conference had been replaced by despair. The ILP delegates recognised that the 'Socialism in Our Time' campaign would be less important in scope and effect than originally planned. Also, trades unions' opposition to family allowances had been underestimated by the ILP. Concerned that their impact could affect workers' wage levels, it was clear that union votes would make their adoption impossible at the conference.[182] For ILP delegates wanting to promote their 'Living Wage' proposals, it was a 'bleak prospect'.[183]

Before the conference started, Minnie attended four full NAC sessions that considered the restructuring of the ILP, the roles and responsibilities of its main officers and Brailsford's [forced] resignation. As power shifted, Brockway took over the editorship of the *New Leader* as well as becoming political secretary. Then, with Minnie apparently in the meeting, Pat Dollan raised the issue of her health breakdown, saying she had medical advice to take a complete rest for not less than twelve months with a sea voyage as part of her cure. The NAC agreed to approach the Keir Hardie Trust to defray her expenses and the Party covered her travel costs, doctor's fees and paid £29 loss of wages for one month.[184]

Although a furlough was agreed, Minnie remained fully engaged and succeeded in being elected to the Labour Party National Executive Committee (NEC), where she joined Lansbury, Morrison, Dalton and MacDonald. *Lansbury's Labour Weekly* marked the occasion with her cartoon caricature, describing her election as that of 'the beloved propagandist of the ILP'.[185] While accurate, this description failed to capture the scale of her achievement. To be elected to the NEC required backing from both unions and constituency parties, not only the socialist societies. In the ballot, Minnie obtained 1,764,000 votes, which presumably included those of the Miners' Federation of which Arthur Cook was now General Secretary and which had 800,000 votes. Her work through the lockout would have only enhanced her strong and long-standing relationship with the miners. She would also probably have secured the support of the Iron and Steel Workers, which had 75,000 votes. Minnie therefore garnered 889,000 votes from others, presumably including many constituency parties. This was a strong base across the movement, not just within the ILP, on which to build an influential position. In contrast, Ellen Wilkinson who had stood each year, nominated by her union, NUDAW, for one of four reserved women's seats on the NEC, did so without success. Now Wilkinson was beaten by Minnie, who won at the first time of asking.[186]

Minnie was the first woman from Wales elected to the Labour Party's highest body. The *Western Mail* recognised Minnie's achievement, describing it as a mark of confidence the Party had in her abilities and declared that her next Parliamentary candidature would be for an industrial seat.[187] The paper may have been aware that, after being approached by other constituencies, Minnie had been unanimously selected as prospective Labour candidature for the marginal Faversham seat in Kent, and had stood down from Bournemouth. Recognising that it was in the movement's national interest, the Bournemouth Party reluctantly agreed.[188] Why, though, in view of her poor health did Minnie pursue the Faversham seat? While the selection process would have started before she became aware of the seriousness of her illness, by continuing was she hoping for some miraculous reversal of her condition? Was she seeking to avoid making public her illness? Was she acting in the hope that the specialist was mistaken? Perhaps she was just in denial. It could not though be denied for long,

On the last morning of the Labour Party conference, Minnie was scheduled to move the ILP's resolution in support of family allowances paid for by direct taxation of high incomes and to propose that the NEC present a scheme of allowances to the next conference. Apparently leading in this key policy area for the ILP and now elected to membership of the NEC, she would have been well placed to pursue the policy through. However, with trades union opposition meaning that family allowances were seen as 'obstacles to unity' within the Labour Party, the NEC supported the watering down of the resolution by adopting the age-old tactic of setting up a committee to consider the impact of allowances in various industries, thereby ensuring union opposition could hold sway.[189] The miners were the only large union to support the ILP as entrenched union resistance ensured that the spoiling amendment was carried.[190] In the event, Minnie was too ill to move the resolution and she was replaced by Pat Dollan.

Although she did not know it, Minnie's political career was over. Overwhelmed by illness, she would never attend an NEC meeting and her resignation was announced at its meeting in February 1927. At the subsequent Labour Party conference, Minnie's NEC position was taken by Wilkinson, finally successful in the endeavour, who was also appointed to the Party's Living Wage Enquiry.[191] Neither would Minnie attend another NAC meeting. After she stood down, Francis Johnson, the ILP Financial Secretary, scored through Minnie's name in the list of NAC members in his diary and scribbled the name of Oswald Mosley in her place. Mosley's biographer described his NAC elevation alongside such veterans as Kirkwood, Shinwell and Wallhead as 'an astonishing achievement'. Unlike Mosley, Minnie had been elected as a young woman, who was not an MP, or a member of the aristocracy. It makes her achievement all the more astonishing.[192]

Just as she was showing what she might be capable of, she was gone. On 29 October, Minnie embarked as a first-class passenger on a ship bound for Tenerife. When she returned to Liverpool on 1 December after a month in the Canary Islands, the miners were returning to work defeated. The demoralisation across the labour movement reflected Minnie's personal circumstances. With so much potential unfulfilled, her political career lay in ruins and she would never return to the main stage of British politics. The meteor first spotted in Norwich in 1915 had burnt out in little more than a decade.

[1] *ILP Chronicle*, 'Headlights from Headquarters', 'For Private Circulation Only', Nos 1 & 2, January & February 1923, ILP Small Collections Misc 371/2. It was initially called the 'Great ILP Campaign'.

[2] NAC Report to the 1923 ILP Annual Conference, pp. 13, 19 & 27/8; Pallister, *Cabbage...*, p. 6.

[3] *New Leader*, 16 March 1923; 'Looking Back'; *ILP Chronicle*, 1923 issues. Patricia Hollis describes the life of the ILP organiser, later lived by Jennie Lee, as 'a male life, the only public life possible'. (Patricia Hollis, *Jennie Lee*, Faber & Faber, 2014 edition, p. 151.) Minnie would have not considered it so. There were sufficient ILP women organisers across generations and across Britain, including Katherine Bruce Glasier, Jessie Stephen and Minnie, to demonstrate a counter view.

[4] Minnie was charged out to Divisional Councils at one guinea per meeting, but her burden was considerable as the number of bookable visits was not limited to five a week and, alongside political meetings, branches were also invited to organise social gatherings where Minnie would perform. Asked to sing at one event, she complied but responded that requests were usually for her not to sing.

[5] *New Leader*, 19 January, 2 & 16 February, 16 March, 20 April, 18 May 1923; *ILP Chronicle*, No 1, January, No 2 February & No 5, May 1923; *Derby Daily Telegraph*, 14 April 1923.

[6] Lucy Cox, 'The Flowers That Minnie Pallister Planted', *WH*, 27 March 1961; Stephen, *Submission...*, p. 93.

[7] Morris, 'The Flowers...'.

[8] *ILP Chronicle*, No 1, January 1923.

[9] *ILP Chronicle*, No 1; Conveyed by G. V. Dowding to Mr Gielgud, 6 October 1938, BBC WAC RCONT1 Pallister (Talks 1).

[10] Cox, 'Flowers...'. Unfortunately, when comparisons were made of speakers, female orators were compared with other another, rather than with males, so it is not possible to judge Minnie against the best male speakers. A year after Minnie left the national stage, Jennie Lee made her mark at the 1927 ILP conference, as had Minnie in Norwich twelve years earlier. (Patricia Hollis, *Jennie Lee*, Faber & Faber, 2014, p. 27) Interestingly, Cox did not include Ellen Wilkinson in her comparison of the great woman speakers of that period, in spite of her reported abilities. (See Vernon, pp. 84–5.)

[11] These comments were used in a different context by Morris, 'Flowers...'.

[12] 1923 ILP Annual Conference Report, pp. 19 & 79–80; Jessie Stephen, *Submission is for Slaves*, unpublished, p. 93, AG/Working Class Biography, Box 3, WCML.

[13] Stephen was candidate in South Portsmouth in 1923, 1924 and 1929 and in Kidderminster in 1931.

[14] Brockway, H. N. Brailsford, who became editor of the *New Leader*, and Paton, the Scottish divisional organiser, were similarly recruited. (Marwick, ILP thesis, p. 138; Dowse, p. 85.)

[15] *New Leader*, 16 March 1923; *ILP Chronicle*, No 5, May 1923; 1923 ILP Annual Conference Report, p. 101.

[16] Cox, 'Flowers...'; *New Leader*, 24 May 1929 & 23 November 1923.

[17] Dowse, pp. 76 & 89.

[18] Marquand, p. 395; *New Leader*, 2 November 1923.

[19] Marwick, *Clifford Allen*, p. 77.

[20] Dowse, pp. 82–3 & 99.

[21] *New Leader*, 28 September 1922; Marwick, ILP thesis, p. 79.

[22] Dowse, p. 82; Gilbert, *Plough...*, p. 180; Bullock, *Under Siege*, p. 360, fn 43; Hamilton, *Friends*, p. 147; June Hannam, 'Debating Feminism in the Socialist Press: Women and the *New Leader*', eds. Catherine Clay, Maria DiCenzo, Barbara Green & Fiona Hockney, *Women's Periodicals and Print Culture in Britain, 1918–1939*, Edinburgh, 2018, p. 376; F. M. Leventhal, 'Brailsford, Henry Noel', *DLB*, Vol II.

[23] *Labour's Who's Who*, Labour Publishing Company, 1927; John Saville, *DLB*, Vol V, pp. 100–102; Hamilton, *Friends*, p. 79.

[24] Quoted in Bill Schwarz, *West Indian Intellectuals in Britain*, MUP, 2003, p. 79.

[25] See MacDonald, Diary, Thursday 8 February 1923, RMD/2/20.

[26] Pallister, 'Now We Are Ten', *People's Weekly*, 5 July 1930.

[27] Mark Clapson, 'From Garden City To New Town: Social Change, Politics and Town Planners at Welwyn, 1920–1948' in eds. Helen Meller & Heleni Porfyriou, *Planting New Towns in Europe in the Interwar Years: Experiments and Dreams for Future Societies*, Cambridge Scholars Publishing, 2016.

[28] Robert Beevers, *The Garden City Utopia: A Critical Biography of Ebenezer Howard*, Macmillan, 1988, pp. 28 & 109–112.

[29] *Labour Woman*, June 1920 & November 1922; *New Leader*, 3 September 1926.

[30] Stephen V. Ward, *The Peaceful Path: Building Garden Cities and New Towns*, University of Hertfordshire, 2016, p. 120.

[31] They included Frederick Osborn, the secretary of the Welwyn Garden City Company, who was a member of the ILP, uncompromisingly anti-war and who went on the run rather than be enlisted. Other company directors included the author and drama critic C. B. Purdom and Richard Reiss, Labour candidate for Colchester in the four general elections in the 1920s. Beevers, pp. 146–7, & 175; Celia Reiss, *R L Reiss*, reproduced at http://cashewnut.me.uk/WGCbooks/web-WGC-books-1965-1.php accessed 9 July 2016

[32] Stephen V. Ward, p. 92.

[33] Declan McHugh, *A 'Mass' Party Frustrated? The Development of the Labour Party in Manchester, 1918–31*, University of Salford, Ph.D, 2001, p. 172.

[34] Beevers, p. 120; Clapson, pp. 1 & 10.

[35] Roger Filler, *A History of Welwyn Garden City*, Phillimore, 1986, p. 81.

[36] C. J. Wrigley, *A. J. P. Taylor*, Bloomsbury Academic, pp. 52 & 54; *Labour Who's Who*, 1927, p. 22; *Labour Party Annual Report*, 1923, p. 271; *Welwyn Garden City News*, 16 October 1925. Fifteen years older than Minnie, Wallhead was a Londoner who trained as a decorator before becoming manager of the *Labour Leader* in 1906. In 1922 he became MP for Merthyr, Hardie's old seat, whereupon he moved to WGC. Cove had been a miner and Marxian schoolteacher in the Rhondda before the war. He became the youngest NUT President in 1922 and MP for Wellingborough in 1923.

[37] Clapson, p. 22.

[38] Stephen V. Ward, pp. 63–4.

[39] Filler p. 81; *WGC News*, 5 January, 9 & 23 February, 20 April & 12 October 1923, 14 March & 7 November 1924 & 6 March 1925.

[40] *WGC News*, 13 June 1923.

[41] *SWDN*, 6 May 1923.

[42] *New Leader*, 2, 9 & 16 March 1923.

[43] *New Leader*, 15 June 1923.

[44] Jessie Stephen, *When I Became a Parliamentary Candidate*, unpublished, PP/BIOGA/1/943, WCML; Stephen, *Submission...*, p. 194.

[45] Bartley, digital copy, 20 & 29.7 of 918.

[46] *New Leader*, 18 May 1923.

[47] *Labour Leader*, 20 July & 21 September 1923; 'Twenty-One Years After', *Tea Time Talk*, 11 May 1939; 'Election Experiences'.

[48] John Paton, *Left Turn*, Secker & Warburg, 1936, pp. 273–4. That year, Miles Malleson read poetry, with Bertrand Russell and R. H. Tawney, the socialist historian, also present, while the ILP's own lecturers (normally including Minnie) provided students with grounding in Party policy.

[49] *New Leader*, 31 August & 14 September 1923.

[50] *ILP Chronicle*, No 9, September 1923; *New Leader* 21 & 28 September 1923; *Bournemouth Times and Directory*, 20 October 1923.

[51] Marquand, pp. 246–7; *New Leader*, 5 & 19 October 1923; *Bournemouth Times and Directory*, 29 September, 13 & 20 October 1923.

[52] *Bournemouth Times and Directory*, 13 October & 15 December 1923; *New Leader*, 5 & 19 October 1923.

[53] Mrs A. E. Hookey to Dear Comrade, 16 December 1934, Middleton papers, JSM/LH/37.i, PHM.

[54] *Bournemouth Times and Directory*, 15 December 1923.

[55] *Bournemouth Times and Directory*, 29 September & 13 October 1923.

[56] *The Vote*, 6 July, 28 September, 19 October & 23 November 1923.

[57] *Bournemouth Times and Directory*, 24 November & 1 December 1924.

[58] Women's Freedom League NEC Minutes, 3 November 1923, 2WFL/1/8, Women's Library, LSE.

[59] *ILP Chronicle*, No 9, September 1923; New Leader, 14 & 21 September, 19, 26 October & 9 November 1923.

[60] Allen & Brockway, circular letter, 'The Condition of Europe', 2 November 1923, Box JX 1963, TUC Library; *Sunderland Daily Echo and Shipping Gazette*, 2 Nov 1923; *New Leader*, 9 November 1923; *Aberdeen Journal*, 15 Nov 1923.

[61] *Bournemouth Times and Directory*, 17 November 1923; 'Election Experiences'.

[62] *Bournemouth Times and Directory*, 24 November & 8 December 1923.

[63] 'Life Story (3)'.

[64] 'Life Story (3)'; 'Election Experiences'; *Illustrated London News*, 8 December 1923; *Bournemouth Times and Directory*, 27 October, 3 & 24 November, 8 & 15 December 1923.

[65] *Bournemouth Times and Directory*, 15 December 1923.

[66] *Bournemouth Times and Directory*, 8 December 1923.

[67] *Bournemouth Times and Directory*, 13 October & 15 December 1923; 'Bournemouth Blossoms Out: A Message From Minnie Pallister', *The Labour Woman*, 1 January 1924.

[68] Marquand, p. 284.

[69] Marwick, *Clifford Allen*, p. 86, fn 8; Sheldon Spear, 'Pacifist radicalism in the Post-War British Labour Party: The Case of E. D. Morel, 1919–24', *International Review of Social History*, 1978, Vol 23 (2), pp. 209–10.

[70] 'Life Story (3)'.

[71] *Yorkshire Evening Argus*, 11 February 1924.

[72] *New York Times*, 12 February 1924; *Washington Post*, 12 February 1924; *Atlanta Constitution*, 15 February 1924.

[73] Kenneth O. Morgan, 'The Labour Party and British Republicanism', *E-rea* 1.2 | 2003, [En ligne], 1.2, 2003, mis en ligne le 15 octobre 2003, accessed 23 April 2020. URL: http://journals.openedition.org/erea/347

[74] *New Leader*, 28 March 1924.

[75] Dan Griffiths, *What is Socialism*, Grant Richards, 1924.

[76] This label was used in 1920s Parliamentary elections by some former supporters of David Lloyd George, instead of more traditional Party labels. It was intended to signify that Labour, with its belief in socialism, was against the constitution.

[77] *New Leader*, 28 March 1924; *Bournemouth Times and Directory*, 22 March 1924.

[78] KBG Diary, 25 January & 24 February 1924, GP 2/2/14.

[79] *New Leader*, 18 January, 22 February & 7 March 1924; *Lincolnshire Echo*, 26 Jan 1924; *Grantham Journal*, 26 Jan 1924.

[80] *Methodist Recorder*, 28 February 1957; Pallister to Brailsford, nd, [1926] HNB/1/20.

[81] *Socialism for Women*, ILP, 1924, p. 6.

[82] See Hannam & Hunt, *Socialist Women*, p. 99. A decade later, when women in the Australian labour movement used Minnie's analysis and arguments to understand Australia's situation, develop their own thinking and shape their responses, they quoted whole sections of *Socialism for Women* verbatim. See Chapter 7 below.

[83] *Bournemouth Times and Directory*, 15, 22 & 29 March 1924.

[84] *Labour Leader*, 24 May 1912; *Bournemouth Times and Directory*, 22 March 1924. She probably knew Hoffman, now an MP, when he was its South Wales organiser before the Great War.

[85] Vernon, p. 70.

[86] *Bournemouth Times and Directory*, 26 January & 20 December 1924.

[87] Criticising negative perceptions of their status, Minnie argued that they should have defined hours of work, a definite hourly rate of pay, be properly trained and provided with the latest tools for their work.

[88] *New Leader*, 15 June 1923 & 4 April 1924.

[89] *New Leader*, 25 April 1924.

[90] Paton, *Left Turn*, p. 212; *New Leader*, 25 April 1924.

[91] Paton, *Left Turn*, pp. 174-5 & 211; Dowse, pp. 122-3.

[92] NAC Report to 1924 ILP Annual Conference, pp. 22 & 23.

[93] *New Leader*, 18 April 1924; *Bournemouth Times and Directory*, 19 April 1924; *Daily Herald*, 21 April 1924.

[94] *New Leader*, 16 May 1924; *Daily Herald*, 15 May 1924.

[95] BBC Bournemouth was launched in October 1923. It was the eighth station and formally had a limited distance of around twenty miles; in practice it could be heard across much of the country. (*Bournemouth Times and Directory* 27 October 1923 & 19 January 1924; Genome.ch.bbc.uk/search 6BM Bournemouth, 30 June 1924, 20.00 hours; Alban Webb, 'The Invention of General Election Broadcasting: Part 1: 1922–1950', *History of the BBC*,
http://www.bbc.co.uk/historyofthebbc/elections/invention-1
Accessed 6 September 2017; Marc Settle, 'Are Election Broadcasts a Turn Off?',
http://news.bbc.co.uk/1/hi/uk_politics/8036645.stm Accessed 23 May 2018.)

[96] *New Leader*, 6 June 1924; *No More War*, June 1922.

[97] Pallister, *Rain on the Corn*, ILP, 1928, p. 54; *Bournemouth Times and Directory*, 27 September 1924.

[98] Pallister, *Cabbage...*, pp. 139–41

[99] 'Minnie Pallister's Diary', *WH*, 27 November 1951; R. J. L. Kingsford, *The Publishers Association 1896–1946*, CUP, 1970, p. 98.

[100] Pallister, *The Orange Box*, pp. 8 & 10.

[101] Pallister, *The Orange Box*, pp. 48–51.

[102] I am grateful to Angela John for this point.

[103] *Bournemouth Times and Directory*, 13 & 20 December 1924.

[104] *New Leader*, 10 October 1924.

[105] *Daily Herald*, 14 October 1924; *Bookman*, December 1924.

[106] *New Leader*, 17 & 31 October 1924; *Man and Metal*, November 1937.

[107] *Bournemouth Times and Directory*, 1 November 1924; 'Election Experiences'.

[108] *Daily Herald*, 15 October 1924.

[109] *Bournemouth Times and Directory*, 18 October 1924; *Daily Herald*, 27 October 1924.

[110] *New Leader*, 23 October 1924.

[111] Brockway, *Inside the Left*, p. 156. Purported to be from the Communist International to the Communist Party of Great Britain, it implicated the Labour Government's support of the Soviet Union in seeking to radicalise British workers.

[112] *Bournemouth Times and Directory*, 1 November 1924.

[113] *New Leader*, 14 & 21 November 1924.

[114] *New Leader*, 5 & 12 December 1924 & 9 January 1925; *Northampton Mercury*, 14 November 1924; *Lincolnshire Standard and Boston Guardian*, 13 December 1924; *Grantham Journal*, 20 December 1924.

[115] *Daily Herald*, 4 October 1924.

[116] Stanley Harrison, *Poor Men's Guardians*, Lawrence & Wishart, 1974, pp. 174 & 183; Richards, pp. 19, 22, 25 & 68.

[117] George Lansbury, *My Life*, Constable, 1928, pp. 294–5.

[118] *Hull Daily Mail*, 17 February 1925; *Labour Leader*, 13 March & 3 April 1925. It included a public meeting in Kirriemuir that 'wishes there were more Minnie Pallisters in the movement, but gives thanks to the gods for the existence of even one!'

[119] *New Leader*, 15, 22 & 29 May & 12 June 1925.

[120] Other members of the WAC included Katherine Bruce Glasier, Margaret Bondfield, Mrs Eleanor Barton, who was General Secretary of the Women's Co-operative Guild, and Dorothy and Dr Violet Jewson. *New Leader*, 8, 15 February 1924, 27 February & 24 April 1925; Hannam & Hunt, *Socialist Women*, p. 95.

[121] *New Leader*, 24 April & 5 June 1925; *Daily Herald*, 28 May 1925; Mary D. Stocks, *Eleanor Rathbone*, Gollancz, 1949, p. 101; Dowse, p. 130, fn 2, referring to Stocks.

[122] *New Leader*, 17 July 1925.

[123] Hannam, 'Debating Feminism...', p. 381.

[124] *New Leader*, 17 July 1925. This mirrored the Presidential address, 'The Old and the New Feminisms' that Eleanor Rathbone had given to the Council of the National Union of Societies for Equal Citizenship (formerly the National Union of Women's Suffrage Societies) two months earlier. Identifying family allowances, birth control and housing as needed for women to control their lives and fulfil individual potential, it committed NUSEC to a 'particular interpretation of what it meant to be a feminist'. (Pedersen, pp. 187–8.) Although at this stage Minnie looked only to work through the ILP, rather than through women's organisations outside the labour movement, in their support of oppressed working mothers, the positions of NUSEC and ILP women were aligned.

[125] *New Leader*, 4 September 1925.

[126] *New Leader*, 17 July 1925.

[127] *New Leader*, 14 August 1925; Robert Skidelsky, *Oswald Mosley*, Macmillan, 1975, pp. 130 & 168–169.

[128] See Paton, *Left Turn*, pp. 178–9 & 336 & Bullock, *Under Siege*, p. 108.

[129] KBG Diary, 18 August 1925, GP 2/2/15. Bruce Glasier recorded it as being M. Jewson but *Labour Woman* and *New Leader* named Dorothy.

[130] *New Leader*, 28 August 1925.

[131] *Labour Woman*, 1 August 1925; *Daily Herald*, 18 August 1925; *New Leader*, 21 August 1925; Katharine Bruce Glasier, *The Glen Book*, Hutchinson, p. 63. Originally Minnie was also to be one of eleven ILP delegates to the main Congress, as well as attend the women's conference, but the Labour Party ruled that the ILP was only entitled to eight full delegates. (Brockway to Gillies, 6 July 1925, LP/L51/13/4/1; Gillies to Scott, 16 July 1925, LP51/13/2/6.1, PHM.)

[132] *New Leader*, 28 August & 4 September 1925.

[133] *Labour Woman*, 1 August 1925; *New Leader*, 28 August & 2 October 1925. Hannam & Hunt, *Socialist Women*, p. 178, inaccurately stated the ILP delegation comprised Bondfield, Dorothy Jewson and Swanwick. Minnie was a delegate with Bondfield and Jewson, Swanwick was not. (See Brockway to Gillies, 6 July 1925, LP/L51/13/4/1, PHM; also *Labour Woman*, 1 August 1925.)

[134] *New Leader*, 28 August 1925.

[135] Pugh, pp. 69 & 135.

[136] Wilkinson as a fellow traveller at this time is based on my reading of Laura Beers, *Red Ellen*, Harvard, 2016 and Vernon.

[137] Howell, p. 338.

[138] Pugh, p. 75.

[139] Beers, p. 163.

[140] Paula Bartley, *Ellen Wilkinson*, p. xiii. See 1924 and early 1925 press cuttings in Ellen Wilkinson Scrapbook, Labour Party papers, Microfilm Reel 30, W1/1–3, Cardiff University Special Collections.

[141] Stephen, *Submission...*, p. 93.

[142] Vernon, pp. 69, 82 & 95–6.

[143] See 'Socialism in Our Time: Ways and Means, *New Leader*, 9 April 1926.

[144] Minnie Pallister, *Socialism, Equality and Happiness*, ILP, nd; *The Candle In The Pumpkin: Why Be Afraid Of Bogies?*, ILP, 1926.

[145] Advert, *New Leader*, 19 February 1926.

[146] Hannam & Hunt, *Socialist Women*, p. 79. The contribution of Minnie's pamphlets to the development of thinking on the relationship between women and socialism is recognised by Hannam and Hunt. See, for example, pp. 72–3. As they did not examine women in the ILP in Wales, they could not consider Minnie's writings in relation to her organisational roles before, during and after the Great War or her work with women.

[147] Royden was considered 'eminent in the religious life of the nation' for which she was made a Companion of Honour in 1930.

[148] Julie Gottlieb, '"The Women's Movement took The Wrong Turning": British Feminists, pacifism and the politics of appeasement', *Women's History Review*, Vol 23, No 3, 2014, p. 455.

[149] Maude Royden, *Bid Me Discourse*, unpublished autobiography, Box FL 224 7/AMR/1/44; Guildhouse Ecclestone Square, Box FL 255 7AMR/1/05; Ecclestone Guildhouse Visitors Book, Box FL 225 7AMR/1/54, Maude Royden papers, Women's Library, LSE.

[150] *Daily Mirror*, 23 November 1936.

PROPAGANDIST

[151] Pallister to Brailsford, nd [1926] HNB/1/20, Brailsford papers, PHM.

[152] 'South Wales and The ILP'.

[153] Dowse, pp. 121 & 130; Bullock, *Under Siege*, pp. 57 & 103.

[154] Huw Richards, *The Bloody Circus: The Daily Herald and the Left*, Pluto, 1997, p. 82.

[155] Marquand, p. 455; Howell, p. 270.

[156] Having heard G.D.H. Cole, Minnie felt the last thing craftsmen wanted was to be attending committee meetings on how their product was distributed. (*New Leader*, 15 November 1929.) Howell repeatedly reduces Minnie to being MacDonald's 'loyal supporter'. (Howell, pp. 63, 230 & 243.) While this was accurate for some periods, there were times, particularly during Macdonald's second Labour administration, when she was very critical. See Chapter 5 below.

[157] *New Leader*, 12 & 19 March 1926; Pugh, p. 161.

[158] *New Leader*, 6 & 13 November 1925; 29 January, 26 February & 12 March 1926; The Editor, 'Family and Wages', *New Leader*, 2 April 1926; *Socialist Review*, June 1926, pp. 38–43.

[159] *Northampton Mercury*, 2 April 1926.

[160] Marquand, p. 450; ILP NAC minutes, 6 April 1926; 1926 ILP National Conference Report, p. 26; *New Leader*, 26 February & 12 March 1926.

[161] Marwick, ILP thesis, pp. 210–5 & 213–4; Dowse, p. 138; Marquand, p. 452; Bullock, *Under Siege*, pp. 3–7.

[162] *Socialism in Our Time* Committee minutes, 16 April 1926, & Brockway to Paton, 21 April 1926, ILP 3/66 NAC papers, LSE.

[163] *Journal of Education*, Vol 57, 1925, W. Stewart and Co., p. 92; *Spectator*, 30 April 1926. See Pallister to Quigley, Tuesday evening, nd, but late March 1940, BBC/WAC /RCONT1 Pallister (Talks 2).

[164] *New Leader*, 11 June 1926; Minutes of Consultative Committee, 20 May 1926, ILP 3/66 NAC papers, LSE; Howell, p. 272.

[165] Pallister, *Cabbage...*, pp. 1–3.

[166] *Methodist Recorder*, 28 February 1957.

[167] Around 1941 she identified it (probably incorrectly) as myasthenia gravis, an illness which made the muscles limp. (Interview Mrs D. J. Williams by Hywel Francis, 14 August 1973, SWML.) Based on the symptoms Minnie described, it was more likely a rare subtype of Guillain Barre or a demyelinating polyneuropathy like CIDP, diseases that chronically affect the sheath around the nerves in the body. I am grateful to Drs Abboud Alhallak, Bindu Desai, Gordi Schiff and Mardge Cohen for their assistance in understanding the nature of Minnie's illness.

[168] In her 1934 book, *Cabbage...*, pp. 1 & 2, Minnie said it was June, mistakenly I believe, because of Katharine Bruce Glasier's diary entries for 29 & 30 May 1926. (KBG diary, GP 2/2/16), Katherine Bruce Glasier, 'Looking Towards Christmas, 1933 A.D.', *Labour's Northern Voice*, December 1933 (copy held in Glasier papers, GP/4/1/ 208); 'Life Story (3)'; 'Looking Back', pp. 212–3; 'Reading Your Letters and Answering Your Questions', *WH*, 18 February 1958.

[169] The demands that the ILP placed on propagandists – or that they placed on themselves – were so heavy that they often worked until they were literally capable of no more. Fred Brennan was hospitalised in 1925. In March 1926 the ILP granted Bruce Glasier £100 'to rest from propaganda work, say, for three months in the year'. (*Labour Leader*, 16 January 1925; Johnson to Brockway, 11 March 1926, ILP 4/1926/21, LSE.) Of course, as one propagandist fell by the wayside, the burden fell on the two who remained.

[170] *New Leader*, 18 June 1926.

[171] *New Leader*, 4, 18 June, 2, 23 July & 27 August 1926.

[172] NAC minutes, 27 August 1926, ILP 6/14/5; *New Leader*, 3 September 1926.

[173] Paton, *Left Turn*, p. 270.

[174] Dowse p. 128.

[175] *New Leader*, 5 November 1926; *Port Talbot Guardian*, 12 August 1938.

[176] *Bulletin to ILP Women's Groups*, August 1926, ILP 6/14/5; *New Leader*, 10 September 1926.

[177] Stephen, *Submission...*, p. 93.

[178] *New Leader*, 10 September 1926; *Bulletin to ILP Women's Groups*, August 1926; Howell, p. 274.

[179] Head Office Letter to Branches, September 1926, ILP 6/14/5; *New Leader*, 18 June 1926.

[180] WAC minutes, 16 September 1926; NAC minutes, 9–12 October 1926.

[181] Pallister to Brailsford, nd [1926], HNB/1/20. For Paton and Brockway's accounts see *Left Turn*, pp. 179 & 287–92 and *Inside the Left*, pp.186–7.

[182] Private and Confidential: Organising Report Summary of Divisional Organisers Reports, nd; 'An Interim Report on the Living Wage Policy of the ILP' by its authors Brailsford, Hobson, Creech Jones and Wise', NAC papers, ILP 3/66.

[183] Howell, p. 273.

[184] NAC Minutes, 12 October 1926; Pallister to Buxton, 28 October 1926, ILP 4/1926/42, LSE archive.

[185] *Lansbury's Labour Weekly*, 23 October 1926.

[186] *New Dawn*, 5 July 1924 & 4 July 1925.

[187] *Western Mail*, 26 October 1926.

[188] *New Leader*, 9 July 1926; *Portsmouth Evening News*, 12 July 1926; *Dover Express*, 20 Aug 1926; *Bournemouth Times and Directory*, 8 January 1927.

[189] J. S. Middleton biography typescript, 1960–2, drawn up by E. H. T. Robinson, p. 190, Middleton papers, MID 136, PHM.

[190] *New Leader*, 22 October 1926; 1926 Labour Party Conference Report, pp. 274–5.

[191] Labour Party NEC minutes, 8 February 1927.

[192] 1926/7 ILP Diary, Francis Johnson collection, ORG/ILP/5, WCLM; Skidelsky, pp. 168–169. Mosley and Shinwell replaced Minnie and Jowett, who became Party treasurer.

Minnie Pallister with a friend, Mary Macdonald Taylor, in Brynmawr wearing saris presumably sent from India by her sister Julia.

Portrait of Minnie Pallister bearing the prison arrow symbol of the No Conscription Fellowship.

ILP Delegation to Labour Party conference, Margate, 1926. Already stricken with illness, it was Minnie's last political appearance for many years. Minnie is in the middle row fourth from right, next to David Kirkwood, third from right. Lucy Cox is second from the left in the front row, next to H N Brailsford. Fenner Brockway is in the centre of the back row.

Minnie, far right, at a meeting of the Peace Pledge Union with Alex Comfort, Sybil Morrison and Pastor Niemoller, Friends House, London, April 1958.

MISS MINNIE PALLISTER, WHO IS A GREAT FAVOURITE AMONG THE MANY WHO LISTEN TO B.B.C. WOMAN'S HOUR, IS THIS WEEK'S "RECORDER" PERSONALITY.

BBC Radio Personality 1957, from the archive of the *Methodist Recorder*.

PART TWO
DARING TO BE

CHAPTER FIVE
Invalid

After Minnie's return to Britain, first reports of her condition were not good. Bill Hookey visited her over Christmas and confirmed her failing health saying that, although she had all the gifts for a successful political career, her sacrifices made her another martyr to the cause.[1] On 8 January, Katharine Bruce Glasier travelled to Welwyn Garden City armed with Nature Cure Books on Diet. However, Minnie's situation was beyond such remedies. In early 1927, her incapacity obliged her to go and live with her mother and sister in a street of large, handsome, bay-windowed houses in Bournemouth, near where her parents had retired. Cared for by Gladys, her sister took it in turns to push Minnie and their mother around, alternately, in a bath chair. So physically stricken was she that, while glad to hear from political friends, she was not able to reply to letters.[2] Largely confined to bed, she was not cut off or lonely, as it was a flat. Minnie told MacDonald that her plan was to stay in Bournemouth for a year before returning to WGC.[3]

There was a steady pilgrimage of visitors from South Wales. Two miner friends who had 'fought' with her during the war sat by her bedside and told her of the dreadful conditions in the coalfield and Minnie wrote to MacDonald of the suffering and devastation of the valleys.[4] However, after the 'first rush of acquaintances who rallied round', the longer the convalescence lasted, the smaller the circle became until those left were 'a choice little band who bear the sacred name of "friend"'. Minnie said they saved the invalid from 'the hell of self, the bogey of depression, the fear of mental inertia, and deadly boredom'.[5] Without the distractions of constant activity, Minnie had to lie there, dealing with the reality of just being. For someone who had a phobia about being inactive, coming to terms with herself and the illness was an enormous challenge.

Minnie's lengthy account of her breakdown and recovery in her 1934 autobiographical *Cabbage for a Year* is misleading. Its unreliable chronology offers false leads, disjointed links and telescopes nearly a decade of life into one year. That smooth, humorous, inaccurate version was produced for popular consumption, rather than to relate the horrors of life as she lived it. Later accounts conveyed her invalid years differently. Bedridden for months at a time, she could not walk, talk or even swallow except with difficulty. Periods were spent in hospital. Alongside the physical pain was the prospect of pending death. Several times she thought she was dying and in panicked moments she expected to die shortly.[6]

After the first shock, Minnie resented her fate but had to learn to accept it.[7] She felt trapped by her total dependence on the goodwill of others for simple tasks but was conscious that the household revolved around the sick person, so she made efforts to avoid becoming unpopular and her development of a sense of humour about the situation was indispensable for survival.[8] Without meetings and other activities, she experienced how many people lived their lives and found evenings strange.

As well as Bruce Glasier, MacDonald remained loyal. Throughout 1927 and 1928 he regularly enquired about her health, complaining that he had not heard from her. One reply was stark: 'I was sure I was dying some time ago, & I composed an affecting farewell letter to you, & moved myself to tears by the pathos of my own eloquence.' However, Minnie added, after a good weep she cheered up and 'decided not to die after all'.[9] During this period, MacDonald was himself in hospital in Philadelphia, having contracted a mysterious throat infection which almost killed him.[10] Minnie admonished him for being a 'pig-headed idiot' for his intention to carry on as before, adding 'However, as I am not your boss now, I suppose it is no use saying anything.' She envied MacDonald 'going back into harness', lamenting 'I do not think I shall ever be of any use again, I still have to do nothing but lie about, & sometimes the future looks very dark.' She concluded that perhaps MacDonald was right after all for to 'go on & then drop is a warrior's death...[better] than the horrid slow death in-life'.[11]

MacDonald was generous in supporting Minnie. He provided money for a much-needed eiderdown, while his gift of a wireless evoked her faux rebuke, before adding that it would take a lifetime to repay all the unexpected kindness coming her way.[12] Although physically broken, Minnie's mind was alert and the radio became an indispensable companion, helping to make life tolerable by allowing her to escape to worlds of music, literature and travel. She also passed time reading novels. By mid-1927 unconvincingly she told MacDonald that she had almost forgotten about politics and hardly knew which government was in power.[13]

There were moments when she seemed to flicker into life. Her essay 'Women and Socialism: My Politics', originally published in the *South Wales News*, reappeared in the *New Leader*.[14] Starting with 'My Politics Are Me', she argued that socialism was based in 'eternal moralities' including how the world's resources were used, the ending of exploitation and the principle of service. She was also one of seventy 'representative leaders of thought and action' who stated in print why they believed in the No More War Movement.[15] Pacifists at this time still carried a stigma of being perceived as 'fanatics and freaks' and it took courage to renounce war before 1928, when there was an outpouring of anti-war literature.[16] However, Minnie no longer defined herself only by her politics as her illness caused her to reflect on her wider beliefs. Previously, her Christian faith had meant being unwilling to accept a standard of living for herself without also demanding it for others. By 1927, after a dreadful year, she reluctantly discovered that she cared more about herself than others. While she became a socialist because of the movement's commitment to building equality, and while the ILP was about feeling other people's suffering as much as their own, she now had to accept that she was, understandably, more worried about her illness than about other people.[17]

The *New Leader* carried regular updates on Minnie's health. The column 'From the Diary of a Socialist Politician' (presumably the editor, Brockway) declared in July that Minnie was considerably better. Her first letter in many months had stronger handwriting; speech and eating were reported as being '*much* better in the last week', the warm weather was having a positive impact, and Minnie held out the possibility of writing articles for the *New Leader*.[18] MacDonald seized on the report, saying he was pleased that she was making satisfactory progress and hoped that it would not be long before she was well again before plaintively requesting that she contact him from time to time.[19] But any minor improvement was met by a setback and she would be back to square one. Her only hope was to keep enough strength to write a little.[20]

There was renewed improvement into early autumn. Katharine Bruce Glasier visited twice in mid-September. On the first occasion, she and Minnie went for a walk and to a concert and she noted mystically in her diary: 'A.T.A.C' 'Allow the Angels Charge'. During her second visit they discussed events and Bruce Glasier recorded: 'go & see Minnie & *wrestle* with her – for her splendid powers.'[21] Prompted by the visit, Minnie became a little more active. A *New Leader* article started with an upbeat 'Hello Everybody! Minnie Pallister calling' where she said she had been scolded by one of her oldest friends for having done nothing for anybody for a year; she was a slacker, and the least she could do was write so that people heard from her. Minnie thanked everyone for the kind thoughts and gifts. She admitted to having had black days when she thought only of 'the dread of life' and 'the awful possibility of being shut away' but she had 'once more picked primroses in the forest, I have sat by the sea, I have walked in the heather and seen the glory of nature, which even the world's worst summer could not spoil.'[22] In November, she attended a bazaar held by Bournemouth ILP where she was presented with bouquets, fruit and chocolates. The *New Leader* offered the visit as evidence of her recovery, noting 'few enjoy quite the intensity of personal affection' that Bournemouth ILP had for its former candidate.[23]

A flurry of articles over the winter marked a temporary re-emergence. 'An Open Letter to A Trades Unionist's Wife', about the Government ending the political levy as part of union subscriptions explained to women why it was important that husbands pay the levy, as it affected what tax money was spent on, including education, housing, unemployment benefit, maternity and child welfare, or war. However, Minnie wrote as if no women were trades unionists, which was something of a blind spot. Also, although she had stood down as its candidate, Minnie sent a message to Faversham women urging them to support Labour in the next election.[24]

It was a false dawn. In January 1928, Minnie reported she had developed 'acute rheumatism in *every* square inch of me from top of skull to littlest toe joint'. She added: 'Last week could not turn an inch & never imagined anything like the pain' before concluding 'Nature is a nasty, unforgiving, un-Xtian like person.' The whole winter was spent in bed in agony.[25] Ivor Thomas, who had received a letter from Gladys, told MacDonald that Minnie was becoming 'a complete cripple' and opined, 'I fear the dreadful disease is doing its deadly work.' MacDonald responded that he feared it was something rather more serious than the 'rheumatism' Minnie had suggested.[26] Katharine Bruce Glasier, too, feared for Minnie, but she was herself bereft. Having lost her husband John to cancer in 1920, now, aged 60, she had lost her son Glen, who died when playing football at school. She recorded privately that she could not eat or sleep and that her whole life seemed in ruins.[27] Minnie lamented Glen's death but was unable to support her closest friend.

Only sporadic *New Leader* articles appeared in the spring and summer of 1928 and mentions of her ceased as she again disappeared from view. As Minnie slid into political obscurity, a new generation, including Jennie Lee, rose to replace her. Minnie's loss of position in the Party must have made her question her self-worth. She was no longer consulted by others on issues of the day, though MacDonald occasionally made passing reference to current events, such as dealing with the fallout from Zinoviev's expulsion from the Communist Party of the Soviet Union. More common were his requests for health updates.[28]

Concerned at Minnie's situation, Ivor Thomas and others launched a private appeal, but they did not include MacDonald, who was already providing generous support. MacDonald asked to be kept informed of progress, adding 'in any event you can be assured that she will not want for anything.' MacDonald had apparently sent about £70 in 1927, and passed on £50 at Christmas 'from a friend' in 'a very private arrangement'. MacDonald's unconditional support was reiterated in March 1928 when he asked Minnie to let him know if he could help in any way. A month later he hoped that she was all right 'so far as filthy lucre is concerned' and to let him know 'if there is any trouble'.[29] Such ongoing concern and open-ended commitment, in effect offering to underwrite all her needs, was remarkably generous. The approximately seventy letters that are saved from between 1927 and 1937 make clear the special affinity between them. Their close, relaxed familiarity, deep and enduring personal loyalty, full of affection, teasing and banter, were part of a bond that was more than that between comrades-in-arms.

In early 1928 Minnie told MacDonald that she was considering publishing a collection of 'little Welsh sketches', thirty essays from the *Daily Herald* and *Daily News* she had done long ago, 'as a souvenir for the folks who probably won't see me again'. She explained, 'I love doing it because doing nothing is awful' and writing was the one thing her 'fingers would let her do'. After he agreed to write a foreword, MacDonald offered to help in any way, including obtaining a publisher, and advising that the ILP handling the orders would save her a lot of trouble.[30] Minnie had not thought of getting a publisher as she had not considered the book of sufficient interest, adding, 'Probably the only thing of any value in it will be the foreword!'. She signed off: '& thanks & thanks & thanks ──────'.[31]

Rain On The Corn received supportive reviews in the labour press. *Labour Woman's* brief paragraph said, 'Minnie Pallister is especially beloved amongst the women in the movement, and her many friends will rejoice that she is again well enough to write,' missing the point that the book was a collection of reprinted essays. In June 1928 a *New Leader* review said Minnie's great gift was 'to realise the drama and romance in common things and to reveal them in a flash'. In the *Daily Herald* 'C E B' commented that Minnie wrote 'with an ease and grace which makes her opinions the more acceptable', concluding: 'Nothing that Miss Pallister has written in this book impresses me particularly by its originality. She has, rather expressed truths which we are all apt to forget...' MacDonald took offence, telling Minnie, 'I was furious with the silly note you had in the "Daily Herald". These smart young people understand nothing except what they call modern.'[32] The book, though, lacked the coherence and power of *The Orange Box*. Her writing had not yet matured sufficiently for a loose collection of articles to be compelling and the muted reviews were justified.

Even so, *Rain On The Corn* quickly went to a second edition. At his own behest MacDonald sent a copy to the publisher, W. Blackwood, at the Amalgamated Press, saying he found the sketches extraordinarily good, and wondered whether Blackwood could use more of Minnie's work. Out of friendship, Blackwood agreed to meet Minnie and 'do my best to encourage her'. However, Blackwood did not share MacDonald's view of Minnie's writing[33] and confirmed the view that his introduction was the best thing in the book. Undeterred, MacDonald supported Minnie's endeavours, suggesting she contact E. T. Brown of Rotherfield, as an agency always looking for material, and identified Sunday papers that might take short pieces.[34] At a time when he had considerable national political responsibilities, the support he offered, unbidden, to Minnie reflects well on him.

In May Nantyglo representatives, fundraising for their District Distress Fund, visited Minnie. They were so concerned that she was almost virtually confined to bed and reduced to writing books for a livelihood, that they contacted MacDonald. After all she had done for the labour movement, they declared, MacDonald and the Labour Party should take the lead as 'she deserves to be placed in a secure financial position for the rest of her life'. MacDonald replied that Minnie was writing not because of economic necessity, but to keep herself occupied, that full provision had been made for her for over a year, and that a private fund had been established to which they could subscribe.[35] Katharine Bruce Glasier visited and once more recorded mystically: 'Bournemouth & Minnie Pallister – A fight for her Cosmic Consciousness.'[36]

Minnie of course was not the only invalid at home. Rose was highly emaciated and the sisters thought at one stage their mother was dying. However, both Minnie and her mother rallied and Minnie cheerily reported she had been 'much better in health', including getting out to a tennis match and even an outdoor meeting. By the autumn her health improved sufficiently for the family to leave Bournemouth for her home in Welwyn Garden City.[37]

Minnie retained a soft spot for Bournemouth and a commitment to its comrades. She was proud of the 'comfortable little hall' that she inspired, constructed by volunteer socialist craftsmen and which would show a profit each year.[38] Minnie, the local activists who built it, and Annie Hookey, her close friend and secretary of the hall, were painted into its cream-bricked walls in coloured cement.[39] In early 1929 Minnie invited MacDonald to open it as 'that would make me feel very happy' and sent him photos, applying gentle pressure through faux guilt. In a much stronger and more confident hand than a year earlier, Minnie teased:

> A long time ago you made me a promise (and I am the only person in the whole world to whom you have broken a promise). I don't reproach you. I know that you were Prime Minister & that things intervened, *but* when a certain Wm Bennett became Lab. Candidate, you gave *him* the meeting you promised *me* [underlined three times]. (No, I have not forgotten the TUC met @ B'mouth -) Still I am not reproaching you, only giving you a chance to make reparation. You leave Waterloo @12.30 any Sat afternoon in February, March or April you can open my hall, catch the 630 & be in Town before 9.

She wound up saying:

It would be an awful thing if I died one day because you would say 'Oh dear. Minnie Pallister's dead & I *never* gave her that meeting' & when you were PM again you wouldn't be able to do any Prime Ministering, because you would always be thinking 'I *wish* I'd done that meeting for MP –'.

She was not asking him to do a meeting, she declared, only opening a hall, adding it would give the Bournemouth people a big start '& make me so happy'.[40]

MacDonald answered in kind:

My dear Old Ladye, I had quite forgotten I was so simple as you make out. I am afraid that your argument is something of the kind that they manufacture on the Clyde and is not respectable in Welwyn Garden City... Having established the truth of this matter let me examine your new proposition...

Saying he would be delighted to do it, he proceeded to list his commitments for every weekend from 2 February to 27 April, concluding 'the only glimmer of hope' was he might find himself wandering about the south coast sometime over Easter 'and could run in and do the ceremony'. He signed off, 'You do not say a word about yourself. How are you and what are you doing? I have just got back to this treadmill.'[41]

MacDonald and Minnie enjoyed jousting. One senses this harked back to a time when informal sparring was their means of relating to each other. His address 'My dear old Ladye' echoed his letter of years earlier when he addressed her as 'Your Laidieship'.[42] MacDonald then provisionally offered Saturday 6 April, though a car full of friends, including Oswald and 'Cimmie' Mosley, were 'up in arms', because he would be hijacking them on their return from Cornwall to London, which required their going considerably out of their way. MacDonald promised to give Lady Cimmie a vote of thanks if she would agree to perform the ceremony.[43] Minnie would have got to know Cimmie at Labour Party and ILP events between 1924 and 1926, and the two became friends. Daughter of Curzon, former Viceroy of India and Foreign Secretary, Cimmie was an establishment figure, and 'a thoroughly modern girl'.[44] Although without roots in the labour movement, she joined the ILP with her husband in 1924 and received the privileged access possible for those favoured by successive generations of Labour leadership, being selected for Stoke Parliamentary constituency in 1929, aged 30.[45]

Minnie's reply has not survived but it evoked MacDonald's response, 'I am glad you feel that way. You are a terror!'[46] Minnie then phoned MacDonald from WGC Post Office to leave a message, only to be put through to speak to MacDonald himself. Minnie burbled: 'The commotion you heard at my end, was the entire staff of the WGC Post Office succouring me when I swooned away with joy.' MacDonald immediately sent a note saying he was 'so glad' to hear her voice on the phone, 'It sounded very good and strong and I hope it means that you are gaining vigour.'[47] In the event, evidently wishing that a woman perform the ceremony, MacDonald arranged for Lady Annesley (half-sister of Constance Malleson/Colette O'Niel) to open the hall, but Minnie was too ill to be there. MacDonald moved the vote of thanks and later told Minnie he wished she had been able to hear the way her work in Bournemouth had been referred to: 'It would have done your heart good to have heard the references made to yourself.'[48] That he was prepared to divert a car full of friends a considerable distance out of their way says everything about his closeness to Minnie. That she did not attend indicates how poor her health was at that time.

*

By the time Minnie moved back to WGC, the realisation would have dawned that perhaps she was not going to die in the near future. Instead, her suspended two-year death sentence was commuted to the prospect of a life of invalidity. Having to face the economic consequences of surviving, Minnie put out feelers to obtain some form of employment. Aware of how little she could physically do, she concluded that one possibility was journalism, so turned for help to her comrades. The *New Leader* was supportive and from October 1928, Minnie's articles appeared regularly. In November, the paper's front cover featured photos of its prominent contributors who included Cole, Laski, Tawney, Nevinson, Brailsford, Wilkinson, Maxton, Lansbury and Minnie, who was to write about 'the fundamentals of Socialism in her own inimitable way'.[49]

From his official position in the Labour Party hierarchy, Middleton strongly supported Minnie. An ILPer who had opposed the Great War, he approached labour journals, contacted publishers and suggested outlets to which she should submit work, including the co-operative *Millgate Monthly* and *Co-operative News*, adding 'nothing would please me better than to be able to secure some regular reviewing for you'.[50] He asked the *Daily Herald* to consider taking her lighter sketches, but Minnie was sceptical, saying that even when she was a Parliamentary candidate and full-time official, she had huge difficulty getting anything in 'my own paper'. When its editor told her she needed to become a member of the National Union of Journalists to write for the paper, it was to Middleton she turned for help in getting a union card.[51] Next, Minnie proposed drawing on her experiences as an organiser as a theme for her writing, including winning Aberavon for MacDonald. She commented to Middleton, there had 'not been *many* full-time woman politicians', so such an account would not be commonplace. She also wondered whether a contact of Middleton might be interested in a series of autobiographical sketches, and sent him a series on her organising experiences for *Labour Magazine*.[52] When Middleton approached MacDonald to help, MacDonald's reply was not hopeful, saying he had already tried but had failed to get her any work. He ended, 'The really important question with her is what is to be the state of her health.'[53]

Often confined to bed or lying flat on her back and without the strength in her fingers to be able to type, Minnie wrote everything in longhand.[54] However, her physical incapacity did not blunt her edge. From 1929, through the *New Leader*, *New Clarion*, *Daily Herald* and elsewhere, she wrote forty to fifty articles a year on war and peace, and the iniquities of capitalism including poverty, slums and disease. Her pieces in the co-operative movement's *People's Weekly* were small cries for social justice.

Many of Minnie's articles and reviews in the *New Leader* addressed women's issues. From March 1929, for a period, her weekly column carried the byline 'The Woman's View'. 'The Young Woman and the ILP' was aimed at the cohort who had just become enfranchised when women's voting age was reduced from 30 to 21, and it was used to lead a fundraising campaign for the ILP.[55] In 'How Dare Men Treat Women Like This', Minnie's glowing review of Ray Strachey's *The Cause* said its depiction of women's suffering was so compelling it made her 'blood boil'. However, Minnie and Strachey differed as to the remedy. Strachey resisted the women's movement becoming aligned with Labour, whereas Minnie's believed that women's interests were best served through the ILP, rather than through separate women's organisations outside the labour movement. Happy, however, to appropriate Strachey's analysis, Minnie even suggested the book be subtitled 'A vindication of the policy of the ILP'.[56] She was also glowing about Vera Brittain's 'Women's Work in Modern England' as being valuable in addressing issues of women seeking to work.[57]

Minnie's consideration of Viscountess Rhondda's 'Leisured Women' was less complimentary. While admitting there was 'just cause for indignation', Minnie described Rhondda as 'indignant almost to the point of incoherence'. She likened her to 'a peppery colonel, longing to tell some miscreant what he thinks of him, but almost too choked with wrath to give himself full expression.'[58] Minnie's gender-based critique argued that Rhondda's criticism of 'idle women' was a problem of idleness in both men and women who had unearned income, not just women. She also argued that Rhondda left unexplored the 'problem of the relationship of the married woman to the community'.[59] Over the next two years, Minnie developed these arguments, saying the status of married women determined the status of all women. The economic basis of marriage was haphazard and was the chief stumbling block in organising women workers. It was necessary to 'face the economic consequences of motherhood' as well as 'the economic implications of Christianity' as those looking after children had the lowest status of workers, along with agricultural labourers and transport workers, and it was necessary to address the inequalities of income and class distinctions that resulted.[60] When considering single and married women and the employment market, Minnie had long commented that no one should be allowed to be idle and that all should work and contribute to society as much as they were able. Her position was not 'She's married: why should she be allowed to go on working?' or even 'She's married: why should she not be allowed to go on working?' but 'She's married: why should she be allowed to stop work just because she's married?'[61] It may well be that Lady Rhondda did not forget Minnie's review for when Minnie later sought to publish work in the feminist journal *Time and Tide*, owned and edited by Lady Rhondda, she made no headway in spite of influential support from Norman Angell. It would not be the only time that Minnie showed a capacity to rub up the wrong way influential women with whom she disagreed, nor the last time she would have to deal with the consequences.

Minnie's writing on women brought a consistent, and at times acerbic, perspective. Her assault on Meyrick Booth's *Woman and Society* was titled, 'Woman, The Scapegoat'. Perceiving the book as blaming feminists for social problems, Minnie countered that the issue was related to women moving from being appendages to citizens, and she chided the author for skimming over 'the crux of the modern woman problem, the difficult, delicate problem of the relation of the mother to the community, her income and how to assess it.' Before concluding 'is there anywhere an Adam, however cultured and however learned, who could resist the temptation to blame Eve?' Booth challenged Minnie's interpretation, saying he mainly blamed men for existing social troubles leading Minnie to counter by presenting a case for family allowances.[62] Henry Savage's 'How to Manage Our Women' earned the riposte: 'It will be a great day for the world when it grasps the idea that women are just people', rather than something to be managed like a tea shop or a poultry farm.[63]

At home, the sisters' situation worsened. When Rose died, aged 76, in February 1929, their personal grief was compounded by the loss of their mother's widow's pension which left them 'completely without resources', except for anything Minnie could pick up from writing.[64] Such were their financial difficulties that they could no longer afford their WGC house.[65] Desperate for income, Minnie contacted Francis Johnson about publishing through the ILP a reworked version of *Socialism for Women*.[66] Minnie also asked Middleton if he could help Gladys, a qualified dispenser, find employment and Middleton contacted Drs Salter and Ethel Bentham, whom Minnie had defeated three years earlier to be the women's representative on the Labour Party NEC.[67] Ivor Thomas, after visiting WGC and finding Minnie 'none too grand', went to see MacDonald and asked him to act. MacDonald contacted Dr Hector Munro, an ILPer whose volunteer ambulance corps MacDonald had sought to join in France in December 1914, telling him he would earn MacDonald's gratitude if he could help Gladys.[68] However, nothing came of it.

Timely support came from Wilson Midgley, who had accepted

Minnie's first article years earlier for the *Daily News* and who now started publishing her articles in *The Star*. A London evening paper established to fight for social justice and champion the needs of working-class families and the underprivileged, *The Star* supported trades unions in industrial disputes and in the 1930s stood out for its opposition to Nazi Germany. Decades later she remembered Midgley 'was such a loyal friend when my life lay in ruins at my feet' and credited him with starting her new life in journalism.[69]

An advantage of returning to WGC had been the chance to see friends and former comrades who visited the town to speak. Lansbury, Cook, Morgan Jones and Mosley addressed Labour Party meetings in early 1929.[70] Once Minnie would have been central to such events; now she was on the sidelines. In marked contrast to Brynmawr or, later, in Bexhill, Minnie was not mentioned in political, social, religious or cultural newspaper reports on WGC activities. Whereas up to 1926 she had been too busy to participate, now she was too ill.

During her stay in Bournemouth, close links had developed between WGC and South Wales. Minnie's former comrade Ted Gill addressed the town's 1928 May Day demonstration and a door-to-door collection was made to relieve the distress suffered by the miners and their families.[71] A Joint Coalfields' Distress Committee was established in WGC with all political parties represented, as well as the trades union federation, various churches, Rotary Club, Folk Players, the Boy Scout and Girl Guide Movements. The Society of Friends collected money and clothing. After H. B. Pointing, the editor of *Land Worker*, the journal of the National Union of Agricultural Workers, and neighbour of Minnie's, toured the South Wales coalfield and wrote an article for the *Welwyn Times*, the distress committee focussed its relief on Brynmawr.[72] Minnie later drafted a letter for MacDonald to send to Peter Scott, the leader of the Quaker settlement in Brynmawr, commending him on the work.[73] However, considering the focus on South Wales and WGC's support for Brynmawr, what stands out is Minnie's lack of involvement, another indicator of the depth of her ill health.

A cause Minnie managed to continue to promote was family allowances, which she had been advocating for a decade. The ILP's campaign had faltered then stalled due to union opposition. In late 1927 Minnie argued, in an article on citizenship and the child, that family allowances should be a state, rather than an industry, responsibility.[74] In April 1929 she was one of the signatories, with Bruce Glasier, Dorothy Jewson and Wilkinson, of an Open Letter to the delegates of the National Conference of Labour Women. Expressing disappointment that the trades union movement was not sufficiently united in its support, ILP women called on the National Conference of Labour Woman for a 'clear and unmistakable lead' on the issue.[75] Later that year, when the unions voted at the Labour Party conference in Brighton against a living wage, including family allowances which they believed would undermine the wage (and position) of the male earner, Minnie wrote a caustic piece entitled 'Dear Brutus', stating that the Churchills and the Chamberlains need not worry about labour transforming society when a 'conference of working men' could go against their own interests.[76] For her, at the core of a socialist society, each citizen should be responsible to the community as well as receiving full privileges from it. It would, though, take the transformative experience of another world war for the unions to overcome their antipathy to the proposal and for Minnie's vision of the world to be realised.

Minnie was very disappointed to learn that MacDonald had decided to leave Aberavon and transfer to the Seaham Harbour Parliamentary seat. She had retained her closeness to Aberavon and would have been aware of the bitterness felt locally towards MacDonald over his departure.[77] Her decade-long relationship with the constituency with strong friendships, a network of contacts and the great esteem with which she was held meant she was uniquely placed to help anyone seeking to replace MacDonald. Bill Cove, MP for the marginal Wellingborough seat, who lived around the corner from Minnie, was eying MacDonald's seat and would have been alert to her potential influence.[78] Minnie and 'Billy' Cove's paths had been crossing for years.[79] Born in Treherbert, he had been a miner before becoming a schoolteacher. As a prominent teachers' leader in the Rhondda, he associated with the 'advanced men' of the Unofficial Reform Committee at a time when Minnie was addressing them. Minnie also would have known of Cove's efforts to bring organised teachers closer to the rest of the labour movement.[80] Whether Minnie played a role in Cove's selection is unknown, but she was drawn into the political intrigue. MacDonald told Minnie he had seen Ivor Thomas and other Aberavon comrades who were 'a little bit disturbed' as local labour activists were 'not too enthusiastic' about Cove and were concerned for their election prospects. 'If you whisper this in Welwyn,' MacDonald said, 'I shall take your head off.' One suspects, though, that MacDonald was privately delighted at the opportunity to gossip about and criticise his successor.[81]

During the spring of 1929, Minnie suffered a heavy cold which drained her of energy. Prone to panic at the prospect of setbacks, she became wary of even seemingly innocuous symptoms as they could portend a relapse with months of pain and weakness. As a general election loomed, MacDonald counselled that Minnie would 'have to do your best to keep quiet during the election. All your friends know where your heart is.'[82] For Minnie it was not easy: 'I am aching to talk just now. Those Liberal women doing stunts are driving me crazy.'[83] Unable to walk or speak, all she could do was write. During the election, Minnie urged women to get others to the polls to vote. Even those who were not good speakers or canvassers could help by spending the day getting other women to the polls, taking shy women with them, she said, or minding babies so their mothers could go to vote.[84] Yet even in the heat of electoral battle, her need to think about work and income was to the fore. Middleton was supportive, acknowledging 'it must be very worrying to continue in such an uncertain way as you have had to do for so long.' She considered joining an agency for which she would have to write exclusively to get her articles placed.[85]

In the May 1929 general election, Labour, for the first time, won more seats than any other party, although it failed to get an overall majority. In Aberavon, Cove was elected MP, a seat he still held twenty years later.[86] Nine Labour women won seats, including Jennie Lee in North Lanarkshire, Cimmie Mosley in Stoke and Molly Hamilton in Blackburn. On 5 June MacDonald formed his second minority Labour Government. Minnie immediately wrote to Middleton, beginning her letter, 'I am afraid you will feel like cursing when you read this...'. She said she had been commissioned to write 'an important article for a religious weekly' and asked him for information on the religious persuasion on each new Cabinet member. She requested the information by return of post, adding, 'It is a chance for me as you can guess' and concluded by saying how 'jolly' it was to be the Government again.[87] Such was Middleton's esteem for Minnie, as well as his trust in her, that even though it was 'rather an awkward moment', he sent a three-page analysis, with enclosures, on the religious tendencies of Cabinet members. He explained that it had not been easy to gather that material for, while 'Crime Sheets' were held on them, they did not include religious affiliations, and with some Cabinet members they 'are buried very deep indeed'. To go to such lengths at the moment the Cabinet was being formed was an act of exceptional solidarity by Middleton.[88]

The following week Minnie wrote 'An Open Letter to Liberal Women Who Grieve'. The rise to power of the Labour Party, she said, was not an insult to Liberalism, but a continuation of the radical work of their forefathers. Arguing that Labour represented progress, she appealed to Liberal women to join the socialist movement. Liberal radicalism had provided the freedom through which socialism could now address contemporary problems: it was a compliment to Liberalism. Her smooth argument was unlikely to win many converts in the *New Leader*, however.[89]

While pleased for Labour and MacDonald, Minnie must have felt regret. Had ill health not intervened there is every chance that Minnie could have become an MP and held ministerial office in 1929. This is not fanciful. In the 1928 Faversham by-election the Unionist candidate received 12,997 against 11,313 for Labour's replacement candidate, a majority of 1,684. In the 1929 general election, the Unionist majority over Labour was reduced to 944. It is reasonable to suggest that had Minnie had the opportunity to 'nurse' the constituency for three years, with her vibrant personality and capacity to appeal to and mobilise women voters, and with her Aberavon and Woolwich experiences and Bournemouth performance behind her, she could well have been elected to Parliament in 1929. Given her ability, intelligence and drive, and her closeness to MacDonald, as one of a small number of outstanding woman Labour politicians, it is reasonable to assume that, had she become an MP, she might well have obtained a ministerial post in his Government.

Minnie's gifts would have made her particularly suited to being a member of parliament, both in the constituency and in the House of Commons. She had the attributes to retain the support of local activists and to conscientiously undertake case work. With her fluency and wit, Cox considered that 'she would have captivated and delighted the House of Commons'. As MP for Plymouth Sutton for ten years, Cox was well placed to judge. Minnie would not have confined her Parliamentary contributions to those narrower areas of most interest to early women MPs, but would have engaged with a wide political agenda, including international questions, war and peace, economic and social policy, all from a feminist perspective. While she could have been a highly successful Parliamentarian and made a lasting mark, it is unknown as to whether she had the skills needed for ministerial office. She could lead, and provide a clear vision of what she wished to achieve, inspire loyalty in those working with her, and she had the necessary intellect. However, she had never managed staff, much less overseen a government department. Alternatively, she could have used her position on the NEC to build a power base within the Labour Party, as she had within the structures of the ILP. Cox concluded that but for her illness a great future lay ahead of her adding, 'It's impossible to guess today, how far she might not have gone.'[90]

Instead, Minnie was on the sidelines. She analysed women's Parliamentary representation across the political parties for the *New Leader*.[91] Labour had nine female MPs, the Conservatives three, with one Liberal. It must have been hard for Minnie to read articles such as 'The Revolution in British Politics: Will Women Take Control?' about the impact women Labour MPs were making.[92] Moreover, the election of Bondfield, Hamilton and Wilkinson brought increased competition to the arena of the published Labour woman's voice.

The new Prime Minister continued to do what he could to help Minnie. Although he wrote to say his efforts to obtain work for Gladys had so far failed, that same day he had a private letter sent on his behalf to Greenwood, whom he had just appointed Minister of Health, saying that he would be grateful if Greenwood could help Gladys obtain work.[93] Two days later, Ivor Thomas asked Rose Rosenberg, MacDonald's close aide, whether there was a position in the Board of Health or elsewhere for Gladys. Thomas reported Minnie to be in a weak state and overtaxing herself in her efforts to get editors to take her work. Getting work for Gladys was key. Rosenberg replied that she had spoken privately to Greenwood about it and he would do his best.[94] Minnie's friendships with people in positions of influence in the labour movement, and sometimes in government, meant she was more fortunate than others as at times they proved the difference for her situation between barely surviving and complete destitution. On this occasion, however, their combined efforts came to nought, so the sisters still depended on Minnie's writings for income.

For two weeks in August 1929, Minnie was present throughout the ILP national summer school held on her doorstep in Digswell Park. She attended a Saturday social gathering, saw comrades and friends, and heard Maxton's opening lecture on Sunday. She participated in sessions with sages like George Bernard Shaw as well as newcomers like Jennie Lee. Her sketch of Shaw, whose writing she felt had given her life direction when a child, expressed surprise to discover him a normal human being, rather than as he was caricatured; and was taken by his 'gentle kindness and tolerance' and humility.[95] It was an infusion of her old life, which she relished.

MacDonald's second Labour Government proved a source of disappointment to many on the left. While there was initial support from the ILP, it became frustrated at what it saw as the Government's timid domestic policies, especially in sacrificing the unemployed to economic orthodoxy.[96] Minnie shared some of the frustrations. Her articles in the *New Leader* argued for clear socialist policies that differentiated Labour from other parties.[97] She was also disappointed that the Government achieved so little internationally. As MacDonald had argued since 1914 that peace could only be secured by disarmament, why, she asked, did the state not organise for peace instead of war?[98] Sensitive to criticism, MacDonald would not have appreciated her arguments.

Nationally and locally a split developed in the ILP. A minority continued to support the MacDonald Labour Government but the majority was hostile towards it and at times the ILP Parliamentary group acted as an insurgency.[99] In Briton Ferry, Ivor Thomas's lack of sympathy for the extremism of ILP leaders had already seen his emphasis shift. The number of paying ILP members in the town fell from over 700 in 1924–5 to 250 by 1929, mirrored by a growth in Aberavon Divisional Labour Party.[100] The significance of the role of the ILP in South Wales was over. When those who supported the Government, including Cove and D. L. Mort, were defeated by its critics at the Welsh Divisional ILP conference in January 1930, Mort, the Division's representative on the NAC, immediately resigned. In February MacDonald resigned from the ILP.[101] A year later, Ivor Thomas, who remained loyal to the Government, said he could take no more and resigned as Treasurer of the South Wales Division, a post he had held for twenty-two years, although he said he would stay in the ILP.[102]

During spring 1930, Minnie showed signs of becoming active

once more when she made a concerted effort to participate for the first time in over three years. After years of near public invisibility in WGC she wrote two articles for the local paper, arguing for official financial support for a Home Help scheme and on the need for a nursery school.[103] In March, Minnie addressed a conference on architecture and town planning in association with the 'Beautiful England' Movement. Revisiting a theme of the previous year when she responded to an article on protecting England by the prominent architect Clough Williams-Ellis, Minnie maintained that houses had to be lived in, not just looked at.[104] Showing she had lost none of her oratorical powers, to laughter and cheers from the conference audience she said: 'Comfort and health, which architects sometimes sacrificed to their frontal elevations, were often preferable, in her opinion, to the little draughty houses perpetrated in the name of garden villages.'[105] Her criticisms were in contrast to the various homages she had written in the late 1920s, where she had described the town as the 'last word' in Garden Cities and captured some of its citizens in little vignettes. Her chiding did not prevent her writing separately as one of the 'hard-bitten veteran pioneers' commemorating the tenth anniversary of WGC[106] or appreciating the town's other attributes in reviewing the annual drama festival, when sixteen companies performed each night over four nights.[107]

In April, Minnie chaired a meeting of the NMWM at 'her' Bournemouth Labour Hall, where Wilfred Wellock, MP for Stourbridge, spoke. She was once again in her element as women from churches, co-operative societies, the Labour Party, ILP and Women's Guilds debated 'Will disarmament cause unemployment?'.[108] Wellock was a plain-spoken Lancashire man, dogged in his convictions. He had been a Methodist lay preacher and an NCF member gaoled during the war. Described as the 'most remarkable Christian socialist pacifist of the inter-war period',[109] he would become Minnie's collaborator in the peace movement for decades.

The most inexplicable aspect of her attempted comeback was Minnie's nomination as one of forty-seven people standing to be national members of the ILP NAC. That she allowed – more likely arranged for – her name to go forward seems fantastical. After the previous three years, how could she think she was well enough, or had the energy for the role? Was it hope? Desperation? Self-delusion? A combination of all three? Or did she feel sufficiently on the road to recovery to lay down a marker for the future?[110]

If so, it was another false dawn. Her burst of activity ended in her being hospitalised in June and put under observation in the Boys' Ward of London's Royal Free Hospital. Too ill to eat, she was so incapacitated she was unable to wash or care for herself.[111] MacDonald took time from Prime Ministerial duties to write. She replied that she had 'such a violent attack in April and May that the Dr thought I ought to come in and try to get a real examination.' It had been heartbreaking to leave her garden, but her desperation was clear. 'I really was disheartened this time it is the first time I have quite lost heart...' Knowing she was not going to die, but with a crippling infirmity that prevented any quality in life, this was Minnie's lowest point. She felt 'horribly ashamed' for not being better after all that had been done for her, and she hoped to see 'a nerve-man' tomorrow and get 'electric treatment or something else, that will relieve me immensely'. She added she had 'everything I want (except the only thing I want)'.[112]

Minnie's relapse came at a bad time. She had just taken on a literary agent and had reviewed for the *Spectator*. Expressing her disappointment, Minnie hoped to make a fresh start when she got out of hospital.[113] Remarkably, although unable to speak or walk, and 'too weak to sit up or even lift my arm', she was later proud that, while in hospital, she was able to 'scrawl a series of articles on hospital life'.[114] Rather than revealing her darkest thoughts, her articles contrasted the experience of being a pampered invalid at home with being just one more in the sick community in a hospital. While she had a horror of going to hospitals, at least the burden was shifted from an already overburdened relative to somewhere where a machinery of care looked after sick people. Her article in *John Bull* observed that hospitalised working mothers, away from serial daily domestic demands, got their first ever proper rest and were waited on for the first time.[115]

Minnie adapted to hospital life. As an obedient person, she '*liked*' the routine – 'that queer, self-contained life of the hospital ward, as divorced from the outside world as the life of a nunnery.' Beyond the personal, the experience reinforced Minnie's view that the state should provide hospital care, rather than an 'obsolete and ungainly' voluntary system. A year later she argued for socialised medicine saying, 'Sickness is not an affair of the sick person only; it is an affair which affects the whole community.'[116]

She was released from hospital after more than three weeks, but the pattern was set. She would spend 'weary months in bed, weeks in hospital' with any progress followed by a relapse.[117] In search of a cure, Minnie received every kind of treatment. For years her struggle for health kept life in abeyance. When Minnie was struggling with ill health, but not bedridden, she considered herself 'crocked'. By the time she wrote to Angell in September 1931, asking him to put in a word with editors, she had been an invalid for nearly five years, was confined to house and garden, 'and cannot do anything but read and write'.[118] Sometimes unable to walk, talk, use her hands, or even turn a tap, her 'deadly foes' were '[C]old, fatigue, exertion, noise [and] worry'.[119] Her account of struggling upstairs showed the physical and emotional effort needed:

Right foot sloped to next step. One.
Back leg straightened, two.
Back leg drawn up, three.
Left foot placed with right, four.[120]

When she could eventually meet people Minnie recalled how exhausting it was to answer questions about her health. She did not need reminding about how tired she looked.

She thought a lot about her looks and deeply appreciated a compliment about her looking nice in a black frock, at a time when she was incapacitated. It was she concluded, 'much easier to face one's fate' wearing a nice bed-jacket and with nice make-up.[121]

It is remarkable that she was able to keep writing while stricken. She challenged negative portrayals of women, and suggested that modern woman seemed to be 'one of the few bright spots in today's dark picture'.[122] She explored the multiple meanings in the clothes women wore, and the relationship between clothes and freedom. Discussing whether it was appropriate for women to dress 'for decoration' rather than just to keep warm or cool, she lauded the freedom of contemporary women's clothing compared to the 'instruments of torture' made of steel, whalebone, gigantic safety pins, tapes and strings and gadgets to keep things in place she had to wear when younger. She implored women not to return to 'the pit from which they have been digged', and warned young women not to be 'bullied, or coaxed, or ridiculed' into wearing uncomfortable 'feminine' clothes for fashion's sake.[123] She also tackled male behaviours. Taking as her starting point the 'idiotic phrase' that 'boys will be boys', she applied a gender and class-based critique to bad behaviour among privileged young male students. She judged that 'one of the sexes, for the first twenty or so years of life, takes pleasure only in destruction, cruelty, rudeness, and idleness', with social rules 'framed to fit in with this quite baseless assumption' – a description that still fits for some a century later.[124]

Minnie's criticisms of the churches and organised religion remained sharp. Since the war she had despaired of religious leaders 'laboriously explaining to their congregations week by week that... Christ said things he didn't really mean... Killing didn't include Germans; usury doesn't mean modern business.'[125] In 1919 she had implied the Church 'combine[d] the ethics of a bishop with the economics of a burglar'.[126] Now she looked at the economic implications of two biblical injunctions not to amass riches, or lend money at high interest rates as examples of how religious principle related to current practice.[127] Minnie concluded that churches considered Christianity all right for Sundays, little old ladies and children, but not for the real world.[128] She continued to complain about churches' objections to holding peace discussions on a Sunday because they said disarmament was political. In 'When Is Murder Not Murder?', Minnie tackled the Catholic Church's belief that the abortion of a foetus was murder. She pointed out that when that child grew to man and committed murder on behalf of the state for, among others, the 'Glory of empire, love of country, the need for increased markets, the protection of investments', the Catholic Church was silent. Why, she asked, if 'Thou Shalt Not Kill' was a divine command, did it only apply to the unborn child? She questioned 'Who gave the Church the right to pick and choose?'[129] These were compelling arguments from a committed Christian and attending church member.[130]

The essential issue for Minnie was that Christianity had to address the present world, and not just relate to some future, unspecified time. If it could not operate 'in the market place, the place of sale...in the home, in the street, where men and women meet and carry on their ordinary affairs' it was 'better dead'.[131] In the *Daily Herald* she wrote almost bitterly that if Christianity could not be aligned to everyday life 'then it is a folly and a lie, and every symbol of it, every trace of it, should be wiped out of our national life.'[132] The depth of her feelings showed how much Minnie had changed her position on the role of organised religion over two decades. Now she was less challenging it to change as much as acknowledging that it could not. A more secular framework had displaced it.

*

Minnie saw cinema as providing a strong challenge to chapels in an area where they should have been strongest, the Sunday religious service [as well as to pubs]. Churches would need to adjust because 'a religion of water-tight compartments is of no use to-day' but had to attract people by its own virtues. They were on notice as cinema was 'a fairy tale come true' that brightened the lives of ordinary people and for the first time provided them with a new alternative on a Sunday night. However, her recognition of people's relationship with the cinema and her love of film were offset by her incapacity to visit the cinema at this time. Even so, scholars have noted Minnie's writings on film[133] and argue that her reviews and those by Winifred Horrabin and Ellen Wilkinson in the *New Leader* can only be understood as 'part of a feminist critique of everyday social practice and popular culture'.[134]

Literature provided an escape from confinement as did her love of her garden, which became the main source of colour in her life. In a brilliant evocation, she explained the relationship that developed between the invalid and her garden as 'no one but an invalid can appreciate a garden to the full'. Cataloguing the changing nature of the association with each different stage of invalidism, Minnie described how, while other gardeners had a range of non-gardening things to do and talk about, for the invalid the garden was the only non-health related topic of conversation. The first stage, being bedridden, brought the torture and worry of knowing what jobs needed to be done but being unable to do anything about it, apart from reading seed catalogues and relying on the goodwill of visitors to help. 'Coming down' allowed her to look at the garden and stare at the bees and the birds. When still unable to leave the house but able to walk around, the invalid got to know every aspect of the garden and developed what felt like personal friendships with each single vegetable. An important stage was reached, the 'exquisite relief from that boredom which is the cruel fate of the invalid' when she was able to arrange the flowers in a vase – although someone else was needed to cut them first.[135]

Since she was remote from the lived experience of others, and especially the rough and tumble of politics, the number of topics she could write about at first hand was reduced. As other areas of life closed, her health, her books and her garden became the only themes she could knowledgably write about for publication. The *People's Weekly* published 'The Pudding Basin Garden' and the *Star* an illustrated gardening article.[136] Presenting WGC from the perspective of its gardens, Minnie was commissioned to write a promotional leaflet, *Seeing the Garden*, as part of the town's efforts to attract residents and industry.[137] Occasional short stories based on gardening, such as 'The Lettuce', about the daughter of an itinerant minister arriving in a valleys town, found its way into the *Auckland Star*.[138] 'Heaven for Twopence' described the anticipation of the January appearance of Ryder's seed catalogue. The catalogue's arrival was a high point of the winter that made the months of darkness more bearable. Perusing it and deciding which 'tuppenny' flower and vegetable seed packets should be purchased for spring was a serious matter.[139] When her essay was included in a collection bearing the title 'Heaven for Twopence', Ryder paid her 10 guineas to use it as a slogan. At the time it depressed her but she later recognised it as a generous act.[140]

Heaven for Twopence was her second collection of sketches, published in 1931 by the ILP, which drew on newspapers and journal articles from a range of publications including the *Co-operative News*, the *Sunday School Chronicle* and *London Opinion*. If *Rain On The Corn* was compiled in 1928 to occupy her time, *Heaven for Twopence* was published out of economic necessity, and one more way of trying to scrape together an income. A review in *Labour Woman* implied it would be a charitable act to buy the book as Minnie had been too ill to do any public work since 1926.[141]

Whilst 'Prime Ministering', MacDonald stayed in contact. That autumn Minnie was invited to Chequers but, as she started the journey, the car broke down and she did not reach her destination. Perhaps a suitable metaphor for her life at that stage; she hoped to be able to rearrange her visit for another time.[142] As Minnie's economic situation deteriorated, she traded on her relationship with 'the People's Premier' to get work. *People's Weekly* printed her reminiscences of how, years earlier, the people of Glyncorrwg had received MacDonald with a torchlight procession, carrying him shoulder high in an armchair through the village to a local chapel.[143] The trades union journal, *The Typographical Review*, published her adulatory review of Tiltman's biography of MacDonald.[144]

By November 1930, her financial crisis was acute. Bernard Langdon-Davies sent a series of handwritten private letters covering a 'Strictly Confidential' circular appeal about Minnie. Langdon-Davies had known Minnie since the Great War. He had been President of the Cambridge Union, secretary of the National Council Against Conscription and managing director of the Labour Publishing Company throughout the 1920s.[145] His appeal spoke of Minnie's work as a loyal and untiring organiser whose personality and abilities were not forgotten. Langdon-Davies explained that her 'unsparing devotion' to the movement had left her stricken with incurable paralysis of the throat which was gradually extending, it was difficult for her to keep in touch with the world of active people, so it was proving difficult for her to obtain work. Her only income was £1 per week sickness benefit and she was living in a house loaned to her while the owners were abroad; she would have to leave in a few weeks when she would face 'poverty and semi-starvation'. Langdon-Davies explained that a widespread appeal on her behalf was inappropriate, as Minnie was very sensitive on the matter and still hoped, 'without very much foundation alas', to be able to support herself. Langdon-Davies sought a subscription of £10 from twenty of her friends that he and Ivor Thomas would handle. Minnie would be tactfully made aware of those who had provided the support. To Langdon-Davies's appeal to Leslie Plummer, General Manager of the *New Leader*, he added in a handwritten PS 'she always says she is getting on well, partly so as to get work to do and partly so as to not seem a burden on the Movement, but I have carefully ascertained the facts.' [146]

The period after the Wall Street crash was not the most propitious time to fight off poverty or look for work. The sisters lived a precarious existence, dependent on the kindness of others, moving from loaned house to loaned house.[147] A spacious dwelling they occupied from early 1930 had ten rooms, two huge attics and two garages, although they had no car. Two years later they had to move again, but hoped to remain in Welwyn.[148]

*

By August 1931, the failure of MacDonald's Government to manage the economic crisis led to it being engulfed by a political crisis. MacDonald, who with Snowden, the Chancellor, was a prisoner of an economic orthodoxy that required a burden of spending cuts to be borne by the unemployed, was not up to the scale of the challenge. Confronted by the Labour Party, trades unions and some of his Cabinet colleagues not prepared to countenance cuts in unemployment benefits, his divided Government was reduced to paralysis.[149] It was expected that he and his Government would resign, but he surprised his Party by dissolving the Labour Government and established what some saw as a temporary expedient of a National Government with Liberals, Conservatives and a National Labour rump. In the immediate confusion, Ivor Thomas trusted MacDonald:

> The wolves will be snarling, you will be abused, misrepresented and misunderstood. But we who know you, who fought with you, we understand. May God's blessing rest with you, and comfort you in your days of seeming darkness.[150]

Even so, it was difficult for many in the Labour fold to come to terms with events. After the first days, 'the full floods of bitterness' against MacDonald's perceived 'treachery' burst open and he came to be seen as committing betrayal in the eyes of much of the labour movement.[151] Of Minnie's former associates, only Clifford Allen followed MacDonald in supporting the National Government.

In the immediate aftermath, Minnie's articles contained no overt political comment on those climactic events. However, one week after the National Government was formed, she used her weekly column in the *New Leader* to send a coded message of personal support to MacDonald that only he could have understood. On 4 September, 'My Best Hike' recalled cycling to Llanthony Abbey down 'honeysuckle-scented lanes' before climbing the steep side of the mountain to the ridge above; it was the trip she had made with MacDonald fifteen years previously.[152] The choice of topic and timing can hardly have been coincidental or without intent and the surreptitious method allowed her to send a personal message while avoiding commenting on the politics of the crisis. Even so, while prepared to offer personal support to MacDonald, Minnie did not support him politically. She wrote to Angell, 'I suppose you are frightfully upset at the political situation. I feel as if I [live] in a perpetual nightmare.'[153]

In October, MacDonald called a general election. The Labour Party suffered an overwhelming defeat at the hands of his National Government, with the ILP reduced to three MPs. MacDonald's closest friends ostracised him. Ivor Thomas changed his view; Molly Hamilton, whom MacDonald had made a delegate to the League of Nations in 1929, when she was MP for Blackburn, had her final, painful conversation with him in 1932. When MacDonald sought to share fond memories with Katharine Bruce Glasier she thought him deluded.[154] Unlike Hamilton and Bruce Glasier, Minnie differentiated between the person and his politics. Three days after the election, she offered a forthright defence of the need for a socialist party in 'Party Politics', while avoiding mentioning MacDonald or his actions.[155] While distancing herself politically, she chose to maintain personal links with MacDonald and not let political difference outweigh their relationship or her gratitude for his support. At the same time as she made clear her distress to Angell, she sent MacDonald a copy of her collection of essays *Heaven for Twopence* saying, 'I hardly like to send you this footling little book, but I like still less the idea of not sending it.' She chose not to refer to the momentous political events through which they were living.[156] This gesture is likely to have been deeply valued by MacDonald who was generally being treated as an outcast. Feeling 'desperately lonely – deserted, as he saw it' and needing 'sympathy and affection as never before', MacDonald hugely appreciated the few friends who maintained contact.[157]

It would seem that Minnie did not broach with MacDonald his break with Labour for some time. In 1933 she ventured to raise the subject in an understanding way:

> It would be an impertinence of me to attempt to discuss anything now, when I am so out of everything, but *I understand very well,* [Minnie's emphasis] that nothing on earth would make you do anything which you felt to be wrong, or prevent you from doing what you felt to be right. Someday if you are allowed to be private again, which I sometimes doubt, it would be good to have a few moments with you about various happenings.[158]

However, while she did not address their political differences on her own account, she explained how others felt. In spite of Ivor Thomas's initially supportive letter, he subsequently became personally and politically estranged from MacDonald. Minnie explained: 'I understand too just how some of the others feel. Ivor is a one-man-dog as you know, and to him it is simply that he worshipped a god for many years, and then suddenly and unaccountably he was deserted...I think that is just simply what he feels.'[159] Minnie and MacDonald remained close until his death in 1937.

*

In late 1931 Minnie went to Champney's in Hertfordshire where she spent two months. Established shortly before by Stanley Lief as a nature cure centre, it was a pioneering facility for neuro-muscular therapy.[160] Lief had trained in the United States as a chiropractor and naturopathic physician and the integrative discipline he developed sought to balance the central nervous system with the structure and form of the musculoskeletal system.[161] Lief was still testing his theories and techniques when Minnie became one of the first people to attend the clinic.[162] Her treatment involved a combination of manual therapy and soft-tissue manipulation, fasting, diet, hygiene and hydrotherapy.[163] After fasts, salt rubs and spinal treatment, she felt 'the accumulated poisons of a life of near [?] fatigue and nervous strain were drained away.'[164] As she told MacDonald: 'they took gallons of wickedness away, & made me what they call "clean".'[165]

This time it was not false hope. Home again and feeling fit she undertook a 'strenuous course of diet & exercise & hope[d] to be quite strong very soon'.[166] While there was not much of her at that moment, she could already walk quite a long way and felt she would be much better when she had built herself up again.[167] Being able to turn a tap rather than have her fingers bend backwards was a moment of pure happiness and soon she would be able to type once more.[168] Although the accumulated damage to her nervous system left her permanently partly lame, Minnie's recovery began at Champney's.[169]

On 30 March 1932, Vera Brittain told Winifred Holtby that Monica Whately had phoned that evening 'in great excitement (on your behalf)' having seen Minnie who was back from 'the place in Tring'.[170] After speaking to Minnie, Whately, the Labour candidate for St Albans (which included Welwyn Garden City) in the 1929 and 1931 general elections, was convinced that the ailing Holtby should try Champney's.[171] Although Minnie would have close links with Brittain in the 1940s and 1950s, particularly through the Peace Pledge Union, in the early 1930s Minnie's links were with

Holtby, a pacifist, feminist and ILP member. A journalist, who contributed to a variety of outlets, including the *New Leader*, she was also a novelist who wrote about strong, independent, single women. In many ways Minnie and Holtby were kindred spirits. While Holtby was fourteen years younger, Minnie would have admired the withering rigour in Holtby's 1934 book *Women and a Changing Civilisation*, which looked comprehensively at women's condition over time. As well as advocating rights and opportunities for women, the book was a bold and sustained denunciation of the barriers and inequalities they faced. Minnie would have identified closely with Holtby's arguments on the status and roles of single and married women, gender power relationships, and on the psychology of clothes. Holtby's defence of the single woman 'Are Spinsters Frustrated?' echoed Minnie, who had already written of the spinster, saying she had the right to choose a mate worthy of her, and if she could not find one, to refuse to marry anyone.[172] Minnie too would have shared the analysis that women's capacity to have a greater degree of control over their lives depended on contraception.

It is not known when or how Holtby and Minnie first came into contact, though Holtby introduced Minnie to *The Bookman*, leading to Minnie becoming a reviewer from March 1931.[173] In her first *Bookman* review, Minnie considered six novels by women, including Holtby's *Poor Caroline*, which Minnie complimented for its 'brilliant style'. Perhaps unsurprisingly, one of its characters, a spinster who 'sits on a committee of the End All Wars movement or something, and feels that the Chancellories of Europe stagger when she sneezes', caught Minnie's attention.[174] Apart from their commitment to pacifism, socialism and women's rights, it was perhaps the experience borne of catastrophic illness that they had most in common. Holtby's 'Doctors and Patients' in *Good Housekeeping* incorporated a review of Minnie's book about her illness, *Cabbage for a Year*. By that time Holtby's own health had seriously deteriorated. Reflecting that 'illness and death constitute the great periodic dramas', Holtby noted the sense of bereavement Minnie must have felt at losing her way of life, her ambitions at having to abandon the 'valuable and individual work' she was undertaking. In identifying with what Minnie had lost, Holtby may well have been lamenting the many realisable goals that she knew she too would not attain.[175] When Holtby died in September 1935, Minnie wrote to Brittain of the 'unbelievable shock' and acknowledged the debt she owed Holtby.[176]

When Minnie left Champney's, she was barely eking out an existence. An out of work freelance socialist propagandist, she led a precarious life, without the means to pay her rent. Although *Heaven for Twopence* had gone into a second edition and was being a 'very present help', the financial pressures were clear.[177] There was a hint of desperation in her wondering if Mrs Barton, the General Secretary, had stuck to her promise of pushing it within the Women's Co-operative Guilds.[178]

Affairs deteriorated further for Minnie in early 1932 as the national political crisis impacted heavily on the ILP. Its April 1932 conference split on whether the ILP should remain affiliated to the Labour Party or should disaffiliate. By the time of its special Bradford conference in July to decide the issue, Brockway, editor of the *New Leader*, as well as Chairman of the ILP, had written to Johnson saying: 'I want to get the Minnie Pallister position settled as soon as possible.' Although Minnie and Brockway had shared struggles at least dating back to the Great War, any residual loyalty was laid aside as he made clear he wanted to use Minnie's *New Leader* column for another purpose.[179] As the paper became more ideological, with a harder industrial and political edge, it is unsurprising that Brockway should want to replace Minnie's homilies and morality tales.

Minnie, though, was still capable of hard-hitting articles. After the 1931 economic crisis, she wrote a series addressing aspects of social injustice.[180] A serious piece on individual freedom and the state under socialism challenged the 'grotesque' assumption that capitalism gave freedom and opportunity for spiritual development whilst socialism did not. Six months later, she challenged the assumption that most people were free under capitalism. People lacked the freedom to live where they wished or eat what they wanted, and they had no access to land or right to work.[181] Her series of articles on socialist policies towards children and families continued the argument that the introduction of family allowances by the state would be a simple yet revolutionary change which would alter the whole basis of family life.[182]

However, while some articles were effective, they were not consistently so. Much of her writing was out of step with the increasingly doctrinaire *New Leader* and its readership of around

20,000 committed socialists. Her seven articles in the series 'Socialism Explained', published between January to March 1932, might bear titles like 'Scientific Distribution' and 'The Ownership of Capital', but their simple, personalised, educative style were of a different hue from John Middleton Murry's 'Fundamentals of Marxism', published between March and May. Furthermore, having been away from frontline politics for years, she did not enter into the debates raging in the paper's pages about what should be the role and position of the ILP and whether or not it should be affiliated to the Labour Party.[183] While this might have been positive for her emotional health, it would not have brought her closer to the political dynamics of the ILP. Although Brockway could still use her occasionally for reviews in the paper, he wondered whether Minnie's services would be used for any other role in the ILP, such as writing straightforward propaganda pamphlets and leaflets, though he added, 'honestly, I cannot see her being a great deal of value'.[184] In October it was announced that Minnie's articles would in future appear monthly, not weekly.[185] In practice, she all but disappeared from the paper's pages. A casualty of the ILP's left turn and its disaffiliation from the Labour Party, nothing seems to have come of Brockway's suggestion of a Trust Fund allowance, and her personal financial circumstances worsened.

Disaffiliation from the Labour Party led the ILP into the political wilderness.[186] After it abandoned ethical socialism and adopted a sectarian approach, Katharine Bruce Glasier protested, 'I never left the ILP, the ILP left me.'[187] The ILP had difficulties as it sought to 'struggle towards a revolutionary socialist position', as Brockway described it.[188] Minnie considered the ILP's withdrawal from the Labour Party mistaken, and forever felt the ILP was her party lost. While her future efforts would be channelled through the Labour Party she believed that, had the ILP remained affiliated, the Labour Party might not have drifted so far from internationalism and pacifism.[189]

As Minnie's relationship with the *New Leader* ended, she developed a link with another labour paper, the *Clarion*. For decades it occupied a distinct space in the labour movement and created its own tradition. With its motto 'Politics: Books: Drama: The Open Road' and with adverts for bicycle tyres and saddles, its political articles were leavened by cartoons and jokes. Molly Hamilton was a regular contributor and on the editorial board. A cycling page written by 'Kuklos' (Fitzwater Wray), Minnie's vegetarian neighbour in WGC, gave itself the dual purpose of 'making socialists of cyclists and cyclists of socialists'.[190] When, in June 1932, the *New Clarion* launched as a weekly, instead of a monthly, with the not so modest ambition to 'clear away the debris of worn-out thought and to provide the foundation for a new world', it featured articles by the heavyweights of the movement including Henderson, Bevin, Morrison and Greenwood.[191] Minnie became the main writer of 'The Home Page', a new feature with regular articles and book reviews to accompany recipes and household hints. Although a marginal paper, she used her niche position within it to develop a blend that avoided party politics, but advised women to make the most of opportunities, such as studying at the Working Women's College, advocated nourishing food and a balanced diet to the very young and denounced the absence of nursery provision for working families.[192]

In spring 1932, Minnie and Gladys were required to move house again. When they first saw 5 Brockett Close, Minnie considered the four-roomed cottage 'so small that nothing could be taken into it except essentials'. Without spare rooms or cupboards, Minnie was obliged to sift through piles of old letters to decide which to keep and which to discard. Being forced to confront and relive her past was not easy. She claimed that life was 'suddenly a simpler and tidier affair', but the extent to which physical uncluttering really was the removal of a burden is open to question. Although a tiny cottage, a compensation was its big, though neglected, corner plot garden.[193]

As the sisters settled in their new home, in some ways her situation was stabilising. With her health improving, Minnie could start to take advantage of the social and cultural opportunities that WGC offered. She provided the front-page article of a supplement to the *Welwyn Times*, covering WGC's fourth drama Festival of twenty-four plays and an essay won the adult literature category in the St Albans Divisional Labour Party eisteddfod.[194] However, even as her health recovered and social opportunities opened up, work activity waned further. As Minnie entered 1933, aged 48, economically she was at rock bottom.

INVALID

[1] *Portsmouth Evening News*, 10 January 1927.

[2] KBG Diary, 8 January 1927, GP 2/2/17; *New Leader*, 7 January 1927.

[3] Pallister to MacDonald, nd but spring 1927, PRO 30/69/749 & nd but post 27 April 1927, PRO 30/69/1172 Pt II.

[4] *New Leader*, 23 January & 23 September 1927; Pallister to MacDonald, nd but post 27 April 1927, PRO 30/69/1172 Pt II.

[5] Pallister, *Cabbage...*, pp. 18–9.

[6] 'Life Story (4)', *WH*, 26 June 1952; 'Through An Invalid's Eyes', *Man and Metal*, April 1938.

[7] 'Through An Invalid's Eyes'.

[8] 'Life Story (4)'.

[9] MacDonald to Pallister, 22 February & 22 March 1927, PRO 30/69/749; 23 March & 30 April 1928, PRO 30/69/1173; MacDonald to Thomas, 20 February 1928, PRO 30/69/1173; Pallister to MacDonald, 'Monday' nd but post 27 April 1927, PRO 30/69/1172 Pt II.

[10] Marquand, p. 396.

[11] Pallister to MacDonald, 'Monday' nd but post 27 April 1927, PRO 30/69/1172 Pt II.

[12] MacDonald to Pallister, 22 March 1927, nd, PRO 30/69/749.

[13] 'Life Story (4)'; Pallister to MacDonald, nd but post 27 April 1927, PRO 30/69/1172 Pt II.

[14] *New Leader*, 4 March 1927.

[15] *No More War*, February to April 1927.

[16] Ceadel, *Pacifism...*, p. 67.

[17] *New Leader*, 23 September 1927.

[18] *New Leader*, 15 July 1927.

[19] MacDonald to Pallister, 18 July 1927, PRO 30/69/749.

[20] Pallister to MacDonald, 'Monday' nd but post 27 April 1927, PRO 30/69/1172 Pt II.

[21] KBG Diary, 12 & 18 September 1927 (emphasis in original); Thompson, p. 236.

[22] *New Leader*, 23 September 1927.

[23] *New Leader*, 11 November 1927.

[24] *New Leader*, 9 December 1927; *Daily Herald*, 21 January 1928; *Dover Express*, 1 April 1927.

[25] MacDonald to Pallister, 18 January 1928 & Pallister to MacDonald, nd, 30/69/1173; 'Life Story (4)'.

[26] Thomas to MacDonald, 14 February 1928 & MacDonald to Thomas, 20 February 1928, PRO 30/69/1173.

[27] KBG Diary, 26 March & 22 August 1928, GP 2/2/18; Bruce Glasier, *The Glen Book*, p. 10: Pallister to MacDonald, 15 March 1928, PRO 30/69/1173.

[28] MacDonald to Pallister, 13 March 1928, PRO 30/69/1173.

[29] Thomas to MacDonald, 14 February 1928, MacDonald to Thomas, 20 & 29 February 1928, MacDonald to Pallister, 16 March & 30 April 1928, PRO 30/69/1173.

[30] Two letters Pallister to MacDonald, nd but both March 1928, MacDonald to Pallister, 9 February 1928 & 13 March 1928, PRO 30/69/1173.

[31] Pallister to MacDonald, 15 March & nd but March 1928, PRO 30/69/1173. 2,000 copies were printed, including a bulk supply for ILP head office to distribute to branches for May Day.

[32] *Labour Woman*, 1 July 1928; *New Leader*, 1 June 1928; *Daily Herald*, 16 May 1928; MacDonald to Pallister, 17 May 1928, PRO 30/69/1173.

[33] MacDonald to Blackwood, 7 June 1928, Blackwood to MacDonald, 8 June 1928, PRO 30/69/1438/1.

[34] MacDonald to Pallister, 14 May 1928, PRO 30/69/1438/2.

[35] Gus Walters to MacDonald, 7 May & o/b MacDonald to Walters, 10 May 1928, PRO 30/69/1173.

[36] KBG diary, 14 May 1928, GP 2/2/18.

[37] Pallister to MacDonald, nd but late spring 1928, PRO 30/69/1173; *New Leader*, 10 August & 12 October 1928.

[38] *New Leader*, 20 September 1929; *Daily Herald*, 3 December 1934; *Man and Metal*, November 1937.

[39] Hannen Swaffer, *Daily Herald*, 3 December 1934.

[40] Pallister to MacDonald, nd but January 1929, PRO 30/69/117 (Emphases in original).

[41] MacDonald to Pallister, 22 January 1929, PRO 30/69/1174.

[42] Marquand, pp. 241 & 827, fn 14.

[43] MacDonald to Pallister, 12 & 18 March 1929, PRO 30/60/1174.

[44] Skidelsky, pp. 8–54.

[45] For an interesting insight see Wertheimer's comments in Howell, p. 309.

[46] MacDonald to Pallister, 18 March 1929, PRO 30/69/1174.

[47] Pallister to MacDonald, nd & MacDonald to Pallister, 26 March 1929. PRO 30/69/1174.

[48] MacDonald to Pallister, 8 April 1929, PRO 30/69/1174; *Daily Herald*, 3 December 1934.

[49] *New Leader*, 23 November 1928.

[50] Pallister to Middleton, nd, & Middleton to Pallister, 7 November 1928, JSM/PAL/1 & 3; Middleton to MacDonald, 7 November 1928, JSM/PAL/2; Middleton to Pallister, 17 December 1928, JSM/PAL/6; Pallister to Middleton, nds, JSM/PAL/1 & 4 & 10.

[51] Middleton to MacDonald, 7 November 1928, JSM/PAL/2; Pallister to Middleton, 7 May [1929], JSM/PAL/16.

[52] Pallister to Middleton, nds, JSM/PAL/4 & 7; Middleton to Pallister, 17 December 1928, JSM/PAL/6 (Emphasis in original).

[53] Middleton to MacDonald, 7 November 1928, JSM/PAL/2; MacDonald to Middleton, 8 November 1928, PRO 30/69/11173/2.

[54] *Methodist Recorder*, 28 February 1957.

[55] *New Leader*, 12 October 1928. For a consideration of the *New Leader* and women's issues see Hannam, 'Debating Feminism...'.

[56] *New Leader*, 7 December 1928.

[57] *New Leader*, 5 October 1928.

[58] *New Leader*, 5 October 1928.

[59] Angela V. John, the biographer of Rhondda, suggests that it was her intention to stimulate a debate about women, not men, and the particular problems that women faced and that the relationship of the married woman to the community was not part of

Rhondda's brief or intention. John discussed the articles and subsequent debate in her *Turning the Tide: The Life of Lady Rhondda*, Parthian, 2013, pp. 411-415; email exchange with author 21 November 2017.

[60] *New Leader*, 25 October 1929.

[61] *New Leader*, 7 February 1930.

[62] *New Leader*, 14, 21 & 28 June 1929.

[63] *New Leader*, 19 September 1930.

[64] Pallister to Middleton, nd, JSM/PAL/11.

[65] MacDonald to Dr Munro, 23 April 1929, PRO 30/69/1174.

[66] Pallister to Johnson, nd, ILP 4/1929/91, LSE archive.

[67] Pallister to Middleton, nds, JSM/PAL/10 & 1; Middleton to Pallister, 12 March 1929, JSM/PAL/12; Middleton to Bentham and Salter, 13 March 1929, JSM/PAL/13 & 14.

[68] Thomas to Rose [Rosenberg], Sunday, nd; MacDonald to Munro, 23 April 1929, PRO 30/69/1174.

[69] 'Minnie Pallister's Day', *WH*, 25 January 1956; *Methodist Recorder*, 28 February 1957; http://thestarfictionindex.atwebpages.com/the.htm accessed 2 January 2019.

[70] *Welwyn Times*, 13 December 1928, 14 & 21 March 1929.

[71] *WGC News*, 11 May 1928.

[72] *Welwyn Times*, 11, 18 & 25 October, 1, 15 & 29 November 1928 & 3 January 1929.

[73] Pallister's draft letter for MacDonald to send to Scott; MacDonald to Scott, 15 Nov 1929, PRO 30/69/117.

[74] *New Leader*, 4 November 1927.

[75] *New Leader*, 12 July 1929.

[76] *New Leader*, 18 October 1929.

[77] Cox, 'The Flowers...'; Marquand, p. 482. For one perspective on MacDonald quitting Aberavon see Howard, 'The Focus of the Mute Hopes...'.

[78] Described as 'a Socialist of unswerving loyalty and idealism', with a penetrating intelligence and at his best in debate, Cove was considered a pugnacious politician who did not know the meaning of the word compromise. (*New Leader*, 11 October 1929).

[79] In December 1924, at Cove's request, Minnie spent a week undertaking pioneering activities in his Wellingborough constituency, establishing ILP branches where previously there were none. (*New Leader*, 5 December 1924.)

[80] Williams, *Democratic Rhondda*, pp. 109-110; J. T. Ozga & M. A. Lawn, *Teachers, Professionalism and Class*, Falmer Press, 1981, pp. 94-7; M. Lawn, *Organised Teachers and the Labour Movement 1900-1930*, PhD, Open University, 1982, p. 75; Martin Lawn, 'Syndicalist Teachers: The Rhondda Strike of 1919', *Llafur*, Vol 4 No 1, 1984, pp. 91-8.

[81] MacDonald to Pallister, 18 March 1929, 30/69/1174.

[82] Pallister to Middleton, nd, JSM/PAL/8; *Man and Metal*, 'Through An Invalid's Eyes', April 1938; MacDonald to Pallister, 18 March 1929, PRO 30/69/1174.

[83] Pallister to MacDonald, nd but March 1929, PRO 30/69/1174.

[84] *New Leader*, 24 May 1929.

[85] Pallister to Middleton, 7 May [1929] & Middleton to Pallister, 8 May 1929, JSM/PAL/16 & 17.

[86] *Welwyn Times*, 10 October 1929.

[87] Pallister to Middleton, nd, JSM/PAL/18.

[88] Middleton to Pallister, 7 June 1929, JSM/PAL/19. Margaret Bondfield who 'At the moment of writing, I think...is sure to be in the Cabinet' [she did indeed become the first woman Cabinet Minister], was formally a Congregationalist, with 'something of a mystic in her make up'. Arthur Greenwood had been 'a good little Baptist' in the 'dim recesses of his past', but having 'shed the youthful enthusiasms', had been '"dry" ever since'.

[89] *New Leader*, 14 June 1929.

[90] Cox, 'The Flowers...'; see Brian Harrison, 'Women in A Men's House The Women MPs, 1919-1945', *Historical Journal*, Vol 29 No 3, 1986, pp. 623-54.

[91] *New Leader*, 7 June 1929.

[92] *People's Weekly*, 6 July 1929.

[93] MacDonald to Pallister & letter o/b MacDonald to Arthur Greenwood, 2 July 1929, PRO 30/69/1174.

[94] Thomas to Rosenberg & Rosenberg to Thomas, 5 July 1929, PRO 30/69/1737.

[95] *New Leader*, 14 June, 9 & 16 August 1929; *Welwyn Times*, 8 August 1929.

[96] Bullock, *Under Siege*, pp. 159-63; Paton, *Left Turn*, pp. 321-2.

[97] *New Leader*, 3 & 31 January, 12 September, 3 October & 7 November 1930.

[98] Marquand, p. 501; *New Leader*, 9 January 1931, quoted in Obituary, *Socialist Leader*, 9 April 1960; Cox, 'The Flowers...'.

[99] Paton, *Left Turn*, pp. 334-5; Bullock, *Under Siege*, pp. 159-63 & 166-70.

[100] Marwick, ILP thesis, p. 235.

[101] Howell, p. 292; Bullock, *Under Siege*, p. 165.

[102] *New Leader*, 23 January 1931.

[103] *Welwyn Times*, 17 October 1929, 6 February & 17 April 1930; KBG diary, Monday 3 February 1930, GP 2/2/20.

[104] Clough Williams-Ellis, 'The Ruin of the Countryside', *Socialist Review*, March 1929; Pallister, 'To Look At Or To Live In?' *Socialist Review*, June 1929.

[105] 'Architecture And Town Planning', *The Times*, 24 Mar 1930, (retrieved from *The Times Digital Archive*, 26 Mar 2018).

[106] 'Our Sunday' (reprinted in *Heaven for Tuppence*, ILP, 1931, pp. 49-51); 'Now We Are Ten', *People's Weekly*, 5 July 1930.

[107] *New Leader*, 4 July 1930.

[108] *Western Gazette*, 18 April 1930.

[109] Ceadel, *Pacifism...*, p. 50.

[110] *New Leader*, 4 & 25 April 1930.

[111] *New Leader*, 8 August 1930; Pallister to MacDonald, nd, PRO 30/69/752; *John Bull*, 11 March 1933.

[112] Pallister to MacDonald, nd, PRO 30/69/752.

[113] Pallister to MacDonald, nd, PRO 30/69/752.

[114] 'Life Story (4)'.

[115] *New Leader*, 'June - In Hospital', 27 June 1930, 'Alice in Hospital Land', 11 July 1930 & 'The Fellowship of Suffering', 8 August 1930. 'Hospital Opened My Eyes', *John Bull*, 11 March 1933, by a 'Grateful Patient', though anonymous, has all the detailing of being Minnie's and fits with her undated letter to Katharine Bruce Glasier (GP/1/2/681).

[116] *New Leader*, 28 February 1930 & 12 June 1931.

[117] 'Life Story (4)'.

[118] Pallister to Angell, 22 September 1931, Box 20, Norman Angell papers, Ball State University.

[119] *Daily Mirror*, 27 February 1936; 'Looking Back', p. 213; 'Minnie Pallister Speaking', 8 February 1954.

[120] *Daily Mirror*, 27 February 1936.

[121] *Man and Metal*, April 1938, *Daily Mirror*, 4 December 1935.

[122] *New Leader*, 29 May 1931.

[123] *People's Weekly*, 8 February 1930. See also *New Leader*, 7 December 1928, 18 July 1930 & 27 November 1931.

[124] *New Leader*, 18 April 1930 & 6 November 1931.

[125] *New Leader*, 1 April 1932.

[126] *Labour Leader*, 24 April 1919.

[127] *New Leader*, 6 February 1931.

[128] *New Leader*, 10 January 1930 & 1 April 1932.

[129] *New Leader*, 16 January 1931.

[130] *New Leader*, 19 December 1930 & 23 August 1929.

[131] *New Leader*, 29 July 1932.

[132] *New Leader*, 1 April 1932; *Daily Herald*, 13 April 1933.

[133] Minnie's work was included in Antonia Lant and Ingrid Periz, *Red Velvet Seat: Women's Writings On the First Fifty Years of Cinema*, Verso, 2006, pp. 339–340.

[134] Ian Taylor, 'The Film Reviews of Winifred Horrabin, 1927–1945', *Screen*, Vol 33, No 2, Summer 1992, p. 175. Horrabin was a feminist, socialist, activist and writer and committed to independent working-class education. Generally, though, Minnie's role as a cultural commentator has largely escaped notice.

[135] Pallister, *Gardener's Frenzy*, pp. 88–93.

[136] *People's Weekly*, 21 December 1929; Pallister to Molony, 12 December 1945, BBC/WAC/RCONT1 Pallister (Talks 3b).

[137] Sir Frederic Osborn collection, DE/FJO/B159/55 & DE/FJO/K442, Hertfordshire Archive.

[138] 'The Lettuce', *Auckland Star*, 18 May 1936.

[139] *New Leader*, 14 March 1930; Pallister, *Cabbage...*, pp. 105 & 108.

[140] Pallister to Miss Wilson, 8 May 1947, BBC/WAC/RCONT1 Pallister (Talks 4); Pallister to Quigley, 9 February [1952] BBC/WAC/RCONT1 Pallister (Talks 5); 'Minnie Pallister's Day', *WH*, 25 January 1956. Although Ryder died in 1936, Minnie maintained a relationship with the company, producing the introductory 'On Keeping a Diary' in *Ryders' 1938 Diary for Gardeners*. Ryder is now best known for having founded the Ryder Cup golf tournament.

[141] *Heaven for Twopence*, ILP, 1931; *Labour Woman*, October 1931.

[142] Pallister to MacDonald, nd, PRO 30/69/1174; Middleton to Pallister, 12 October 1929, JSM/PAL/24.

[143] *New Leader*, 12 January 1923; *People's Weekly*, 12 October 1929.

[144] *The Typographical Review*, October 1929.

[145] Pat Francis, 'The Labour Publishing Company, 1920–9', *History Workshop Journal*, Autumn 1984, Issue 18, pp. 115–23; Norman Angell, *After All*, Hamish Hamilton, 1951, p. 309.

[146] B. N. Langdon-Davies to L. Plummer, 1 December 1929, ILP/4/1929/88i & ii, LSE. MacDonald sent £20 (which Langdon-Davies considered 'unexpectedly kind') and told him since she had become ill he had anonymously donated 'pretty heavily' around £100 to various funds to support her, but he wished such information to be kept 'absolutely private'.[146] (Langdon-Davies to MacDonald covering 'Strictly Confidential' appeal, 29 November 1929, & MacDonald to Langdon-Davies, 29 November 1929, RMD/1/15/141; Langdon-Davies to MacDonald, 1 December 1929, RMD/1/15/142.

[147] *People's Weekly*, 26 April 1930.

[148] Pallister to MacDonald, nd, PRO 30/69/1754; *New Leader*, 22 April 1932.

[149] Robert Skidelsky, *Politicians and the Slump*, Macmillan, 1967, pp. 387 & 392–5.

[150] Quoted in Marquand, p. 649.

[151] Marwick, *Clifford Allen*, pp. 112–4.

[152] *New Leader*, 4 September 1931.

[153] Pallister to Angell, 22 September 1931. Angell's response to MacDonald's forming a National Government had been, though, equivocal. Pressed by MacDonald, and especially Allen, to join them, Angell vacillated then stayed with Labour, mainly he said because he could not face being seen by his fellow comrades as betraying the cause; he also mistrusted MacDonald on international affairs. Hamilton, *Friends...*, p. 246; Allen to Angell, March 1932, quoted in Gilbert, *Plough...*, pp. 249–50; Angell, *After All*, pp. 256–9; Ceadel, *Illusion*, p. 287.

[154] Hamilton, *Friends...*, p. 125; Thompson, p. 239.

[155] *New Leader*, 30 October 1931.

[156] Pallister to MacDonald, nd, PRO 30/69/1176.

[157] Marquand, p. 690.

[158] Pallister to MacDonald, nd but 1933, PRO 30/69/754. This is incorrectly filed in the PRO, so attributed by Marquand p. 681 as 1932.

[159] Pallister to MacDonald, nd but 1933, PRO 30/69/754.

[160] http://www.naturopathy.org.uk/history.asp https://en.wikipedia.org/wiki/Champneys & https://nmtcenter.com/history/ accessed 30 September 2017.

[161] https://www.google.co.uk/search?q=stanley+lief+neuromuscular+therapy&rlz=1C1CHWA_enGB595GB599&oq=stanley+lief+&aqs=chrome.0.0j69i57j0l4.12368j0j7&sourceid=chrome&ie=UTF-8 accessed 30 September 2017.

[162] https://nmtcenter.com/history/ accessed 30 September 2017.

[163] Leon Chaitow, *Naturopathic Physical Medicine: Theory and Practice for Manual Therapists*, Churchill Livingstone, 2008.

[164] 'Life Story (4)'; Pallister to Knowles, 27 November 1959, BBC/WAC/RCONT1 Pallister (Talks 10).

[165] Pallister to MacDonald, 'Tues', nd, PRO 30/69/754.

[166] Pallister to Johnson, March 1932, ILP 4/1932/24, LSE.

[167] Pallister to MacDonald, 'Tues', nd, PRO 30/69/754; Pallister to Katharine Bruce Glasier, nd but 1933, GP/1/2/ 681.

[168] Pallister to MacDonald, nd, PRO 30/69/1176; Pallister to Quigley, 5 September [1953], BBC/WAC/RCONT1 Pallister (Talks 6); 'Minnie Pallister Speaking', 8 February 1954.

[169] Gladys Pallister, 'The Flowers That Minnie Pallister Planted', *WH*, 27 March 1961.

[170] Brittain to Holtby, 30 March 1932, Holtby to Brittain, 1 April 1932, eds. Vera Brittain and Geoffrey Handley-Taylor, *Selected Letters of Winifred Holtby and Vera Brittain (1920–1935)*, 1960, Bath, Cedric Chivers, pp. 212–3.

[171] A member of the ILP as well as the NMWM, Whately was a long-time supporter of women's rights, and a supporter of the Women's Freedom League. (Pugh, pp. 49 & 69; Julie V. Gottlieb, *'Guilty Women': Foreign Policy, and Appeasement in Inter-War Britain*, Palgrave, 2015, pp. 40–1.)

[172] *New Leader*, 21 November 1930.

[173] Pallister to Brittain, 6 October 1935, Series J Incoming Correspondence, 1935, Brittain papers, McMaster University.

[174] *The Bookman*, March 1931.

[175] Winifred Holtby, 'Doctors and Patients', *Good Housekeeping*, February 1935.

[176] Pallister to Brittain, 6 October 1935.

[177] Pallister to MacDonald, 'Tues', nd but after beginning of February 1932, PRO 30/69/754. (The reference is from Psalm 46.)

[178] Pallister to Johnson, March 1932, ILP 4/1932/24, & nd, ILP 4/1932/59, LSE. With orders 'gathering slowly', Minnie asked Johnson whether the ILP had sold enough of its batch of 455 of the 1,400 print run to justify making her a payment, and pushed him to sell extra copies at imminent ILP conferences.

[179] Brockway to Johnson, 10 June 1932, ILP 4/1932/39.

[180] *New Leader*, 18 September to 16 October & 13 November 1931.

[181] *New Leader*, 20 November 1931 & 20 May 1932.

[182] *New Leader*, 27 May, 3 & 10 June 1932.

[183] See, for example, Allen and Brockway, *New Leader*, 29 January 1932.

[184] Brockway to Johnson, 10 June 1932, ILP 4/1932/39.

[185] *New Leader*, 7 October 1932.

[186] Ceadel, *Pacifism...*, p. 114.

[187] *Socialist Leader*, 24 June 1950.

[188] Brockway, *Inside the Left*, p. 237.

[189] *Peace News*, 24 November 1950.

[190] Kuklos was one of the most widely read cycling journalists both in cycling journals and national newspapers and through his writing ran the conviction that 'on every real bicycle there is the unseen pennant of progress, the standard of democracy, (and) the banner of freedom.' https://en.wikipedia.org/wiki/William_Fitzwater_Wray Accessed 28 July 2017.

[191] *Clarion*, June 1932.

[192] *New Clarion*, 24 September & 12 November 1932.

[193] Pallister, *Cabbage...*, pp. 13 & 14; *New Clarion,* 16 July 1932.

[194] *Welwyn Times*, 16 June & 15 December 1932.

CHAPTER SIX
Writer and Journalist

In January 1933, Minnie 'felt downed'. Her income for the month was 8/6d. In desperation, she again asked friends and former comrades if they could help her find work. Having contacted many of 'our people', and received replies saying, 'they would never forget my marvellous work', she suddenly thought of 'old George Lansbury' and wrote to him.[1]

Minnie and Lansbury had known each another at least from the Great War. In 1933, he was leader of the Parliamentary Labour Party, one of only 49 Labour and ILP MPs who had retained their seats after Labour's decimation in the 1931 election. Minnie's heart sank when Lansbury replied that he had 'spoken to a friend', and she thought, 'That's the end of *that*'. However, two days later she was summoned to meet John Dunbar, the editor-in-chief of Odham's Press, and former left-winger, at their offices near Covent Garden. Odham's now owned the *Daily Herald*, of which Lansbury had been such an integral part, after acquiring it in 1930, although the TUC retained editorial control. Odham's publishing expertise transformed the paper's fortunes. At a time when national newspaper circulation wars were in full swing, the *Daily Herald*, after a revamp, was turned into the world's best-selling newspaper, with a circulation rising from hundreds of thousands to over two million in June 1933.[2]

For Minnie the meeting with Dunbar was transformative. She was given a daily slot in the *Daily Herald* under the editor, W. H. [Will] Stevenson, a former South Wales miner, who had previously been editor of *Llais Llafur*.[3] From 13 February until late March 1933 she wrote a series of twenty-eight 'Slogan Cameos' which provided the basis for a competition that was part of Odham's promotional strategy to increase sales.[4] To enter the competition to win £25,000, readers paid sixpence and sent in a coupon, with profits going to hospitals. Minnie's short stories addressed people's ill health, poverty and overcrowding, or were little morality tales about people out of work, unable to buy Christmas presents for the children or go out socially because their clothes were shabby. As the series developed, her writing became increasingly bold. A sharp-edged commentary on the burden of war debt observed that although the war was becoming a memory, with battlefields overgrown by nature, war debt remained, even for those who fought it, asking, 'How long is this madness to continue?'[5] With her writing being both popular and principled and grounded in many people's everyday realities, Minnie noted, 'I *am* rather proud of the slogans as they were dashed hard to do and I tried to keep our socialist programme to the front.'[6]

The 160 pieces written for the *New Leader* from 1929 to 1932, her first sustained writing, served Minnie well and she now had sufficient journalistic ability to work on national papers. The *Daily Herald* commissioned Minnie to write a 1,000-word article on the Parliamentary Bill for the preservation of wild birds, an issue that was important to her, and she published a short story and an article on St David's Day for its Welsh edition.[7] Dunbar got *John Bull* to take an article on what Minnie had observed while hospitalised, for which she received 6 guineas.[8] Lord Riddell, another newspaper magnet, arranged regular reviewing for *John O'London's Weekly*, which he owned, and the Cadbury-owned *News Chronicle* from 1930 gave her reviews about twice a month. She may have been fortunate that her historic contacts provided the initial connections for her to get work but, once the introductions had been made, it was her abilities rather than personal favours that allowed her to maximise the opportunity.

Dunbar also read the manuscript of *Gardener's Frenzy*, a gardening book she had written, and recommended it to Methuen. It had been previously rejected by two agents and one publisher. When Minnie went to Methuen's offices, its head immediately asked if she was willing for them to publish it. The company would pay an advance of £25, and very good royalties after the first 2,000 sales. In a daze, she answered questions about a timetable and illustrations, and left 'feeling very drunk, and seeing everything in a rosy mist'. Minnie later described it as the happiest day of her life.[9] *Gardener's Frenzy* was an imaginative, engaging and quirky alphabetical approach to gardening, with an attractive dust jacket illustrated by the artist Dorothy Burroughes. The *Daily Herald* gave it a positive welcome, offering Minnie its lead page, and published a section 'G is for Gardener' as a free advert. *The Bookman* complimented Minnie for being both a born gardener and a born essayist, and the conservative *Morning Post* gave it a good review.[10]

Reviewers did not mention Minnie's feminist analysis in the section 'E is for Eve', where she applied the gender-based scrutiny to gardening she brought to all aspects of society. She described women's traditional work in pre-industrialisation agriculture, where they grew food as well as prepared it. She linked it to perceptions that modern women had a 'wicked determination to lead an "artificial" life', with their 'shameless demand' to do interesting work for a good salary, rather than accept the worst-paid or unpaid jobs, 'as Heaven plainly intended'. Then she reprised the argument that women's shortcomings were just as much 'news' as they had been for Eve in the Garden of Eden. In *Gardener's Frenzy*, Minnie widened the scope of what books on gardening could consider.[11]

One chapter, 'O is for Onion', developed a life of its own. Described as being filled with 'merry audacities' and 'needs to be read to be believed', an adapted version was published widely, including as far away as New Zealand.[12] Minnie was very proud when it appeared in a small collection located between Mrs Gaskell and H. V. Morton.[13] She would have been equally proud of another essay being published with Trevelyan and Chesterton in a 1954 Canadian collection.[14] As well as syndication across journals and newspapers of the empire, *Gardener's Frenzy* would have other spin-offs, including providing an opportunity for travel that would have a profound effect on Minnie's life.

Not everyone was gushing. 'J. L.' thought the book's title was wrong, and that many of its pages were written in an exasperating style. While pleasurable and profitable, it was written for ordinary citizens, who had just enough land to grow some familiar flowers and to keep the kitchen supplied with fresh vegetables, rather than for 'real' gardeners. This comment confirmed Minnie's later point that if gardeners had a fault it was that they took themselves too seriously.[15]

The sense of disbelief at her change in fortunes, and her relief, are palpable. She told Katharine Bruce Glasier she had had 'such an exciting time lately'. After six years of acute economic hardship, for the first time she had some money. In comparison with January's pittance, Minnie earned £25 in February. Also, she had something of her health back. 'I can't grumble, for ever since I went to

Champneys I have not had a single morning in bed & I have been going alone to town nearly every week.'[16]

Minnie's other news was equally dramatic. Gladys had obtained a job for life in Bexhill-on-Sea in West Sussex with a 'ripping firm of Doctors'. Minnie underlined the sentence for emphasis, and prefixed it with 'shout out for joy old darling'. The position came with a free flat for them both, had free electric light and paid £150 per year. It was to start in mid-July. With Gladys' steady income and free accommodation, and with Minnie's increased earnings, the sisters' fortunes turned.

Minnie yearned to spend a few days with Bruce Glasier. She wanted to discuss the Nazis, who had just won what were to be the last contested elections in Germany, the Moscow show trial of British Metro-Vickers employees on charges of sabotage and espionage, and India. It was too funny for words that they would both be home for Easter and that she hardly remembered that the ILP conference was being held. Observing, 'Once I hadn't a thought apart from it, it was all my life' she added, 'how times change!!' Then, probably alluding to the difficulties of the ILP's disaffiliation from the Labour Party, she lamented, 'Things do seem to go to pieces.'

Minnie quickly adjusted to life in Bexhill. Each day seemed like a holiday as she walked the short distance down the hill to swim in the sea, drink coffee, lie in a deckchair and sunbathe. She said she had never felt as young before – certainly not when a serious, priggish child.[17] She believed sun and sea bathing considerably aided her recovery, as 'I very very gradually built up a new body'.[18]

Their new tied flat was very old, with violently sloping floors that left a six-inch gap under the sitting-room door, but it was sunny and south-facing. There was no bathroom or pantry, and the 'powder closet' wasn't big enough to be converted into a bathroom, so a bath was installed in the bigger bedroom and curtained off. Hot water was carried in relays from the kitchen to the bath. The powder closet, with a bookcase and new typing table, became a perfect writing room where Minnie's litter could be hidden away. Its narrow window got sun all day. Also the flat was upstairs, and Minnie had always wanted to live upstairs.[19] After they moved in, Minnie described herself as becoming a 'fully fledged housekeeper with an allowance and a notebook'. However, her duties could not extend to cleaning. Although her health was somewhat restored, she was still unable to exert herself physically. A charlady, Mrs Tidey, was paid half a crown for three hours' work each day and treated Minnie 'with that indulgent tolerance afforded to those not quite like other people'.[20]

The move to Bexhill meant forsaking her half-acre corner plot. Minnie's tiny new garden faced north and was overshadowed by buildings so that much of it lay permanently in shade. Even so, Minnie was still sufficiently incapacitated for a gardener to be needed to sort it out.[21]

After the move to Bexhill, MacDonald, feeling out of touch, wrote:

> I have often been thinking about you and wondered where you were and, seeing a paragraph in a paper yesterday, I am having a shot at you. How are you really keeping? I wish I could come across you.

He understood that although her health was not good, 'life still remains tolerable' and wondered if she had got the letter that he had sent to her in Wales. His letter comes over as from a man lonely in both office and life as well as someone genuinely wondering about, and glad to be able to chat to, a close friend. Minnie replied immediately. Her only mention of health was of her throat. She still could not speak in public, 'otherwise it is quite a good throat'.[22]

Minnie had learned of the death of 'Cimmie' Mosley, who had died, 'fearful and defeated' of peritonitis in May, aged 34.[23] Cimmie had been uneasy with Mosley's turn to fascism, and suffered 'hell incarnate' through Oswald's affair with Diana [Mitford], who had left her husband to begin a public relationship with Mosley, of which 'the whole of London' seemed aware.[24] Minnie told MacDonald she would always regret not seeing Cimmie that year because 'from what I now know of her last few months, I think that perhaps she might have been quite glad to have had a tiny chat with an old friend'.[25] In spite of Cimmie's 1931 defection from Labour to support her husband's New Party and her banishment from Labour ranks, as with MacDonald, Minnie's preparedness to sustain friendships showed the value she placed on personal loyalty over political difference.

Compared with Brynmawr and Welwyn, Bexhill was conservative

and traditional. Minnie was much less in her natural habitat than anywhere she had previously lived. However, there were groups with which Minnie could identify. In October 1933, she attended a meeting of the local branch of the Women's Freedom League, where she was welcomed by the President, the redoubtable Mrs Dora Montefiore. The Bexhill and Hastings WFL branches were particularly active, supporting relief for Russia in 1922 and the Peace Makers' Pilgrimage in 1926 as well as opposing animal cruelty.[26] Montefiore was a legendary figure and had been active in the Social Democratic Federation and the suffrage movement, her home had been seized by bailiffs and she had been gaoled in Holloway prison for the suffrage cause. The pairing of Montefiore and Minnie would have been a formidable combination, and may well have been the renewing of an earlier acquaintanceship.[27] Now she said it was a pleasure to have Minnie there, with her promise to help the local branch whenever possible.

Minnie still experienced 'longings for a life that is over for ever, regrets that will not be silenced'. These could make her depressed. She wrote in the *Daily Herald*: 'There are times when the darkness of desolation still comes upon me. Sometimes there comes a great longing for movement and excitement.' Then, she said she would write a long letter to her blind friend [Willie] or think of other people with broken lives. 'I think of other[s'] clouds so black that there is not a vestige of silver lining. I remember these things, and turn to face life again.'[28]

Her regret at losing her political life is evident. However, for the first time in a long time she could now look at others and reflect that their circumstances were worse than her own.

While Minnie might lament the loss of her political life, her journalistic life was flourishing. *The Daily Herald* was sufficiently impressed by her writing that from July 1933, as well as regular general articles, she contributed on women's matters to a page of home tips and health and beauty. The *Herald* was no longer the radical campaigning paper of the Lansbury years, but writing for its two million readers was exhilarating. Minnie's light pieces about social justice, often based in human interest, fitted well with the paper's popular left-leaning style. Whereas she had been increasingly ill-fitted to the *New Leader*, her down-to-earth approach perfectly suited the less ideological *Daily Herald*.[29]

Minnie's articles addressed a range of issues related to women.

Two short pieces argued that women were martyring themselves to housework and should take opportunity to rest while working at home.[30] Another paid tribute to the contribution of 'maiden aunts'. The modern spinster, she argued, was regarded with suspicion and sometimes fear for taking men's jobs, having a career rather than home building and shirking motherhood. At a time of 'vehement anti-spinster rhetoric', she noted how the war had turned them from being viewed 'with mild pitying contempt, even a tolerant affection' and figures of fun, into being 'bachelor girls', who were 'emphatically not on the shelf' and considered by some as 'a Menace'.[31]

Minnie wrote of the former struggle for women's franchise rights by saying that women were not using their vote in order to achieve better homes and conditions, peace and social justice with the zeal with which they had fought for it. Pointing to fascist countries where women were being told to return to the home, she argued that women must use their votes or risk going back two hundred years. She argued that their children's futures and the housing, education and health care they received were in the hands of the women voter. For all its power, the piece developed into something of an anti-climax, an appeal for women to vote in the forthcoming country council elections because medical inspection, free milk, clinics and a host of other services that determined the quality of people's lives were the responsibilities of the councils now being elected. The end of the piece though was chilling: women had to take a stand against the forces of reaction, 'For let woman make no mistake, if she does not deal with reaction, it will deal with her.'[32]

In October, Minnie asked whether, in order to be able to aspire to equal pay for equal work with men, professional women should employ others to undertake domestic duties in their homes. The article provoked a tremendous response. Hundreds of readers replied for or against Minnie's position that women should not be conscientious, trying to do everything, but should overcome their guilt and employ someone else to do the housework, so allowing themselves time to rest and relax. Single women would then have the same energy for work as single men and married women should recognise that they should not expect to hold down a full-time job and be 'a cook, housemaid, housekeeper and nurse as well'.[33] [Ms] Cooper of Manchester responded: 'it slowly came to me that I was reading about myself... Thanks Miss Pallister for making me realise.'[34]

The *Daily Herald* was quick to appreciate Minnie's popular appeal. Recognising that her articles chimed with readers' lived experiences and evoked strong responses, the paper requested readers' views on Minnie's articles. It invited them to contact her at the paper to seek her advice on confidential and personal matters, as someone with 'an intimate knowledge of human affairs'.[35] At a time when the genre hardly existed, Minnie invented herself, almost by accident, as an agony aunt for the largest newspaper in the country. The themes she addressed resonated with her audience and elicited lively responses, including single women having affairs with older married men and older women marrying younger men.[36]

The mid-1930s was the time when such columns became a central feature of daily journalism.[37] Although others claimed to have originated the genre, Minnie's column preceded those of Ann Temple in the *Daily Mail* and Dorothy Dix in the *Daily Mirror* by a couple of years.[38] Minnie's was consciously located on the women's page, whereas Temple's was aimed equally at women and men.[39] Both approaches allowed women to raise issues they found impossible to discuss with relatives, friends or neighbours,[40] as such columns became 'an important source of advice and guidance on personal and sexual questions'.[41] Minnie's column had ceased by the time agony aunts entered their golden age.[42] However, at the very least she can be claimed as one of the pioneers.

As well as addressing personal issues, her column delivered social and economic messages. Gender imbalances were never far from the fore. In an exquisite play on words, Minnie's 'Unequal Home Work' argued that girls at school were entitled to the same interrupted time to do their homework as boys, rather than being expected to do 'Home Work' in helping their mothers around the house in the evening, while the boys' school homework time remained sacred. The responses to an article about a boy who did housework led to Minnie writing about how mothers could reduce the domestic strain they suffered by training their sons to do cooking, sewing and housework. After all, she pointed out, the most highly paid cooks, clothes makers and domestic workers were all men.[43] Minnie also wrote that housewives should do a little less around the house so that they had more energy to share companionship when the husband returned home from work.[44] Although expressed in the somewhat stilted language of interwar Britain, she called for greater sharing of domestic responsibilities between the sexes, and women becoming more inspired and emboldened to assume wider, fulfilling, roles.

Minnie appeared knowledgeable about complex areas of which she had no personal experience, such as parenting and constructing and sustaining a happy marriage,[45] but she also wrote on topics that carried the authority of direct experience, such as becoming a middle-aged woman. She repeatedly challenged the notion that the 'best days are over' for a woman in her fifties, for 'with all her rich experience, [she] is one of the most valuable people in the world'.[46]

Such themes were developed in a column Minnie wrote for the *Daily Mirror* between 1935 and 1937. Initially called 'A Cottage by the Sea', and later 'Housewife's Corner', it addressed 'the problems of women in later middle age' and was 'a kind of country women's diary', focussing on housekeeping and fashions, especially for aging women.[47] Her 'Autumn Comes to Us All', was a significant piece for middle-aged women who felt their lives had become 'stale'. On reaching 50, women did not need to resign themselves to 'middle-aged spread of both mind and body'; they should not bitterly resent lost youth as life could still be good. Although the word menopause was unmentioned and unmentionable, she argued that after the family had grown up, as her domestic responsibilities and the demands of motherhood reduced, a woman whose life had been spent serving the family could regain her personality and explore new interests. Rather than being seen as a sign of her losing her 'charm', middle age was an opportunity for a woman to become a person in her own right.[48] At one with herself at this stage of her life, Minnie was also a voice for other women of her generation.

*

The changes in the politics of the ILP meant that Minnie had lost her spiritual home. Consequently, from 1933 a decisive shift occurred in the way she channelled her energies. Henceforth she would engage in the two causes that would dominate her life: working with and through independent women's organisations in pursuit of woman-centred politics and pacifism.

Minnie recognised the potential in being involved with and speaking to all forms of women's organisations and she engaged at all levels. This included undertaking practical work, the delivery of services, promoting citizenship, and advocating feminist policies of radical social, economic and political change. Her choice of collaborators ranged from organisations that did not identify themselves as feminist to those that were avowedly feminist and was based on her assessment for achieving change, either with individuals or at a societal level.[49] Their range and scope was extensive. Minnie was chair of the Bexhill Labour Party women's section, was involved with the Women's Freedom League, and supported the Over 30s Association. Through much of the 1930s, she served on national committees of the Association of Girls' Clubs.[50] Her *Daily Herald* article promoting their work was a PR coup for the Association's 4,000 clubs.[51] Early in the Second World War, Minnie started speaking at meetings of Women's Institutes (WI) and remained committed to them and Townswomen's Guilds for the rest of her life. From 1943, shortly after it came into existence, she was associated with Women for Westminster, and became a speaker for the Open Door Council, which sought equal economic opportunities for women. Immediately after the Second World War, Minnie promoted Equal Citizens and became involved with the National Council of Women.

Minnie was impressed at how women ran conferences with 'amazing efficiency'. She made the point that when they went to conferences, women had to pay a price for attending, doing double the work the day before, then getting up early to prepare everything for the family and feed the children before leaving home. She mischievously wondered if it might be a 'good idea to put every able bodied male on the land or in a workshop where he could be producing something useful and be out of mischief comparatively, and hand over all administrative work to our Women's Organisations'.[52]

Her other great cause was pacifism. Although Minnie had been occasionally involved in the No More War Movement, her pacifism had not been to the fore. However, Hitler's coming to power on 30 January 1933 was a watershed moment. International politics and the rise of fascism required pacifists to examine their politics and principles in deciding how they should respond. Paradoxically, an upsurge in pacifism in some was paralleled by many others accepting the need to give it up in favour of some form of deterrence to fight fascism.[53]

The politics of British pacifism was complicated by the political crisis of 1931 and the July 1932 disaffiliation of the ILP from the Labour Party.[54] Just as the ILP's political problems had affected Minnie in the *New Leader*, so it impacted on the No More War Movement (NMWM), which was split between a purist ultra-leftist majority who saw a revolutionary situation emerging, and a pro-Labour faction which supported the League of Nations. The majority on its national committee was unwilling to compromise with what they considered a League of imperialist and capitalist governments.[55] Considering themselves to be a vanguardist leadership, the majority dismissed 'paralysing unity' with "pacifists" [their inverted commas] who interpreted events differently.[56] It hardly provided a platform for building peace within pacifism.

The situation was not helped when, in September 1932, 'Reggie' Reynolds became NMWM General Secretary at the age of 27. Although a Quaker associate of Gandhi, he was described as 'arrogant, intransigent, cantankerous and altogether a pain in the neck'.[57] He joined the ILP as it split from the Labour Party, and he accompanied the NMWM down its revolutionary road.[58] By late 1932, absolute pacifists like Minnie could barely make their voices heard above the revolutionary rhetoric.[59]

The NMWM was ailing.[60] Runham Brown, (who Minnie had been identified to replace in the NCF in 1916) had been on the NMWM national committee since its foundation, but he now resigned, recommending either 'admit[ting] defeat' and shutting down the organisation, or dramatically reducing its operations, including closing its paper.[61] By the end 1933, the NMWM had stopped most of its propaganda activities and its *New World* had ceased publication.[62] There was also strain between the federations and the national committee, with the Midlands Federation exercising its independence of mind and strength to become autonomous and free-standing.[63]

It was into this tangle that Minnie stepped, probably unwisely, in January 1934, to revive and edit the *No More War* journal. She would need all her wits to cope. Sponsored by the Midlands Federation, against a backdrop of a fraught international situation, Minnie was now editing the only large-scale pacifist paper in the country. This may have been facilitated by Katharine Bruce Glasier, who was on the editorial board and had 'done' forty peace meetings in the Midlands the previous October and November. Minnie worked under the management of Will Rowe, the area secretary and organiser.[64] Centred on the Midlands but with a perspective that was also national and international, Minnie made 'our little paper', which initially had a print run of 5,000 copies, into a journal of substance. Calling on friends, collaborators and contacts, including Angell and Russell to provide articles, Minnie garnered support from a galaxy of prominent literary, civic and political figures.[65] The paper wove articles by prominent pacifists with the work by churches, Sunday schools and youth groups and made evident the potential power of the movement with its demonstrations, meetings, events and conferences. Minnie's uncompromising editorials were rallying cries in favour of democracy and against fascism. The gravity of political events in the summer of 1934 meant the demand for speakers was as high as during winter months.[66] By November circulation had doubled to 10,000, 'which I think is marvellous for a small voluntary paper' and it made a profit.[67]

From the beginning there was anxiety within the NMWM National Committee about Minnie's editing of the journal. Concern that her editorial line did not represent NMWM policy led the national committee to nominate Wilfred Wellock, the NMWM chair, to 'co-operate closely' with Minnie to insist on its contents reflecting agreed policy. When she 'practically ignored' paragraphs written by Reynolds and substituted her own, she was seen to have seriously erred.[68] Things got worse when she provided space for others from outside the NMWM to present views counter to the NMWM line. Angell, the doyen of international affairs and prominent in the League of Nations Union wrote a two-page spread supporting collective security, necessitating Wellock to counter, arguing for unilateral disarmament.[69]

In July, Minnie was among delegates from twenty-one different countries who attended the War Resister's International conference at Digswell. Reynolds spoke against the collective security approach of the labour movement. The conference adopted an impossibilist plan for mobilising anti-war forces across countries, including refusing military and non-combatant service, or any other work which contributed to war and refusing to pay taxes. Proposals included unarmed mass opposition, direct action, general strikes, and encouraging disaffection amongst the military.[70] How such resistance would be implemented was left for individual countries to consider. It cannot have been easy for Minnie who, while an ardent pacifist, was realist enough to despair at such ultra-leftist posturing.

Not that Minnie's own position was without contradictions. For while her pacifism was based in a refusal to fight and an unerring application of Christian principles, she thought that working for peace through the League should not be discounted. This view was shared, it seems, by most pacifists in 1934–5, for they broadly accepted some collective security actions, whilst not being prepared to carry them out themselves.[71]

As well as being editor of *No More War*, Minnie undertook other pacifist activities. In January, a ferocious article in the *Daily Herald* railed against 'the cant of war'. War, with its 'mystic, spiritual, cleansing' of courage, sacrifice and endeavour, was instead based in cruelty, filth and slaughter. Peace was not 'a flabby, spineless affair', which made men 'soft', nor an easy coward's way out. It was war that was flabby and spineless. War could come about easily through a 'policy of drift', weakness, corruption and greed. Avoiding war was more difficult. It required diplomacy, foresight, knowledge and skill. War, which had nothing to do with honour, national security or saving civilisation, could only be stopped when people believed that war itself was wrong and when Christians and others were prepared to obey the command 'Thou Shalt Not Kill'.[72] H. R. Tadgell wrote to the paper praising Minnie's article as 'one of the finest, simplest and plainest articles on peace I have ever read'. He had bought copies for various people in positions of authority, adding it should be reprinted in pamphlet form and distributed to every head of a religious denomination and to every youth leader in the country.[73] In spite of the praise, there was nothing original in her words. While cogently argued, forthright and articulate, she had made the points repeatedly over previous decades. Now the timing gave them punch.

That summer a Peace Ballot supported by the League of Nations Union was announced. Minnie joined the Bexhill committee to conduct it. It had wide popular support.[74] During the months it took to organise the Ballot, considerable propaganda work was undertaken. Norman Angell spent one of the most satisfying months of his career on the road promoting it. As he appeared in Bexhill he learned he had been awarded the Nobel Peace Prize. Minnie thought his speech 'magnificent', adding, 'I had no idea you were so eloquent, eminent people aren't always!'[75]

Minnie's editorship of *No More War* lasted a year. The factors that made the paper attractive to readers, including its freedom from dogma, were anathema to the National Committee. Simultaneously envious of the journal's success and appalled at Minnie's deviation from 'the line', the sectarians on the committee determined to take it over.[76] On 3 November a representative of the National Committee met the Midlands Council to oversee the journal's transfer from January 1935. For appearances sake, Minnie was to be included on a small board which would control the paper.[77]

Minnie explained to Angell:

> The National Committee is now taking it over so I shall not be doing it anymore. I am not altogether sorry as it means a lot of work, and also I am not altogether in agreement with some of my people, who I think are too censorious towards the League and the Labour Party... I of course take the view that personal repudiation of war is of the utmost importance, as no war can be entered into without the support of public opinion, but that does not mean that I do not think that every kind of work is also important. [78]

It is interesting that, in spite of profound political differences, through loyalty and historic bonds, Minnie still identified the ultra-leftists as 'my people' even as the non-communist but revolutionary NMWM continued down its futile path.[79]

The NMWM's narrow dogmatism proved disastrous. Under a new editor, from January 1935, the paper followed a sectarian line.[80] NMWM membership, and the circulation of *No More War*, declined.[81] After the Italian assault on Abyssinia in late 1935 and the forces of war gathering strength, the NMWM reported that the 'voice of pacifism has become a voice crying in the wilderness'.[82] However, the foundation of the Peace Pledge Union in 1936 would prove that there was ample opportunity for a loud pacifist voice, but that the shrill sectarianism of the NMWM was striking the wrong note.

Minnie retained her close affinity with South Wales. From 1933, Minnie visited each summer, writing regularly about the plight of the valleys. A moving St David's Day piece chronicled 'the deadness of despair' as South Wales 'lay in chains, waiting'. A year later she wrote of 'a land of dead souls', moving George Barker, former miners' agent and the MP for Abertillery until 1929, to write to the *Daily Herald* that Minnie's article was 'unsurpassable'.[83] When the miners at Nine Mile Point Colliery in Cwmfelinfach attracted worldwide attention in 1935 by conducting a week-long Stay in Strike against 'scab' unionists, Minnie wrote that the strikers were being treated 'almost like outlaws', and described the different forms of hardship suffered by miners' wives in times of employment and unemployment.[84] In her accounts of Wales, Minnie often featured the National Eisteddfod. Pointing out it was not divorced from ordinary lives, she described people attending wearing shabby and threadbare suits. Timbermen, electricians and fitters no longer had need to make elaborate arrangements to switch shifts to compete at the festival, for they would not have worked for some time and had no prospect of working again.[85]

Minnie used her intimate knowledge of Brynmawr, one of the earliest areas to suffer economic hardship and where 60 per cent of miners had been unemployed for a prolonged period, to present sympathetic portrayals.[86] She had left for Porthcawl just before Brynmawr's local economy collapsed. Now, so desperate had the situation become, that books were being published about the suffering of the communities of Brynmawr, Blaina and Nantyglo.[87] Minnie's articles 'Beauty from a Rubbish Heap' and 'Transforming a Devastated Town' looked at the plight of Brynmawr and the efforts of the Quakers to ameliorate the situation.[88] While the Quakers' role in interwar South Wales could be seen as negative in disempowering communities capable of organising themselves without the need for outside intervention, Minnie supported such efforts, recognising that 'the experiments in communal working and living...were carried out by groups of men driven to them by unbearable sorrow'.[89]

On 1 November 1934, Minnie published a memoir, *A Cabbage for a Year*, about her illness and recovery. The book omitted her years of being bedridden or invalided between 1927 and 1932, and fast forwarded from her diagnosis in 1926 to the first year of her recuperation in Bexhill in 1933. Even so, it was an early example of an 'illness memoir', a phenomenon that was comparatively rare at the time, with book-length accounts of such personal suffering only becoming common in the 1950s.[90] The flyleaf described the book as a bridge between having been 'on the threshold of a brilliant political career' and having a completely different existence when incapacity struck. Minnie gave the book a light and positive tone. Only later in the decade, when she was well on the way to recovery, would she write fully and openly about the physical and psychological impact of her illness. *A Cabbage for a Year* could be seen as the first stage in a process of repair.

The deal with Blackie's was good. Minnie received £30 on the date of publication, plus 12½ per cent royalties on the first 2,000 copies and 15 per cent thereinafter, plus 12½ per cent on worldwide sales, except in the USA.[91] On publication day she wrote to MacDonald: 'Tomorrow...I succumb in desperation to the Spirit of the Times, and have my first "perm"', perhaps as self-reward.[92] However, a few weeks later she expressed concern to Angell at the book's muted reception in the press.[93] A sympathetic review in the *Times Literary Supplement*, complimenting her shrewd and witty observations and deftly sketched characters, broke the silence. A glowing review in the *Bookman* offset the brief mention in the *Daily Herald*.[94] However, in time, *Cabbage* was picked up and amplified far and wide, particularly across the Empire.[95]

For decades Minnie's writings reached huge audiences through worldwide syndication.[96] Even in remote and obscure publications, such as in *Kaja* in Estonia or *UFA – the Official Organ of the United Farmers of Alberta, the Alberta Wheat Pool and Other Provincial Marketing Pools*, her work challenged perceptions.[97] One article from the *New Leader* on the length of women's skirts was picked up, for example, by the *Hanover Evening Sun* of Pennsylvania, the *Toronto Daily Star* and the 'Woman's World' page of the *Auckland Star*. With a turn of phrase which could always attract attention, Minnie said skirts were 'stupid' because they 'attempt[ed] to join together what Nature has put asunder', adding the sooner skirts disappeared the better. The article's humour carried a serious message – that unlike the Victorian artificial flower, post-war women were real people whose lives would not permit the return of such clothing. She advocated wearing knee breeches saying the way you dressed shaped the way you thought and acted. 'Freedom of limb is as important as freedom of mind – indeed it is doubtful whether it is possible to have full freedom of mind without freedom of limb.'[98]

Minnie's writings had an impact on women in other countries. Some examples from the Australian women's labour movement indicate that they were used repeatedly to frame debates and illuminate issues. When May Holman, the first woman in the Australian Labour Party and its second woman parliamentarian, broadcast on 24 October 1933, to coincide with the annual conference of the Western Australian Labor Women's Organisation and the 21st anniversary of the First Conference of Labour Women held in that state, she based her talk heavily on Minnie's *Socialism for Women*. Even though it was by then nearly a decade old, Holman's talk recited its foreword verbatim. Two months later the *Westralian Worker*'s 'Women's Sphere' again quoted from it under the subtitle 'A Maxim for Women', as did 'Everywoman's Health' in Brisbane's *The Worker*.[99]

Australian women did not simply copy Minnie's writings, they analysed, adapted and applied her thinking to the Australian context. In October 1934 the 'Of Interest to Women' page of *Voice of Hobart*, Tasmania, drew on a *Daily Herald* article of February 1934 called 'Women Must Use Their Votes' to set the context for a piece on women's voting in the recent Australian Federal elections.[100] Three years later, Minnie's article 'Can Women Be Non-party?', published in the British TUC journal *Labour*, made an immediate impact in Australia.[101] Her argument, that too many women saw the granting of the vote as the end in itself, which would automatically bring peace and security, rather than recognise that it only provided the means to build a future, was reproduced on the 'For Worker Women' page of *The Australian Worker*, and adapted to Australian circumstances to ask whether a Woman's Party should be formed in New South Wales.[102] Although Minnie's own efforts by this time were being invested primarily in the British peace movement, her earlier thinking continued to help shape the Australian national labour women's agenda.[103]

In late 1934 Minnie told MacDonald that her publisher, Blackie, wanted her to do a 'short autobiographical sketch' of her time in Wales, including 'the Aberavon adventure'. She said she contributed nothing 'to the spate of words which was written after the fight as

I did not like the idea of appearing in any way to make use of my work there for journalistic purposes.' While it seemed 'rotten' to write about people, she said, a Prime Minister could not be private, so she asked MacDonald's permission. She proposed giving 'the world a picture of you during those three years', emphasising that his career and return to the House of Commons after the war formed an important part of history. She suggested a personal and intimate account of their work but 'with no political controversies much'. Addressing MacDonald's concern that it would be about 'happy crusading times' rather than 'politics being a dirty game', she posited it as a 'statement of the feeling in the valleys and its gradual surrender to you'. She intended to finish the book about the time of the General Strike 'when I died'. If he objected, she would try writing a novel instead, though she acknowledged she could not write fiction. MacDonald replied that he hoped to write an autobiography himself at some point that would have no spiteful or nasty comments on anyone, but was sure that she would also write in that spirit. He encouraged her to go ahead and hoped that it would bring her a reasonable income.[104]

By May, Minnie had nearly finished her manuscript. Wanting to ensure that she was reflecting MacDonald's views on Aberavon correctly, she requested to see him. When offered an appointment at 10 Downing Street for 30 May, Minnie accepted but raised with Rose Rosenberg rumours that MacDonald intended to reshuffle his Cabinet during the Whitsun recess. Minnie quipped:

> Well he just can't *do* that, because there mustn't be any political crises or anything until the book is ready. So if you have arranged anything for Whitsun, it is definitely off!!!!![105]

Having sent MacDonald advance rough copies of the chapters that referred to him, by the time she went to see him, her publisher had already said they liked the draft manuscript.[106] The Downing Street meeting occurred as MacDonald planned the reshaping of the Government. A week later he gave up the premiership and became Lord President of the Council. However, for reasons that are unknown, the book did not proceed.

Minnie was getting back into her stride. Years of pain and weakness were slowly replaced by a sense of 'coming back to life'. Physically revived, New Year's Eve 1935 was spent in Piccadilly

Circus and she saw John Gielgud playing Hamlet.[107] Now the simplest action was an adventure. She described running all the way to post a letter and back 'for the sheer joy of being able to run again'.[108] MacDonald noted the spring in her correspondence.[109] A five-day music festival in Hastings was used by Minnie to frown on the folly of countries 'speaking to one another with guns and bombs' instead of with strings. With conductors from Germany and Russia and the works of great masters and modern composers, she claimed music as an international language. She also looked forward to music, art and travel being a normal part of ordinary people's lives, not just the privilege of the elite.[110] On the same day that the *Bexhill Observer* reviewed *Cabbage,* Vera Brittain addressed an exceptionally large audience on the *Testament of Youth* for the Bexhill Lecture Society.[111]

While no royalist, Minnie loved pomp. During the 1935 Jubilee of King George V and Queen Mary she stood on a box from 7 am to 11 am outside Coutts Bank in Piccadilly, to which she reported having just transferred her overdraft, to watch MacDonald pass. Applying it to pacifism she later wrote: 'I like grandeur in civic life. I don't see why peace should be content to trail about in a limp nightgown, while war glitters with scarlet and gold.'[112] However, while she might love ceremony, with her eye for ordinary people, rather than the occasion itself, the focus of her *Daily Herald* Jubilee article was not on the majesty, but on the street cleaners who afterwards spent hours collecting tons of litter.[113]

By 1936, with a regular column in the *Daily Herald* and occasional columns in the *Daily Mirror*, her journalistic career was becoming established. Although her pieces in *The Bookman* had tailed off in 1934, she had articles in Odham's lively weekly magazine, *The Passing Show*, as well as in *Labour* and *Labour Woman*, including a review of Barratt Brown's *Great Democrats*, in which she praised the builders of democratic institutions such as trades unions and organisations that promoted women's rights for taking pain and poverty from lives. Women had reached undreamed of heights of freedom and a 'new dignity has come to Labour'. 'Suffering today' she argued, was 'maintained only by our own slackness' in not using the powers already won for ordinary people. Five years earlier, she had written of fascist and communist dictatorships being a result of democracies being unable to live up to their responsibilities.[114] Now she argued that reform should not be enforced but built on the will of the people. This approach was superior to seizing factories and institutions by force and avoiding the hatred and violence that ensued. There were no shortcuts, as all forms of dictatorship disregarded the individuals who made up the masses. War, poverty, insecurity, ignorance and disease could be conquered by the twin weapons of industrial combination and political power, claimed Minnie in her manifesto to the future.[115]

From December 1936, Minnie edited and wrote the 'Woman's Page' of *Man and Metal*, the monthly journal of the trades union, the Iron and Steel Trades Confederation.[116] Much of the journal's content was centred on the numerous metal-working plants in South Wales. Unlike coal, tinplate employed many women and Minnie wrote knowledgably about the different stages of tinplate production and the skills, dexterity and intelligence of the women employed there. She sought to strike a relationship with them through her pages and wished to discuss problems affecting their homes, industry, market place, leisure and children, and she invited feedback and comments.[117] To those hundreds of mothers from whom she had received letters over the years who said they had no time of their own, were unable to get out in the evenings and had become out of touch with the outside world, Minnie's articles encouraged their active involvement. She proposed they attend meetings of the labour and co-operative movements to find an interest outside of themselves as well as to learn. She prompted them to attend classes and also suggested they visit art galleries to study the lives of previous generations of women.[118]

Minnie had the freedom of the Women's Page to unashamedly promote her socialist, Christian and feminist views. Fusing her faith and politics, she explained Christian doctrine in terms of trades union, co-operative and Labour Party work. She wrote of the dignity of ordinary workers such as the milkman, fisherman or postman, and of the importance of being in a union. When she realised that many local bakers would not recognise the union and provided inferior wages and conditions rather than unionised bakeries, she started baking herself (an added benefit was that kneading exercised her arms and shoulders).[119] She considered social questions including providing a class analysis of child delinquency that was rooted in her understanding of ordinary lives. As it was difficult to get working women organised in trades unions, she attended the Domestic Services Exhibition to visit the stalls dealing with the drive to unionise domestic workers. She also suggested work areas women could occupy, such as preaching.[120]

As international events worsened, Minnie continued to argue unapologetically for peace, opposed militarism and was implacably against any involvement in another war, saying that the focus should be on poverty, slums and hunger. Echoing a moving piece by Margaret and Rachel McMillan and their advocacy of nurseries as women and children needed protection from everyday issues of overcrowding, fear and anxiety, and illnesses, for they were just as deadly as air raids, Minnie called on the Government to spend as much money building homes as on battleships.[121] Uncomfortably for the readers of *Man and Metal*, who had been suffering unemployment in the metal industries, Minnie criticised rearmament as a waste of resources that could be better invested elsewhere, such as building roads and homes.[122] An article encouraging voting in local elections perceptively argued that the main enemy was not those with extremist views but the apathetic who had no particular views at all.[123]

Writing for a wide range of publications with a diverse range of audiences involved using a variety of styles, Minnie's shorter and lighter pieces in the *Daily Herald* contrasted with the longer and more serious articles in *Man and Metal*. Her political journalism, woman's pages, book reviews or short stories, like those of Holtby, Brittain and Macaulay, brought together politics and writing, melding them to shape opinion.[124]

Time and Tide was the most significant periodical for women writers and an obvious outlet for Minnie. In February 1935 she asked Angell to help her get published in its pages. His review, *Foreign Affairs*, had been incorporated into *Time and Tide* in 1931 and he continued to edit it as a supplement for the next decade. Claiming, disingenuously, that she did not want special treatment, she asked him to use his 'great influence with Lady Rhondda' and 'put in a word for me'.[125] Reminding Angell of her own political profile, Minnie argued that 'as one of the representative women of the political life of the country for some years, I think a paper like *Time and Tide* might consider taking something of mine or at least letting me do a little reviewing', arguing that she was qualified for the work.

The owner, editor and driving force of *Time and Tide*, Lady Rhondda, Minnie felt, was outwardly committed to promoting equal opportunities for women. However, between two-thirds and three-quarters of the review's writers had always been men, some of whom were published anonymously, and in later years Rhondda felt obliged to go through drafts of the magazine removing women's names, as she believed to include them would negatively affect circulation and advertising.[126] While Minnie enjoyed *Time and Tide*, her feelings were thinly masked. She fulminated that much of its output was given to 'well-known men who are already snowed under with work and have more than they can do as well as all the money they can possibly want'. Saying she couldn't help but be amused at its feminist attacks on men, Minnie expressed indignation at '[t]he feminist [who] has such a lot to say about women being given no chance by selfish man'. Instead she countered, 'I don't know what would become of some of us if the man had not more consideration for us than our sister women.'[127]

As Holtby, who had helped Minnie obtain work at *The Bookman*, was one of the directors of *Time and Tide* until her death, Minnie had not been without allies. However, having been in touch several times with various women associated with the publication, Minnie had 'never received the slightest encouragement to contribute in any way'.[128] Angell replied straight away saying that he was 'passing on immediately a little hint to Lady Rhondda and I hope that it will be taken' and that something might come her way as a result.[129] However, even with the support of Angell, Minnie was unable to break into the magazine.

Could Minnie's lack of success have been based on Lady Rhondda having not forgotten Minnie's stinging review of her *Leisured Women* in the *New Leader* seven years earlier? Or perhaps it lay in the criticism in *No More War* when, less than a year earlier, Minnie said that Lady Rhondda had not wanted the 'best man' to win the Great War, but 'England', and she didn't want the war to stop until 'England' had won.[130] Perhaps Minnie should have expected being passed over by Rhondda.

In March 1935, Minnie reached 50 years of age and was at a stage to reflect. Over the previous decade, her health, economic circumstances and housing had provided huge handicaps. Having lost her career, she was rebuilding her physical life after years of illness and was embarking on a new professional life. Looking back, she was now able to identify her insecurities and talk about them. After a decade of experiencing real difficulties, she realised that her earlier anxieties, such as worrying over her thick ankles when younger to the point that she could not see her other virtues, had been needless. Even so, she could still be crippled by insecurity and depression, and even in older age still could not sleep in a house on her own.

It is impossible not to read her advice columns referring to the impact of a chronic lack of self-confidence or of the importance of crying as a means of easing disappointment, sorrow or bitterness, without seeing them as in part based in personal experience. As she put it: 'All life is a process of growth and struggle, of trial and error, of seeking out the best paths. Experience can only be gained at a price, the price often of suffering.'[131] When she wrote of baring one's soul and admitting to past indiscretions with disastrous results, she said it was people who had led comparatively blameless lives who suffered most from the shame of having departed slightly from their own high standards. Now she believed it was wiser to bury the past 'if the matter is past and over and can have no bearing whatever on present behaviour'. She counselled against sharing confidences with friends that were much better kept private. She concluded:

> What living person has nothing at all to regret? After all, it is far more important to live well in the present than to brood over the mistakes of a dead past.[132]

If in coming to terms with herself Minnie had forgiven herself for past errors and was determined to live for the day, her openness with others about her own personal struggles was part of her process for coping with them.

*

Minnie's life took an unexpected turn when a friend sent one of her books to his cousins in Germany. Consequently, Minnie was invited to stay with the Schwarbs, a Jewish family, in their gigantic flat in Frankfurt.[133] What a time to go! In August 1936, the Berlin Olympics were underway and weeks earlier the Nazi regime had started to provide military support to Franco against the republican government in Spain. Telling MacDonald she hoped to sail on 7 August, she said:

> am taking my courage in my hands firmly, and going, all by myself. I shall try to keep my eyes open and my mouth closed,

but in case I get into prison, I shall rely on you to hop into an aeroplane and fly to my rescue![134]

For three weeks Minnie shared the Schwarbs' life, which 'combined modern culture with something of the patriarchal life of the Old Testament'.[135] Although she had a marvellous time, ominous signs were all-pervasive. In spite of the Nazi regime being on its best behaviour during the Olympics, Minnie saw cafe signs that read 'Jews Not Welcome Here', and the Schwarbs were no longer allowed in the swimming baths or tennis club. Although the family had been in the town since the fifteenth century and had been great patrons of the arts, the host and his wife could not accompany Minnie to see the State Opera perform *Der Rosenkavalier*.[136] Of Jews being banned from holding certain occupations Minnie commented:

> Magnificent men who had held good positions in public medical services etc sacked. Can't see the end of it. They lavished every sort of kindness on me, and I feel I can make no return.[137]

In spite of the warning signs, the Schwarb family stayed in Germany, hoping that the situation would improve. Minnie's time would come.

Back home after the summer, she sold 'House Proud in a Flat', on the Schwarbs home, to the *Passing Show* and wrote for the *Daily Mirror* about the food she had eaten. However, while she told friends, other than passing reference in her account for *Man and Metal*, she made no public comment about what was happening to the Jews in the Nazi state.[138] Minnie's Frankfurt visit and seeing fascism through the eyes of Jewish friends made clear to her the nature of Hitler's regime. Yet her attitude towards Germany was complex. She wished to build bridges to an 'enemy' perceived to have been treated unfairly over the Versailles treaty and reparations.[139] Over the next three years Minnie wrestled to avoid war while supporting victims of Hitler.

1936 was a key year for the pacifist movement. The Italian invasion of Abyssinia of October 1935 was followed by the remilitarisation of the Rhineland in March and the outbreak of the Spanish Civil War in July. With the limitations of the League of Nations exposed, the peace movement polarised. Some saw the need to confront fascism, and the Spanish Civil War caused the vast majority of socialists to change their position and resist. Minnie was among a tiny minority of socialists who remained pacifist.[140]

The founding meeting of the Peace Pledge Union occurred on 22 May 1936. Although initially only open to men, membership was opened to women after a month and Minnie became one of its first female members.[141] Local PPU groups were organised across the country. Bexhill and District group developed a programme of monthly meetings, a weekly study circle and a library of pacifist literature. As part of a national strategy, the group donated *Peace News* to the public library each week.[142] Although Ceadel discounts the PPU as being a 'minority movement without political influence', by October 1937, membership reached 120,000. *Peace News*'s circulation reached 20,000, which makes the 10,000 circulation of Minnie's *No More War* journal, without a national organisation behind it, all the more remarkable.[143]

Minnie supported the central PPU position that nothing was worse than war. Pacifism was an alternative in all circumstances and complete disarmament the best defence to deter aggressors. The PPU did not support reducing armaments, instead believing in a complete renunciation of war, with men refusing to fight and women refusing to support the machinery of war.[144] Minnie fitted within that section of the PPU identified as being puritan activists – non-smoking, vegetarian, teetotallers with an inclination towards self-righteousness – although increasing numbers of secular, humanitarian pacifists were also attracted.[145]

By early 1937 Minnie considered herself 'very fit'.[146] As she grew stronger she gradually did more in the garden, including what she described as 'real gardening' – digging, planting and watering. Previously in order to sow a few seeds, first the gardener had to undertake all the preparations and spread the soil afterwards, leading her to comment to MacDonald that she was a hypocrite in writing about gardening while other people did the work (as well as admitting to 'turn[ing] a thoroughly dishonest penny by writing about housekeeping, knowing less than nothing of the subject').[147] But she found her limits. On a cold November day she dug up 'very obstinate' roots in the garden and the following day washed clothes. As a consequence, the ulnar nerve in her left arm seized, resulting in severe pain in her elbow. Twisting and turning in bed at night, she resorted to painkilling tablets and had to hold her arm in a sling. Painful attacks of neuritis could last for weeks. Although her health continued to recover, she lived under the constant shadow of possible relapse.[148]

Minnie had been meaning to write to MacDonald for some time, and now responded to a message from him. Methuen (who had published *Gardener's Frenzy*) was interested in Minnie's 'South Wales' book with MacDonald the highlight in some chapters. Minnie considered Tiltman's 1929 biography of MacDonald 'rather stodgy' and references in other biographies not 'very generous'. She suggested that if they talked for a few hours she could produce 'some fine chapters' and wondered if he had any letters and documents she could see.[149]

On Sunday 11 April she arrived at Hampstead for supper, wearing a new coffee-coloured coat with Renaissance sleeves 'that will surprise you' as it made her 'look like Queen Elizabeth at her most hag-like'. She had instructed MacDonald: 'don't let anyone else come because I want you to talk and talk' and set an agenda for them to follow. She stayed late and hoped she had not kept him up.[150] However, in spite of Methuen's interest, for reasons unknown, again the book did not proceed.

Blackie's still wanted a historical biography. Minnie preferred to do a study of the seventeenth century Lady Anne Clifford, who had spent much of her life in a prolonged legal battle to gain her inheritance of the family estates. Minnie considered the story of a brave, determined and resourceful woman, who fought against the odds for decades, to be 'very out of the ordinary' but Blackie's thought Lady Anne 'too unknown' and suggested alternative subjects. However, Minnie decided to proceed anyway and went to Cambridge for background research.[151]

In early September, Minnie travelled via Paris to Switzerland for three weeks' holiday. She had a 'fleeting glimpse' of the Paris exhibition – the Exposition Internationale des Arts et Techniques dans la Vie Moderne. It was a 'highly charged political atmosphere... with the pavilions of the USSR and Nazi Germany glowering opposite each other'; the Spanish pavilion exhibited Picasso's *Guernica*[152] and the unofficial Peace Pavilion and Tower of Peace, built near the main entrance, received 30 to 40,000 visitors a day.[153] Minnie had come to regard such visits as 'part of the ordinary life'. As she sat in open-air cafes watching the world go by, she now thought

Paris, with its teeming street life, cosmopolitan rather than tawdry.[154] The city, though, highlighted her insecurities. She realised, 'I can stand on my own feet more or less in England, but abroad I'm a completely clinging female.'[155]

MacDonald died on 9 November on board a ship, bound for a South American holiday. Minnie's sense of loss at the sudden ending of a decades-long relationship would have been heavy. Between 1926 and 1937 each had demonstrated unwavering personal loyalty when the other faced adversity. After his death, two new biographies contested his legacy. L. MacNeill Weir, MacDonald's Parliamentary Private Secretary, wrote a highly critical *The Tragedy of Ramsay MacDonald*. Lord Elton described it as 'not a biography but an embittered attack' and countered with his own sympathetic *The Life of Ramsay MacDonald* which Minnie and Ivor Thomas supported, providing Elton with information, anecdotes and correspondence.[156]

Four years later Minnie reviewed Howard Spring's *Fame is the Spur* about a poor boy who rose to become a Labour Cabinet Minister. Hamer Shawcross, the lead character whose motivation was 'to work for the under-dog' becomes tainted by his own ambition and love of the limelight. Whilst not mentioning that the character was supposedly based on MacDonald, she observed, 'His tragedy is that of the man who, when he himself tastes the [sweets] of the system he attacks, cannot keep his hatred of it, a tragedy which has happened too often in real life.'[157] And that is probably as close to Minnie got to publicly judging the political trajectory of her friend MacDonald.

When Gollancz published George Orwell's *Road to Wigan Pier* in March 1937, Minnie added it to her list of books to read, although she did not buy a copy until January 1938. Then she read it straight away and became so engaged that she wrote immediately to Orwell, explaining that while she did not 'often bother strangers with long screeds', for *Wigan Pier* she made an exception.[158] Orwell would have been aware of Minnie from her regular articles and reviews in the *Daily Herald* and *New Leader*. Saying she was particularly drawn to his final chapters 'with which I don't altogether agree', she acknowledged some of his points were well made. It belied what was to follow. As with Bertrand Russell two decades earlier, Minnie tackled Orwell head-on, addressing his arguments point by point, before informing him how out of touch he was.

Explaining her conversion to socialism, Minnie addressed his comments on middle-class socialists and on relations between the working and middle classes. She did not mention that she had lived and worked for twenty years in industrial areas, that more than a decade earlier she had written about conditions in Wigan from a woman's perspective, nor that in 1934 she had visited the unemployed of the Wigan district.[159] Instead she argued those who came to socialism through poverty sometimes held the mistaken idea that capitalists and capitalism were to blame, which resulted in a 'great waste of time and ammunition'. For them the 'real position' was obscured by their hard conditions. Instead, the early movement was based on seeking 'justice and liberty', while 'the class war in its narrow and often utterly untrue sense was superimposed and never part of our own movement'. She considered 'the parrot back-chat of the communists ha[d] much to answer for' in shaping Orwell's views.

Her distaste of the Communist Party was evident as, perhaps more surprisingly, was her continued identification with 'my own ILP', which Orwell too would join that summer.[160] She blamed 'the present deplorable condition of the LP [Labour Party]' on both the Communist Party and the 'foolish action' of the ILP in 'flirting with Russia', the result, she said, of weakness and vanity on the part of some ILP leaders who wished to stand large on the international stage. Minnie would later broadcast that the decline in influence of the ILP resulting from its disaffiliation from the Labour Party was a major tragedy and that the united front with the CP was disastrous.[161]

Orwell had not long returned from Spain, where he had been wounded fighting for the Republic. When his *Homage to Catalonia* was published, three months after her letter, he recounted having to go on the run from the Communist Party. There his antipathy to the Communist Party found full expression. When she read it, Minnie would have realised that in their criticisms of the Communist Party she and Orwell were as one.

However, Minnie took exception to Orwell's depiction of those socialists about whom he was dismissive as 'sniffily superior, middle class, pacifist, feminist, teetotaller, vegetarian food-cranks and eccentric sandal-wearing creeping Jesus types', and 'Nature Cure quacks' who attended ILP summer schools and lived in Welwyn Garden City. This broadside was so close to home it could have been written about Minnie personally.[162] She criticised Orwell for 'your continuous use of "Fruit juice drinker"' as a term of reproach, adding, 'I think you are almost as lacking in reality as the communist with his prattle of ideologies etc.' She said, 'far from socialists being inferior people, all the nicest people I know seem to be socialists, so much so that it always comes a shock to me when I find a decent person who is a conservative.' However, Minnie's comments on some working-class people displayed just as much prejudice as Orwell had showed towards middle-class socialists. She wrote, 'I really can't see that the man whose horizons [are] bounded on one side by a glass of beer and on the other by a football pool, is going to be of much use in fighting for justice and liberty.' In her wide-ranging analysis, Minnie also said Orwell was 'a bit confused' over machines, pointing out the contradiction in his arguments about industrialisation. Minnie stated that she was going to buy all Orwell's other books and reread *Wigan Pier* and enclosed a stamped addressed envelope, although it is not known if he replied. The issues addressed by Minnie reflected the concerns of Gollancz, the book's publisher, who found Orwell's comments so 'provocative' that he wrote a foreword to the Left Book Club edition, distancing himself from the author.[163]

The one area where she coincided with Orwell was as a fellow creative spirit: 'I think there is a swing towards creative work which I agree with you is absolutely necessary for happiness.' Art, music and literature had provided Minnie with outlets. Surprisingly though, for Minnie, it was not found through writing. Relating Orwell's arguments to her own existence, she explained, 'I have to earn some sort of a living by writing and therefore must sit down to the typewriter sometimes, but I could quite well dispense with writing.'[164] Creativity, then, was essential for her happiness, but not through the written word. Instead it was the spoken word that was her inspiration. However, she had been denied use of that elemental force for over a decade. Now, within weeks of her letter to Orwell, a new opportunity offered the means to harness her voice once again...the radio.

[1] Pallister to KBG, nd but (pre-Easter) 1933, GP/1/2/ 681.

[2] Richards, pp. 136, 138–142, 147 & 149; Marwick, *Clifford Allen*, p. 106.

[3] Pallister to KGB, nd but 1933; Richards, p. 102.

[4] Harrison, p. 201.

[5] *Daily Herald*, 24 February 1933.

[6] Pallister to KGB, nd but 1933. Emphasis in original.

[7] Pallister to KGB, nd but 1933; *Daily Herald*, 21 June 1933.

[8] Pallister to KGB, nd but 1933; *John Bull*, 11 March 1933.

[9] Pallister to KGB, nd but 1933; Pallister, *Cabbage...*, p. 138; Pallister to Quigley, 21 November [1939], BBC/WAC/RCONT1 Pallister (Talks 1) 'Minnie Pallister Speaking', *WH*, 8 February 1954.

[10] *Daily Herald*, 27 July 1933; Pallister to KGB, nd but 1933; *Bookman*, September 1933; Pallister to MacDonald, nd, & MacDonald to Pallister, 24 August 1933, PRO 30/69/754.

[11] Pallister, *Gardener's Frenzy*, pp. 44–5; *Time and Tide*, 26 August 1933.

[12] KBG, 'Looking Towards Christmas...'; *New Zealand School Journal*, April 1938; Pallister to Quigley, 15 December 1937, BBC/WAC/RCONT1 Pallister (Talks 1).

[13] Pallister to Quigley, 15 December 1937, BBC/WAC/RCONT1 Pallister (Talks 1).

[14] W. F. Langford, *Essays Light and Serious*, Longman, 1954.

[15] *The Tablet*, 12 August 1933; *Daily Herald*, 26 November 1936.

[16] Pallister to KGB, nd but 1933. The exceptional nature of the letter must have registered with KBG, as it was one of the few from Minnie she kept. Its richness and detail help knit together the main events in Minnie's life, revealing 1933 as a pivotal year.

[17] Pallister, *Cabbage...*, p. 32; *Daily Herald*, 10 August 1937; *Daily Mirror*, 28 August 1935.

[18] 'Life Story (4)'.

[19] Pallister, *Cabbage...*, pp. 7, 22–8, 55, 58 & 96–7.

[20] Pallister, *Cabbage...*, pp. 72–4 & 112.

[21] Pallister, *Cabbage...*, pp. 60–1 & 191–2; *Daily Mirror*, 28 August 1935.

[22] MacDonald to Pallister, 26 July 1933, Pallister to MacDonald, nd, PRO 30/69/755.

[23] Anne de Courcy, *The Viceroy's Daughters, The Lives of the Curzon Sisters*, e-book, loc 3125.

[24] Nicholas Mosley, *Rules of The Game: Sir Oswald and Lady Cynthia Mosley, 1896–1933*, Secker & Warburg, 1982, pp. 241–2.

[25] Pallister to MacDonald, nd, PRO 30/69/754.

[26] Eustance, pp. 360–3, 385 & 388–9.

[27] In April 1918, Montefiore had spoken at an 'enthusiastic meeting' of the New Era Union in Abertillery. Three years later, she returned during the 1921 miners' lockout to go into hiding and avoid arrest as a member of the Communist Party Executive. Disguised in a nurse's uniform, and using her mother's maiden name, Montefiore helped feed miners' children. (Dora B. Montefiore, *From a Victorian to a Modern*, Archer, 1927, pp. 199 & 208–9; *The Vote*, 27 October 1933.)

[28] *Daily Herald*, 2 December 1933.

[29] Hazel Kent, 'A paper not so much for the armchair but for the factory and the street': Fenner Brockway and the Independent Labour Party's *New Leader*, 1926–1946', *LHR*, 2010, Vol 75 No 2, p. 219.

[30] *Daily Herald*, 29 July & 18 August 1933.

[31] *Daily Herald*, 8 August 1933 & letter S J G, 10 August 1933; Tanya Evans, review article, Katherine Holder's *'The Shadow of Marriage: Singleness in England, 1914–60*, *Reviews in History*, 2009, pp. 1–6.

[32] *Daily Herald*, 22 February 1934.

[33] *Daily Herald*, 14 October 1933; Minnie repeated this argument when a broadcaster – 'The Knitting Complex', *Woman's Page*, 12 November 1943.

[34] *Daily Herald*, 4 November 1933.

[35] *Daily Herald*, 18 & 25 November 1933.

[36] Other issues included the loneliness and boredom of old age; being dependent on others, sick visiting and inter-generational relations.

[37] Adrian Bingham, 'Newspaper Problem Pages and British Sexual Culture since 1918', *Media History*, Vol 18, No 12, 2012, pp. 51–63.

[38] In January 1936 the managing editor of the *Daily* Mail asked Ann Temple to establish her 'Human Casebook' column. In her autobiography Temple claimed that no other national newspaper had allocated such a space for 'the human problem'. She claimed: 'Rivals soon followed suit with similar features of their own.' (Ann Temple, *Good or Bad – It's Life*, Nicholson & Watson, 1944, p. 7.) Temple's account may have contributed to historians overlooking Minnie's role.

[39] Temple, pp. 1–9. Another difference was methodological: Minnie initially did not publish readers' questions verbatim before publicly advising them on the problem, as later became the norm. Instead, Minnie corresponded directly and privately with individual readers who had written to her with their problems, though there were exceptions. (See, for example, *Daily Herald*, 8 December 1934.) By October 1934, Minnie was quoting at least part of readers' letters. By early 1936 Minnie was seeking feedback from readers on other individuals' problems. Later that year, 'We Welcome Worries' was part of the paper's 'Home Page Service Bureau'.

[40] Robin Kent, *Agony Aunt Advises*, W. H. Allen, 1979, pp. 246–7.

[41] Bingham, 'Newspaper Problem Pages...', p. 5. Irma Kurtz of *Cosmopolitan* suggested that giving advice to a woman was the least important element of the work. What mattered was to 'give her the chance, possibly for the first time ever, to write her problem down' and to get her thoughts in order. (Quoted in Rosalind Coward, *Female Desire, Women's Sexuality Today*, Paladin, 1984, p. 135.)

[42] Bingham, 'Newspaper Problem Pages...', p. 51.

[43] *Daily Herald*, 6 January & 3 March 1934.

[44] *Daily Herald*, 24 February 1934.

[45] *Daily Herald*, 17 November 1934, 9 & 30 November 1935.

[46] *Daily Herald*, 2 November 1936.

[47] See, for example, *Daily Mirror*, 13 April 1936; Pallister to Molony, 12 December 1945, BBC/WAC/RCONT1 Pallister (Talks 3b).

[48] *Daily Mirror*, 21 October 1936; *Daily Herald*, 10 March 1934, see also 9 November 1937.

[49] See Catherine Blackford, 'Wives and Citizens and Watchdogs of Equality', ed Jim Fyrth, *Labour's Promised Land?*, Lawrence and Wishart, 1995, pp. 59–60.

[50] The absence of National Council minutes between 1932 and 1948 precludes understanding Minnie's full involvement, though it is known she served on the Council's Publicity and Publications Committee from 1933 until the outbreak of the Second World

War. (National Council of Girls' Clubs Annual Reports, 1933/4 – 1939/40, MS 227/5/11/1–8, Birmingham University Archive.)

[51] *Daily Herald*, 13 September 1935. It referred to girls and young women having time on their hands after work or work in the house, and of the clubs looking beyond just recreational activities, drama and libraries to encourage girls and women into active citizenship as they promoted women's status in society, worked with the unemployed, and became involved with issues such as hours worked by shop assistants.

[52] 'Minnie Pallister's Diary', *WH*, 11 April & 27 November 1951.

[53] Ceadel, *Pacifism...*, pp. 134, 147 & 123.

[54] Ceadel, *Pacifism...*, p. 108.

[55] Ceadel, *Pacifism...*, pp. 74–7.

[56] Recommendations on Policy by the National Committee of the No More War Movement for Consideration by the Annual Conference at Sheffield, November 1932, Temp MSS 573/2, No More War papers, Friends House.

[57] NMW National Committee, 13 February, 9 April, 10 & 11 September 1932; description by Laurence Housman, quoted in Robert Huxter, *Reg and Ethel*, Sessions, 1993, p. 70.

[58] NMWM, *Annual Report*, 1931–1932.

[59] Ceadel, *Pacifism...*, p. 117.

[60] Ceadel, *Pacifism...*, p. 169.

[61] Runham Brown to Wellock, 11 February 1933, Temp MSS 573/2.

[62] Ceadel, *Pacifism...*, p. 120.

[63] Runham Brown to Wellock, 11 February 1933.

[64] NMW National Committee, 19 November 1933; KBG, 'Looking Towards Christmas; *No More War (NMW)*, January 1934.

[65] *NMW*, June 1934.

[66] *NMW*, March & July 1934; NMWM, *Annual Report*, 1933–4.

[67] Pallister to Angell, 23 November 1934, Box 200, Angell papers, Ball State University

[68] NMW National Committee, 3 February & 24 March 1934. Martin Ceadel, upon whose work so much of the sections on pacifism have been based, underplayed the paper's significance in describing it as 'a local newssheet'. Ceadel, *Pacifism...*, p. 171.

[69] *NMW*, April 1934.

[70] *NMW*, September 1934; Devi Prasad, *War is a Crime Against Humanity: The Story of the War Resisters' International'*, WRI, 2005, pp. 146 & 149–157.

[71] Ceadel, *Pacifism...*, p. 147.

[72] *Daily Herald*, 18 January 1934.

[73] *Daily Herald*, 23 January 1934.

[74] Many local organisations were associated with it ranging from Toc H and the Rotary Club to the League of Women Helpers and the Trades and Labour Council. (*Bexhill Observer*, 20 October & 22 December 1934; Ceadel, *Pacifism*, p. 156.)

[75] Pallister to Angell, 23 November 1934; Ceadel, *Living...*, p. 320. Nationally the majority overwhelmingly supported Britain remaining a member of the League of Nations, and favoured economic and military collective security while reducing armaments and abolishing military and naval aircraft by international agreement.

[76] NMW National Committee minutes, 14 Oct 1934.

[77] Notes of Agreement, Midlands Council and Allen Skinner, 3 November 1934; NMW National Committee, 1 December 1934. See also 'No More War' entries 2423 and

2424, Royden Harrison, Gillian B. Woolven & Robert Duncan, *The Warwick Guide to British Labour Periodicals*, Harvester, 1977, p. 369.

[78] Pallister to Angell, 23 November 1934. Following the takeover of the journal and Minnie's removal as editor, Rowe – the organising secretary who had made the Midlands area so vibrant – resigned from the NMWM, which the Midlands Area considered a cause of 'profound regret'. *NMW*, December 1934.

[79] See Bullock, *Under Siege*, especially chapter 14.

[80] *NMW*, January and February 1935; Ceadel email to author, May 9, 2016.

[81] Huxter, pp. 72–3; Ceadel, *Pacifism*, p. 172; NMWM, *Annual Report*, 1935–6, p. 1.

[82] NMWM, *Annual Report*, 1935–6, pp. 1 & 3.

[83] *Daily Herald*, 1 & 5 March 1934 & 1 March 1935.

[84] *Daily Herald*, 17 & 24 October 1935; see Francis & Smith, pp. 115–133.

[85] *Daily Herald*, 6 August 1934.

[86] Figure quoted by Duncan Tanner, 'The Pattern in Labour Politics in Wales, 1918–1939', in eds. Duncan Tanner, Chris Williams and Deian Hopkin, *The Labour Party in Wales 1900–2000*, UWP, 2000, p. 115.

[87] Hilda Jennings, *Brynmawr: A Study of a Distressed Area*, Allenson, 1934; Blaina and Nanytglo was described as 'a dreary scattered wilderness of colliery tips and broken down dilapidated over-crowded gloomy hovels'. (Phillip Massey's *Portrait of a Mining Town*, Fact, November 1937, p. 7.)

[88] *New Clarion*, July 1932; *Millgate Monthly*, February 1933.

[89] *Daily Herald*, 1 March 1935. See also my 'A "Subtle Danger"? The Voluntary Sector and Coalfield Society in South Wales, 1926–1939', *Llafur*, Vol. 7 Nos. 3 & 4, 1998–1999, pp.127–41.

[90] Arthur W. Frank, 'Illness and Autobiographical Work: Dialogue as Narrative Destabilization', *Quantitative Sociology*, Vol 23 No 1, 2000; Neil Vickers, 'Illness Narratives', Summary of Chapter 27, Part 5 *Kinds of Community, A History of English Autobiography*, Cambridge, 2016, citing Anne Hunsaker Hawkins.

[91] Author's Agreements, Vol 3 1919–1937, p. 257, Blackie's Collection, Glasgow University Special Collection, GB 248 UGD 061/6/1/3.

[92] Pallister to MacDonald, 1 Nov [1934], PRO 30/69/1444.

[93] Pallister to Angell, 23 November 1934.

[94] *Times Literary Supplement*, 13 December 1934; *Bookman*, December 1934; *Daily Herald*, 8 November 1934.

[95] For example, it was featured in 'Books of the Week' in the *Brisbane Courier-Mail*, it was mentioned in, among others, the *West Australian*, and listed in Perth's *Western Mail*'s book club selection. (*Brisbane Courier-Mail*, 16 March 1935; *West Australian*, 30 November 1935; [Perth] *Western Mail*, 11 February 1937.) All Australian references through Trove sourced 5 October 2016.

[96] Minnie's articles for the *Daily Herald*, or clips of BBC broadcasts after the Second World War had similar reach. Minnie was probably unaware of the many newspapers, magazines and labour journals in which she appeared from the 1920s to the 1950s, whether the *Blue Mountains Advertiser* of Katoomba in New South Wales in January 1952, or *MacDonald's Farm Journal* of Canada in February 1959. Apart from BBC broadcasts, I have seen no reference to her receiving syndication fees.

[97] *Kaja*, Estonia, 4 January 1928; *UFA*, Vol. VIII No. 25, Calgary, Alberta, 1 November 1929.

[98] *Hanover Evening Sun*, 03 January 1928; *Toronto Daily Star*, 14 January 1928; *Auckland Star*, 3 March 1928.

MINNIE PALLISTER: THE VOICE OF A REBEL

[99] *Westralian Worker*, 29 December 1933; *The Worker*, 15 November 1933.

[100] *Voice of Hobart*, 6 October 1934.

[101] *Labour*, October 1937.

[102] *Australian Worker*, 1 December 1937.

[103] Whether her influence on the women's labour movement in Australia was reflected in other countries might be answered through the future digitisation of national newspapers.

[104] Pallister to MacDonald, 1 & 3 November [1934], MacDonald to Pallister, 2 November 1934, PRO 30/69/1444.

[105] Pallister to MacDonald, 17 May [1935], PRO 30/69/757; Pallister to Rosenberg, 27 May 1935, PRO 30/69/1445.

[106] Pallister to MacDonald, 21 May [1935], PRO 30/69/1445.

[107] *Daily Herald*, 5 January 1935; http://theshakespeareblog.com/2011/10/shakespearian-stars-3-john-gielgud-as-hamlet/ accessed 8 May 2018.

[108] 'Through An Invalid's Eyes'.

[109] Pallister to MacDonald, 1 November [1934], MacDonald to Pallister, 2 November 1934, PRO 30/69/1444.

[110] *Daily Herald*, 21 February 1935.

[111] *Bexhill Observer*, 26 January 1935.

[112] 'Minnie Pallister Talking', *WH*, 20 October 1954.

[113] Pallister to MacDonald, 17 May [1935], PRO 30/69/757; *Daily Herald*, 18 May 1935.

[114] 'The Years After the War', *People's Weekly*, 29 November 1930.

[115] *Labour Woman*, April 1935.

[116] Another contributor to the journal was David Mort, with whom Minnie had worked closely in opposing the war and then in the Aberavon campaign. He was now a senior official in the union and may have helped Minnie obtain the role.

[117] *Daily Herald*, 24 October 1935; *Man and Metal*, February 1937.

[118] Though where the nearest art gallery was to my grandmother who was working in Abercarn tinplate works at the time, I am unsure....

[119] *Man and Metal*, December 1936, January, June & July 1937, February 1938.

[120] *Man and Metal*, January & September 1937; February, March, October & November 1938.

[121] *Daily Herald*, 10 September 1935.

[122] *Man and Metal*, April 1937.

[123] *Labour Woman*, November 1936.

[124] Clay, pp. 210–1.

[125] Pallister to Angell, 12 February 1935.

[126] John, pp. 308, 311 & 321.

[127] Pallister to Angell, 12 February 1935.

[128] Pallister to Angell, 12 February 1935

[129] Angell to Pallister, 14 February 1935

[130] *NMW*, April 1934.

[131] *Daily Herald*, 9 February & 30 March 1935.

[132] *Daily Herald*, 13 April 1935.

[133] Pallister to Walker, 31 January 1957, BBC/WAC/RCONT1 Pallister (Talks 8).

[134] Pallister to MacDonald, 29 July 1936, PRO 30/69/758.

[135] 'Life Story (4)'.

[136] Pallister to Derville, 4 January [1959], BBC/WAC/RCONT1 Pallister (Talks 10).

[137] Pallister to MacDonald, 17 September [1936] PRO 30/69/758; scored through lines in script of 'Life Story (5)'.

[138] *Passing Show*, 21 November 1936; *Daily Mirror*, 23 October 1936.

[139] Pallister to Knowles, 12 January 1960, BBC/WAC/RCONT1 Pallister (Talks 10).

[140] Ceadel, *Pacifism*, pp. 193–5.

[141] Ceadel, *Pacifism*, p. 214; William Hetherington, *Swimming Against the Tide: The Peace Pledge Union Story 1934–2014*, PPU, 2015, p. 10; Morris, 'The Flowers...'.

[142] *Peace News*, 25 July 1936 & 27 February 1937.

[143] Ceadel, pp. 263, 264 & 272.

[144] Mariel Cardew, 'What the Peace Pledge Union Stands For', *Peace News*, 10 July 1937.

[145] Ceadel, pp. 228. Minnie was no longer a strict vegetarian. She described herself and Gladys as 'vegetarians of sorts'. They would cook meat when they had visitors and ate fish. Possibly the change in diet had been to aid her recovery. (Pallister, *Cabbage...*, pp. 72–3 & 98; *Daily Mirror*, 13 April 1935.)

[146] *Man and Metal*, February & June 1937; Pallister, *Gardener's Frenzy*, pp. 88–93; 'Looking Back'.

[147] Pallister to MacDonald, 16 February 1936, PRO 30/69/758.

[148] *Daily Herald*, 2 January 1937; *Man and Metal,* February 1937; 'Looking Back'. A lump on her arm terrified her until she realised that it was not a malignant growth but a muscle from gardening.

[149] Pallister to MacDonald, 19 March PRO 30/69/759 & Pallister to MacDonald, 29 March 1937 PRO 30/69/758 [this latter is misfiled in PRO as 1936].

[150] Pallister to MacDonald, 29 March [1937] & nd, [written from Selfridge's].

[151] Pallister to MacDonald, 19 March & 29 March 1937; *Daily Herald*, 24 May 1937.

[152] *Man and Metal*, October 1937; Pallister to Quigley, 26 September 1937, BBC/WAC/RCONTI Pallister (Talks 1); *The Story of the Artists International Association, 1933–1953*, p. 37, quoted in Margaret Glover, *Images of Peace in Britain*, Vol 1, Ph.d, University of Reading, 2002.

[153] Glover, pp. 128–131.

[154] *Man and Metal*, October 1937, 'The Beauty of Cities', *WH*, 30 May 1958.

[155] *Daily Herald*, 15 October 1937; 'Minnie Pallister Talking', *WH*, 1 June 1955.

[156] Elton, pp. 10–11.

[157] *Man and Metal*, June 1941.

[158] Pallister to Orwell, 16 January 1938, ORWELL/H/2, UCL Special Collection.

[159] *Daily Herald*, 7 November 1934.

[160] Bernard Crick, *George Orwell: A Life*, Penguin, 1980, p. 364.

[161] 'South Wales and The ILP'.

[162] George Orwell, *The Road to Wigan Pier*, Left Book Club, Gollancz, 1937, pp. 194–5, 206–7, 214 & 254.

[163] Michael Shelden, *Orwell*, Minerva, 1992, pp. 301 & 310.
[164] Pallister to Orwell, 16 January 1938.

CHAPTER SEVEN
A Pacifist in Total War[1]

From the mid-1930s, Minnie sought an introduction to the BBC. By then she was largely restored to health. Although she still had a 'tired throat', and so could not speak on public platforms, she hoped broadcasting might allow her to speak 'just for five minutes at a time... slowly and quietly'.[2]

In March 1935, Mary Adams raised with John Green of the Talks Department of the BBC the possibility of Minnie talking about amateur gardening, based on *A Cabbage for A Year*, saying she would be 'awfully popular'. Green asked whether Minnie was an entertaining speaker and about her knowledge of gardening. While the internal BBC memos from Green and Adams are signed, a third unidentified person, presumably the invisible hand of the security service, underlined Minnie's name and wrote 'Labour Party organiser' next to it.[3] MI5 had a permanent presence in Broadcasting House and, from the Corporation's earliest days, undertook routine political vetting on job applications, known by the code name 'formalities'. At a time when the Corporation was under pressure for being too left-leaning, Minnie's background as a former labour organiser would have been considered sensitive.[4] She was not hired.[5]

The introduction of Minnie by Adams may not have helped. Adams was seen as a highly able producer of talks, and became its first woman television producer. However, she was also viewed with suspicion within the BBC for being 'a wild unruly, Bolshevik sort of person'.[6] How did Minnie know Mary Adams? Like Minnie, Adams went to university in Cardiff, graduating with a first-class degree in 1921. During her years in South Wales – the most febrile industrially and politically – the young student firebrand may well have known the vibrant ILP organiser.

In June 1937, Molly Hamilton, who had been MP for Blackburn, then a BBC Governor until 1936, commended Minnie to Janet Quigley of the Talks Department as capable of giving 'good, light

5 min talks'. She had 'a great sense of humour, a real knowledge of how the ordinary person lives'.[7] Since their first meeting fifteen years earlier, Hamilton and Minnie had followed parallel political and career paths. They were two of a small number of ILP/Labour women Parliamentary candidates in 1923 and 1924. When Molly became deputy editor of the *New Leader* in the mid-1920s, Minnie was already a contributor. They had shared an admiration for MacDonald, who nominated Hamilton to the BBC.[8] Both were members of the 1917 Club. Those connections now paid off, with this particular recommendation to the Corporation evading the attentions of the security service.

Meeting Quigley on 15 July 1937 irrevocably changed Minnie's life.[9] Educated at Oxford University, Quigley joined the BBC in 1930, and had responsibility for content aimed at women. She was considered 'formidable'[10] but was a sympathetic woman with a low, calming voice. Like Minnie she had a disability which gave her a limp. Quigley was 35 years old and Minnie 52. Quigley, who was later producer, then editor of *Woman's Hour*, became Minnie's supporter, mentor and friend, and opened up opportunities for her. The two women shared values and outlooks, and a strong personal bond developed that extended beyond work to shape the course of Minnie's next two decades.

The Talks Department, particularly women's talks, was one area of the BBC where women were involved in the creative process, and where consideration was given to how the female audience should be engaged. The remarkable early women at the BBC have been noted.[11] However, attention has centred on BBC staff, including Adams, Hamilton and Quigley, but has not extended to programme contributors such as Minnie, who have eluded consideration. Yet, as in politics, through her work with Quigley on radio, Minnie pushed and often challenged the boundaries of *what* women's issues were presented, as well as *how* and *why*. Over the next two decades, in a prominent and successful career that lasted until her death, Minnie showed she too was a remarkable broadcaster. Under Quigley's tutelage, Minnie transferred her popular touch from the printed page to the broadcast word, building a new means for her to connect with millions of women.

Minnie barraged Quigley with proposals but it was Quigley who identified 'Sickness in the House' as the subject for Minnie's first transmission. In contrast with the polished gloss of *A Cabbage for a Year* which had addressed her recovery, the script covered the most traumatic period of Minnie's life, looking at illness through the eyes of the invalid. Minnie's draft needed no alteration.

The fifteen-minute talk was transmitted on Friday 4 March 1938 and Quigley thought it 'extremely good'.[12] After twelve years of almost complete silence, the studio microphone gave Minnie voice again. Minnie later recalled: 'I could not be sure that after the first few sentences my throat would not lock and I should be absolutely speechless.' She reflected, 'I don't think I shall ever have quite such a nerve-racking experience again.' Initially Minnie talked too fast and suffered from 'mike [sic] nervousness'. These problems were quickly overcome. Minnie realised that the art lay in not thinking that the broadcast was to millions of people. Instead, the aim was a relationship where the listener thought that Minnie was speaking just to her or him.[13] Minnie's openness and willingness to talk about sensitive, personal issues struck a note with listeners. Her sincerity and humour became the foundation for her radio career. The BBC assessment found her an 'unusually sympathetic' broadcaster who received a 'considerable number' of appreciative letters. With the 6 guineas fee Minnie immediately bought a new cooker.[14] However, her informal platform style, to which she aspired on radio, still eluded her.[15]

The *Bexhill Observer* advised its readers to listen in. It lamented though that, while Minnie was always helpful, it was a shame that she did not apply her 'powerful and practical aid' more in local life.[16] Over the next two years, Minnie became a high-profile presence in the town, though not always in ways that earned the newspaper's approval.

In March, Minnie chaired a local meeting of the Over 30s Association with a view to setting up a branch in Hastings.[17] It was a cause with which Minnie closely identified. She repeatedly raised employers' demand for youth, thus making the lot of women over 30 a hard one[18] and had written two years earlier of the spinster who was told she was 'too old at thirty' but not included in schemes for widow's pensions or children's allowance.[19] Highlighting the difficulties faced by independent woman who 'after years of service are thrown out of employment to make room for girls leaving school', personal experience gave her direct appreciation of the economic and social precariousness of 'older' single woman living on a pittance who 'quietly starved in tiny rooms'.[20]

Broaching the issue with Quigley, Minnie presented 'the freedom of the spinster without the loneliness' as at the crux of the career question for women.[21]

Minnie once more had an active social life based in public engagement. Over one week she attended an Over 30s Association meeting, saw a film on the distressed areas; went to a performance in aid of the Spanish Relief Fund, and joined the devoted band of comrades for the annual Labour bazaar in Bournemouth, held in their hall in the heart of Toryism. Her driver was a woman who had just returned from Austria, annexed by Nazi Germany two months previously, where she witnessed queues of Jewish people struggling to escape Nazi tyranny. Minnie protested, 'How can men, in the name of God and justice, persecute others for no fault except race, for which they are not responsible?'[22]

As fascism cast a dark shadow, Minnie was one of 540 delegates who attended the May conference of Labour Women. Barbara Ayrton Gould, member of the National Executive and Vice Chair of the Labour Party, moved a resolution condemning the National Government for its conduct in international affairs. Gould, a former pacifist, now believed the people of the Spanish Republic should be able to defend themselves. She called for the suspension of non-intervention and the lifting of the arms embargo on the Spanish Government. In her first appearance on the national Labour stage for twelve years, Minnie supported an opposition amendment that war was futile in all circumstances. It was heavily defeated.[23]

Meeting friends she had not seen for years, the conference allowed her to reflect on when she first became active in the labour movement. Then, there had been few Labour members on elected bodies and labour conferences were tiny. She claimed that now, through hard work and using political and industrial power, they had created the greatest political party in the world that was transforming conditions.[24] To Minnie, the Labour Party, trades unions and co-operative movement were 'three aspects of the same truth'.[25]

Issues of peace and war were markedly different from those of two decades earlier. With fascism rampant in Germany and Italy, and an ILP contingent fighting for the Spanish Republic, Brockway, who had led the NCF during the Great War and had been imprisoned for his principles, abandoned his pacifism over Spain. For most, socialism and pacifism were now incompatible. For Minnie, with her beliefs underpinned by her Christian faith, there was no contradiction.[26] She dismissed the 'get-rich-quick' methods of the Popular Front and presumably supported non-intervention.[27]

Even though (as Minnie said) fascism posed a direct threat to the women's movement and feminism and to individual women's social, economic and political freedoms, newly enfranchised women helped shape international relations by providing the most solid grassroots support for appeasement.[28] Minnie was one who identified the opportunity to apply pressure and called on women to build a future that avoided bloodshed. Mass Observation found that women were much more concerned about the deprivations of war than the menace of fascism. So widespread was this feeling that appeasement became recognised as a feminine policy.[29] There was a gulf between the sexes.[30] While women were more inclined towards 'anything for peace', men felt Hitler should have been challenged sooner.[31] In 1941 Richard Baxter's wartime rant, *Guilty Women*, castigated those who supported disarmament, no more war and appeasement. Minnie would have been such a target, but she would have rejected his negative depictions.

The backdrop of international events was everywhere. Minnie's visit to Cambridge in July was accompanied by the drone of bombers on practice flights from the aerodromes that had sprung up like small towns. She lamented that in wartime money could be found to get people back in employment and earn good wages and 'houses spring up like magic', whereas in peacetime men are 'left to eat their hearts out on the dole'. She read David Lloyd George's memoirs, recalling the folly of the Versailles Peace Treaty as a bad dream.[32]

From late 1937, Minnie was increasingly active in the PPU. The NMWM had merged with the PPU earlier that year, although the ever-independent Midlands Council initially refused to join.[33] In September a national pacifist convention regretted Labour supporting rearmament and, in April 1938, over 1,000 delegates attended the PPU AGM where a manifesto described as 'a plan for real peace' offered 'complete and constructive pacifism' as a defence of democracy and a way to confront fascism.[34]

At the AGM, John Barclay, the national organiser, called on PPU groups and members across the country to 'systematically contact every important body of public opinion in their areas'.[35] By the time Barclay visited Bexhill a month later, Minnie, Gladys and three dozen other members of Bexhill PPU, as part of the national house-to-house campaign, had delivered the manifesto to the people of the town as an 'alternative to a policy of rearmament and war'.[36] Bexhill was an active PPU branch and its Peace Shop displayed an exhibition, 'War, the Personal Problem'. A joint committee with the League of Nations Union, Labour Party, Liberal Association, Women's Co-operative Guild, and free and Anglican churches called a public meeting about a local canvass for the National Peace Council petition.[37]

Minnie used *Man and Metal* and the *Daily Herald* to argue for pacifism. She was also a warrior on the letters pages of the *Bexhill Observer*, defending PPU positions in relation to opposing air raid precautions because they fostered a 'war mentality', as well as its refusal to take part in practice blackouts and gas drills. Rather than build shelters, she argued, the only way to protect the civilian population was to abolish war and its causes; the solution, she proclaimed, lay in international economic cooperation, rather than in using force to defend national interests.[38]

*

In what became an annual visit to Wales, in 1938 Minnie made a triumphant return to Aberavon. Receptions and social evenings organised in her honour were filled to capacity and attended by dignitaries. She was greeted with enthusiasm as the person who had done more than any other to win Aberavon for Labour and credited with giving Aberavon the stability and strength to stay solid after Labour's 1931 crisis. Bill Cove MP had travelled from London specifically to pay tribute to Minnie and referred to the 'deep affection, love and trust' that existed for her in Aberavon. Ivor Thomas, to whom much of the credit was actually due, said it was good to have her well enough again to revisit the scene of her early accomplishments. Minnie answered that in spite of the setback of 1931 every sacrifice that they had made for socialism would bear fruit.[39] Finally, local women in 'a shabby little hall', out of loyalty and affection for when they had worked together fifteen years earlier, brought gifts, but after ten years of economic and emotional hardship, Minnie observed, the women too looked shabby.[40]

Minnie's interactions with the BBC were less positive. After her first broadcast, she bombarded Quigley with suggestions, but none were accepted. Until that point, Minnie had relied on her own contacts, often from her political life, to generate work. Perhaps interpreting Quigley's response as holding out little hope, Minnie appointed an agent to represent her.[41] When Quigley raised the issue, Minnie poured her heart out, saying the occasional appearance on-air 'makes all the difference in the world to my life'. The jolt seems to have worked. On Friday 30 September, Guy Burgess of the Talks Department phoned Minnie to offer her a six-minute talk on 'Rebuilding Life in Later Years', in the *At Home Today* series.[42] That same day, Chamberlain arrived back from Munich, where he had agreed the fate of Czechoslovakia with Hitler, declaring 'Peace for Our Time' to enthusiastic celebration. It was a women's peace[43] and Minnie, the committed appeaser, would have been delighted. Burgess, a committed re-armer, was appalled.

On Tuesday 4 October, after Minnie scribbled a note to Quigley to say that, rather than rely on collective security, the only hope, and first step, should be to give up fighting and renounce war, she travelled to London.[44] There she rehearsed with Burgess, who that day reported back to the Talks Department on his 1 October visit to Churchill in Chartwell, where they had discussed the international situation.[45] Minnie and Guy Burgess, the strong appeaser and arch re-armer, were both forthright believers in their opposing causes. Could they have avoided discussing the big issue of the day that autumn day in 1938?

They did not work together long. Two months later Burgess resigned from the BBC and joined MI6, so Minnie was not overly exposed to his erratic style (or chaotic private life). He had already been a spy for Soviet intelligence for three years and he would pass secrets to the Russians from MI6 and the Foreign Office as part of the Cambridge spy ring along with Maclean, Philby and Blunt, until he and Maclean defected to Russia in 1951. During the biggest crisis in pre-war international affairs, Minnie worked with Burgess, unaware of his double life.

In March 1939, the German army invaded Czechoslovakia in breach of the Munich agreement. Assumptions about women being able to stop war were shown as hollow, although Minnie, as ever convinced that she was right, did not accept the point. Such obduracy allowed her to adopt and maintain brave, isolated positions that at times win admiration. This however was not one of them.

Unrealistically, she placed the blame elsewhere, seeing it as a tragedy that the political coming of age for women who could have ensured peace coincided with conscription. For Minnie, the outcome was 'Hitler appears to have won.'[46]

When working with Burgess, Minnie never ceased pitching ideas direct to Quigley. Over the years, her notes, often scribbled on scraps of paper while travelling, or in the cinema, fizz with ideas, organisational issues, politics and personal detail. Whatever the subject, Minnie sought to primarily use a woman's perspective to engage the audience. What she described as her 'one small gift' – to be able to talk about 'worthwhile things in a light way' – was to drastically understate her contribution.[47] Sharing an outlook on women's issues, Quigley and Minnie were complementary. Feeding off one another creatively, two sharp minds honed ideas and worked through what should be promoted and how. In Minnie, Quigley found a highly intelligent presenter who could draw on personal experiences to promote their shared gender perspective and popularise their ideas in ways that appealed to ordinary women. At times between 1938 and 1945 Minnie and Quigley wrote to each other almost daily, and their correspondence shows a close personal bond. After Katharine Bruce Glasier, Quigley provided the second closest relationship of Minnie's professional and personal life. If Brittain and Holtby's friendship was 'an example of feminist achievement, specifically in terms of women's triumph in the field of professional work,'[48] that description could apply in minor key to what Minnie and Quigley achieved over much of two decades.

Minnie's easy charm could be winning. Complimenting Quigley over her education, her intelligence, her value, she said she assumed Quigley probably needed to eat, though had 'the appearance of living on honey dew'.[49] Minnie's use of language towards Quigley could be flirtatious, at times almost romantic, and a counterpoint to Quigley's professional formality. When a friend said that Minnie did not sound happy in one broadcast, Minnie wrote to Quigley 'that was missing you'; she bought a copy of *Woman* 'as it had a picture of you, a very poor one, but still—'.[50] Occasional summer Sundays would be spent together. Minnie was doubtless sincere when she said Quigley was one of the people who made the times through which they were living less hellish. When war was declared, Minnie described Quigley as 'a ray of light on a dark world'.[51]

Quigley got to know well the chatty and excitable Minnie who 'blew in like a storm tossed seagull', giving the 'impression of being slightly mentally deficient, but I am always like that when I am thrilled'.[52] Always accident-prone but increasingly neurotic, Minnie portrayed life at this time as one long series of misadventures.[53]

Enthused to be back after months off-air, in order to convey the reality of women's lives and domestic conditions, Minnie's approach was to use cooking, gardening and clothes and link them to national circumstances and economics. Forsaking a serious, technical approach, her sketches aimed to be 'comforting for women who don't get much fun'. She acknowledged, 'I think perhaps we should keep the comforting note to the fore, so many women do seem to have a rotten time.'[54] The first opportunity to use this approach came when Minnie was contracted at short notice to give three talks on 'Housekeeping for Fun'.[55] Allocated her own slot, Minnie brought thoughtful insights to matters of everyday life that affected women, framing them consciously from a gendered viewpoint. Her broadcasts drew letters from all over the country, and from men as well as women.[56]

Minnie then proposed talks on practical issues that addressed power relationships between husband and wife that she had first raised on public platforms nearly two decades earlier, including control of the domestic economy and 'payment for wives'.[57] Minnie had an eye for altering conditions affecting women and proposed a feature on the changing nature of Sundays, as less emphasis placed on preparing heavy Sunday meals offered greater potential for recreation and picnics. While recognising that most women had no hot water, bathroom or indoor toilet, Minnie appreciated the potential that technology offered for transforming ordinary women's domestic lives.[58] Chauvinistic men were given short shrift. One, who published Minnie's gardening books, and thought 'with rare exceptions woman's place is nursery and kitchen' was dismissed with 'Attaboy'.[59]

Not all of Minnie's suggestions struck home. Sometimes they were discounted as 'rather too light' or lacking substance. Quigley also rejected Minnie's 'little moral essays'. Minnie's regular efforts to insert religion and pacifism into scripts were often done baldly. At times Minnie's world view was shown as narrow, with her middle-class assumptions earning rebukes.[60] She was, though, no elitist. She represented the experience of ordinary people, acknowledging the contribution of 'the million unknowns', whether working in sewers or on trawlers, who made her life and the lives of others possible and comfortable.[61]

*

Immediately after a fourth 'Housekeeping for Fun' broadcast, Minnie set off for Frankfurt.[62]. After her visit in 1936, the Schwarbs had regularly invited her back and she eventually agreed to a holiday in November 1938. Passage was booked for a night sailing on 12 November. As Minnie was preparing to travel, the 'single instance of large-scale, public and organised physical violence against Jews in Germany before the Second World War' occurred on the night of 9–10 November. Kristallnacht – 'the night of broken glass' – saw windows in Jewish shops smashed, businesses and synagogues burned and homes ransacked. Continuing in broad daylight, the pogrom saw tens of thousands of Jewish men arrested in their homes or picked up on the streets and sent to concentration camps.[63]

Frankfurt had 26,158 Jewish residents in 1933, the second largest Jewish population in Germany, after Berlin.[64] When the Nazis took power in 1933, the state followed a 'legal and bureaucratic strategy for persecuting Jews'.[65] Harassed, arrested, beaten and often deprived of their livelihoods and denied rights of citizenship, many fled. On 28 May 1938 the Jews in Frankfurt were subjected to a day of intimidation when their caricatures were painted on their windows and gangs warned them to leave Germany.[66] Matters came to a head with the street violence and destruction of the Kristallnacht pogrom. By 1939, such had been the threat that the number of Jews in the city was reduced to less than half.[67]

With newspapers full of stories of action taken against Jews, friends cautioned Minnie against travelling as it was unsafe – especially as she would be staying with a Jewish family. She could have been in no doubt about what might await her. Her decision to go, and her conduct in the days she was there, attested to an obituarist's description of her as 'fearless'. Minnie arrived with fires 'still smouldering' and 'signs of looting and rioting'.[68] In Frankfurt alone twenty-three synagogues and chapels were destroyed. In one synagogue that was not gutted, the fire was rekindled four times in subsequent days, as crowds gathered, until the task was complete and the building demolished on 17 November.[69]

Minnie found the Schwarbs in real trouble.[70] The women were terror-stricken and in despair. All the male relatives whom Minnie had met two years earlier had been taken, though the women had no idea where they were or what would happen to them.[71] In fact, her host Dr Alfred Schwarb and his son Hans, along with all other adult Jewish males in Frankfurt, were taken to the Frankfurt Convention Hall, before being roughly herded onto trains to the accompaniment of beatings and insults, and sent 170 miles through Weimar to the Buchenwald Concentration Camp. Shaved bald, and given concentration camp numbers, they were made to wear striped prison uniforms, and held prisoner.[72] Housed in five intolerably overcrowded barracks, in appalling and degrading conditions, they were held without drinking water or sanitary arrangements until the prisoners themselves dug the first latrines.[73]

Minnie spent her time going around police stations and shipping companies in the city, trying to arrange the men's release and obtaining passage for family members. The British Consulate was besieged by desperate, terrified people seeking to leave Germany.[74] Consular staff, who worked round the clock, advised Minnie to return home as 'the only thing in the world which could get anyone out of a concentration camp was an invitation to England'.[75]

After only three days, Minnie returned to Britain, much earlier than planned, to arrange permits. She took a few of the family's belongings in case they escaped and 'as many messages as I could carry in my head', as they were afraid that any written messages might be intercepted if she were searched at the frontier. She was scared as she crossed the border under the eye of storm troopers, but the journey passed without incident.[76] Reflecting that women in Germany lived in fear of another visit from the secret police, she declared that thousands of them would be glad to leave behind their homes and all they cared for in order to begin life again in their middle age, 'if they may take their men with them unharmed'.[77]

Although visas could be issued on the understanding that refugees were nominally in transit to the United States, those seeking refuge still required a British citizen to act as guarantor for accommodation and financial support during their stay.[78] *Peace*

News urged individuals to immediately invite Jews from Germany into their homes for three or six months and act as surety to help overcome government objections.[79] It was, though, easier said than done. Minnie spent a week 'of hectic clamouring at Home Office doors' to obtain permits.[80]

Hans was held for five weeks, a week longer than his father. As their visa approvals trickled through, prisoners were released in batches of forty.[81] They had to pay their own way back to Frankfurt by coach. Their bald heads made the prisoners easily identifiable.[82] Alfred, Alice and Hans Schwarb eventually arrived in Britain in February 1939.

The eleven months after Munich was one of prolonged international crisis for the people of Britain. The countdown to war was described as a sense of emergency that each felt personally.[83] Minnie noted people were living day to day.[84] This was more than a 'war of nerves'. Minnie's friends would receive fewer Christmas presents as her money was diverted to filling a stocking for stricken children in Spain and China or to meet the needs of refugees. Distress funds were set up for them in Bexhill and Minnie appealed to everyone to channel their money to alleviate suffering, rather than indulge in Christmas excess.[85]

In contrast with the grim international situation, Minnie's personal circumstances were bright. Her health was largely restored after a near decade-long hiatus of impairment and she was no longer haunted by poverty. By her mid-50s, Minnie had rebuilt her personal and professional life, and was once again fully engaged politically, socially and culturally. She served on national committees of organisations including animal welfare and children's institutions.[86] She was a regular writer for the *Daily Herald* and *Man and Metal*, and was embarking on a new career with the BBC. Receiving a fee of 8 guineas for each of her three October talks, Minnie had a decent, if somewhat erratic, income and the Pallister sisters' domestic economy was in balance. With over 500 articles, a clutch of pamphlets and five books, including two collections of essays, plus work syndicated across the world, Minnie rightly described her occupation as journalist.[87] While it was a quite different life from the one she had lived until the mid-1920s, by the late 1930s it was palpably the old Minnie once again living it.

In Bexhill, Minnie became a central figure in the town's cultural life. Although she described herself as 'at best a low to middling brow where music is concerned', she was secretary of the Bexhill Friends of Music Society, which had around sixty members, and organised a concert of Mendelssohn, Mozart and Beethoven at the De La Warr Pavilion in December and another in February.[88] Underwriting the second event personally, Minnie had to fill the new De La Warr Pavilion or 'drop £80'.[89] The Pavilion, built and opened in 1935, was designed by a German Jewish refugee from Nazism, Erich Mendelsohn, and his associate Serge Chermayeff. It was one of the most impressive modernist buildings in Britain.[90] The activities of the Society led the *Bexhill Observer* to comment that the town could 'no longer be reproached with being "not interested in high class music" and of having a superb hall without music worthy of it.' The concert must have been financially successful as another was put on in June with the programme once more comprised exclusively of Germanic composers, Mozart, Schubert and Beethoven.[91] In small ways Minnie tried to build bridges.

As chair of the Hastings Writers Club, a social was held in the sisters' 'delightful old-world residence' where Minnie's 'famous' date and nut sandwiches were served.[92] She was also part of a small group which sought to establish a John Galsworthy Society and present his plays at the De La Warr Pavilion. For those on the left, Galsworthy was an advocate for 'the weak, the helpless, and the oppressed'. Another risky venture, it required an attendance of 3,000 people over a week to be financially viable.[93]

When the Schwarb family arrived in Britain, Minnie did all she could to help settle her German friends.[94] She noted 'after a nightmare of humiliation and fear' that the family was now finding freedom and friendship. She enjoyed showing Sussex to Alice, who she had last seen 'sobbing with terror' in her Frankfurt apartment.[95] Although the Schwarbs stayed in the sisters' flat for a week, it was too small to accommodate everyone, so they were found lodgings elsewhere, returning each day to study English.[96] During their stay Alice was disoriented by British foods, which gave Minnie the idea that Alice, who had 'a deep pleasant voice', be offered a slot to broadcast on the differences between German and British cooking, and Quigley agreed. After Alice's broadcast, Minnie thanked Quigley saying: 'They have suffered such humiliations during the last five years that it means a great deal to them to be treated like human beings.'[97]

However, not all of the Schwarb family were safe. In March,

Minnie received 'frantic calls' from Alice worried about friends and family still in Germany, as new permit regulations meant people were being turned back at the frontier. It may have been Alice's frantic calls that led Minnie to make a sudden journey to Frankfurt, probably between 28 April and 3 May. Anticipating possible problems, she told Quigley she would next be at the BBC on 4 May, 'D and Hitler willing'.[98] Her comment to Quigley, 'I don't know what will be the end of it all', was chillingly prophetic.[99] The purpose and outcome of the journey are not known. However, by the outbreak of war, all the extended Schwarb family had managed to escape.[100] On 19 April 1939, Alice, Alfred and Hans left Waterloo Station for the SS Europa on which they sailed to the USA.[101] Conscious that the German ship had Hitler's agents on board, they were nervous about other passengers until their arrival in the United States.

It is not known if Minnie was involved in a structured rescue programme or if she acted alone.[102] At a little concert given by a refugees' club, chaired by a learned Rabbi, a 'pathetic little band of refugees' performed to thank, in some small way, those who had helped them. A pianist from Dusseldorf played, a young actress from Berlin performed, and a young Jewish woman sang.[103] The last person she helped escape from Germany was a Jewish boy for whom she stood surety, who arrived in Britain during the final week of peace.[104]

Meanwhile, the PPU took measures to go 'underground'. Anticipating police raids under Emergency Powers legislation that could deem PPU activities to be 'opposed to the nation's war effort', and based on the experience of the Great War, the PPU prepared to operate semi-clandestinely. An April emergency meeting of sponsors, with representatives from all over Britain including Bexhill determined to decentralise finances to the areas.[105] As group leader, Minnie would have been involved.

Although it was not pursuing a policy of active war resistance, it is not surprising that the PPU anticipated action by the authorities. *Peace News* in the early months of 1939 was conciliatory towards Hitler and highly critical of British rearmament. Moreover, in a spectacular lapse of judgement in early 1939, the PPU included two pro-Nazi organisations among those with whom it encouraged international friendship. Although the PPU retracted, the damage was done, and the name of the PPU tarnished.[106]

After Germany seized Prague in March 1939 most supporters of appeasement became disillusioned, leaving only the PPU and pro-fascists supporting the policy. Even so, while the police continued to monitor the PPU, the expected raids did not materialise.[107] Locally Minnie projected a softer tone, writing a letter about the blackout on behalf of the PPU branch to the *Bexhill Observer*. Members did not 'wish to give the impression that they are merely carping critics, opposing for the sake of it, or that they are always obstructing'. It was, she argued, dangerous for the civilian population to be led to believe that they could be protected from air attack as defensive precautions were in reality a step towards war. Instead, government outlook and policy should be directed towards ensuring peace.[108] In chairing a session at the annual peace weekend of East Sussex PPU branches, she stated that working for peace was far harder than averting war.[109] Minnie decried social services being robbed to pay for ammunition,[110] and at a conference of women that considered the establishing of a state medical service, Minnie argued it was surely as important to have national defence from ill health as to have national air defence against bombing.[111] The PPU, though, was out of step with the national mood. Addressing kindred spirits within the PPU was one thing; taking the message to the streets was another. When Bexhill PPU undertook a poster parade in the town, they met with a hostile reception.[112]

As the international crisis deepened, Minnie called for a more spiritual approach to politics. Religion should be brought into laws, especially international problems, and Labour should become a crusade again.[113] Perhaps in an attempt to find a new outlet, Minnie became active in Moral Rearmament, a movement established in 1938 that identified the international crisis as fundamentally a moral one. Its central message was to change yourself first, then the people nearest to you, then your town, then the country. At a time when almost all her friends gave up their pacifism to oppose fascism, Minnie looked within. She also looked to the utopia provided by small self-selected alternative communities that provided a space to 'create the nucleus of a new social order'.[114] She visited people who had recently settled on the land, to seek a simpler form of life and escape from a 'world sickened of mass production, of noise and show, and useless luxury' and to get away from war.[115] But escape from that 'dark, dishonest decade' was easier wished for than achieved.

MINNIE PALLISTER: THE VOICE OF A REBEL

*

To mark the coming of age of women obtaining the vote in 1918, Minnie suggested 'Twenty-One Years After' as the topic for a BBC talk. Wanting her script to convey 'the immense importance of political power to women, as it is in some ways their only power', she sought to infuse the punchy draft with 'excitement, rush and glamour'. The theme was a variation on 'Can Women Be Nonparty?', an article she had written for the TUC publication *Labour* in 1937, with the content adjusted to be acceptable to the BBC. Quigley was enthusiastic and suggested Minnie address the use that women had made of the vote. Assuming that Minnie was going to be 'rather critical of the present-day young woman and her attitude to politics', Quigley anticipated that the talk would provoke a response 'and may serve to show us how much or how little interest there is in this subject amongst the women who listen'.[116]

The discussions around the draft script were as significant as the final version. As heavy revisions occurred in April and May, one issue considered was 'Does this generation display the same intensity in *using* the vote, which the last generation displayed in *demanding* it?'[117] Another referred to the role of women seeking to bring peace, although the final script only touched on the international crisis.[118] The broadcast criticised women's magazines and women's pages of newspapers for their content, but not as bluntly as did Minnie's private note to Quigley: 'I feel that there is something a trifle sinister in the sickly atmosphere of froth and frivol [*sic*] not to say drivel which pervades the magazines and pages devoted to women.'[119] Minnie would still be strongly arguing this case twenty years later. Transmitted as a tea-time talk in May, it was such a success it was repeated in August.

In July, the BBC's Overseas News Editor asked to meet Minnie. The German News service wished to include talks of direct interest to women listeners and Quigley had proposed Minnie to write scripts.[120] Anxious to do anything she could to reduce war tensions, Minnie suggested bringing in positive links with Germany, such as a 'small touch about Wagner at Covent Garden... perhaps comparing it with a performance seen in the Opera House in Aachen.' She suggested finishing her talk with a poem on peace and friendship, composed by a friend in the Great War that had been translated by a poet from Vienna. But Minnie realised that it would not be easy to get approval as 'snags simply stick out and that every comma has to be vetted remorselessly'.[121]

Now that paid holidays were obligatory, Gladys and Minnie had to vacate their flat in mid-August so it could be used by her sister's locum, which was the only time that Gladys would leave Bexhill each year.[122] Minnie found herself 'marooned in wilds of Somerset' before going to stay with an old ILP comrade, Bill Collins, in Cardiff. Then she intended to be with Ivor Thomas in Swansea until 3 September, 'unless war comes', but would return to London early if the international crisis worsened.[123]

Her final days in Swansea were completely overshadowed by the international situation and with war imminent Minnie was told that her talks for the German Service could no longer be used.[124] Minnie returned to London a day early and on the following day, Sunday 3 September 1939, Chamberlain declared war on Germany. With the outbreak of war, Minnie wrote that so great was the suffering of the Jews that it would rebound on the rest of the world for 'the whole world is kin and an injury to one must sooner or later be an injury to all'. She concluded, 'What will be the end of this persecution we cannot see.'[125]

The declaration of war brought immediate dislocation. Ordinary life stopped 'for the duration'.[126] The BBC's adoption of wartime broadcasting arrangements, with one single Home Service, resulted in Minnie's broadcast of 4 September being cancelled. Quigley apologised, saying that when things settled down Minnie might be asked to broadcast again but she could not be more definite.[127] Bexhill Labour Party suspended its activities and the Writers Club, which Minnie chaired, now held joint fortnightly, rather than weekly, meetings alternately in Hastings and Bexhill and in the afternoon rather than evening.[128] Newspapers shrank, though Minnie's articles in the *Daily Herald* and *Man and Metal* continued.

Minnie spent little time in London that autumn. By the end of October, after six weeks of war, so many incredible things had happened that she found it impossible to decide what to write about. As pages became dominated by official announcements on men being called up for military service, fuel rationing, and other restrictions, Minnie quickly adjusted her writing to wartime themes, albeit in a typically Pallister way. Explaining that everyone was needed in wartime, she focussed particularly on the contribution of mothers; although they were not 'in special uniforms, they will not appear on parades, or be photographed', their work of giving birth, looking after the home, and growing and preparing food were eternal, whereas the calamity of war 'bringing new duties, new dangers, new sorrows' must pass in time. She also highlighted people's mutual dependence: 'the fate of the world hangs on the integrity of its unknown citizens for... as never before...we are all members one of another'.[129] She marked the 1939 Armistice Day bitterly lamenting that the promises made to the dead soldiers of the previous war had been so easily forgotten.[130]

At different points after Hitler's rise to power in 1933 and the summer of 1940, many pacifists renounced their previous position. Hitler's behaviour made war unavoidable or even just for many pacifists including women who realised that Hitler had to be forcibly opposed. Eleanor Rathbone took an early position against appeasement, seeing the need to confront fascism as soon as Hitler came to power.[131] Ellen Wilkinson left the PPU in March 1938, when Hitler took Prague. At the outbreak of war, Lucy Cox, former stalwart of No More War, recognised the need to confront Hitler and gave up her pacifism.[132]

Minnie was of a generation of women who viewed the build up to the Second World War through the eyes of the First. Despite having seen Hitler's regime at much closer quarters than most, Minnie was unable to imagine that there might be a greater evil than war. Although she had personal experience of the impact on Jewish people, and a clear sense of the implications of fascism for women, she failed to grasp the depth of malevolence in Nazism and her view that killing was wrong prevailed. She had long believed that if women really wanted to stop the war, they had the power to do so.[133] This precept was shared with part of the women's pacifist movement who thought women were naturally more peace loving, and so could lead the opposition to war.[134] It was a chimera and for Helena Swanwick, whose WIL peace tour Minnie had helped organise in 1916, and who like Minnie supported a position of peace at any price, the internal conflict became too much. In despair, Swanwick took her own life in November 1939.[135]

Paradoxically, war brought an influx of new members into the PPU as the actor Sybil Thorndike became a sponsor for the first time. With appeasement seen to have failed, pacifism became a faith rather than a policy and many pacifists shifted towards advocating a negotiated peace.[136] Stuart Morris, the PPU chair, recognised that, in renouncing all wars, members were cutting themselves off from those who were generally opposed to war but thought that it was necessary to fight this one.[137]

In the first days of the war, Talks Department staff in the BBC found themselves 'hopelessly constrained' by the Ministry of Information (MOI).[138] However, when 'normal' BBC schedules resumed, Quigley and Minnie discussed 'little heartening talks to women' that would be sympathetic and sincere whilst addressing the daily problems and worries that most women were encountering. Minnie immediately submitted two ideas. The first would look humorously at everyday life in 'making the best of wartime conditions'; the second would look towards the coming of peace, which Minnie doubted would get past the censor 'but...might be able to insert bits gently later'.[139]

Quigley counter-suggested that she wanted Minnie to start off the new series, *Talking It Over,* with a fifteen-minute slot giving 'some thoughts and impressions that have occurred to you since the outbreak of war', and bring in some memories of the start of the last war. Minnie accepted, making clear she wanted to get away from the idea of 'women "giving" their sons for a noble cause', and instead focus on how quickly war becomes the central pivot of life and the normal state of things.[140]

Starting gently, Minnie contrasted the two world wars: how, although the Great War had come 'like a bolt from the blue', wartime *conditions* [Minnie's emphasis] came very slowly. This second war had long been foreseen and preparations had been underway for a long time, so that when war came, the change from peacetime to wartime conditions was 'startlingly sudden'. People's 'outward lives' completely altered almost overnight, as sandbags, the blackout, and gas masks 'were instantly part of our everyday existence'. Minnie was even more surprised at the speed with which people had become accustomed to them. It now felt hard to remember when it wasn't necessary to put up the blackout.

It was important to remember though, Minnie argued, that war was not normal life, any more than having an accident was normal life. War, she said, was an enormous accident, a calamity which disunited human beings. Listing the constant things in life for all peoples, such as literature, sowing and reaping, music, labour and friendship which existed in peace and war, and recognising it was important to adapt to current hardships, she argued it was also important to keep 'the lovely normal things', as such values would provide the basis for peace. Minnie suggested that it was not too early to think about the kind of peace that was wanted. She warned that a peace made with a wartime mentality could be unworthy and called for the best [Minnie's emphasis] of wartime mentality, rather than the worst, to be carried into peacetime. Women specifically had to do something about it. If the same level of organisation was brought to organising 'national life' as to the organisation of the evacuation and blackout, and if women were prepared to take strangers into their homes; and give up their money and time for war, then they could also be willing to 'accept the change in social, political and economic life which alone can bring peace'.[141]

Broadcast during the 'Bore War' (or 'phoney war' as it was later described), when the RAF was dropping leaflets and not yet bombs on German cities, Minnie's talk, far from falling foul of the censor, fitted with the BBC's cautious policy of 'attacking Hitler but offering a conciliatory tone to the German people'.[142] After her broadcast, Minnie was contacted by two German women who said 'how they wished that all German women could have heard my talk'. Minnie then sent a shortened form to the German Department of the BBC in case it could be used. She was told it was not the sort of talk that would appeal to German women as 'the Germans are on the whole feeling rather cock a' hoop about...the Polish campaign'. Minnie countered that if a German woman had a son in the war she cared 'not two hoots for ten thousand Polands' and many German and English women felt only hopeless despair.[143]

The failure of appeasement had exposed the limitations of Minnie's faith in women to bring peace. Yet Minnie could still applaud the work of The Women's Peace Campaign, with its adapted position that a just peace could be negotiated 'now'.[144] Established in late 1939 and the only specifically women's initiative of the PPU, the feminist and uncompromisingly pacifist Women's International League participated in it.[145] In December the campaign organised a march which was banned by the Metropolitan Police Commissioner, with the agreement of the Home Secretary. It went ahead anyway, with no action taken. Demonstrations and meetings, including one in Hastings, took place in bitter weather across the country, as part of a Women's Peace Day in February 1940.[146]

Before the first months of war were out, Minnie laid out her vision for the post-war world and identified women as the motive force to achieve it.[147] From the platform, in print and over the air she called on women to use the war to build a new world. They must never again be content to ameliorate the worst social conditions but must alter the whole system that created them. It was for women to ensure that slums were abolished, prison conditions were improved and health safeguarded. Giving examples of what was deemed impossible in peacetime but quickly achieved in wartime, Minnie declared that never again should women accept being told that resources were not available for ordinary peacetime activities, when they were always available for military purposes. The evacuation scheme for children most showed clearly the iniquities of war. Minnie found it difficult to believe that as soon as war was declared, allowances were paid to billet evacuated children with strangers while parents contributed nothing; before the war the means test had forced families in the distressed areas to split up as the Government would not pay an allowance for children of the unemployed. Showing how soldiers' wives were struggling to maintain their own children, while evacuated children were paid for at a much higher rate, she used the opportunity to argue that children should be treated as citizens in their own homes with a family allowance, just as when they were evacuated.[148]

Domestically, things were very quiet in Bexhill. After a long and hard winter, Minnie wrote that 'like everyone else in civilian life', she was coping with the rationing, and thankful for lighter evenings. She passed her time knitting, going to the cinema and reading.[149] Minnie volunteered as a fire-watcher, albeit an unenthusiastic one, but the night skies were yet quiet.[150] Bearing in mind her earlier stated opposition to air raid precautions, it is intriguing that she undertook the role. Pacifists volunteering for fire-watching could either be seen as 'an almost apologetic' act and a means of 'atoning', or more generously as eagerness to volunteer services to the community.[151]

From her office in Broadcasting House, Quigley asked Minnie to do a talk soon on 'something that you had a real urge to speak about'. Minnie, who was 'starving for a sight of London', suggested Russia or 'war nerves'.[152] Although radio was central to everyday life, much of the BBC's early wartime broadcasting was out of touch and patronising. Its talks struggled to find an appropriate tone and the Corporation was reluctant to put trust in personalities.[153] Minnie's provided an authentic contrast and her 'Kitchen in Wartime' on producing economic meals, was accepted for the *At Home Today* series as 'Catering for Two'.

Her *Talking It Over* broadcast in April gave practical advice on the contribution each person could make, even the old or infirm who considered themselves a burden during wartime. W. E. 'Bill' Williams, the 'Spoken Word' critic in *The Listener*, the BBC's house journal, described it as 'a kind of wireless parish-visitation, with Minnie Pallister trebling the roles (so to speak) of parson, district nurse and the friend-who-has-dropped-in-for-a-chat'. He found Minnie's advice about how to keep up morale in wartime 'worth a dozen of the sententious gentlemen who lecture us from the Front Bench, the High Court and the Clubs of Pall Mall'.[154] Williams, at that time and for three decades until the mid-1960s, was editor-in-chief and 'cultural force' behind Penguin Books. He was instrumental in setting up the Committee for the Encouragement of Music and the Arts in 1940 and from 1951 to 1963 was secretary-general of the Arts Council. He was therefore a shrewd judge.

After war broke out, some of Minnie's friends and colleagues took jobs in the Ministry of Information. Mary Adams was appointed Director of Home Intelligence in December 1939 and Molly Hamilton joined in February 1940. Minnie, with her background as a political propagandist, organiser, print journalist, author and broadcaster, would have been ideally suited for such work. From early in the war, the MOI sought to recruit writers to its ranks. Vera Brittain was asked to refrain from undertaking any other form of national service but decided on 'a conscious and deliberate withdrawal from popular acclaim and material reward' by declining the opportunity to do war propaganda.[155] With her contacts in the MOI and the media, Minnie would have had little difficulty securing a post but she adopted the same position as Brittain, albeit less grandly expressed. Her connection to the MOI would take a different form.

The Ministry's Home Intelligence Division was responsible for monitoring civilian morale, using a new regional structure for collecting intelligence. The Division was linked to Special Branch and MI5, with whom it shared information. H. S. Banner was Regional Information Officer (RIO) in the South Eastern Region and he prepared reports for headquarters. Initially intelligence gathering was haphazard, apparently relying as much on opinion and gossip as hard evidence. The historian of the MOI concludes that in the first two years of the war the Ministry was widely criticised for its inefficiency and subject to ridicule. Some RIOs were 'straining at the leash' and they 'tended to magnify local instances of anti-war agitation into symptoms of a seditious, nation-wide conspiracy'. In particular, Hubert Banner in the south-east was highlighted.[156]

In his first report, Banner noted that pacifist activity in Kent and Sussex were 'pretty bad' with black spots in West Sussex, where Minnie lived. His report wondered whether the pacifist realised that s/he 'would undoubtedly be the first victim of the concentration camp' adding, 'The Nazis, for all their faults, hate and despise cowards and traitors.'[157] By March, in spite of national PPU protestations to the contrary, Banner concluded 'it appears to be a matter of common knowledge in West Sussex that a local alliance between the... [PPU and the British Union of Fascists] does exist'.[158] However, when little evidence of such an alliance was forthcoming, he pointed to 'certain of the PPU members' in the region having a 'spiritual affinity' with the BUF 'which may perhaps be of greater significance' and pointed directly to Minnie Pallister, the President of Bexhill PPU, as proof.[159]

Banner reported that during discussion at a PPU meeting, Minnie 'spoke with warm admiration of Hitler, asserting that Czechoslovakia was a State which ought never to have been formed, and that partition had been the best possible solution to the Polish problem'.[160] For the second time in two wars Minnie was considered pro-German, but this time also pro-fascist. The MOI's source is not revealed, nor where and when the alleged comments were said to have occurred. Uniquely, therefore, in the same month that Minnie was praised by Bill Williams in *The Listener* for her contribution to morale, she was fingered by an MOI official as supporting Hitler.

Was Minnie an apologist for Hitler? For Minnie the shadow of Versailles hung heavily, and she and other peace women were very sensitive to German attempts to save themselves from the humiliation of the treaty. Early in the conflict, the boundaries were blurred between liberal pacifism and fascist opposition to the war. There is no newspaper coverage of a meeting of John Barclay, which Minnie chaired, in November 1939. The only reported PPU meeting was when Minnie chaired Maude Royden's meeting on 'The Peace We Want' in February 1940. The detailed report of the PPU meeting and the subsequent 'small war' that took place in the letters pages of the *Bexhill Observer*, where Minnie's beliefs came under close scrutiny and criticism, carried no suggestion that Minnie supported Hitler or fascism.[161] Royden was one of the 'leading ideologues and idealists' of a feminist internationalism forged in the experience of the Great War. Made a Companion of Honour in 1929, she had left her position as Guildhouse minister in November 1936 to devote herself to peace work.[162] Within the ambiguous relationship that existed between fascism and some women in the PPU, Royden had recently started flirting with the pro-fascist splinter group, the British People's Party (BPP), which attracted a number of former ILPers.[163] No evidence has been found that Minnie associated with the BPP.[164] In their opposition to war, there may have been an overlap of interests between most PPU women and those of the British Union of Fascists, but there were also marked differences. Minnie would have had no truck with the BUF's description of a 'Jews war'. Mary Adams, the Director of Home Intelligence, would have received Banner's report. She knew Minnie well, having previously tried to get her a job at the BBC. If Adams responded to Banner's report, it is not in the files.

The ever-enthusiastic Banner undertook operations to counteract the activities of the PPU in Sussex and Kent by deploying local information committees that 'are eager to take the field'. He confidentially contacted the editors of local newspapers to seek their cooperation in thwarting the PPU, ludicrously suggesting that much of the PPU's propaganda was suspected of being derived 'not from genuine abhorrence of war but from enemy sources'.[165] Unfortunately for the Regional Officer, his hapless exuberance did not pay off. One of the editors gave a copy of his confidential letter to the PPU which promptly published it in *Peace News*. Anxious to make a bad situation worse, Banner then sought permission for the MOI to use its PPU contacts to find out which editor had leaked the letter. Mrs Adams with good sense replied 'NO!'[166]

These incidents can have done little to reassure Adams as to the intelligence-gathering capacity, interpretative skills, or sound judgement of her South East regional head, including his views on

Minnie Pallister. In spite of his best efforts, the South Eastern Area of the PPU continued to produce its *Bulletin* throughout the war, in contrast to the PPU elsewhere whose publications were largely in abeyance.[167] As no copies are extant, it cannot be confirmed that Minnie was involved in its production, though with her track record it seems probable that she was at the heart of it.

The German invasion of Denmark and Norway in April 1940 severely shook the PPU. Membership, which had reached 136,000 that month, immediately began to fall as attitudes hardened against pacifists. The invasion of Luxemburg, Belgium and Holland the following month proved decisive. A rally in support of a negotiated peace scheduled for Hyde Park on 18 May was abandoned, membership plummeted and sponsors and prominent members resigned. A. A. Milne, a poet, playwright, novelist, creator of *Winnie the Pooh* and author of the 1934 anti-war book, *Peace With Honour*, to which Minnie had dedicated her last *No More War* editorial in December 1934, disavowed his pacifism. So did Bertrand Russell, who resigned his PPU sponsorship.[168] Even an historian of the PPU, a committed pacifist, questions the validity of continuing to urge a negotiated peace in those circumstances.[169] One of the few who retained their pacifist beliefs, George Lansbury, President of the PPU, died three days before the invasion of the Low Countries. With his passing Minnie lost a vital supporter and ally. Minnie's eulogy described him as a pacifist who never ceased to fight.[170]

A week after Lansbury's death, Minnie attended the 1940 Labour Party conference in Bournemouth where delegates were in a state of nervous excitement at the prospect of a German invasion. A few days earlier, Attlee and Greenwood had been invited to join the Government under Chamberlain. They replied that they needed to consult the Party before responding, which they did at Bournemouth. Labour declined to serve under Chamberlain, precipitated his resignation and brought Churchill to the premiership.[171] In her conference account, Minnie did not refer to the noisy protests that took place by pacifists and some on the left. She limited herself to saying that while everything was focussed on winning the war, several delegates 'reminded the conference that the world, whatever it may be, will still be here when the war is over, and that the future depends on the kind of peace which is made...'.[172] Minnie would have been in the thick of the group delivering that message.

As the situation in France became grave, the German army reached the Channel ports. With the fate of the British Expeditionary Force in the balance, an intelligence report of the Royal Sussex Regiment dated 21 May was alert to members of the PPU seeking to circulate *Peace News* among the troops in the county. In view of the paper's contents, and the fact that some of its soldiers were already members, it is clear that the army would want to prevent *Peace News* reaching more of them. A military intelligence file from December 1939 to August 1940 that covered 'offshore flares, air raids, suspicious vehicles, bacteriological warfare, treatment of enemy parachutists and wounded, civilian passes, rounding up aliens, measures in event of enemy invasion, sentry duties, construction of defences, leave arrangements and the possible use of gas' also catalogued the activities of the PPU.[173] Had she been aware, Minnie would have been pleased that their modest local PPU actions had registered within the military.

The concerns of the military were understandable. Some positions taken in *Peace News* were wrong-headed and potentially dangerous. In January 1940 it argued that continuing the war would be a disaster for civilisation and would lead to totalitarianism in Britain, no matter who won. On 2 August, while the Battle of Britain raged, it declared that even ignominious terms would be preferable to prolonging the war. A week later 'A Pacifist Commentary' by 'Observer' on the front cover stated, 'Personally, I don't believe that a Hitlerian Europe would be quite so terrible as most people believe it would be.'[174] Not surprisingly, the paper was criticised as pro-Nazi.

In the circumstances, the shrewd and sober assessment of the Home Office that it shared with the MOI Home Intelligence Division at the end of May 1940 was remarkable. It concluded that the PPU was 'stupid and mischievous but not actually dangerous'.[175] That such tolerance could be shown at the height of the Dunkirk evacuation, the Fall of France and the Battle of Britain, when the future of the country hung in the balance, displayed an acute sense of judgement and professional detachment by the Home Office. It also demonstrated a capacity to assess where real dangers lay in differentiating between BUF women opposed to the war, who were interned, and PPU women opposed to the war, who were allowed to continue with their lives.[176]

Minnie was part of the 'handful' of absolute pacifists, including

Brittain and Sybil Thorndike who stuck resolutely to the view that any war, whatever the circumstances, was too high a price to pay, and that there was no moral difference between the First and Second World Wars.[177] As Brittain recorded, their stance required accepting that invasion, defeat or death might be preferable to armed resistance or hating the enemy.[178] To use Baxter's pejorative 1941 phrase, Minnie was of the '"peace at any price" clique' of feminist appeasers.[179] She was out of step with her Great War pacifist comrades, as every major leader of the NCF, except Alfred Salter, concluded it was necessary to fight to defeat Nazi Germany.[180] Even Royden, who had perhaps been closest to Minnie in pacifist beliefs, in spite of her links to the far right, came to believe that Nazism was worse than war. She had given up her PPU membership within weeks of the Bexhill meeting that Minnie chaired and her faith in 'women's power to deliver peace' was also shattered.[181] The changes of position by those close to Minnie, as well as Swanwick's suicide, must have weighed heavily on her. It would have been much easier to fall in with the majority who had recanted in the summer of 1940, and avoid the social isolation and rancour she knew was to come. Brittain noted it was around this time that 'pacifist' became a term of abuse.[182] Although Minnie did not have to experience the options of invasion, defeat or death, she was prepared to pay a price for her beliefs. When the moment came, she did so uncomplainingly.

Unlike in the Great War, Minnie was not now part of a collective cause to prevent war but rather acted as an individual, through personal faith. Arguing from a position of moral rearmament, that the only person she could change was herself, she worked to retain the values upon which a future peace could be built.[183] It would be easy to denigrate Minnie's choice. To put herself apart from society at its moment of deepest danger was the most profound decision that Minnie took in the second half of her life. At a time when the overwhelming majority of the population were supporting the fight for the survival of their country, she stood back. History shows Minnie did not have right on her side. That she later referred little to her experiences as a pacifist in the Second World War, in contrast to her multiple reflections on the Great War, says much. In a rare comment a decade later, she said that while pacifists were now held in part responsible for the war, a pamphlet should be published of quotations from national newspapers extolling

Hitler's virtues at a time when pacifists were rescuing his victims.[184] However, that was a comment at a PPU meeting, rather than an open statement. In public, she was silent.

*

From June 1940, the south-east coast of England was a restricted area, and visitors were barred.[185] Although the south coast had initially been designated as a reception area for children evacuated from London, the risk of bombing and the real threat of invasion meant plans were reversed.[186] Non-essential people were encouraged to evacuate voluntarily and the town's population fell sharply with the number of ration books issued reduced by nearly two-thirds, from 29,000 at the beginning of 1940 to 10,198 a year later. Minnie and Gladys were part of the skeleton population that stayed in Bexhill for the duration of the war. Surprisingly, in view of intelligence reports on Minnie and the role of the PPU, she was not required to leave the restricted area. She reported it was strange shopping in deserted streets. The *Bexhill Observer* described how defence restrictions made the town's ordinary commercial life impossible. Industries were suspended and the local authority's income so markedly reduced that central government was asked to help in order to maintain its services.[187] The local paper reproduced advice from the Government about what to do in case of invasion and fighting in the immediate vicinity. Without irony, it said that if enemy tanks or soldiers were seen, the guidance of the local police or ARP should be sought.[188]

In September 1939, Minnie's enigmatic wish had been for a very different form of military intervention. 'We are very quiet but I am hoping that we shall soon have the place *filled* with troops and the *noisiest* aeroplanes and tanks in the Army (for private reasons of my own!!)'[189] [Minnie's emphasis]. Whatever her reasons, now lost, her wish was in some senses fulfilled on 2 June 1940 when 56th Heavy Artillery Regiment was posted to Bexhill to strengthen coastal defences against the prospect of imminent invasion. D Battery contained recently conscripted Gunner Terence 'Spike' Milligan of the Royal Artillery.

It seems very likely that at this key moment in British history, Minnie got to know Milligan. As secretary of the Bexhill Friends of Music Society that put on concerts at the De La Warr Pavilion, she would have met Milligan, who had formed a jazz band that was looking to perform. They each had a love of music, a love of performing and a sense of fun. Milligan's band played first at a 'village dance affair' in the Old Town Church Hall – about 100 yards from Minnie's flat – before graduating to the De La Warr Pavilion. According to Milligan, his band provided the focus of social life for the town in the winter of 1940. It is hard to imagine Minnie missing a musical event in a town that Milligan described as empty, blacked out and 'entertainment-starved'.[190] In the two and a half years Milligan was based in or around Bexhill, before he and his comrades were sent to North Africa in January 1943, 55-year-old Minnie made a considerable impression on 21-year-old Milligan, as later events were to show.

The summer of 1940 was spent gardening. Minnie was loaned a friend's border and sowing vegetables was followed by 'fighting the caterpillar plague' and picking blackberries between air raid warnings. Minnie was also involved in a group which made blankets for war victims from scraps of wool. On Sunday 1 September, with the Battle of Britain at its peak, Minnie wrote to Quigley, 'London sounds ghastly just now'.[191]

As a German invasion seemed imminent, Minnie's pacifism told against her in the BBC. On 4 September 1940, the Director General informed staff that no one who belonged to an organisation whose policy was 'inconsistent with the national effort' would be allowed to broadcast.[192] The following day Quigley wrote to Minnie, 'I am afraid that this note will surprise you, but I have to ask you whether you are still a member of the Peace Pledge Union?' She explained that new wartime regulations required the BBC to know whether speakers belonged to such organisations.[193] The BBC was aware of Minnie's historic links. In January 1938 a press cutting from the *Manchester Guardian* on the activities of the PPU had been inserted in Minnie's BBC personal file. Although the article did not refer to her in person, and was without comment, whoever inserted it – presumably the security services – was making clear her association with the PPU. Minnie replied, 'I should much dislike sailing under any false colours', saying that she had been a pacifist in the last war and had been ever since.[194] Although it was acknowledged that Minnie was a popular broadcaster and that what she said on-air was 'quite unobjectionable', the BBC decided that Minnie should be barred.[195] Minnie accepted the situation and made no protest or complaint. Quigley observed 'she fully realises our point of view on such matters.'[196]

As no exceptions to the ruling could be made without the agreement of the Director General, two months later Quigley made the case for Minnie to be able to broadcast saying she had a 'real contribution to make in present circumstances when more people than usual are suffering and lonely and sad'. She excelled as 'a sympathetic, sincere speaker' on different topics and the 'gentle uplift' she introduced was 'much appreciated by elderly ladies and invalids'. Quigley's request worked its way up through the BBC's hierarchy, gaining qualified support, until Sir Frederick Ogilvie, the Director General, ruled that Minnie could not be exempted from the ban.[197] After Minnie's broadcasts ended, her communication with the BBC fell away and from November 1940, there was only sporadic contact. An occasional letter to Quigley talked about life but not work.[198]

Although opposed to the war, Minnie was not defeatist and she did not sow alarm or despondency. Her *Daily Herald* pieces were cheery. Finding beauty in the roof garden on an air raid shelter softened the reality of the moment.[199] In 'Life Goes On' she wrote of thousands of women leaving their homes and possessions to take on 'unaccustomed work, new responsibility, service and comradeship'. In losing their material comforts they found themselves, Minnie suggested.[200] Although her *Daily Herald* articles made as much of wartime conditions as circumstances would allow, they ended when wartime restrictions on newsprint reduced the paper from twenty pages in the 1930s to four pages.[201]

In *Man and Metal*, Minnie continued to draw on the prevailing spirit to set an agenda for the future. She noted how quickly change could be achieved when a country puts its mind to it, and how war had brought people closer together. Unlike the Great War, which was about the armed services, this war involved every citizen. Everyone now helped one another, taking in evacuees, and the bombed out. They bore one another's burdens, and should be doing the same in peacetime.[202]

September and October were dry and sunny. Crops were bountiful, and the sea and sky were perfect, so it was hard to believe there was a war on 'even when the bombs whistle past'.[203] Friends and neighbours continued to leave Bexhill, abandoning houses, gardens and pets. Minnie was free to take advantage of the crops in their deserted vegetable gardens and orchards. Life between raids was 'one long gathering of apples and pears and vegetables', though it left her stiff. A bumper harvest provided enough for the winter. A supply of blackberry jelly offset a national jam shortage. With the 'gardens and cats...odd brothers and husbands' left behind 'we don't get a chance to be bored'.[204] In October there was a run of good films in the cinema including Shirley Temple in the *Blue Bird* and *The Grapes of Wrath*, which 'showed the whole tragedy of civilisation'.[205]

Being a pacifist did not exempt Minnie from being on the front-line. German military plans identified Bexhill as a suitable point for invasion. Beaches were no-go areas and barbed wire and artillery lined the seafront.[206] Raids and unexploded bombs disrupted the routines of life. Meals for guests who failed to arrive remained uneaten.[207] Unlike six months earlier, fire-watching was no longer a quiet affair. The risk of death heightened Minnie's sense of being alive. Hit-and-run raids were so quick there was no warning of attack. High-explosive bombs wrecked houses in Bexhill and killed a number of people. As she was writing her Women's Page for *Man and Metal*, a bomb whistled down and exploded nearby 'with the familiar crash and sound of splintering'. Minnie had another narrow escape when sat in the window. Hearing a low noise, which she thought was a noisy bus coming up the hill, she looked up to see 'an enormous bomber just coming straight for the window, so low that when he dropped his bombs at the end of the road they made no thud and didn't go off.' The sisters also escaped lightly when an incendiary bomb dropped in their garden; neighbours' houses were set alight. 'We live from one raid to the next, and so far have been lucky in having no more than a tile or two knocked off.'[208] When the Luftwaffe switched to night bombing London, Minnie wrote to Quigley: 'We hear the planes droning over night after night, and know they are coming your way.' Minnie's 'chief grouse' was that the enemy planes were so loud that they drowned out the evening's radio programmes.[209]

Minnie's writings capture the circumstances of late 1940. With the nightly blitz of Britain's cities underway, she felt uplifted by the sense that 'none of us know whether we shall survive to see another day when we go to bed at night'.[210] Life required adaptation but Minnie remained positive. Facing 'long dark evenings when it was not safe to go out', although it would be difficult to go to the cinema, theatre, meetings and lectures, Minnie counselled readers that winter was not something to be feared, but provided opportunities for service, courage, endurance and the chance to read books or take correspondence classes.[211] She urged them to overcome the prejudice against sleeping at odd times to make up for broken nights and disturbed sleep, for while they could get by without much food, they needed rest. Minnie was now eating communal meals that were economical and helped develop bonds with people living nearby. Seeing an opportunity to extend socialised services, she hoped they would continue in peacetime.[212]

Banished from the airwaves, Minnie's written appeals for 'a change of system and a change of heart'[213] paralleled those of J. B. Priestley on the BBC. As the war took its toll on towns and cities, Minnie condemned the inequality of sacrifice between rich and poor, and argued, 'If we do not change this system the very moment the war is ended...then we will have lost the war.'[214] Minnie praised Priestley's Postscript talk, which captured the national mood. People must not think only of victory as being just about destroying Hitler, but also as an opportunity to destroy the conditions that created him. Both understood that the war would change the world for ever and saw it as a platform for constructing a new society, arguing that people should expect to serve the community in peacetime just as much as in wartime.[215] Her ode to the common man declared the nation was no longer represented by 'small groups of people at the top, the champagne-and-Rolls-Royce class' but by the ordinary woman with the teapot who offered it to victims of bombing, to firefighters, to people in the shelters. It was for them to show the same courage in meeting the challenge of peace and building the new world that they showed in the face of fire and high explosive and it was for the Labour Party, trades union and co-operative movements to be ready and big enough to provide the leadership when peace came.[216] Workers should have enough faith in their own cause to take on 'the job of running the world'.[217] Moreover, people had to have the courage to tackle the class privilege which was insidious in British society.[218] Where Minnie diverged from Priestley was in saying that war itself was the enemy.[219]

Although Minnie kept the pacifist flag flying, as the war intensified, the PPU crumbled.[220] Members were harassed or arrested for selling *Peace News* in the street or for public speaking.[221] It became an offence to publish statements which could 'foment opposition to the prosecution of the war to a successful issue' and publishers and printers were cowed by the risk of guilt by association with the paper.[222] Newspaper wholesalers refused to distribute it and circulation fell to less than 16,000, so it relied on an unofficial network of volunteers for distribution.[223] Middleton Murry, its editor, commented that the pacifist movement 'now exists precariously in a sort of no man's land on the fringe of a democratic-totalitarian society', while failing to acknowledge that its activities were allowed to continue.[224] By the end of 1940 the MOI noted that the PPU had lost considerable ground.[225] As pacifists became remote from the rest of the population, the Women's Peace Campaign suspended its activities and other pacifist organisations started to shut up shop.[226]

In late 1940, the MOI issued a leaflet where Bertrand Russell, Maude Royden, A. A. Milne and others, some ex-collaborators of Minnie, renounced their pacifism saying the situation the country faced was 'different now'. The PPU countered with a pamphlet quoting Thorndike and Ponsonby who had not changed their views.[227] Although it was not an even contest, Minnie took to task erstwhile colleagues who publicly recanted former beliefs. Molly Hamilton's vigorous denunciation of her own earlier pacifist views and those of her friends who still held them, received a solid rejoinder from Minnie. While avoiding commenting on their differences over the Second World War, Minnie criticised Hamilton's retrospective views on pacifism during the Great War, retorting 'she eats humble pie so heartily for some of her beliefs during and just after the last war, that one feels she is sometimes eating more pie than there is.'[228] The historian of women's appeasement noted that in recanting of previous positions, which they had sometimes held for two decades, individuals were often vindicating themselves and 'rewriting their histories to cohere with current political moods'.[229] Hamilton was described as wrenching herself from a pacifist position and condemning those who 'chatted about "moral rearmament"' thereby polishing her own 'patriotic' credentials.[230]

While in the Great War Minnie had been 'hated by the public, ostracised by family and friends', she had 'the exhilaration of being in a small minority fighting with our backs to the wall' and 'with a burning conviction that we were right'.[231] Feeling part of something dynamic and important did not exist for pacifists during the Second World War. Many felt guilt at their position.[232] The overwhelming majority of people, including friends, were committed to resisting Hitler. How odd it must have felt to be living the war first-hand, with bombs landing around you and taking part in fire-watching, yet putting yourself apart from active resistance.

It is likely that Minnie's experiences paralleled those of Brittain, who sensed mistrust from the authorities. Brittain believed there was a black mark against her name as a writer and citizen, as government offices refused her work and authors attached to the MOI attacked her writings. Suggesting the authorities were unable to tell the difference between 'religious conviction and political treachery', she said she was monitored by police, and her mail was intercepted and read. She incurred the animosity of friends, was shunned by editors and fellow writers and received letters of abuse. She was told unofficially by a source in the MOI that the objection lay in her PPU membership.[233] Minnie differed from Brittain in two ways. She was told overtly that her exclusion from the BBC was due to her PPU membership. Neither was Minnie aggrieved. She appears to have been reconciled to her position and did not consider herself persecuted.

Something of how Minnie and other pacifists were perceived, and the climate they endured, is depicted in the film *Unpublished Story*. Released in 1942, before the war had turned in Britain's favour, it was set against the Fall of France, Dunkirk, the Battle of Britain and the suffering of the people of the East End during the Blitz of 1940–41. Highly critical of the pacifist movement, the film contrasted the 'rats and mules' of the People for Peace Society with the heroism of soldiers, firemen, women ambulance drivers and the bravery of the civilian population. The lead character, Randall, a journalist played by Richard Greene, considered the pacifists to be defeatists, and dupes of Hitler, who should be exposed. When, under German bombing of innocent citizens, the leading pacifist and sincere secretary of the Society, Trapes, recanted his pacifism, the Peace Society was exposed as a front for paid agitators and German fifth-columnists whose aim was spreading rumours and causing panic and division.

The immediacy of the film, dealing with such recent events, must have been a source of discomfort for Minnie and her equally sincere fellow pacifists. The film's sense of paranoia and propagandising overreaction towards the perceived pacifist threat contrasted with the Home Office's shrewd assessment of the PPU as 'stupid and mischievous but not actually dangerous'. However, the words of *Peace News* and the actions of the PPU had provided all the material needed to inspire the script. If Minnie went to see the film, it would have made uneasy viewing.

A probable example of Minnie being singled out by the MOI occurred when Minnie wrote to Routledge and Keegan Paul (RKP), which acted for the Labour Book Service, proposing a book on women after the war called *Women and the New World*. Formulated 'in an easy style' to appeal to the woman voter, Minnie said she would be able to write it quickly.[234] Established in the spring of 1939 as a rival to the Communist-inspired Left Book Club, about which the Labour Party was concerned, the Labour Book Service was a joint initiative with the TUC to publish monthly books.[235] T. Murray Ragg, the Managing Editor of RKP, considered the series important for when the war ended 'and the work of transition to a planned society in peace time begins'.[236]

Ragg liked Minnie's idea and requested a detailed synopsis for a 40 to 50,000-word book, although he advised her that the final decision would rest with the Selection Committee. Minnie submitted the outline, but a week later Ragg replied that it had been turned down.[237] Oddly, the minutes of the Selection Committee make no reference to Minnie's book having been placed before it. Was Minnie's pacifism an issue? Did Brittain's 'black mark' against pacifists have an impact? MOI members on the Committee included the recanted pacifist Molly Hamilton and Francis 'Frank' Williams, ex-editor of the *Daily Herald*, who in 1941 was Controller of Press Censorship and News in the Ministry.[238] It seems likely that representatives of the MOI ensured the proposal was not considered.

In spite of Minnie's concerns about the prospect of a 'long dark winter', it passed quickly due to the speed of events with 'problems of shelters, of canteens, of evacuation, of bombed houses, of burst pipes', and spring coming early.[239] She did not go far afield. An exception was her annual pilgrimage to Bournemouth for May Day where, in spite of war conditions, the local labour movement held its bazaar in 'her' hall, though it was a shadow of its pre-war self.[240] Minnie kept in loose touch with Quigley, sending her flowers. She occasionally suggested an idea or discreetly sounded out whether talks on the BBC were limited to those who believed in outright victory as a way out of the military impasse.[241] While

Quigley always expressed pleasure in hearing from Minnie, she regretted the BBC's policy regarding broadcasters remained unchanged.[242]

Minnie used her one remaining print outlet, the 'Women's Page' of *Man and Metal*, to raise social and political issues. Over months, she analysed the relationships between women, work and home in wartime. She defended the right of married women to work in factories, saying they were not being made to work, but welcomed the real wages, the comradeship of other women and reasonable conditions it provided, and gave the opportunity for a woman to be 'a "person" in her own right'. Minnie also called for homemaking and motherhood to be seen as a career by those women who wanted it, and given the dignity it deserved, instead of being considered 'worth nothing at all'. Again she returned to the issue of family allowances. Now that women were needed for war work, they were less impractical and Minnie saw their extension to civilian homes after the war as a way of removing anxiety and laying a foundation for building a better society. Minnie warned against men and women being played off against one another in the post-war jobs market. She objected to employers expecting women to do twelve-hour shifts and run homes, only for them to accuse women, when peacetime returned, of taking men's jobs, and send them back to the kitchen. Women, she said, must have the freedom to occupy places in public life, and she looked forward to 'some dim and distant future' where a woman receiving a family allowance could also be seen as important as a civil servant in a responsible job. Taken together, Minnie's writings in 1941 were a manifesto for women in work and home.[243]

In favour of rationing, Minnie advocated its continuation in peacetime to ensure fair shares for all. She reminded readers that there had always been a form of rationing through people not having money for food and called for miners and workers in other heavy industries to be given the same access to meals in work as affluent people had in hotels and restaurants. Prefiguring twenty-first-century fair and ethical trading, she wrote of the 'real price' of goods, highlighting the 'human suffering' in digging coal or fishing in the North Sea or the child labour and 'woman slavery' involved in the supply chains of goods. It was, she said, part of the housewife's job to ensure overseas workers were not exploited so that they too received their share of resources. She also called for boycotts of non-rationed foods sold at inflated prices.[244] In one of her last articles for the *Daily Herald*, Minnie complained of inefficiency in agricultural production. 'The Ministry of Food is doing its best, but it is a man's best', she lamented and called for a woman to be put in charge so that the production and distribution of foodstuffs was done more effectively.[245]

By the second year of war, Minnie was grateful that in spite of war disruptions, including paper shortages, labour difficulties, transport hold-ups and bombed offices, books were still being published. They reminded Minnie of the important, elemental aspects of life, otherwise lost in a focus on materialism or warfare. There was also cinema. She regularly reviewed books and films in her 'Women's Page' and urged readers to see Chaplin's *The Great Dictator*, drawing attention to its plea at the end for 'brotherhood, sympathy, love, and justice'.[246] By the end of 1941, though, she had lost her last remaining publication when *Man and Metal* was considerably reduced and the 'Women's Page' ended.

*

In spring 1941, almost fifteen years exactly after she became ill, Minnie made a major talk in public. Thrilled, and delighted that she still had her old ease of speech, she wanted to try herself out on a bigger platform with an hour-long lecture. The opportunity came in her annual September visit to Aberavon where, as well as visiting the towns and villages of the constituency, she gave a large set-piece talk.[247] The experience provided hope for a new start in public speaking and she declared, 'I feel I am once more alive.'[248]

Local speaking engagements provided a timely alternative to radio and newspapers as Minnie found a new audience, or a new way to reach her existing audience. The Women's Institute (WI) had grown to over 300,000 members by the late 1930s, promoting the ideal of the active woman citizen, supporting campaigns for equal pay and family allowances, and encouraging women to become involved locally and stand for elections. As the WI straddled the boundary between citizenship and feminism, it was the perfect fit for Minnie.[249] From the autumn of 1941, as confidence in her voice returned, the WI became an increasingly important outlet. Her talks included her experiences in Germany before the war and Russia, which since the Nazi invasion of June, had dominated attention.[250]

From March 1942, in village halls across the south of England, she addressed women on what they should want after the war, spreading the word about what post-war reconstruction should look like, promoting state control, strong public services and social justice. She told seven combined Sussex WIs that women now had the opportunity to build a future and it was for women to determine what happened in their communities and the country by working out what to do with their vote. People had to learn to share goods with other peoples of the world; British people should not have a priority claim. Also 'money' had to be brought under public control.[251] While the messages were, in essence, the same as she had presented for decades, the radicalising effect of the war gave them resonance. No longer a party propagandist, and not speaking to political audiences, Minnie spent the next three years evangelising her politicised messages to middle England.

When Russia and America entered the war, the threat of invasion lifted and there was a let-up in bombing. Not accustomed to it, Minnie commented, 'One gets rather suspicious of long lulls these days.'[252] As the frontline shifted away from Britain, there were signs of Bexhill returning to life and the local Labour Party revived its activities.[253]

After the RAF introduced a new policy of area bombing of Germany that targeted the morale of industrial workers, Minnie addressed a 'Stop Mass Bombing' meeting convened by Christianity Calling, supported by the Bombing Restriction Committee,[254] organisations that were later described as 'The Voices of Conscience'.[255] However, as the war had not yet turned in the Allies' favour, at the time bombing was generally seen as a necessary way of attacking the Nazi regime from Britain, so anti-bombing views were unpopular. Minnie actively supported Christianity Calling, a 'Union of Christian progressives', which had been established by Arthur Belden in the first month of the war. Operating in parallel with the official churches, it aimed to take more 'advanced' positions than the Anglican, Roman Catholic and Free Churches, which were perceived to be failing to address 'the gravest social crisis of all time'.[256]

Minnie continued to do fire-watching, although she was under no obligation to do so. When the junior minister Ellen Wilkinson made it compulsory for women up to 45 in August 1942, Minnie was already well over the age limit.[257] Fire-watching proved deeply unpopular with conscripted women – up to 80 per cent claimed exemption – but Minnie persevered. Occasional mornings were spent getting hot from stirrup pump practice and nights spent fire-watching dragged as there were fewer alerts and the hated blackout made them feel even longer. While some people were able to work through the night, Minnie could not, so coped by reading a light novel or magazine, accompanied by a pot of tea.[258] One day, feeling 'mouldy' as she usually did after a night of fire-watching, she prepared the curriculum for a six-week lecture course on 'The World in Books'. Contracted by the Workers' Education Association (WEA) with only a few days' notice, she decided to talk on the books of Russia, America, China, Germany and India, declaring that it was 'not too bad' as she then had a week to prepare for each.[259]

A change in the BBC's policy about hiring pacifists provided an opportunity for Minnie's rehabilitation. In September, Quigley requested a re-examination of Minnie's ban. She argued that as a good, popular broadcaster, liked by women listeners, Minnie would be 'particularly useful' on 'training for citizenship', without appearing to preach or educate.[260] The Controller (Home), Sir Richard Maconachie, and Director of Talks, George Barnes, concluded that Minnie did not fall foul of the new criterion which was 'opposition to the National war effort'.[261] While they would have welcomed her collecting for the families and dependents of British servicemen, had they known about her efforts to stop RAF bombing, they would have been less happy.[262]

Quigley immediately invited Minnie to contribute to the *Mostly for Women* series. Broadcast in a prime slot, just before the 1 pm news on Sundays, when families were settling down for dinner, Quigley's idea was that through pleasant and entertaining, rather than heavy and serious talks, to get women to think for themselves, becoming more consciously responsible citizens.[263] Minnie replied that the subjects 'every decent woman' should be thinking about were 'post-war planning and a new basis of Society' as well as 'relations between peoples of different countries'.[264] However, her suggestions did not appeal to Quigley. Disappointed, Minnie responded that if she were 'just...one more woman giving one more talk, there's no point in it...' She continued that while 'I have never been a feminist in the sense that I want women to go down the mines...I do feel that women have given enormous contributions to public life which are never recognised, and I would like to make that a sort of signature tune.' As her 'one small gift' was 'to be able to swallow rather technical principles...and regurgitate them in a palatable form', Minnie proposed including 'a little gentle economics' in her broadcast as it was essential to overcome the idea of women as the 'spending sex'.[265] It took four months before Minnie struck a note that resonated, when Quigley was happy with a 1,200-word script 'I'm Not Interested in Politics', a straightforward appeal for women to engage with the subject.[266]

On Sunday 18 April 1943, after an absence of nearly three years, Minnie was back on the air. Quigley thought Minnie's talk came over well, if a little fast. Her highly accessible follow-up talk on local government was also good and Quigley invited Minnie to draft a talk on party politics to be broadcast in June.[267] They discussed how to overcome women avoiding anything overtly political and Minnie suggested not advertising the talk as political, but instead including the material 'naturally into a women's magazine, in another form [so] they would be almost sure to listen.'[268] Minnie's script arrived when Quigley was on leave. Instead it was read by Barnes, who complained to Maconachie of the talk's lack of balance. He did not doubt Minnie's sincerity or popularity, but he considered sections of the script on common ownership to be unfair, and thought the absence of the Liberal Party from the narrative to be unjust. There was 'plenty of time for the script to be altered and for a new script on a different subject to be written.'[269]

Although the Government had asked the BBC to help create an environment for debate on democracy and reconstruction, in 1942 the Corporation continued to be chary. In the 1930s, the Talks Department had come in for criticism for supposed left-wing bias, and, as a result, it was reorganised, and its senior staff dispersed.[270] Maconachie, a former British Minister to Kabul, had been appointed as Head of BBC Talks in 1936 in a move perceived to be to the right and towards caution. He had an aversion to political issues.[271] Now Maconachie responded to Barnes that the subject of party politics did not seem 'altogether appropriate' in wartime. If there were to be such a broadcast, the BBC would need to 'have someone with a harder and clearer head than M.P.'.[272] Even though a contract had been issued for Minnie's talk, Barnes told Quigley that Maconachie had agreed that the 'Party Politics' talk should not go ahead, 'particularly at this moment when there is a vote of censure on the B.B.C. for Left-Wing bias'.[273] At a time when the BBC was nervous of broadcasters becoming personalities, Minnie made the BBC hierarchy uneasy.[274]

Quigley explained Barnes's and Maconachie's decision, while distancing herself from it without stating so openly, ending the letter with, 'I know that by this time you are used to our strange ways.'[275] Minnie breezily acknowledged that 'I seem to be the bad girl of the family as far as talks go', adding: 'Should hate to see on your tombstone "Died of an overdose of Minnie Pallister".'[276] Minnie recognised that the Party Politics talk was 'stone dead' [277] and suggested a programme on books as 'reading is the next most neglected thing to politics', adding as if the issue had not happened, 'in fact one can bring in political reading'.[278] Quigley thanked her for being so uncomplaining and afterwards fed back that the 'Reading' broadcast had come over well.[279] Minnie still hankered after a book review slot and raised it regularly with the BBC. A decade later she was still making the case without success.[280]

Minnie planned to spend the week before the broadcast in Bournemouth with the Hookeys for the annual bazaar. They provided 'a shrine of friendship' where she could just be herself and stay as long as she wanted. However, on arrival Minnie found her old friend dangerously ill, and Annie Hookey died a few days later.[281] Her death was a tremendous loss, still keenly felt over a decade later.[282] Despite her pain and grief, Minnie spent a 'ghastly' week working in the bazaar before participating in a huge Co-operative conference on Saturday. After the event, Minnie travelled to Broadcasting House for the transmission.[283] Although she retained links with Bournemouth, Minnie had lost her second home.

Mid-1943 was also significant for the resumption of Minnie's publishing career. Her friend Wilson Midgley was appointed editor of the literary journal *John O'London* and a few months later Minnie was back in print as a reviewer. In the magazine, Minnie specialised in books on Asia, reviewing them particularly from the perspective of Britain's role and relationships, and the lives of people, rather than considering Asian countries as allies or enemies. Midge said of Minnie that while she 'talked like a Poll Parrot' she reviewed like an angel.[284] She also used her column to highlight outstanding women from British and other cultures. Minnie continued reviewing until Midgley retired in 1953, after which she would occasionally contribute until late 1959.[285]

There were other signs of Minnie's wartime rehabilitation and she began appearing again in Labour Party events. At a women's conference, Minnie said the Beveridge Report, whose principles provided the foundation for establishing the welfare state, was the 'first glorious idea there had ever been in this country in which the citizen was recognised as part of the state and had rights'.[286]

The war on the Home Front was now a matter of endurance. In Bexhill, though the immediate dangers of 1940 and 1941 had passed, Minnie suffered war fatigue as life became a matter of coping with frustrations and inconveniences. The clothing ration had come 'like a bolt from the blue', and Minnie foresaw a period of drawing on the skills of mothers and great-grandmothers to patch and darn, alter and cut down.[287] Constant themes were where to get food, what was available, and how long it took to queue for it. The availability of sugar became the subject of complex barter arrangements, and Minnie hoarded typing paper because of shortages. Morning trains from Bexhill to London were problematic.[288]

Throughout 1943 Minnie supported Christianity Calling and was a member of its council. In February, one week after victory at Stalingrad and with the tide of war turning decisively in the Allies' favour, she was one of twenty-eight Christians and pacifists, who signed an open letter to the Prime Minister calling for peace to be offered to the Axis countries.[289] During her annual visit to South Wales, Minnie spoke on behalf of Christianity Calling at a Port Talbot conference, chaired by Bill Cove. In the evening she preached in the Baptist Church, before attending a social hour with 700 to 800 people then stayed up talking until nearly midnight.[290] In August, seeking to avoid what it considered unnecessary deaths, Christianity Calling objected to Allied governments' demand for unconditional surrender and called on the British public to offer 'a big peace gesture resulting perhaps in an armistice'.[291] The following Easter, Minnie was a signatory to 'a manifesto and an appeal' that condemned the Government's indiscriminate 'destruction of whole cities' and criticised the 'silent acquiescence' of the official denominations 'in this iniquity'.[292] Such calls were whistling in the wind. In the House of Commons there was a call to restrict the activities of those opposed to the RAF's bombing strategy and to intern its leaders for their pro-German activities. Herbert Morrison, the Home Secretary, replied he did not doubt the sincerity of those involved and that their impact was in any case limited.[293] Once again sound judgement prevailed.

Within the BBC, Quigley and Minnie persevered. Quigley asked Minnie to make a special journey to London to hear plans for *Woman's Page*, a new women's magazine programme, and to exchange ideas for the autumn. As correspondence buzzed back and forth, ideas tumbled over one another as each struggled to keep up with the other. Apologising for a three-page 'screed' that was 'trying to clear my own mind at the expense of yours', Minnie suggested the themes of the woman's duty to her home and friends, including home work as a career, duty to the community 'which gives us our political angle', and duty to herself.[294]

An early assumption was that Minnie would be a key presenter of *Woman's Page*. Minnie suggested that the first talk would be very general, instigating 'several trains of thought', each to be developed later. Explanatory talks on economics, including money, were essential. She also wanted to challenge the gendering of roles in domestic and work environments – 'it is all wrong for girls to be always expected to sew and wash up, while boys are expected to play football' – and recalled an earlier unbroadcast talk on outstanding women being squeezed out of 'so-called men's jobs'. Distancing herself from what she saw as 'The tendency in feminist circles [is] to treat women as if all were alike, and all wanted to be engineers and so on...', Minnie argued that women had different wants and should be able to fulfil diverse roles, whether in the home or at work. Quigley marked these comments with a tick.[295]

Minnie promised to have the opening political talk ready by the time Quigley returned from a visit to Ireland, and suggested presenting the viewpoints of feminist Women for Westminster and the 'Six Point Group', which supported equality for women.[296] For Minnie, promoting women of all political persuasions was now as important as party allegiance. Women for Westminster had been established in 1942 as a non-party organisation to promote women in political life, although it was perceived as having a centre-left bias. Its focus on civic education chimed with Minnie's approach and a few days later Minnie spoke at one of its meetings in Nottingham.[297]

The week before *Woman's Page* launched, Lady Violet Bonham Carter, a BBC Governor, contacted the Director of Talks, apparently at the behest of Nancy Astor, to ask why Minnie was a contributor to the programme. Whatever the reason for Astor's unhappiness, Bonham Carter might have had her own lingering reason to object as Minnie had attacked her during the Great War for her wealth. Quigley gave a robust defence. Minnie was a good broadcaster who 'always seems to ring the bell' and had a particularly sympathetic approach to people.[298] Barnes, though, would have been alerted once more to Minnie as a person who attracted controversy.

Having not buckled to external pressure, Quigley proposed that Minnie present the first two programmes. *Woman's Page* was launched on 1 October. Quigley was 'not entirely happy' with Minnie's draft so rewrote it.[299] In 'Women and Politics', Minnie broadcast that politics was not just an affair for experts as national government and local government were important to everyone as they influenced children's education and the husband's pension. Women should scrutinise those in power and find out who was their member of parliament. 'Your vote helped to put a man in power. It helped to keep another man out. Are you satisfied with your choice?' She ended by promising 'Next Friday I am going to try and answer the question "What Can I do about it?".'[300]

However, her next broadcast was pulled from the schedules. Listener Research indicated that the new series was 'rather too serious lines for the average woman'.[301] Some considered the programme 'deadly dull', patronising, and smacking of propaganda. Of the four presenters, Minnie in particular found disfavour. She was the only one whom more people considered 'inadequate' rather than 'particularly good', each of the other presenters receiving more than twice as many comments as Minnie.[302] For once Minnie was not considered memorable. The script lacked Minnie's usual chatty and engaging style and was a little hectoring. Responsibility should have been shared. Quigley had been closely involved in the conception and was responsible for its content, while Minnie set the tone. However, it was Minnie who was deemed culpable. Quigley reported internally to the BBC that Minnie's 'attack on the question of women taking an interest in politics was rather too direct and severe' for the audience.[303] Quigley told Minnie she'd have to be more circumspect and 'go a little more gently'.[304] It is her one known failure as a broadcaster.

As the year ended, Minnie was a ship in full sail. For the first time in nearly twenty years, she had fully engaged for a whole year in campaigning, undertaking platform speaking, broadcasting and writing. She was also politically rehabilitated. A grainy image exists of Minnie opening Bexhill Labour Party's Bazaar, where she spoke of the Party's present and post-war policy and its roots in Christianity.[305]

Over the winter, Minnie worked on a challenging script that consciously pushed BBC boundaries, 'because I didn't know how far we can go'. Getting to the heart of the imbalance in gender relationships, the central point of 'The Spending Sex' was that 'nothing will be right so long as any one human being depends on the accidental relationship to another human being for the right to live, or have money'. Acknowledging that women's work had historically been undervalued, Minnie argued controversially that it wasn't the professions as such that women wanted, but the salary attached to them.[306] The script, which evolved into a discussion on the marriage bar for women, was not broadcast.[307] There followed a four-month break in correspondence when Quigley did not use Minnie as a contributor. The cause of their distancing is unknown.

Had Minnie pushed too far on women's issues? When Quigley wrote to Barnes in mid-1944, proposing to bring Minnie back after six months off-air, she emphasised that in future Minnie would speak about a book, film or personal experience 'which will only indirectly bring in the old theme of women taking more interest in things outside their own immediate domestic sphere'.[308] That Quigley had to justify Minnie's return to a senior BBC figure suggests that the original decision to remove Minnie may not have been hers alone. Did the Astor/Bonham Carter axis finally prevail? Were there wider concerns within the BBC that Minnie was overplaying her hand, for example in her handling of the politics of reconstruction?[309] Or was her pacifism a contributory factor? Were Minnie's positions too radical for the BBC to countenance? In her two decades with the BBC, Minnie consciously sought to insert and promote issues and speakers sympathetic to the causes she supported and endorsed individuals without revealing their backgrounds.[310] Whatever the exact balance of reasons for the BBC to pause Minnie's broadcasting career, it was not short of grounds on which to do so. Yet the BBC files are silent on the precise causes.

In March 1944, Minnie displayed a gross error of judgement. At the Bexhill Sisterhood Brains Trust, she was asked whether Russia was as great a tyranny as Nazi Germany. Minnie replied [as she had years earlier about the Soviets] that the original intentions of Nazi Germany had been good, but they went off the rails.[311]

This is inexplicable. Had she not personally experienced enough to be in no doubt about the nature of the regime? By the spring of 1944, the malevolence of Hitler and the Nazi regime were apparent, even if the horrors of the exterminations camps were not yet revealed. Perhaps her failure to grasp the essence of Nazism was rooted in her inability to conceive that any system could be so malign or any individual that evil.

That spring, fellow pacifist Michael Tippett had his oratorio, *A Child of Our Time*, first performed at the Adelphi Theatre. Inspired by the events of Kristallnacht, Tippett started writing it on the day Britain declared war and completed it during the first years of the war, but was advised against performing it in 1942 because of its pacifist overtones.[312] Tippett had become a member of the PPU in November 1940 and, demonstrating the depth of his commitment, refused to undertake non-combatant service such as air raid precautions or fire service, and was sentenced to three months' gaol in 1943.[313] Nothing would have kept Minnie from her friend Tippett's opening night.

At the PPU AGM, Minnie became a member of the National Council and was joined by Tippett the following year. At a time of intense pressure for opening a second front, Minnie flew in the face of the public mood in moving the AGM resolution that demanded the Government immediately declare its conditions for the cessation of hostilities. Minnie told an attendance of nearly 700 delegates that she was not asking the British Government to surrender but to 'save the frightful suffering that will be entailed in the next few months if we go on'. It was passed with no opposition.[314] Minnie became a member of the PPU's Negotiated Peace Campaign Committee, the most active part of the organisation. Having already rejected the Allies' demand for unconditional surrender, by the time of Minnie's first meeting, in June 1944, the Committee was aware that circumstances were highly unfavourable and 'it was now a case of saving what one could from the wreck'.[315]

That week, the Allied invasion of Normandy began. After the D-Day landings, Bexhill became full of wounded. A week later the first V1 'doodlebug' was launched against London from occupied Europe. For five months between June and October, the drone of rockets overhead shredded nerves as over 2,000 'doodlebugs' reached London. Minnie sympathised with Quigley, with whom she was back in contact, over the attacks London was suffering.

Perhaps not realising that the route of the flying bombs was over Bexhill, Quigley advised Minnie against spending more time in the capital than was essential. On the day Quigley advised Minnie to avoid London, nineteen V1s were downed in Bexhill. The sisters had a 'marvellous escape' when a flying bomb brought the ceilings down in the flat and shattered the window in front of which they would normally have been sitting, sending glass fragments over their tea.[316] Weeks later, half the roof tiles were still missing.[317]

D-Day brought further difficulties for the PPU. Printers became reluctant to produce its pamphlets and leaflets, and a rally planned for Trafalgar Square was banned under DORA as likely to cause serious public disorder; it was put on instead in Hyde Park.[318] Undeterred, throughout the autumn Minnie continued to speak, including on 'Pacifism and the Post-War World' to a Cardiff conference.[319] More generally, even when Allied victory was in sight, remembering the impact of the Versailles treaty, *Christianity Calling* pleaded for a generous peace that fell short of overwhelming military victory and seeking revenge, in direct opposition to government policy of 'unconditional surrender'.[320] In the spring she toured both the north and south of England, speaking on 'Conditions of Peace'.[321]

Minnie's period in the BBC wilderness ended – temporarily – in June 1944, when Quigley prompted her to start a regular *Woman's Page* slot with the signature sentence 'I Want To Tell You About...'.[322] Perhaps unaware of the depth of concerns within the BBC, Minnie proposed serious talks with a 'political touch' including the biographies of Beatrice Webb, Margaret Bondfield, Rachel McMillan on nursery schools, and George Eliot.[323] As well as working on a script 'If Peace Comes', about how to carry the impetus of war into peacetime, in anticipation of an election after the end of the war, Minnie proposed writing on women who had fought elections, with a discussion on the women's vote.[324] Their interaction was short-lived. With a strain in their relationship apparent, when Quigley advised her that she would be given plenty of notice the next time she was invited to broadcast, Minnie took the hint. In the last letter between them for months Minnie said, 'I had no idea you owed me anything, and it doesn't matter in the least, anyhow.'[325] Minnie was once more off the air.

During that last phase of the war, Minnie focussed her efforts to remould society into a post-war form by working with organisations to secure women's greater representation and equality. She actively supported Women for Westminster, which was at the height of its influence and Open Door, which for two decades had worked for equality for women.[326] When Quigley broke the silence in March 1945 saying it seemed a long time since they had seen one another and asking if there was anything Minnie might feel like contributing to *Woman's Page*, Minnie replied she would very much like to return if she could do anything worthwhile, but there had to be a point to it. Implying she was not prepared to broadcast unless it was a sufficiently relevant topic, Minnie cautiously sounded out Quigley on whether the BBC would allow her to repeat on air what she had been saying from the platform and tentatively wondered 'if you would consider sometime my speaking about one or two of the organisations which now exist helping women'.[327] Instead, Quigley asked her to give a talk on her election experiences. Satisfied with the theme, Minnie gave a 'very entertaining' talk on 22 June 1945. It also proved timely as the broadcast fell in the middle of the general eection campaign. Still in love with politics, Minnie worked hard for the return of Labour.[328]

When the general election result was announced on 26 July, Minnie was in Bournemouth. It was a double celebration. As well as clearing the debt on 'her' labour hall, Labour gained an overwhelming electoral majority on a socialist programme that included nationalisation of the coal industry, establishing a National Health Service and enacting family allowances. Many of Minnie's friends, including Lucy Cox Middleton, became MPs.[329] The success was giddying. Her faith over the previous decades in the left taking a Parliamentary approach to bringing societal change had borne fruit. It was everything she had hoped for.

---

[1] This title is adapted from a section heading in Andrew Rigby, 'The Peace Pledge Union: From Peace to War, 1936–1945', in Peter Brock and Thomas P. Socknat, *Challenge to Mars: Essays on Pacifism from 1918 to 1945*, Toronto, 1991.

[2] *Bexhill Observer*, 26 July 1952.

[3] Adams to Green, 29 March 1935, BBC/WAC/RCONTI Pallister (Talks 1).

[4] Paddy Scannell and David Cardiff, *A Social History of Broadcasting Volume One 1922–1939*, Blackwell, 1991, pp. 153–161.

[5] For the role of MI5 in the BBC see Paul Reynolds, *The Vetting Files: How the BBC Kept Out Subversives*, 21 April 2018, https://www.bbc.co.uk/news/stories-43754737 Also correspondence between author and Michael Hodder, who was the last MI5 liaison within the BBC, 17 & 18 May 2020.

[6] Kate Murphy, *Behind the Wireless A History of the Early Women at the BBC*, Palgrave,

2016, p. 184.

[7] Hamilton to Quigley, 27 June [1937], RCONTI Minnie Pallister Talks 1.

[8] Brockway, *Inside the Left*, p. 146. The nomination was for BBC Governor, not Director.

[9] Quigley to Pallister, 6 July 1937, BBC/WAC/RCONT1 Pallister (Talks 1).

[10] Paul Donavon, 'Quigley, Janet, Muriel, Alexander', Oxford *DNB*, 2004, article/65432, accessed 22 August 2017; Cliff Michelmore, Jean Metcalfe, *Two-Way Story: An Autobiography*, Chivers, 1988, p. 75.

[11] See Murphy, *Behind...*, particularly p. 7.

[12] See correspondence 12 October 1937 to 2 January 1938, including Quigley to Pallister, 13 December 1937, 15 February & 7 March 1938, BBC/WAC/RCONT1 Pallister (Talks 1).

[13] 'Life Story (4)'; Quigley to Pallister, 17 October & Pallister to Quigley, 18 October & 2 November 1938, BBC/WAC/RCONT1 Pallister (Talks 1).

[14] Quigley, 'Report on January/March Series: "Sickness in the House"', 29 April 1938, BBC/WAC/R51/397/2 Talks Policy April – November 1938 ib. (I am grateful to Kate Murphy for this reference.) Pallister to Quigley, 6 March 1938, BBC/WAC/RCONT1 Pallister (Talks 1); *Man and Metal*, March 1938; 'Life Story (4)'.

[15] Pallister to Quigley, 14 August 1944, BBC/WAC/RCONT1 Pallister (Talks 3a).

[16] *Bexhill Observer*, 26 February 1938.

[17] *Hastings and St Leonards Observer*, 26 March 1938.

[18] Hilary Daniels & Jean Richardson, *A Place of Her Own, The Over Forty Association*, 1983, pp. 8 & 10; *The First Annual Report and Statement of Accounts for 1935–6*. Minnie referred to the work of the Over 30s Association in a *Daily Herald* article on 'The Exhibition of Women's Progress', 29 April 1937.

[19] *Daily Herald*, 4 March 1936.

[20] *Man and Metal*, February & May 1938, & April 1939.

[21] Pallister to Quigley, 18 October [1938], BBC/WAC/RCONT1 Pallister (Talks 1).

[22] *Man and Metal*, May 1938.

[23] Report of Nineteenth National Conference of Labour Women, 10–12 May 1938; Brockway, *Inside the Left*, pp. 338–41. Later that month Gould and Minnie reprised their opposing positions when Minnie chaired Gould's meeting on the international situation at the Bexhill Labour Party Women's Section. (*Bexhill Observer*, 28 May 1938.)

[24] *Man and Metal*, June 1938.

[25] *Forward*, 21 May 1938.

[26] Ceadel, *Pacifism...*, p. 194.

[27] *Forward*, 21 May 1938; Ceadel, *Pacifism...*, p. 277; *Peace News*, 21 August 1937.

[28] Gottlieb, *Guilty Women*, pp. 9 & 154.

[29] Gottlieb, *Guilty Women*, pp. 4, 9 & 13.

[30] Quoted in Gottlieb, *Guilty Women*, p. 89; *Man and Metal*, December 1938.

[31] Gottlieb, *Guilty Women*, pp. 4, 17 & 58–9.

[32] *Man and Metal*, August 1938.

[33] *Peace News*, 13 February 1937; information from Bill Hetherington, 21 June 2016.

[34] *Peace News*, 25 September 1937.

[35] Hetherington, pp. 14–15; *Peace News*, 9 April 1938.

[36] *Peace News*, 7 May 1938; *Bexhill Observer*, 23 April 1938. Although Minnie was a

local celebrity, Gladys was equally well known locally due to her work in the doctors' surgery and her causes, including secretary of the League of Friends of Bexhill Hospital, the East Sussex Association for the Disabled and the PPU.

[37] *Peace News*, 27 November 1937 & 1 October & 9 December 1938; *Hastings & St Leonards Observer*, 12 February 1938.

[38] *Bexhill Observer*, 28 May 1938; see Hetherington, p. 12.

[39] *Port Talbot Guardian*, 12 & 19 August 1938.

[40] *Daily Herald*, 19 September 1938.

[41] G. V. Dowding to Director Talks, 25 July 1938; Director of Talks to Cecil Brooks Ltd, 24 August 1938, BBC/WAC/RCONTI Pallister (Talks 1).

[42] Pallister to Quigley, 8 September & Burgess to Pallister, 30 September 1938, BBC/WAC/RCONT1 Pallister (Talks 1). Guy Burgess was at this time 28 years of age and had been educated at Eton and Cambridge University, where he joined the Communist Party.

[43] Gottlieb, *Guilty Women*, pp. 4, 9 & 13.

[44] Pallister to Quigley, Tues 6 [actually 4] October 1938, BBC/WAC/RCONTI Pallister (Talks 1).

[45] Andrew Lownie, *Stalin's Englishman: The Lives of Guy Burgess*, Hodder & Stoughton, 2015, pp. 93–95.

[46] Pallister to Quigley, 26 April [1939], BBC/WAC/RCONTI Pallister (Talks 1).

[47] Pallister to Derville, 14 March 1947, BBC/WAC/RCONTI Pallister (Talks 4).

[48] Catherine Clay, 'Re-visiting the Friendship of Vera Brittain and Winifred Holtby: a "trade" in work and desire', *Women's History Review*, Vol 12 No 2, 2003, p. 310.

[49] Pallister to Quigley, 25 March [1939], BBC/WAC/RCONTI Pallister (Talks 1).

[50] Pallister to Quigley, 18 October [1938] & 26 October [1939], BBC/WAC/RCONTI Pallister (Talks 1).

[51] Pallister to Quigley, nd but April [1939] & 24 September [1939], BBC/WAC/RCONTI Pallister (Talks 1).

[52] Pallister to Miall, 7 August [1939], BBC/WAC/RCONTI Pallister (Talks 1).

[53] Her interactions with Quigley include a catalogue of apologies for 'all the bother you put up with', 'I sit there babbling!' and 'if you get much more of my distraught appearances you will have a nervous breakdown'. Pallister to Quigley, 10 October, Thursday nd but early October, 1 November [1938] & 14 May 1939, BBC/WAC/RCONTI Pallister (Talks 1).

[54] Pallister to Quigley, 10, 18 & 25 October 1938, BBC/WAC/RCONTI Pallister (Talks 1).

[55] Contract, 13 October 1938, BBC/WAC/RCONTI Pallister (Talks 1).

[56] *Man and Metal*, January 1939.

[57] Pallister to Quigley, 7 January & 29 June 1939, BBC/WAC/RCONTI Pallister (Talks 1).

[58] e.g. *Man and Metal*, December 1938.

[59] Pallister to Quigley, date stamped 27 April 1939, BBC/WAC/RCONTI Pallister (Talks 1).

[60] Pallister to Quigley, 28 November 1938, Quigley to Pallister, 24 March & 26 May 1939, BBC/WAC/RCONTI Pallister (Talks 1).

[61] Pallister to Quigley, 22 June 1953, BBC/WAC/RCONTI Pallister (Talks 6); 'The Stopped Clock', *WH*, 17 July 1953.

[62] Pallister to Quigley, 1 November [1938], BBC/WAC/RCONTI Pallister (Talks 1).

[63] Alan E. Steinweis, *Kristallnacht 1938*, Harvard University Press, 2009, pp. 1, 4 & 5.

[64] http://www.holocaustresearchproject.org/nazioccupation/frankfurt.html accessed 3 August 2016.

[65] Steinweis, p. 5.

[66] Martin Gilbert, *The Holocaust: The Jewish Tragedy*, Fontana Press, 1987, pp. 32–56 & 61.

[67] http://www.holocaustresearchproject.org/nazioccupation/frankfurt.html

[68] Pallister to Quigley, 20 November [1938], BBC/WAC/RCONTI Pallister (Talks 1); 'Life Story (5)'.

[69] Jonathan C. Friedman, *The Lion and the Star: Gentile-Jewish relations in Three Hessian Communities 1919–1945*, p. 254 fn 14; Testimony B48, 24 November 1938, ed Ruth Levitt, *Pogrom 1938 Testimonies from Kristallnacht*, Souvenir Press, 2015, pp. 67–8.

[70] Pallister to Quigley, 20 Nov[ember 1938], BBC/WAC/RCONTI Pallister (Talks 1).

[71] 'Life Story (5)'.

[72] 'In the Beginning: 1919 through 1939', *Memories: The Life and Times of Hank R. Schwab*, http://www.hankschwab.com/beginning.html accessed 15 August 2016.

[73] See testimonies, especially B82 & B216, Levitt, pp. 109–116 & 329–341; Original testimonies taken in late 1938 and early 1939, anonymous report, *The Pogrom in Frankfurt*, 1938, P.II.d.No. 736, 1656/2/4/736, Wiener Library.

[74] Anonymous report, *The Pogrom in Frankfurt*.

[75] 'Life Story (5)'; see Martin Gilbert, *Beyond the Call of Duty: British Diplomats and other Britons who helped Jews Escape from Nazi Tyranny*, https://issuu.com/fcohistorians/docs/hpopub_1, accessed late 2016. I am grateful to Esther Gilbert for this lead.

[76] 'Life Story (5)'.

[77] *Man and Metal*, December 1938.

[78] Hetherington, p. 11.

[79] *Peace News*, 19 November 1938.

[80] Pallister to Quigley, 28 November [1938], BBC/WAC/RCONTI Pallister (Talks 1).

[81] Schwab, 'In the Beginning...'.

[82] Anonymous report, *The Pogrom in Frankfurt*; Testimony B202, Levitt, pp. 298–300.

[83] Gottlieb, *Guilty Women*, pp. 5 & 6.

[84] *Man and Metal*, January 1939.

[85] *Man and Metal*, December 1938; *Bexhill Observer*, 14 March 1942.

[86] These included the National Children's Home and Orphanage in Bexhill and an open-air school at St Leonards which took boys from the East End of London. She served on the management committee of two London County Council deaf schools. Over Christmas 1938 she was involved in arranging three separate children's parties organised by the Labour Party, and by London local authorities. She was also a member of the committee of the East Sussex Cripples Association. (*Bexhill Observer*, 24 June 1939; Pallister to Quigley, 12 September [1940] & 21 November 1950; Pallister to Quigley, 'Friday', nd, but January 1939, BBC/WAC/RCONTI Pallister (Talks 1 & 4); *Daily Herald*, 3 August 1938; *Man and Metal*, January 1939.)

[87] Entry in National Register, 1939.

[88] 'Request Week', *WH*, 17 July 1951; *Bexhill Observer*, 17 & 31 December 1938.

[89] Pallister to Quigley, 'Friday', nd, but January 1939, BBC/WAC/RCONTI Pallister (Talks 1).

[90] Exhibition, De La Warr Pavilion, July 2016.

[91] *Bexhill Observer*, 27 May 1939.

[92] *Man and Metal*, May 1939.

[93] *New Leader*, 22 January 1926; *Bexhill Observer*, 7 January 1939; *Sussex Express & County Herald*, 6 January 1939.

[94] Pallister to Quigley, 4 March [1939], BBC/WAC/RCONTI Pallister (Talks 1).

[95] *Man and Metal*, April 1939.

[96] Pallister to Quigley, 21 February & 28 March 1939, BBC/WAC/RCONTI Pallister (Talks 1).

[97] Pallister to Quigley, 14 March & 5 April 1939, BBC/WAC/RCONTI Pallister (Talks 1).

[98] Pallister to Quigley, 19 & 26 April [1939], BBC/WAC/RCONTI Pallister (Talks 1).

[99] Pallister to Quigley, 16 March 1939, BBC/WAC/RCONTI Pallister (Talks 1).

[100] Stephanie Schwab to author, 22 December 2016.

[101] Hans Schwarb, 19 April 1939, Old Diary Translation, unpublished.

[102] Gilbert, *Beyond the Call...*, pp. 12–3.

[103] *Man and Metal*, September 1939.

[104] In 1952 Minnie saw him and his young bride off from Southampton as they sailed to South Africa to start a new life. ('Life Story (5)'.

[105] PPU Sponsors' Meeting, 20 April 1939.

[106] Ceadel, *Pacifism...*, p. 282; Hetherington, p. 16.

[107] Ceadel, *Pacifism...*, pp. 281–2; Hetherington, pp. 16–8.

[108] *Bexhill Observer*, 8 July 1939.

[109] *Man and Metal*, February 1939; *Sussex Agricultural Express*, 23 June 1939.

[110] *Man and Metal*, August 1939.

[111] *Man and Metal*, February 1939.

[112] *Peace News*, 21 July 1939.

[113] *Man and Metal*, June 1939.

[114] Ceadel, *Pacifism...*, pp. 291–2.

[115] *Man and Metal*, July 1940, p. 122.

[116] Pallister to Quigley, 20, 22 & 28 March 1939 & Quigley to Pallister, 23 March 1939, BBC/WAC/RCONTI Pallister (Talks 1).

[117] Pallister to Quigley, 7 May [1939], BBC/WAC/RCONTI Pallister (Talks 1). Emphasis in original.

[118] Pallister to Quigley, 26 April [1939], BBC/WAC/RCONTI Pallister (Talks 1).

[119] Pallister to Quigley, 7 May [1939], BBC/WAC/RCONTI Pallister (Talks 1).

[120] Overseas News Editor to Pallister, 21 July 1939, BBC/WAC/RCONTI Pallister (Talks 1).

[121] Pallister to Quigley, 7 August 1939, BBC/WAC/RCONTI Pallister (Talks 1).

[122] Pallister to Quigley, 9 July 1939 & 11 September [1951], BBC/WAC/RCONTI Pallister (Talks 1 & 5).

[123] Pallister to Miall, nd, & Pallister to Quigley, nd, [but both August 1939].

[124] Pallister to Quigley, 25 July, 21 & 30 August, & nd, [1939]; Pallister to Miall, nd but August 1939, Sunday, nd but 27 August 1939 & nd but late August 1939, BBC/WAC/RCONTI Pallister (Talks 1); *Man and Metal*, October 1939.

[125] *Man and Metal*, September & October 1939.

[126] *Man and Metal*, January 1940.

[127] Sian Nicolas, *The Echo of War*, MUP, 1996, p. 25; Quigley to Pallister, 5 September 1939, BBC/WAC/RCONTI Pallister (Talks 1).

[128] *Man and Metal*, January 1940; *Bexhill Observer*, 18 November 1939 & 7 March 1942; *Hastings & St Leonards Observer*, 11 November 1939.

[129] *Daily Herald*, 25 September & 16 October 1939.

[130] 'While disabled soldiers went from door to door we raised memorials of stone to the dead.' *Man And Metal*, October 1939 & January 1940.

[131] Julie Gottlieb, '"The Women's Movement took The Wrong Turning": British Feminists, pacifism and the politics of appeasement', *Women's History Review*, Vol 23 No 3, 2014, pp. 47 & 443.

[132] Martin Ceadel, *Semi-Detached Idealists: The British Peace Movement and International Relations*, 1854–1945, 2000, p. 390.

[133] *NMW*, August 1934.

[134] For this 'biologically determined' aspect of 'womanist pacifism' see Gottlieb, 'The Wrong Turning', p. 444.

[135] Gottlieb, *Guilty Women*, pp. 97 & 98.

[136] Ceadel, *Semi-detached...*, pp. 194, 238 & 294.

[137] *Peace News*, 8 September 1939.

[138] Nicholas, *Echo*, p. 32.

[139] Nicholas, *Echo*, pp. 27/8; Quigley to Pallister, 19 September 1939, Pallister to Quigley, 7, 12 & 21 September [1939], BBC/WAC/RCONTI Pallister (Talks 1).

[140] Quigley to Pallister, 22 September 1939, Pallister to Quigley, 12 September & 1 October [1939], BBC/WAC/RCONTI Pallister (Talks 1).

[141] 'Thoughts and Impressions', *Talking It Over*, 11 October 1939.

[142] Nicholas, *Echo*, pp. 41 & 43.

[143] Pallister to Miall, 21 & 24 November, Miall to Pallister 22 November 1939, BBC/WAC/RCONTI Pallister (Talks 1).

[144] *Man and Metal*, March 1940.

[145] Hetherington, pp. 19–20; Gottlieb, *Guilty Women*, p. 22 & 'Wrong Turning...', pp. 450–1.

[146] *Peace News*, 23 February & 1 March 1940; Hetherington, pp. 19–20.

[147] *Man and Metal*, April 1940.

[148] *Man and Metal*, September & November 1939.

[149] Pallister to Quigley, 16 & 23 January [1940], BBC/WAC/RCONTI Pallister (Talks 2); *Man and Metal*, March & April 1940.

[150] Pallister to Quigley, 13 March 1940, BBC/WAC/RCONTI Pallister (Talks 2).

[151] Ceadel, *Pacifism*, p. 307; Rigby, p. 178.

[152] Correspondence between Quigley and Pallister, 15 January to 14 March 1940, BBC/WAC/RCONTI Pallister (Talks 2).

[153] Nicholas, *Echo*, pp. 4–5, 63 & 65; Sian Nicholas, 'The People's Radio: The BBC and Its Audience, 1939–1945', in Nick Hayes and Jeff Hill, *'Millions Like Us': British Culture in the Second World War*, Liverpool, 1999; D. Cardiff, 'The Services and Popular Aspects of the Evolution of Style in the Radio Talk, 1928–1939, *Media, Culture and Society*, 1980, pp. 29–47; Sian Nicholas, '"Sly Demagogues" and Wartime Radio: J. B.

Priestley and the BBC', *Twentieth Century British History*, Vol 6 No 3, 1995, pp. 250 & 252–3.

[154] *The Listener*, 18 April 1940, p. 807.

[155] Vera Brittain, *Testament of Experience*, Virago, 1979, Foreword, p. 15, & pp. 216 & 218.

[156] Intelligence Report No 2, 1 February 1940, Pacifism (General) Reports and Correspondence RIOs, HO 262/2, National Archive; Ian McLaine, *Ministry of Morale*, George Allen & Unwin, 1979, pp. 1, 3 & 57.

[157] Special Report on Organized Pacifism, South East region, 21 February 1940, Peace Pledge Union, HO 262/3.

[158] 'Extract from South Eastern Regional Officer's Intelligence Report', 11 March 1940, HO 262/2.

[159] S Eastern RIOs Intelligence Report to Headquarters, No 5, 1 April 1940, Peace Pledge Union Corres & Reports RIOs, HO 262/4.

[160] S Eastern RIOs Intelligence Report to Headquarters, No 5, 1 April 1940, HO 262/4.

[161] *Bexhill Observer*, 28 February & 2–16 March 1940.

[162] *Peace News*, 7 November 1936 & 24 November 1939; *Bexhill Observer*, 17 February 1940.

[163] Julie Gottlieb, 'Women Blackshirts and the Grey Areas of "Peace"' *Politics in Britain, 1938–1942, Women of the Far Right* conference, Worcester, 9 November 2019; Gottlieb, *Guilty Women*, pp. 96–7.

[164] Minnie did not sign the statement published in the BPP's *People's Post* calling on the British Government to attend a peace conference, which was signed by Maude Royden, Helena Swanwick and Bernard Langdon-Davies. (*People's Post*, October 1939.)

[165] Extract… 11 March 1940, HO 262/2; Hetherington, p. 17.

[166] Handwritten on Macadam to Adams, 26 March 1940, HO 262/3.

[167] *PPU Journal*, No 3, June 1946.

[168] Ceadel, *Pacifism*, pp. 182, 215, 263, 296–7 & 361.

[169] Hetherington, p. 17.

[170] *Man and Metal*, June 1940.

[171] Martin Gilbert, *Finest Hour Winston Churchill, 1939–1941*, Minerva, 1989, pp. 300–1 & 312; John Bew, *Citizen Clem*, Riverrun, 2016, p. 243.

[172] *Man and Metal*, June 1940.

[173] 'Intelligence – Peace News', 21 May 1940, 'Wartime military training pamphlets, administrative papers and intelligence reports December 1939 – August 1940, Intelligence reports and memoranda', Add Mss 48201, West Sussex Record Office.

[174] *Peace News*, 19 January, 2 & 9 August 1940.

[175] A. S. Hutchinson to Adams, 31 May 1940, Peace Pledge Union, HO 262/3.

[176] Ceadel, *Pacifism*, p. 283.

[177] Gottlieb, 'Wrong Turning', p. 454.

[178] See Brittain, *Testament of Experience*, pp. 168, 170 & 173.

[179] Quoted by Gottlieb, *Guilty Women*, p. 96.

[180] Kennedy, *Hound…*, p. 289.

[181] *Sunday Dispatch*, 10 March 1940; Gottlieb, 'Wrong Turning', pp. 458 & 459.

[182] Brittain, *Testament of Experience*, p. 217.

[183] She wrote 'the finest gift I can give my country is to make myself fit to live in a world based on brotherhood.' (*Man and Metal*, July 1940.)

[184] *Peace News*, 22 & 29 April 1955.

[185] *Bexhill Observer*, 15 March 1941.

[186] Many private schools in Bexhill, particularly for 'children of the empire', closed and children evacuated.

[187] *Bexhill Observer*, 25 January 1941.

[188] *Bexhill Observer*, 1, 15 & 22 March 1941; 'Life Story (5)'.

[189] Pallister to Quigley, 25 September [1939]), BBC/WAC/RCONTI Pallister (Talks 1).

[190] Spike Milligan, *Adolf Hitler: My Part in his Downfall*, 2012 Penguin reissue of 1972 edition, pp. 24, 43-8 & 126; Headphone recording of Milligan, Bexhill Museum.

[191] *Man and Metal*, July, August & September 1940; Pallister to Quigley, 1 September 1940, BBC/WAC/RCONTI Pallister (Talks 2).

[192] Private and Confidential Memo W R D 'On Broadcasting in Wartime', 18 September 1940, Policy Employment of Broadcasters in Wartime, BBC/WAC/R34/353/1, 1a 1940.

[193] Quigley to Pallister, 5 September 1940, BBC/WAC/RCONTI Pallister (Talks 2).

[194] Pallister to Quigley, 8 September 1940, BBC/WAC/RCONTI Pallister (Talks 2).

[195] Note dated 12 September 1940 on letter Pallister to Quigley dated 8 September 1940, BBC/WAC/RCONTI Pallister (Talks 2).

[196] Quigley to Maconachie, 13 November 1940, BBC/WAC/RCONTI Pallister (Talks 2).

[197] Policy Employment of Broadcasters in Wartime, BBC/WAC/R34/353/1, 1a 1940, including Quigley to DT [Director of Talks], 13 November, & C (H) [Controller (Home) Sir Richard Maconachie] to DG 15 Nov 1940.

[198] As the BBC's role in the Second World War was to promote national unity and support morale, it is understandable that at a moment of acute national crisis, Minnie and other pacifists should be taken off-air. However, the BBC's blanket ban lacked the nuance displayed by the Home Office in differentiating levels of risk. At a time when ordinary people struggled to identify with impersonal BBC voices using language that felt remote, the Corporation, by removing from the airwaves those not fitting its profile of what constituted national unity, discarded individuals, including Minnie, who might have contributed positively to public morale. (Nicholas, *Echo...*, p. 2; McLaine, p. 99.)

[199] *Daily Herald*, 10 June 1940.

[200] *Daily Herald*, 4 July 1940.

[201] Richards, p. 157.

[202] *Man and Metal*, July, November & December 1940.

[203] Pallister to Quigley, 17 October 1940, BBC/WAC/RCONTI Pallister (Talks 2).

[204] Pallister to Quigley, 8 September & 17 October 1940, BBC/WAC/RCONTI Pallister (Talks 2).

[205] Man and Metal, October & November 1940 and April 1941.

[206] https://www.eastsussex.gov.uk/leisureandtourism/localandfamilyhistory/localhistory/ww2

[207] Pallister to Quigley, 17 October 1940, BBC/WAC/RCONTI Pallister (Talks 2).

[208] David Burton & Alan Beecher, *Bexhill in World War II*, Bexhill Museum, 3rd edition, 2009, p. 18; Pallister to Quigley, 17 October 1940, BBC/WAC/RCONTI Pallister (Talks 2); *Man and Metal*, October & November 1940.

[209] Pallister to Quigley, 17 October 1940, BBC/WAC/RCONTI Pallister (Talks 2).

[210] *Man and Metal*, January 1941.

[211] *Man and Metal*, October 1940.

[212] *Man and Metal*, January 1941.

[213] *Man and Metal*, January 1941.

[214] *Man and Metal*, October 1940.

[215] *Man and Metal*, January, February & August 1941.

[216] *Man and Metal*, October 1940 & March 1941.

[217] *Man and Metal*, June 1941.

[218] *Man and Metal*, October 1941.

[219] She asked why governments lavished 'divine skill' on armaments to kill people when those same resources could be channelled to improving people's lives. Contrasting the training received by air force pilots with their treatment in 'normal times', she looked forward to when every boy and girl would be developed in an equivalent way to serve the community in peacetime (*Man and Metal*, November 1940 & March 1941).

[220] Sybil Morrison, *The Life and Work of Stuart Morris*, PPU, nd, p. 5.

[221] Hetherington, p. 20.

[222] *Peace News*, 5 July 1940; Morrison, *Stuart Morris*, p. 5.

[223] *Peace News*, 31 May, 19 & 26 July 1940; Sybil Morrison, *I Renounce War*, Sheppard Press, 1962, pp. 53–4.

[224] *Peace News*, 5 July 1940.

[225] Home Intelligence to All RIOs, 6 January 1941, HO 262/1.

[226] *Peace News*, 14 March 1941; Gottlieb, 'Wrong Turning', p. 451.

[227] BBC/WAC G 94/41; Hetherington, p. 24.

[228] Hamilton, *Friends*, pp. 100–3; *John O'London*, 29 December 1944. When A. A. Milne produced a book of poetry on the first nine months of the war, Minnie found many of the poems charming. However, she described one poem about a conscientious objector as 'a cruel and utterly misleading jibe' and hoped that one day Milne would be ashamed of it. (*Man and Metal*, December 1940.)

[229] Gottlieb, 'Wrong Turning', pp. 442 & 451.

[230] Gottlieb, 'Wrong Turning', pp. 445–6.

[231] *Peace News*, 3 March 1956.

[232] Martin Ceadel, 'The Case of Interwar Britain, 1918–1945', in Peter Brock and Thomas P. Socknat, *Challenge to Mars: Essays on Pacifism from 1918 to 1945*, Toronto, 1999, p. 142

[233] Brittain, *Testament of Experience*, pp. 250, 262/3, 266, 267, 273, 280 & 289; Paul Berry, introduction, Vera Brittain, *Testament of Experience*, Virago, 1979, p. 10.

[234] See correspondence between Pallister and Routledge Keegan Paul, 30 May to 2 July 1941, Miscellaneous Publishing Correspondence, file O-Pa, 1941–2, RKP 170/9, Reading University Special Collection.

[235] John Lewis, *The Left Book Club*, Gollancz, 1970, pp. 38 & 94.

[236] Ragg to Citrine, quoted in Jennifer Platt, 'The International Library of Sociology and Social Reconstruction and British Sociology', in J. Holmwood & J. Scott, *The Palgrave Handbook of Sociology in Britain*, Palgrave Macmillan, 2014, p. 239.

[237] Ragg (RKP) to Pallister, 2 July 1941.

[238] Selection Committee Minutes, 27 June 1941, LP/LBS/39/1/31, PHM. As well as

A PACIFIST IN TOTAL WAR

Hamilton, other attendees included G.D.H. Cole, Walter Citrine, the General Secretary of the TUC; Hugh Dalton & R. H. Tawney.

[239] *Man and Metal*, February 1941.

[240] *Man and Metal*, May 1941.

[241] Pallister to Quigley, 11 July, 7 August 1941 & 15 September 1942, BBC/WAC/RCONTI Pallister (Talks 2).

[242] Quigley to Pallister, 29 September 1941, BBC/WAC/RCONTI Pallister (Talks 2).

[243] *Man and Metal*, March, April, May, October & November 1941.

[244] *Man and Metal*, March & May 1940, February & September 1941.

[245] *Daily Herald*, 15 April 1941.

[246] *Man and Metal*, September 1940, January & March 1941.

[247] *Port Talbot Guardian*, 12 September 1941, provided by Angela John.

[248] Pallister to Quigley, nd but April/May 1941, BBC/WAC/RCONTI Pallister (Talks 2); 'Minnie Pallister Talking', 3 October 1955; 'Life Story (4)'.

[249] Caitriona Beaumont, 'Citizens Not Feminists: the boundary negotiated between citizenship and feminism by mainstream women's organisations in England, 1928–39', *Women's History Review*, Vol 9 No 2, 2000, pp. 417–8.

[250] *Bexhill Observer*, 18 November 1939 & 6 December 1941; *Hastings & St Leonards Observer*, 23 August 1941; *Sussex Agricultural Express*, 10 October 1941.

[251] *Bexhill Observer*, 21 March 1942; *Mid Sussex Times*, 25 March 1942.

[252] Pallister to Quigley, 7 October 1941, BBC/WAC/RCONTI Pallister (Talks 2).

[253] *Bexhill Observer*, 7 March 1942.

[254] From 1941 Christianity Calling allied itself with Committee for the Abolition of Night Bombing, renamed the Bombing Restriction Committee in 1942. Arthur Belden to Stuart Morris, 19 June 1941; The Area Bombing Directive, 14 February 1942, Thomas Foley papers, Temp MSS 448/1/1, Friends House; *Peace News*, 31 July 1942; Christianity Calling, 'Mass Bombing of Germany: Air Ministry's Defence', 16 Sept. 1942, referred to in Richard Overy, 'Constructing Space for Dissent in War: The Bombing Restriction Committee, 1941–1945', *English History Review*, (2016) 131 (550): pp. 596–622, fn 65.

[255] Grayling, Chapter 5.

[256] *Port Talbot Guardian*, 20 August & 10 September 1943.

[257] Beers, *Red Ellen*, p. 393.

[258] Pallister to Quigley, 4 October & 12 November 1942, BBC/WAC/RCONTI Pallister (Talks 2); 'I Want To Tell You About', *Woman's Page*, 29 September 1944.

[259] Pallister to Quigley, 12 & 24 November 1942, BBC/WAC/RCONTI Pallister (Talks 2); *Sussex Express & County Herald*, 20 November 1942; *Sussex Agricultural Express*, 20 Nov 1942; 'Minnie Pallister', biographical details sent to the BBC, nd but November–December 1945, BBC/WAC/RCONTI Pallister (Talks 3b).

[260] Quigley to Director of Talks, 17 September 1942, BBC/WAC/RCONTI Pallister (Talks 2).

[261] R. N. Armfelt, Assistant Controller (Home) memo 'Conscientious Objectors' to Director Secretariat, M. G. Farquharson, 20 September 1942; Director Secretariat to AC (H), 24 September 1942, BBC/WAC/RCONTI Pallister (Talks 2).

[262] *Bexhill Observer*, 12 September 1942.

[263] Quigley to Pallister, 3 October 1942, BBC/WAC/RCONTI Pallister (Talks 2).

[264] Pallister to Quigley, 5 October 1942, BBC/WAC/RCONTI Pallister (Talks 2).

[265] Pallister to Quigley, 12 November 1942, Quigley to Pallister, 10 November 1942, BBC/WAC/RCONTI Pallister (Talks 2).

[266] Pallister to Quigley, 21 March, Quigley to Pallister, 5 April 1943, BBC/WAC/RCONTI Pallister (Talks 3a). The script was a rewrite of a *New Leader* article of December 1929, though without its conclusion that unemployment was the result of capitalism that could be solved by socialism. (*New Leader*, 13 December 1929.)

[267] Quigley to Pallister & Pallister to Quigley, 20 April–16 May 1943, BBC/WAC/RCONTI Pallister (Talks 3a).

[268] Pallister to Quigley, 6 June 1943, BBC/WAC/RCONTI Pallister (Talks 3a).

[269] Memo Barnes to C (H), 30 June [1943], BBC/WAC/RCONTI Pallister (Talks 3a).

[270] Paddy Scannell and David Cardiff, *A Social History of Broadcasting Volume One 1922–1939*, Blackwell, 1991, pp. 153–161.

[271] Sian Nicholas, '"Sly Demagogues" and Wartime Radio: J. B. Priestley and the BBC', *Twentieth Century British History*, Vol 6 No 3, 1995, pp. 247–66.

[272] Maconachie to Barnes, 30 June [1943], BBC/WAC/RCONTI Pallister (Talks 3a).

[273] Barnes to Quigley, 2 July 1943, BBC/WAC/RCONTI Pallister (Talks 3a).

[274] She was in good company. This was not the first occasion that Barnes and Maconachie had acted in concert over what they saw as left-wing bias in talks. They had previously raised 'deep concerns' over the 'left-wing views' of Priestley before his hugely popular Postscripts series ended in autumn 1940. (Vincent Brome, *J B Priestley*, Hamish Hamilton, 1988, p. 249).

[275] Quigley to Pallister, 5 July 1943, BBC/WAC/RCONTI Pallister (Talks 3a).

[276] Pallister to Quigley, nd but early July 1943, BBC/WAC/RCONTI Pallister (Talks 3a).

[277] Pallister to Quigley, nd, & Quigley to Pallister, 21 July 1943, BBC/WAC/RCONTI Pallister (Talks 3a).

[278] Pallister to Quigley, 6 June & nd but early July 1943, BBC/WAC/RCONTI Pallister (Talks 3a).

[279] 'Reading', *Mostly for Women*, 11 July 1943; Quigley to Pallister, 14 July 1943, BBC/WAC/RCONTI Pallister (Talks 3a).

[280] Pallister to Quigley, 20 October 1942; Pallister to Miss Moore, 5 January 1952 [though dated 1951]; Moore to Pallister 9 January 1952, BBC/WAC/RCONTI Pallister (Talks 3a & 5).

[281] *Daily Herald*, 24 August 1935; Pallister to Quigley, 5 April, Sunday [11 April] 1943, 'Thursday' [presumably 15 April] & Good Friday [23 April 1943], BBC/WAC/RCONTI Pallister (Talks 3a).

[282] 'Mothers and Daughters', *Indian Summer*, 13 November 1957.

[283] 'Diary', 1 September 1952.

[284] Pallister to Quigley, 16 May 1943 & Pallister to Keen, 11 April 1954, BBC/WAC/RCONTI Pallister (Talks 3a & 6).

[285] *John O'London*, 6 September 1946 & 2 April 1954.

[286] *Bexhill Observer*, 5 June 1943.

[287] *Man and Metal*, July 1941.

[288] Pallister to Quigley, Monday 24 [May], 19 September, 23 November 1943 and see 29 July [1944], BBC/WAC/RCONTI Pallister (Talks 3a).

[289] *Manchester Guardian*, 11 February 1943.

[290] *Bexhill Observer*, 18 September 1943; Pallister to Quigley, 9 September 1943, BBC/WAC/RCONTI Pallister (Talks 3a).

[291] *Peace News*, 27 August 1943.

[292] *Christianity Calling In the Name of Christ A Manifesto and an Appeal 1944*, George Orwell Collected Pamphlets, 1899.ss.39, British Library; Thomas Foley papers Temp MSS 448/1/1; *Peace News*, 12 May 1944.

[293] House of Commons Debate, 28 October 1943, Vol 393 cc 363–4.

[294] Quigley to Pallister, 20 August 1943, Pallister to Quigley, 1, 2 & 9 September 1943, BBC/WAC/RCONTI Pallister (Talks 3a).

[295] Pallister to Quigley, 9 September 1943, BBC/WAC/RCONTI Pallister (Talks 3a).

[296] Pallister to Quigley, 9 September 1943, BBC/WAC/RCONTI Pallister (Talks 3a).

[297] Pallister to Quigley, 13 & 22 September 1943, BBC/WAC/RCONTI Pallister (Talks 3a); *Nottingham Evening Post*, 18 September 1943. See Laura Beers 'Women for Westminster: Feminism and the Limits of Non-Partisan Associational Culture', Gottlieb and Toye, *The Aftermath of Suffrage*, Palgrave Macmillan, 2013, pp. 225 & 227.

[298] Barnes to Dear Lady Violet, 22 September 1943, & Quigley, 'Notes for Lady Violet', 23 September 1943, BBC/WAC/R51/645, Talks, Woman's Page 1943–1946.

[299] Quigley to Pallister, 23 & 24 September 1943, BBC/WAC/RCONTI Pallister (Talks 3a); Notes for Miss Pallister: Script No. 2, nd, BBC/WAC/R51/645, Talks, Woman's Page 1943–1946.

[300] 'Women and Politics', *Woman's Page*, 1 October 1943.

[301] Quigley to Pallister, 20 October, 1943, BBC/WAC/RCONTI Pallister (Talks 3a).

[302] A Listener's Research Report, No 2095, Woman's Page, 1 October 1943, BBC/WAC/R51/645, Talks Woman's Page 1943–1946.

[303] Quigley to DT, 11 July 1944, BBC/WAC/RCONTI Pallister (Talks 3a).

[304] Quigley to Pallister, 20 October, 1943, BBC/WAC/RCONTI Pallister (Talks 3a).

[305] *Bexhill Observer*, 18 December 1943.

[306] Pallister to Quigley, nd [date stamp 25 Nov 1943], 23 November & 15 December 1943, BBC/WAC/RCONTI Pallister (Talks 3a).

[307] Pallister to Quigley, 10 January 1944, BBC/WAC/RCONTI Pallister (Talks 3a).

[308] Quigley to DT, 11 July 1944, BBC/WAC/RCONTI Pallister (Talks 3a).

[309] The *BBC Year Book for 1944*'s account of *Woman's Page* formally stated that Minnie and Janet Dunbar 'did their best to rouse their women listeners from what they believed to be an excessive apathy about public affairs' through discussions like demobilisation and post-war reconstruction. That may have been the programme's original intention in 1942/3, and possibly remained the official position into 1944. However, in practice the Corporation did not embrace the discussion on post-war reconstruction until 1944 and did not seek to lead the debate until 1945. (*The BBC Year Book for 1944*, p. 54; Nicholas, *Echo*, pp. 245-55.)

[310] In her last letter before contact ended, on 2 February, Minnie sent Quigley a manuscript from Arthur Belden, saying that he had a lovely speaking voice and was always in town should she wish to invite him for a test. Minnie, however, did not reveal that Belden was a fellow pacifist, a leading opponent of the RAF's bombing of civilian areas and, like Minnie, an advocate of an armistice with Germany. (Pallister to Quigley, 2 February 1944, BBC/WAC/RCONTI Pallister (Talks 3a).

[311] *Bexhill Observer*, 18 March 1944.

[312] Kate Molleson, *Suzy Klein*, Radio 3, 15 February 2019.

[313] Ian Kemp, *Tippett: The Composer and His Music*, Eulenburg, 1984, pp. 40-1.

[314] *Peace News*, 28 April & 5 May 1944; PPU AGM minutes, 22 & 23 April 1944, Friends House.

MINNIE PALLISTER: THE VOICE OF A REBEL

[315] Negotiated Peace Campaign Committee, 29 March & 5 June 1944.

[316] Pallister to Quigley, 23 June, Saturday, nd but late June & 4 July 1944, Quigley to Pallister, 4 July 1944; Pallister to Quigley, Mon, nd late July 1944, BBC/WAC/RCONTI Pallister (Talks 3a).

[317] Pallister to Quigley, 14 August 1944, BBC/WAC/RCONTI Pallister (Talks 3a).

[318] Negotiated Peace Campaign Committee, 25 July, 15 August & 9 September 1944; *Peace News*, 25 August 1944; Hetherington, p. 25.

[319] *Peace News*, 8 September & 27 October 1944; *Port Talbot Guardian*, 13 October 1944; Pallister to Quigley, 8 & 12 November 1944, BBC/WAC/RCONTI Pallister (Talks 3a).

[320] Albert Belden, *The Better Victory*, Christianity Calling, nd.

[321] *Peace News*, 30 March 1945; Pallister to Quigley, 15 March & 16 April [1945].

[322] Pallister to Quigley, 23 June 1944, BBC/WAC/RCONTI Pallister (Talks 3a).

[323] Pallister to Quigley, 8, 16 & 20 November 1944, Quigley to Pallister, 10 November 1944, BBC/WAC/RCONTI Pallister (Talks 3a).

[324] Pallister to Quigley, 17 December 1944, BBC/WAC/RCONTI Pallister (Talks 3a).

[325] Quigley to Pallister, 5 January 1945, Pallister to Quigley, 6 January 1945, BBC/WAC/RCONTI Pallister (Talks 3b).

[326] *Wiltshire Times*, 30 September 1944; *Rochdale Observer*, 14 April 1945; Peter Gordon & David Doughan, *Dictionary of British Women's organisations 1825–1960*, Woburn Press, 2001, pp. 115–6.

[327] Quigley to Pallister, 13 & 16 March 1945, Pallister to Quigley, 15 March & 16 April [1945], BBC/WAC/RCONTI Pallister (Talks 3b).

[328] Quigley to Pallister, 18 April & Pallister to Quigley, 14 July [1945], BBC/WAC/RCONTI Pallister (Talks 3b); 'Election Experiences', *Woman's Page*, 22 June 1945.

[329] Pallister to Quigley, 24 July 1945 & Pallister to Molony, 26 February 1946, BBC/WAC/RCONTI Pallister (Talks 3b).

CHAPTER EIGHT
Broadcaster

The 1945 Labour election victory breathed life into groups and societies that had languished during the war.[1] Minnie was invigorated as she spoke on the National Health Service Bill to women's groups. Directing her energy towards achieving greater women's representation across politics and society, she found a growing platform through Townswomen's Guilds and WIs, which both had mass memberships. Although they were formally, and sometimes rigidly, non-political, through their wide audiences she shared her core messages.[2] Making the most of the moment, the same talk might appear in print, on the platform and over the radio.

The dynamism she experienced in party and women's politics helped offset the 'extraordinary apathy' that existed within the PPU, where activists, without the galvanising effect of war, were initially left empty and exhausted.[3] After some months, the PPU roused itself to launch *A Crusade for a People's Peace* that sought to 'win the peace' in a way that had not been accomplished after 1918. Minnie served on the committee which directed the crusade as it travelled the country. In parallel, she spoke in support of the broader *Save Europe Now* campaign set up by Victor Gollancz to relieve distress across the continent, and which was led within the PPU by Vera Brittain.[4]

The destruction of Hiroshima and Nagasaki at the end of the Second World War saw the issue of nuclear weapons imposed on to the peace agenda. With 'the bomb' occupying attentions, as one of the PPU's most sought after speakers, Minnie toured Lancashire in February 1946, talking on 'How to Avoid the Third World War'.[5] Military conscription was another concern. The PPU had long sought exemption for objectors, supporting those individuals prepared to take action through conscientious objection. At the 1946 PPU AGM, Minnie moved the resolution that opposed military conscription, amended to include industrial conscription. Anticipating the technical assistance programmes of decades later, when addressing a branch of the Women's International League for Peace and Freedom Minnie called for Britain to send out armies of plumbers, doctors and teachers instead of soldiers.[6]

Although 'the long reign of war psychology' seemed over by late 1946, the following year the Government extended peacetime conscription.[7] Upping the ante, the subsequent PPU AGM, rather than limiting itself to obtaining exemption provisions for objectors, voted for the General Council to take a lead in completely destroying the Conscription Acts. It also urged all who were opposed to peacetime military conscription to ignore the Act and refuse to obey it, calling for demonstrations outside Labour Exchanges.[8] The decision, which received considerable press coverage, split the PPU down the middle. The national council divided 12:10 in favour of implementing the decision, with Minnie in the slender majority.[9] The divided leadership was unable to reconcile its differences, and six sponsors and four members of the National Council resigned. With her idealism outweighing her realism, Minnie maintained her firmer line at a special meeting of the National Council, where she seconded the resolution to consider how civil disobedience could be used to help implement the decision.[10] Uncertain over the extent to which PPU groups in the country would follow, the National Council was left confronted with being unable to deliver its own divisive policy.[11]

After the war ended, Minnie's relationship with the BBC changed. Quigley left to get married and moved to Ireland. For Minnie this was a disaster. She admitted 'You have always been the BBC as far as I am concerned, and I can't imagine it without you.'[12] Minnie now pitched a number of ideas to other BBC staff to no avail. Her proposals about the Education Act, the Children Act, women's organisations and how new legislation would affect women went unheeded. No longer did she have the immediate access to which she had been accustomed.[13] Godfrey James, who was in charge of book talks on the Home and Light programmes was polite to Minnie but made harsh private criticisms. He told Roy Campbell, in charge of the *Literary Magazine*, that he was unimpressed with Minnie at interview and that her trial script was '*awful* – incredibly arch and facetious'. Campbell wrote of Minnie, 'Rejection Please'.[14] Unaware of these views, Minnie kept trying but by October 1946 was resorting to sending generic 'Dear Sir' letters.[15]

Without Quigley, Minnie did not have a sponsor within the

Corporation. When Howard Thomas wrote in a woman's magazine that no woman broadcaster had been successful, except for singers etc., Minnie challenged his analysis, saying that women were 'the one bright spot' even though men were given the 'intimate' talks.[16] However, no one at the BBC was attuned to her gendered analysis so it was not picked up. Instead, Minnie channelled her views into *John O'London* where her review of Alexander Gray's *The Socialist Tradition* noted that the character studies of men who had dreams of building a better society were good but that women had been omitted from consideration.[17]

Minnie had been off-air for over a year when *Woman's Hour*, a new magazine programme to help recreate domestic life after the war, was launched on 7 October 1946. As women returned from factories and the forces, the programme's aim was to restore home life and represent women's interests in the post-war world through 'fashion, celebrity news and the home'.[18] Over the next seventy-five years, *Woman's Hour* became an institution in its own right, a cornerstone of BBC broadcasting – 'the Rolls Royce of Radio 4'. It has continued to break new ground, introducing discussions on previously taboo topics including the menopause and female masturbation.[19] Sally Feldman, a later editor of *Woman's Hour*, suggests that, from the beginning, the programme embraced a far wider range of issues than had been originally conceived.[20] It was often Minnie who, in spite of a stuttering start, was at the forefront of efforts to sharpen the programme's focus. In the way she linked the domestic with broader gender issues including women's economic situations and the status of women in the workplace, Minnie used women's domestic roles to subvert and challenge as much as affirm. She became one of the programme's outstanding voices and was indelibly identified with it.

Within a month of the programme's launch, Minnie was commissioned to give a talk on the 'Exhibition of the King's Pictures' at the Royal Academy for which she was paid 11 guineas. Afterwards Minnie apologised profusely for having caused 'trouble' in the days leading up to the broadcast. She became scared at the size of the subject, was deeply ashamed, and hoped at some point to have a chance to retrieve her reputation. Hers may have been an overreaction as BBC staff were complimentary and it did not interrupt her broadcasting.[21]

Minnie's insecurities and vulnerabilities accompanied her constantly. Increasingly unable to handle stress, she became difficult to manage. Successive generations of BBC staff learned that they needed to provide a supportive environment and positive feedback to get the best out of her. Minnie acknowledged she was not a hardy soul who could pursue a path 'unflinching, regardless of other people's opinions'. She was of 'commoner clay, we need bolstering up, appreciation is the breath of life to us'.[22] Even after two decades of broadcasting, she could still feel panicked that she no longer 'belonged' and needed reassurance.[23] The producer Anthony Derville developed an affectionate relationship with Minnie. As confidence with him grew, she became more assured in the way she proposed ideas for broadcasting. The supportive relationship was not one way. Correspondence with Derville and other producers over many years show her gently educating them while also seeking to shape the *Woman's Hour* agenda.

In late 1946, Minnie broadcast a talk that gave parallel consideration to modern professional women and to women engaged in trades in the eighteenth century before regulations were tightened to exclude them. Analysing post-World War II legislation affecting women's roles, including married women in the civil service and as chairs of committees and members of the House of Commons, she drew on historical precedent to show what women had lost and were now trying to reclaim.[24] Another broadcast covered the Society of Women Artists exhibition in the Guildhall, which was a topic that fitted her perfectly. The Society had been a refuge for women artists not allowed to join other professional societies as the art establishment excluded women, just as did other spheres. Also explaining how artists could 'help us to see'; she argued that while many things were scarce due to austerity, art was one commodity that was readily available.[25]

The big freeze of early 1947, with deep snow everywhere, brought the country to a halt. In early February the pipes in the flat burst, requiring her to move to Welwyn for six weeks, presumably to stay with her sister Julia, who had returned from India with her husband. The economy and national morale were at an all-time low when further dislocation caused by the fuel crisis led to *Woman's Hour* being suspended and Minnie's scheduled broadcast being postponed from March until April. Having endured the war, for Minnie to report that life was hard indicates the depth of difficulties faced by the population in those months.[26]

Meanwhile, Minnie continued to press the BBC to look at the women's movement, including the National Council of Women, which had worldwide reach and representation. While she recognised that 'the ordinary tired housewife wants to be amused and seduced into knowledge', Minnie suspected that women had no idea how many women's organisations there were or what they did.[27]

However, before her ideas came to fruition, Minnie was commissioned to present a talk on the Royal Academy Summer Exhibition. She noted it marked a turning away from war and a return to 'life'; she enjoyed that a third of the paintings were by women. She coveted many of the traditional landscapes and observed there was no modern art, with its 'distortions, all triangles and squints and odd eyes'. Derville very much liked the script. However, in what was otherwise a balanced account, the opening section was ill-judged and indiscreet. There, Minnie related how on Press Day she had tailed 'a well-known artist' – the thinly disguised Sir Alfred Munnings, President of the RA – whom she described as being profane. Minnie recounted following him, listening in on his views on various paintings, including those of Winston Churchill, who Munnings judged could have been a very good artist. In her criticism of Munnings, and in repeating on-air to listeners comments she had heard by eavesdropping, Minnie badly misjudged the tenor of her script.[28] (Ironically, while her comments were ill-judged, they were not misplaced. Two years later, in his valedictory speech to the Royal Academy, live on the BBC, a drunken Sir Alfred achieved notoriety by colourfully attacking modernism and quoting a personal conversation with Churchill.) Minnie's broadcast had considerable repercussions and Derville was told not to use her again on *Woman's Hour*.[29] A 'quiet word' was sufficient to remove Minnie from the airwaves.

BBC files give no indication of who spoke to Derville. Paul Bloomfield, who joined the Talks Department in 1937, referred to how the 'Hidden Hand' operated in Broadcasting House, influencing the atmosphere and decision making.[30] Although Derville had already commissioned another script, he informed Minnie that *Woman's Hour* had 'decided to rest you for a little'. Minnie rang him for clarification but, after their conversation, was none the wiser.[31] Her summer was wasted as she was unable to work; she found it difficult to explain to literary agents, lecture agencies or audiences why she was no longer broadcasting as she was 'guilty of some kind of nameless obscenity, for which I am banned'.[32] Unable to find peace of mind, Minnie told Derville that she had a right to know the complaint against her and who had made it. Derville was sympathetic. His draft reply read, 'there is no cloud hanging over you & Please don't feel that there is.' Tactfully, he said he had heard no criticism of her talk from any member of the Royal Academy, though he was silent on whether criticism had come from inside the BBC or from listeners. A phone call with him eased her mind. Reading the script sixty years later, the only surprise is that it was not evident to Minnie why she was taken off-air. Perhaps in response to the situation, she found herself a new woman agent.[33]

Apparently reassured that she was not barred, Minnie sent suggestions for topics to various parts of the BBC, including a talk on Ramsay MacDonald in their 'Famous Men' series – though she could not resist asking whether they also proposed doing a series on 'Famous Women'.[34] She even approached the Forces Programme, without success.[35] It did not need a formal note on her file to say she had a 'black mark' against her. Stock rejections meant she would not broadcast for another three years, except for a talk facilitated by Derville on 'South Wales and the ILP' for the Welsh Home Service.[36] Without the BBC, Minnie concentrated on talks to women's organisations and she submitted work to the *Daily Mirror* through Derville, who knew the editor.[37] She still reviewed for *John O'London* and had published a portrayal of miners and their wives, albeit of an earlier era, in *Everybody's Weekly*.[38]

In spite of her broadcasting ban, Minnie was fizzing with energy and life. Hoping to travel again before she got too old, Minnie, now 63, had been invited to Tasmania by a cousin, who had stayed with her that year. She had many cousins in Australia, and hoped for a speaking tour with the Country Women's Association – the Australian equivalent of the WI. She also hoped to visit the United States, and from 1945 had sought a travel permit, no doubt to visit the Schwarbs. She maintained this hope throughout the 1950s, but it would remain an unrealised ambition.

Minnie strongly supported the domestic policies of the Labour Government and was frustrated with its critics. She wished 'our own people' could be as loyal in accepting change as had been some of their enemies. She was 'sick to death' of their moaning about what hadn't been done and 'stabbing their government in the back'. Minnie's resentment of the Communist Party was also clear. She lamented having gone to a *Daily Worker* conference to which she and Katharine Bruce Glasier had been invited 'so as to use our names abroad'. For Minnie the Communist Party had no connection with any kind of communism as it had been previously understood and she contrasted Russia with Britain, commenting that whatever a capitalist country might be, as long as there was free speech and parliament, change was possible.[39]

Katharine Bruce Glasier died on 14 June 1950. Minnie considered she had been her 'closest friend to the end'.[40] Feeling 'absolutely overcome' and unable to imagine a world without her, Minnie said she felt old and tired with the passing of friends.[41] After her death, Bruce Glasier's closest friends considered what should happen to her home, a cottage in Lancashire, and Minnie proposed that it should be a retreat for the women's movement.[42] Three years later, her judgement of Bruce Glasier was that she had been 'an inspiration without stint' and was still 'a burning flame' at 80.[43]

The loss of Minnie's closest friend was partially offset by the reappearance of another. After five years' absence, on 1 June 1950, Janet Quigley returned to the BBC as Editor of *Woman's Hour*. Minnie drooled, 'I was rather dazed yesterday as it all seemed like a dream...'[44] Quigley quickly returned Minnie to the BBC fold,[45] catapulting her to the centre of *Woman's Hour*'s programming. For its autumn return, Quigley decided that the second series of 'Other Women's Lives' should start with Minnie's own political life and requested that Minnie talk about how far her ambitions and aspirations had been realised, the effect of her illness on her career and how she felt about it now. Giving Minnie four days to send an outline, Quigley added: 'It would make a good come back to broadcasting would it not?' The following day, drawing on six chapters of the eight or nine she had written for her 1934–7 autobiography, Minnie submitted the script saying it had just flowed.[46] The broadcast went well. Appreciative letters from listeners, including some who were themselves invalid, provided the praise upon which Minnie thrived.[47] A further accolade was that an edited version appeared in the annual *Book of Woman's Hour*.[48]

In her preparations Minnie had considered whether to include reference to her sense of loss in not being an MP and whether she regretted it.[49] She chose not to mention it but three years later declared that: 'Every now and then something reminds me that but for the merest chance I should have been in the House of Commons for years, and for a moment I grow so bitter I just can't bear it.' She added, 'then I wonder if I should have been any happier or more useful. You can't be happier than happy, and if you're happy doing what you're doing, why worry because you're not doing something else?' They were, she said, 'Useless regrets!'.[50] In the same 1953 talk, Minnie said she had envied three unnamed people for their health or position before each had died tragically young. Ellen Wilkinson would have been one. Elected in Minnie's place to the Labour Party National Executive in 1927, Wilkinson subsequently eclipsed Minnie as a darling of the ILP and became the only woman in Attlee's Cabinet, before dying of an overdose in February 1947. Minnie's guilty conscience at having held such negative thoughts led her to feel, in all three cases, 'like a murderess'.[51] Thirty years after her political career was ended, Minnie might say she had she had largely come to terms with being denied her political ambitions and it was, in part, true. However, resentment at her situation, and perhaps even jealousy of others who achieved what was denied her, still lingered deep within.

It is not possible to assess the extent of her association with the Labour Government, although she is certain to have taken advantage of her links with its Ministers, many of whom she had known for decades.[52] At its fringes, after Attlee launched a fund in memory of Margaret McMillan, a pioneer of nursery schools, Minnie did a broadcast on the proposed Margaret McMillan Training Centre in Bradford. The Centre's committee heard the broadcast and sought Minnie's advice about Mrs Attlee giving a BBC talk. Minnie suggested that Arthur Greenwood, a former minister in Attlee's Cabinet, approach Quigley and a date was arranged for Mrs Attlee to broadcast. When an association was formed to build the Centre, Minnie retained an involvement.[53]

Quigley and Minnie shared the same outlook on women's issues. In Minnie, Quigley found a presenter who could popularise ideas by drawing on her own experiences in ways that appealed to ordinary women. In turn, the BBC provided Minnie with a medium to promote to huge audiences the same women's issues she had advanced for decades through newspaper articles, books, pamphlets and from the platform, albeit calibrated for BBC consumption. Once more they corresponded almost daily, discussing what should be promoted and how, and recognising 'indirect propaganda' as the most effective way to convey messages.[54]

Quigley and Minnie discussed Minnie having a regular diary slot that looked at life from a women's angle. Minnie emphasised that it should be based on her *own* interests to include her visits to WIs, Townswomen's Guilds, WEA summer schools, conferences of the National Council of Women, meetings of professional or political women, museums, theatre and cinema and talks on books she had read. She was discreet enough to not point out she would be funded for living her own life, but made the point that others would be interested in one woman's 'scheme of life', rather than odd talks. Quigley was 'anxious' for all Minnie's contributions to be 'personality broadcasting' so the focus was not the book or the garden but 'what Minnie Pallister has been doing in her garden and what Minnie Pallister has been reading.'[55] 'Minnie Pallister's Diary' was broadcast once a month from 5 January 1951. At first Minnie found it difficult to overcome her self-consciousness, but Quigley declined proposals that were not based in personal experience. After finding the right tone, Minnie felt the format suited her. The February Diary went 'particularly well', made all the sweeter by her 11 guineas fee for a ten-minute transmission.[56]

Light humorous talks, 'with a bit of advice tucked in', had always been Minnie's strong suit.[57] However, her angst over the Korean War led her to swing between 'thinking it[']s good to take women[']s minds off horrors for five minutes' and feeling it was awful to give light talks at such a time.[58] Minnie therefore worked on a very serious talk for Armistice Day. Unhappy with the script, it accompanied her 'every waking moment' for months until finally Quigley said they should be 'courageous' and put it out at Easter.[59] Her Easter meditation addressed 'the quickening of conscience, in relation to other peoples' needs'.[60] While it was impossible to imagine being a displaced person, a deprived child or a 'coloured' person, there were a small number who felt the suffering of others as much as their own. The majority of the German people did not know about the concentration camps because they did not care, but it was our business to know and care, and do something about it, and Easter was the time for such a conscience to awake. The talk drew so many responses (including a thirty-page letter from a doctor) that Minnie had to tabulate them.[61] After years off-air, this was a triumphant return.

Minnie's broadcasting career, previously episodic, took off. In 1951 she did seventeen broadcasts, previously never having done more than seven in a year. She remained a regular voice of *Woman's Hour* throughout the 1950s and over six years had a number of, sometimes overlapping, *Woman's Hour* series. These were supplemented by broadcasts on specific topics as well as contributions to other programmes and series. The monthly 'Diary', which ran from January 1951 to April 1956, laid the platform. 'I've Been Thinking About...' aired from January to May 1953. 'Minnie Pallister Speaking', which ran from January 1954 to June 1955, freed her from the limitations of the Diary format.[62] Like 'Meanderings', from November 1956 to June 1957, all were essentially open-ended vehicles for Minnie to talk about whatever she wanted. In total, Minnie made more than 100 broadcasts for *Woman's Hour* in the 1950s, as well as numerous non-*Woman's Hour* appearances.

Between three and four million women listened regularly to *Woman's Hour*. Minnie's popularity with the audience and her broadcasting prowess were recognised within the BBC. In the summer of 1951, when *Woman's Hour* went off the air for two months for its summer break, listeners named their favourite speakers over the previous ten months for inclusion in 'Request Week'. Minnie came second in the *Radio Times* poll.[63] In 1952, 1954 and 1955, Minnie again came near the top of listener requests while in 1953 she was selected to present records for a week, each day choosing a different classical music category.[64]

Minnie's popularity was based in her authenticity. Her human qualities, warmth of personality and humour were matched by her honesty about her failings and willingness to show her fallibilities, whether serious or light-hearted. Acknowledging her shortcomings as a person was a strength as a broadcaster. Minnie talked openly about her depression, irrational fears, hysterical outbursts, tears, and low self-esteem. In the way she talked about difficult situations, including dealing with illness or old age, she was without peer.[65]

Listeners identified with Minnie, and could see bits of themselves in her. An increasingly neurotic ditherer who lost coats, gloves and luggage and was prone to panic, she was prepared to admit to the same worries, weaknesses and mistakes as everyone else. She recognised the realities of everyday life, making broader social commentary from the domestic and quotidian, for example in acknowledging that, alongside the official rationing system, it was necessary to develop a network of people with whom you could barter to survive, with tea as the central currency. Minnie reported that wherever she spoke, women told her she made 'all the difference to their lives'.[66] People wrote to her to say she helped them, and hundreds of women approached her in person. 'It is a complete mystery to me, I cannot imagine what on earth I say which helps these women, but I get it all the time, by letter and word of mouth.'[67] She took her audiences seriously though, replying assiduously to every letter and card she received.[68]

Recognising that radio and television meant more to women than men, especially those wives and mothers who spent more of their time at home, Antoinette Fortune, writing in 1959, captured the essence of Minnie as a radio broadcaster:

> Strangely enough, Joyce Grenfell can be disappointing. I always have the uncomfortable feeling she is forcing the camaraderie. She tries too hard. Minnie Pallister has an ordinary voice and a down-to-earth approach. Here, you feel, is the real salt of the earth and all unaware...
>
> Listening to her you realised the influence these programmes must have, the gentle insistent formation of the opinions and outlook of thousands of 'ordinary' women, who in their turn will be the chief formative influence in their own homes.[69]

The favourable comparison with Joyce Grenfell, a star of stage and film, comedian, singer and broadcaster was praise indeed. However, to an old 1920s-style propagandist like Minnie, there could be no higher accolade than Fortune's observation of her as a major influencer of women. From the platform, in print and over the airwaves for fifty years Minnie had worked to bring others to her point of view, so to be recognised for shaping opinion in homes across the country was a real prize.

Creativity, ability and application, fed by ambition, had seen Minnie rise up the political tree. Now she showed equal ambition in her radio career. While there were many interesting things on *Woman's Hour*, she thought there remained a 'vacant spot' for a

Harold Nicolson, Wilfred Pickles or Richard Dimbleby 'to which I aspire one day to fill'.[70] In spite of personal insecurities, her professional confidence allowed her to compare herself with some of the most prominent broadcasters of the era. Though she did not achieve the status of such luminaries, she established herself as a household name of women's radio.

As an interpreter of the woman's position and women's rights, an advocate of pacifism or socialism, or referring to grief and illness, Minnie Pallister was simply one of the best of communicators. On the radio, her calls for social justice and her ability to relay her message made Minnie what she was in real life – a force of nature. Within *Woman's Hour*, Minnie's significance was greater than just as a broadcaster. Her influence on programme content and the way she went about tackling issues consistently pushed the Corporation beyond its comfort zone.

Minnie was delighted to renew her working relationship with Derville, one of the few men on the *Woman's Hour* team.[71] She was always aware of the impact of gender on her working life and those of other women and was ready to point it out. After taking part in a *Woman's Hour* forum on reading, she noted tongue-in-cheek: 'perhaps Margaret Jackson (whose contributions are so fresh and stimulating) and I were a little too polite in letting the male element [Daniel George, a literary critic and Frederick Sinclair, a public librarian] go on a bit too long at some points', then with sweet irony added 'but they *are* two experts after all…'[72] (Emphasis in original.)

Minnie's *Woman's Hour* appearances made her a popular choice for WIs. Her broadcasts helped build her a nationwide profile she would otherwise have found impossible to attain. Equally, to invert the point, Minnie acted as an unofficial ambassador for *Woman's Hour*, taking the BBC and something of its personality out to hamlets and villages across the country, and providing the Corporation with a form of outreach to WI and other women's groups it otherwise lacked. Local women were such fans of *Woman's Hour* that they arrived by the coachload to hear Minnie speak.[73] In response to a listener's request about what she did for an occupation, Minnie responded that she made 'a more or less honest living by talking to women's organisations of all sorts and sizes'.[74] Her meetings with WIs alone probably numbered in their low thousands.

If women's organisations and women's issues were a primary manifestation of her politics, the PPU was now the main expression of Minnie's faith. While people thought of her as a Methodist, 'the Peace Pledge Union is my church strictly speaking now, I give to it the money and time I always gave to church work'.[75] From 1945 to 1951 the PPU had heft. Its influence was shown in the range of subjects it embraced, the seriousness with which it did so, and the people on whom it could call. In 1949 Vera Brittain became PPU chair, seeing the organisation as having 'a revolutionary function to perform in a society still dominated by traditional behaviour'.[76] Minnie joined the PPU Executive Committee the following year, at a time when the organisation was suffering a campaign of vilification.[77] Its members had been described as traitors during the Second World War, and it was still regarded as a fifth column. Having previously been considered pro-Nazi, the PPU was now labelled pro-Soviet.[78] Slurs by local and national politicians, newspapers, and even the London Housewives Association were common. It is remarkable that a peace organisation could be considered so threatening and attract such antipathy. Although unpleasant, the virulence and nature of the attacks were testimony to the PPU's significance early in the Cold War.

As one of the PPU's main national speakers, Minnie's energies were mainly directed outwards. In November 1949, a PPU *Steps To Peace* conference considered how to foster peace through the country's economic, social and cultural life. A series of commissions analysed the pursuit of peace through various lenses, including education, the arts, religion and science. Minnie led the politics commission. Expressing disappointment at the Labour Party's foreign policy, she asked whether a pacifist Foreign Secretary would have done better than Ernest Bevin. Those present agreed that his performance had disappointed the world's hopes and its policy of collective security was 'a great sham'.[79] Despondency about the international position resulted in the conference agreeing that it was necessary 'for pacifism to be vigorously propagated at a political level' and for the PPU to establish a permanent committee to address it. Furthermore, individual pacifists should join the Labour Party to influence its policy.[80] Such ventures stood no chance. Foreign policy lay with Bevin, who dominated his department. Minnie knew his hostility to Russia chimed with the TUC leaders' anti-communism so that grassroots criticism and the pacifism of the PPU were easily dismissed. Nevertheless, she called for Britain to renounce the atomic bomb and give moral leadership to the rest of the world.[81]

As a strong critic of the Labour Government's foreign policies, there was a paradox when she offered a spirited defence against the charge that 'she breaks her pledge of pacifism by remaining a Labour Party member' at a Mock Trial in Westminster.[82] She was more comfortable in accepting the position of Vice-President of the Labour Pacifist Fellowship (LPF),[83] but her disappointment at the Labour Party's response to the Fellowship led her to contrast the Labour Party's outlook with that of the ILP as a Peace Party.[84] Even so, in the 1950 general election, Minnie campaigned for the Labour candidates in Hastings and Eastbourne, which included Bexhill. Just like old times, when Minnie spoke at an eve of poll rally, an altercation broke out, and pandemonium ensued. Minnie, the hardened campaigner, continued speaking despite considerable heckling.[85]

After the return of a Labour Government, Minnie criticised its support for the United States' anti-communist intervention in Korea, its backing of German rearmament as a bulwark against Russia, and for undertaking imperial ventures such as the 'police action' in Malaya.[86] At times, she said, it felt as if supporting the Labour Party was 'a policy of despair'. She continued to support Christianity Calling, but maintained her doubts about the church as it had so often blessed war.[87] In spite of anti-communist propaganda being at a peak, when Minnie was advertised to speak on 'The Asia Crisis: War? We Say No', over 700 people attended.[88] When *The Times* refused to print a PPU letter about the Korean War, Brittain believed the organisation to be subject to a media boycott. In order to break through it, Brittain called for sensational, non-violent actions, pointing to suffragette methods and Gandhi's civil disobedience campaigns for inspiration.[89] Subsequently the PPU arranged meetings with pacifist and non-pacifist journalists and editors to break the boycott.[90]

Once more Minnie's social life was a function of her politics. She went to Glyndebourne to see Benjamin Britten, a committed pacifist, perform his first 'chamber opera', *The Rape of Lucretia*. Britten himself looked 'much too young and innocent to have written the Opera' thought Minnie, adding, 'What a night'.[91] In January 1951 although trains were disrupted by snow and a smallpox scare, Minnie wanted to go to Brighton to see her friend and PPU Treasurer, Sybil Thorndike, in a play. That same month, Minnie picked up Michael Tippett, another friend, from the ancient Sussex farmhouse to which he had just moved to speak to 'a group of us' on world affairs.[92] Tippett's position was that non-violent resistance needed to be made a 'symbol of the hopes of the common man'. It was necessary to ally 'moral force...to the non-violent method'. This was 'not the submissiveness of the weak, but the resistance of the strong'.[93]

Each winter, Minnie struggled against depression as one 'looks back and sees nothing but a long mis-spent life, full of failure and futility'.[94] However, in spite of the cloud that always accompanied the darkest months, she kept functioning. Standing at a bus stop in sleet on a cold February night after speaking at a remote WI, with no fuel to heat the hall, and dependent on the vagaries of unreliable post-war transport, Minnie, now 65 years old, maintained her spirits with the promise of spring.[95]

Minnie's pace of life was extraordinary. In March 1951, for example, as well as attending a Margaret McMillan meeting in the House of Commons, she did four or five 'routine' political meetings, spoke to a Women's Co-operative Guild and a literary society, ran a WEA literature class, attended a lecture on astronomy, went to a weekend school on films 'as I'm still trying to be intelligent about modern art forms', and went a long way one snowy night to see two surrealist films (one of which she was supposed to have studied Freud to understand). She was a guest at the Business and Professional Women's Club annual dinner in Swansea, where she gave a talk on 'Mother and Home Can Give Lead in World Affairs'; participated in the quarterly management meeting of a school for deaf girls; visited an open-air residential school for 'delicate children', (for which she did house-to-house collections) as it was her turn on the rota; saw an exhibition on book design at the National Book League; and attended a large WI conference. When at home her daily routine was to get up at 6.30, have a pot of tea, and work on the garden from 8 am until around 9.30 am, leaving the rest of the morning for work. That month Minnie made kitchen curtains for her new home, went clothes shopping, and picked wild primroses. She read the biography of Robert Blatchford twice, as she had enjoyed it so much.[96] Over Whitsun, as most years, Minnie went on a 'physical, mental, spiritual' retreat, which considered international relations.[97] Also Minnie was always looking for opportunities to visit South Wales having retained her affection for the place and its people.[98]

The last hurrah of Labour in government was the Festival of Britain. Minnie visited often and Attlee had already called a general election for 25 October 1951 when Minnie saw Horovitz play at the Festival Hall.[99] Quigley asked Minnie to talk on her election experiences three days before the election, but had second thoughts and considered deferring the broadcast to four days after. Having fallen foul of the BBC so often, Minnie cautioned about breaking impartiality rules, but wondered whether people would still be interested after the election was over.[100] Concerned, Quigley sent an 'URGENT' message, underlined in red, to Mary Somerville, Controller of Talks, about Minnie giving an innocuous talk about politics in the election period but stated misleadingly that Minnie had suggested the idea. Somerville replied immediately saying 'This really cannot be defended...', so Quigley smoothly wrote to Minnie saying she agreed with her that such a talk would be 'cold mutton' after election day. Minnie replied hoping that before too long, she would be able to give her 'Don't Be Afraid of Isms' talk, when she would spend a minute or two explaining each one 'without the sky falling'.[101]

At the eve of poll meeting, Minnie made a 'fighting speech' to 700 people at Eastbourne Town Hall for the candidate Christopher Attlee, the Prime Minister's nephew. Although there was opposition in the hall, unlike in the previous year the atmosphere was amicable.[102] Despite Labour achieving its highest ever national vote and gaining more votes than the Conservative Party, the Tories won more seats and Churchill's Government was returned to power. After six years, Labour was out, but with the country transformed.

As British post-war life slowly returned to normal, albeit still with dislocations and inconveniences, Minnie did not relish the adjustment. 'Make do and mend' suited Minnie. A puritan at heart, she was psychologically and politically more sympathetic towards late 1940s austerity than the 1950s consumer society. Two world wars made her appreciate that labour and materials should not be wasted on 'frivolous and useless things'.[103] Although she opposed the military imperative, she was at one with the collective endeavour, self-sacrifice and personal disciplines that wartime imposed and wanted them to continue in peacetime.

However, by late 1951, any hope that those values might last were fading as she saw people were once more bribed into buying. When the BBC producer Honor Wyatt suggested Minnie speak on 'Christmas is A Racket', Minnie considered 'the coarseness, the crudity, the insult' of giving any gift at Christmas without thought as just paying money and 'idle mockery'. She saw Christmas degenerating into 'an orgy of waste' and 'an orgy of overeating'. Minnie's view of the retailer in society was that 'Things should meet a need rather than create a need'. She referred regularly to the lives of displaced persons in a Europe devastated by war; now she wished to challengingly portray the child Jesus as a displaced person. Wyatt felt a 'choking rage' at the commercialisation of Christmas and believed that by limiting shopping to necessities, the line between 'legitimate glamour and sheer waste' was all the clearer. She proposed that Minnie discuss the subject with the General Manager of Selfridges. The broadcast went out on 14 December.[104]

Some listeners saw Minnie as a sort of campaigning agony aunt. When one listener wrote on an issue of public concern, Minnie took up the case up with the authorities. This may have inspired her to propose a series called 'What Can We Do About...'. Her idea was that as the world grew bigger, people felt smaller, so individuals should be encouraged to know more, become more active, and address wrongs that should be altered, since nothing was more disempowering than to become indignant over an issue but failing to do anything about it. Seeing the series as an opportunity to work with women to organise and campaign, she wanted to tackle big problems like war and peace, prices, housing, prison conditions, child neglect, cruelty, and juvenile delinquency. Anticipating TV consumer programmes over thirty years later in exposing 'rackets', she aimed to sort out individuals' problems and equip people with the knowledge to resolve problems for themselves, informing women about means and helpful organisations of which they were otherwise unaware.

The sweep of Minnie's scope was impressive. Her talk on prices and shopping prefigured early twenty-first-century ethical, fair trade and environmental concerns.[105] However, she could strike a quite different tone. When a highbrow literary friend said sneeringly, 'Of course, you never read poetry', Minnie was hurt, but knew it was true.[106] Although she had a poetic sensibility, describing cathedrals as 'poems in stone', on seeing the bombed remains of Coventry Cathedral she realised she was missing something that should be ordinary and accessible and wondered if people were put off by so many people using 'a special voice for poetry as they do for religion'. She gave a talk on poetry similar to her earlier introductions to books, paintings and ballet that looked at the disciplined language of poetry and revealed to listeners a way of hearing and reading it.[107] Listeners from as far afield as Ireland and Holland requested a copy of the script and a record company contacted Minnie and made a record of it.[108]

Minnie's stature was recognised when, in spring 1952, *Woman's Hour* staff proposed a new series, 'Minnie Pallister's Life Story'. Broadcast over five days, it was accompanied by a feature in the *Radio Times*. She talked of her childhood, living in Brynmawr, 'The Hurly-burly of Politics', 'Retired Hurt' and 'A New Life'. Minnie was paid 25 guineas for the five episodes.[109] Sadly, the recordings do not survive.

Quigley then invited Minnie to speak about an outstanding woman of her choice in a new series, 'I Knew Her'. Minnie volunteered Katharine Bruce Glasier, the pioneering woman involved in the creation of the labour movement and who, said Minnie, gave it its spiritual tone. She contrasted Bruce Glasier's methods with the bitterness of the revolutionary movements, 'Just now when so many of our own people are going a whoring after strange Communist gods.'[110]

When Quigley asked Minnie to suggest other women who could broadcast on other female subjects, Minnie forwarded extensive lists of subjects and suggested broadcasters. She proposed ending the series with 'The Unknown Woman', paying homage to the thousands of women who worked behind the scenes, 'making it possible for their men to do deeds in public' and 'often making it possible for the outstanding women to be outstanding'.[111] Minnie voluntarily worked on the series for a month, because she believed so much in it. Although no fee had been discussed, Quigley retrospectively arranged a consultant's fee of 5 guineas because, she said, Minnie had very little money.[112] The following year, Minnie sent Quigley publicity material for Vera Brittain's new book *Lady into Woman*, on the struggle for women's rights, and facilitated her appearance as *Woman's Hour*'s Guest of the Week. Minnie then advised Brittain in her preparation for the programme, and their chatty, shorthand style reflected Minnie and Brittain's relaxed familiarity.[113] A joint review of plays with Pearl Binder, the legendary East End artist, writer and supporter of women's rights, earned the accolade of being 'a really successful broadcast'.[114]

When in late 1952 Minnie felt very unwell and fainted, a medical check-up concluded that she was not suffering a heart problem or a stroke as initially suspected, but her condition was a combination of being overtired and overweight. She was told to reduce the number of meetings and go on a diet. Minnie had long had difficulty with her overeating. Throughout the 1950s, her fondness for food stymied her eternal battle with weight. During the war the rationing of food, particularly sugar, had improved her diet. Combined with exercise from growing vegetables and training on the stirrup pump for fire-watching she had lost a stone and a half.[115] Now, with rationing largely over and doing less exercise, losing weight was 'a wretched business'.[116] Since, as she often said, she didn't smoke or drink and claimed not to have love affairs, food was her one indulgence. Drastically cutting out breakfast, elevenses, sweets and eating at teatimes, her diet was always on her mind.[117] Food, and her relationship with it, was a frequent topic in her talks as Minnie shared with listeners her inability to resist temptation.[118] As penance, whenever she ate a small luxury, Minnie contributed an equivalent amount to the Peace Pledge Union.[119] This was a counterproductive strategy because as the PPU coffers swelled, so did Minnie. At one point she could not fit into a size 42. Once more her doctor told her to lose weight.[120] Neither did she reduce her number of meetings.

In spite of appearing in front of live audiences, Minnie displayed a marked reluctance to allow publicity photos. Judging herself too fat and colourless, she quoted a friend who said, 'One day they'll put your photograph in the *Radio Times*, and that will be the end of everything.' Minnie concluded, 'If listeners have any illusions about me, let them keep them.'[121] She was not alone in that view. When she sent her only decent snap to Quigley, someone in the BBC judged that it 'confirms my feeling that Minnie's *face* is worth a photo'. (Emphasis in original.) A suggestion of a photoshoot the following year led Minnie to offer thirty-year-old photos from Bournemouth elections.[122]

Jean Metcalfe, who was often Minnie's producer, provided an entertaining description of *Woman's Hour* in the 'amiable, meandering fifties' and remembered Minnie as a likeable but chaotic person, who spent half her life on the radio broadcasting about her experiences as a WI lecturer and the other half telling WIs about the BBC.[123] While this was a shrewd assessment of the way Minnie made the most of her opportunities, it failed to acknowledge her qualities as a broadcaster, her popularity with the audience or the breadth of her coverage. Tellingly, although Metcalfe described the programme's role as being 'to divert and inform tired housewives' adding, 'we aimed to please. We were not intentionally controversial', Minnie consistently challenged that convention. Her new series 'I've Been Thinking', launched in early 1953, provided an opportunity to pick up some of the residual themes from 'What Can I Do About', including problem families, and the prejudice against social services and their support of what some saw as the 'undeserving poor'.[124] The issue of necessities versus luxuries again surfaced as she argued that 'not a minute of time, not an ounce of material should be used for frivolities, until every child in the world has been fed and clothed housed and educated.'[125] Minnie also finally got to speak about 'isms'. The BBC need not have worried as its sharpest part related to vegetarianism.[126] However, the Corporation always needed to be on its toes.

Minnie's communications with the BBC were often conducted in a scraggly hand on scraps of paper on bus, train and tram journeys, or at a railway station.[127] Although her producers had confidence in her capacity to deliver a script, to a length, on a theme, and on time, they were covered with a barrage of crossings out and littered with arrows, insertions and additions. At a time when live broadcasting was done by reading from scripts, Minnie noted to Quigley, 'I won't ask you not to cry at the chaotic script, because you know me well enough by now, not to panic.'[128] As if being live on-air were not enough of a challenge, Minnie did it working from shambolic scripts.

Managing Minnie was a permanent job. A week after Quigley told her that one particular script was 'better than any you have done for a long time. It is, as they say, "vintage"', Minnie had a 'Nobody Loves Me' outburst.[129] She did not handle stress well and recognised she could become 'frightfully het up'. She was aware that she 'spoiled things by worrying and fussing', as well as wasting time and energy. With a tendency to overreact, she made more mistakes than most 'because that's how I'm made'.[130] On balance though, BBC staff considered the time taken in supporting Minnie to ease her insecurities and get her to perform well as a good investment. Minnie's life was a blur of bus and railway timetables only possible in the pre-Beeching era. Interspersing routine committee meetings with conferences and lectures, she typically addressed women's and pacifist organisations four to five times each week, with three or four long journeys and nights away from home.[131] As she pin-balled from village to village, on tours that required immense coordination, she could have set records for endurance, only matched by the political peregrinations of her younger days. Guided by the Post Office Directory, she criss-crossed southern England with occasional forays into the Midlands, East Anglia and the north.[132] In 1954, ignoring her doctor's advice to ease up, she was away for nine consecutive days. Then she spoke at 45 places in twelve counties from Grimsby to Port Talbot in five weeks – more than one meeting a day.[133] After she turned 70, her pace did not ease: 38 meetings from Canterbury to Yorkshire between 17 October and 21 November 1955. In one week she undertook five meetings in five days, in five different counties – Devon, Hampshire, Hertfordshire, Staffordshire and Essex – and on the afternoon and evening of the sixth day, she held meetings in a Methodist Church in Bradford. By Sunday morning she was lecturing at King's Weigh House Church in central London on 'Woman and the New World'.[134] Even in mid-1959, when she was 74, Minnie could write of coming home from a trip for only an hour or two, frantically answering letters from listeners and doing a bit of clothes washing before she repacked her case and was on her way again.[135] This lifestyle was not greatly different from the one she had forty years earlier with the ILP. Then, after weeks of rushing around, a pause back home was accompanied by a 'black depression'.[136] Likewise, the day after a successful broadcast also carried the danger of anti-climax.[137]

*

During the 1950s, Minnie was one of the main pacifist proselytisers in the country. Her monthly *Peace News* column, 'Around and About', charted some of her travels for the cause. In September 1953 a feature described Minnie as 'In the best sense an "agitator"' with enormous energy and drive, and described her life as broadly being about three sets of initials – the ILP, the PPU and the BBC, to which it could have added the NCF and the WI.[138]

The BBC remained conscious of Minnie's pacifism. One event showed the sensitivity that existed towards her within the upper echelons of the Corporation. In March 1953 she spoke at a PPU event 'It Can Be Peace', in Central Hall, Westminster. Whereas other speakers were advertised by their positions in the church, trades union or as an MP, no designation was given to Minnie. Her comments were confined to the Great War but, in its report of the event, *Peace News* referred to her being a 'popular broadcaster in the BBC's *Woman's Hour*'.[139] R. E. L. Wellington CBE, one of the Corporation's six directors with responsibility for the Home Service, Light and Third Programmes, raised the issue with Quigley. Wellington's knowledge of *Peace News* and Minnie's role would have been at the prompting of the security service. Her personal file that identified her as a Labour Party organiser in 1937 and linked her with the PPU in 1938 indicates her to have been subject to routine monitoring.[140] In her broadcasts, said Wellington, Minnie 'always gets in something on the peace issue'.[141]

Wellington had a valid point. There is ample evidence from the Second World War onwards that Minnie sought to insert elements of pacifism into her scripts and to introduce pacifists as speakers to the BBC. As Stuart Morris said in his tribute to Minnie after her death, as a broadcaster 'she used such opportunities as she could to bring in her pacifism, even if necessarily somewhat obliquely.'[142]

Quigley, however, rejected Wellington's charge, pointing out that Minnie was never invited to broadcast on political subjects. While acknowledging that Minnie had made it clear on-air that she 'regards war as one of the worst evils in the world', an opinion that sometimes found 'indirect expression' in other contributions, Quigley told Wellington that she thought highly of Minnie and considered her a woman of integrity. She added: 'if her appearance at the meeting... is likely to have unfortunate repercussions for her with us, I should like to know beforehand and have a chance of fuller talks with you about her.'[143]

At this time, 'peace', once more, had a bad name as communist-affiliated organisations aligned themselves with peace organisations and pacifists were again suspect, this time as crypto-communists rather than Nazi-stooges.[144] A document, handwritten by Minnie, on her BBC file from around November/December 1952 analyses the different strands of the peace movement in Britain. Unrelated to any programme or script, it was presumably written to brief Quigley on the politics of pacifist organisations.[145] The document is reminiscent of the list Orwell drew up in 1949 of communist fellow travellers for the Foreign Office's Information Research Department. Minnie, though, did not name individuals, she analysed organisations.

Nothing further came from the Central Hall incident and Minnie's pacifism was never raised again, even when there were strong reasons to do so.[146] Might Minnie's briefing to Quigley on pacifist organisations have been connected to the Corporation not acting on the links between her pacifism and the BBC? It is unknown whether Minnie's briefing document was requested or was unsolicited. Was it the issue Quigley wished to raise with Wellington in the fuller talks she requested? Minnie's anti-communist credentials were impeccable.[147] The BBC's MI5 liaison files were mostly destroyed in the 1990s, so it must remain a matter for speculation whether the BBC and the security services regarded Minnie's pacifism as serving the lesser evil and therefore acted with discretion.[148]

Minnie remained a sponsor of the Labour Pacifist Fellowship when it changed its name to the Labour Peace Fellowship to allow it to broaden its activities. She supported its advocacy of Labour foregoing militarism, being non-aligned in the Cold War and backing colonial freedoms.[149] Minnie shared the Fellowship's profound differences with the Labour Party over rearmament, Britain's close alignment with the Pentagon, and providing bases for US nuclear weapons. Her differences with the Labour Party's foreign and defence policies became ever starker as she supported calls to remove US bomber bases from Britain, stop the manufacture of nuclear weapons and withdraw from NATO.[150]

In late 1953, Minnie became ill. She struggled on, fulfilling engagements in spite of a band of iron around her chest and a tendency to topple over when she stood up.[151] Two months later she was still staggering around in five layers of clothing.[152] By then Minnie's doctor was insisting she go away for treatment to lose weight. She would have preferred a fortnight abroad, 'but they give you *food*, and that is what I mustn't have, life is hard'. She went to Champneys, knowing she would hate it. On a diet of fruit juice she lost seven and a half pounds in eight days. Flora

Robson was there at the same time but, even so, for Minnie it was a miserable experience.[153] After a fortnight she came out somewhat lighter but feeling 'a little wan, rather forlorn'. Her sister's delight that she was under ten stone was offset by her unhelpful observation that 'when you lose weight it is your neck which gives you away'.[154] 'Empty of food, but full of good resolutions', Minnie's resolve did not last long.[155] Reducing the number of meetings also failed. For a woman reaching 70, her commitments were so packed together there was hardly a space between them.

Minnie paid little attention to clothes, putting them on just to keep warm and did not look to match up those she wore. She consciously rejected the consumerist ideal of what women should aspire to and the fashion image she was expected to adopt. Shopping brought her no joy, and she never bought clothes unless she needed them.[156] She told her audience of the pain of spotting an advert for a frock that looked appealing. She broke her train journey to visit a shop, but on showing the assistant the photo she was told haughtily 'not in your size' and 'no good to you anyhow unless you've got a very long waist'. She asked to try something else on but was told 'Nothing in your size til next week'. Minnie interpreted this as meaning 'Nothing in your size ever'. She lamented: 'What do they mean, not in my size, I'm only a 41 hip.' So affected was she, she said she felt obliged to eat food, which she later regretted.[157] It was an experience with which many women across the country could identify.

In March 1954, Minnie went to stay with her old friends, the Midgleys, in Kent and was in the garden with Wilson, when he dropped dead, leaving her distraught.[158] After his death, Minnie appeared less in *John O'London*. His demise opened a gap in the BBC line-up and, after a year, sensing an opportunity, she wrote that she had reviewed books for many years for 'Midge', and before that for the *Bookman*, and offered to contribute book reviews – not 'erudite criticisms' but light reviews that would encourage people to read.[159] However, the suggestion was not taken up.

Quigley sought Minnie's advice on subjects and speakers for a series on '20th-century woman', considering it 'very daring' to tackle such a vast subject.[160] Minnie counselled avoiding hackneyed suffragette leaders or doctors, and suggested putting the twentieth-century woman under the microscope for her roles as mother; business executive, author, artist, politician and social worker, and so on. Quigley asked to see a draft of Minnie's introductory talk that would set the context for later speakers in the series. 'Heaven round the Corner' would have set every alarm bell ringing. Setting her talk at the time when 'Political power [was] just coming to women, industrial power coming to mass of workers', Minnie proposed looking at the aspirations held by people at a time when 'Political Utopias became Holy Crusade' to see how those dreams now stood. Minnie concluded that in spite of superficial changes and improved material wealth, the basis of life had not altered and there were still problems in housing, ill health and social anxieties, with huge disparities between rich and poor countries. Would atomic energy be diverted from war to peace in fifty years' time? She answered her own questions 'Were we all wrong? Were we dreamers with heads in [the] air?' by determining heaven was still 'round the corner but we haven't [yet] turned the right corner'.[161]

Quigley's reply was diplomatic. She ignored the talk's highly politicised content and said plans for the series had changed so much that it might not now be possible to take a full-length talk as they had originally discussed. She wanted Minnie to pause: 'I don't want you to spend time working on a long and difficult script until you have had another talk with Joanna.' Joanna Scott-Moncrieff advised Minnie that her talk should be more personal, focussing on her college experiences, and be very short.[162] The eventual broadcast demonstrates the gap between what Minnie wanted to broadcast and what the BBC was prepared to accept. Filleted of politicised content, it became little more than a reminiscence of the early years of the twentieth century, ending at the point that Minnie discovered her political path.[163]

The BBC now managed the risk Minnie posed by consistently shearing her scripts of political substance. Minnie suggested to Derville that as a general election was underway she might start her next talk by referring to women's turnout and how it was the basis of democracy and individual social responsibility. Her proposal was met with copious underlinings in red. Instead Derville suggested Minnie focus on 'holidays abroad'.[164] Her draft of 'My Utopia' included the importance of abolishing war production so that resources could be diverted into building health centres and schools. However, an editorial pen deftly excised the hard edge of the original, leaving just the statement: 'Even the abolition of war will not automatically bring Utopia.'[165] Yet even that emasculated form drew great interest from the audience.[166]

Minnie's relationship with *Woman's Hour* was at this stage contradictory. While the boundaries around what she could speak on were closely patrolled, staff were aware of her tremendous 'pull' with the audience. (All the more reason presumably to keep her off sensitive subjects.) Hence Minnie was a key personality to whom they looked for special occasions. Quigley requested Minnie attend a public performance of *Woman's Hour*, though she was not broadcasting that day, to sit on the platform and meet fans of the programme. For *Woman's Hour* Tenth Birthday Week she was invited to the round-table question-and-answer session.[167] Yet when Minnie suggested to Derville she do a programme on older women marrying younger men, Quigley said it was a good topic, but not one for her.[168]

Dissatisfied at her lack of broadcasting scope, Minnie was 'rather frustrated' within *Woman's Hour* as she thought that much of her material was being wasted. She wanted to make an occasional broadcast to America and looked for the names of producers on other programmes she could approach. Kay Fuller, a Producer in Overseas Talks, commissioned Minnie to record Women's Institutes for *English Magazine*, but her subsequent broadcast did not go well. Afterwards Minnie made an abject apology for 'something which happens in the worst nightmare' and a handwritten note by BBC staff referred to Minnie's 'fluff'.[169]

In spite of her complex relationship with the Corporation, her broadcasting stature was further confirmed when she was made guest editor of *Woman's Hour* for one day. Honoured, yet daunted at the undertaking, Minnie began the extensive process of determining the content of the programme and its guests. This initially involved ruling out options. First she discounted her three main choices for the programme's theme: politics 'my first love', books, or Women's Institutes. Then she dismissed two ideas of working the programme around different sorts of courage and of having Canon Morris of the PPU discuss peace with a non-PPU canon, although she thought it the central issue on women's minds. Instead, Minnie chose to make her programme about friendship, which she considered the greatest thing in her life.[170]

In January 1956, the *Radio Times* featured 'A Muster of Friends' to accompany 'Minnie Pallister's Day'.[171] It was a deeply personal selection. Mrs Tidey, Minnie's 75-year-old char, had supported the sisters for twenty-three years as well as working every afternoon in the local hospital. She was Minnie's 'unknown woman' who allowed her to have a public life. Over the years, Minnie had mentioned on-air Mrs Tidey's importance in freeing her from domestic chores. Her inclusion in the programme recognised and honoured Mrs Tidey's role as being much more than a skivvy. That she was chosen instead of an actress, Dame or a national politician said as much about Minnie as it did of Mrs Tidey.[172] Joan Scarfe was the daughter of Samuel Ryder. She had taken over the troubled seed supply company, with which Minnie had had an association, after her father's death. Gwen Catchpool, the Quaker, had had to leave her pacifist husband, Corder, Minnie's wartime anti-bombing associate, to die on a mountain after he had fallen down a crevasse in the Swiss Alps, while Gwen and the guide descended in a blizzard.[173] Another contributor was Michael Tippett. Minnie had interviewed him the previous year about his opera *The Midsummer Marriage*.[174] Now, he wrote to his friend Anna Kallin about his second appearance:

> I have incredibly stupidly agreed to do 5 minutes on *Woman's Hour* to keep out an old (eccentric) friend, Minnie Pallister. It is the end!![175]

By 16 January, as zero hour approached, Minnie was getting panicky as she had not heard from Tippett for a week.[176] But Tippett appeared and talked about moving house.[177]

Afterwards, for perhaps the only time, Quigley addressed a professional letter to 'Dear Minnie', rather than 'Dear Miss Pallister', to say how good the programme had been. Each item was of quality and Gwen Catchpool 'quite outstanding'. Quigley signed off 'Yours ever'. Minnie was paid 20 guineas for devising and presenting the programme.[178] Minnie was one of the last guest editors for nearly sixty years, indeed until J. K. Rowling was invited in 2014.[179]

Tippett's comments on Minnie's eccentricities, while sharply articulated, were not misplaced. After two decades apologising to producers who had to work with her, as she became older Minnie appears to have become even more disorganised and her foibles more pronounced. No one was more aware of her idiosyncrasies than Minnie herself – except perhaps for Terence Alan Milligan.

For it was the comic genius of Spike Milligan that took the spirited battiness of Minnie Pallister and immortalised her as Minnie Bannister in the 1950s radio comedy series *The Goon Show*. Goons' fans have a clear impression of Bannister as a feeble flirtatious spinster, a sexy senior citizen who loves all things 'modern' including 'modern' music and who regularly breaks out in song or dance. As flirtatious as a girl a third of her age, she has an interesting past, lives in sin with Henry Crun and was once a lover of Major Bloodnok.[180]

John Dowling, retired Deputy Editor of the *Bexhill Observer*, got to know Milligan through his work and visited his house near Rye a couple of times.[181] Dowling, who grew up in Bexhill, had worked on the paper from 1961. When a lad, his mother had proudly told him about Minnie, the Bexhill resident well-known for her BBC broadcasting, and showed him where she lived. He had been a childhood fan of *The Goon Show* of which Milligan was a key member. In one of their meetings, he asked Milligan who were the inspirations for the show's characters. Milligan gave 'chapter-and-verse' the background to Eccles, Bluebottle and other characters, and stated that Minnie Bannister was based on Minnie Pallister.[182]

It was on the cliffs at the edge of town where, during the Second World War, Milligan had his Observation Post, celebrated in his book *Adolf Hitler My Part in His Downfall*. There Milligan located the Goons story of the wartime Batter Pudding attack on Minnie Bannister. The episode, 'The Terror of the Dreaded Batter Pudding Hurler of Bexhill-on-Sea' is set in 1940 at the point of expected German invasion.[183] In the deserted, blacked-out coastal town, Bannister takes an evening constitutional along the cliffs with her beau, Henry, when she is struck from behind by a batter pudding. Bannister, the central character in the script, becomes the target of sustained assaults from the batter pudding thrower. The initial suspect is a soldier from 56th Heavy Artillery Regiment [Milligan's Unit], stationed nearby.[184]

There are too many details connecting the lives of Minnie Pallister and Spike Milligan in wartime Bexhill to draw any conclusion other than they knew one another at that time and in that place. A decade later, when Bannister was brought to life, both Pallister and Milligan were regular radio broadcasters. Was their wartime acquaintance renewed in the canteen queue in Broadcasting House, by which time Pallister was even closer to being the batty old spinster of Spike's portrayal than she had been in 1940? Was Minnie

Pallister aware she was the inspiration for Minnie Bannister, not least as the Bexhill episode would have been the talk of the town? Although no evidence has been found, it is easy to see why Minnie Pallister would have appealed to Milligan's sense of the absurd, and Bannister to Minnie Pallister's sense of fun.

*

As she passed 70, Minnie retained a high public profile. Her commitment to her political causes remained as strong as ever. She never lost faith in the pacifist movement even if she was sometimes disappointed with its 'creaking machinery or human frailty'.[185] She drew lessons for it from her other causes. Speaking on 'The Status of Women' to the United Nations Association in 1956, Minnie said women's improved status, compared with the 'base injustices' they had suffered in earlier eras, gave her hope for pacifism.[186] She also drew on the 'revolution worked by the Socialist movement in this country', arguing that what had happened in political affairs nationally could also happen with pacifism internationally. Their slow approach based on building consent had been vindicated, she argued, even though others had been contemptuous. Having been regarded as 'political fools' she said it was nothing new for the 'so-called "realists"' of today to now call them 'pacifist fools'.[187]

Minnie reflected on whether the path of duty she chose, involving 'heart break and loss, the lonely fight in unpopular minorities', had been worthwhile, but concluded that regret came from falling below standards, not living up to them. Somewhere, Minnie said, she had found 'a standard for measuring life' which acted as 'a kind of sheet anchor'. Her maxim was that unless people assumed personal responsibility 'even a society based on social justice, fall[s] down'.[188] Looking back, Minnie saw how she had changed. Now she felt more tolerant, seeing shades of grey and not just black and white. She felt that she had reached a stage of serenity, and could now 'fill the unforgiving minute, with honest toil, instead of fretting and fuming'. She was still, though, just as intolerant of suffering and injustice and hoped that, if she had to choose, she would still choose the wilderness over faithlessness.[189]

Minnie became a PPU sponsor at the 1954 AGM, joining an accomplished group that included Brittain, Britten, Aldous Huxley,

Thorndike and Tippett.[190] For its 40th Anniversary, the Women's International League for Peace and Freedom acknowledged Minnie's personal association with the organisation that dated back more than thirty years, and invited her to speak on her 'Forty Years in the Peace Movement'.[191] The following year, it became her regular theme across the country, before the PPU used her four decades long commitment to send a letter in her name to all members appealing for funds.[192]

Minnie stood down from the PPU National Council in 1956, but did not reduce her workload. Simultaneous crises in Suez and Hungary squeezed Minnie's column from the pages of *Peace News*, but her appearances on public platforms remained prodigious.[193] She also still sought to mobilise women. Retired women might no longer want to sell *Peace News* in the streets, or take part in demonstrations, she argued, but they could make a major contribution to building a sound movement by taking over the administrative work of PPU groups.[194]

Minnie's range continued to be wide. After a thirty-year hiatus, she once more spoke at the Royal Albert Hall, having last been there before the use of the microphone. She claimed to be 'scared stiff' at the prospect of addressing 'a great Rally of the Sisterhood', attended by women from the length and breadth of Britain,[195] but it did not deter her from returning to the hall eighteen months later for the centenary of the first women's committee of the Methodist Church.[196] To the British Women's Total Abstinence Union Minnie delivered a witty annual lecture entitled 'Is Your Drinking Really Necessary?'[197] Not until she was invited to give the talk did Minnie ask herself why she was still a non-smoker, abstainer, and a bitter opponent of gambling. Over time, she had softened from being 'a rabid and bigoted teetotaller', but she remained resolute on gambling, regarding it as 'a canker in the heart of society'.[198] She might recognise that it offered relief from drab monotony, but she condemned an approach that looked for something for nothing, rather than having allocation based on need.[199] On the radio, she railed against the minority 'who want oodles of money and mink and jewels and high-powered cars and unlimited luxury and unlimited power, who can never think of the world's resources in terms of sharing, but only in terms of grabbing'.[200] The surprise was that such statements sneaked past the invisible boundary of BBC acceptability.

The Corporation though, maintained its vigilance. When friends pressed Minnie to attend an international 'summit' of Moral Rearmament in Caux which organisers claimed had the capacity to bring unity to divisions in the world, Scott-Moncrieff was sufficiently concerned to alert Derville that Minnie had been 'nearly hooked' by the Movement, and cautioned him to look out for it.[201]

Generally, life was good. For the first time since being a teacher in Brynmawr, Minnie was comfortable. She had the BBC to thank for much of the quality of her life and loved combining duty and pleasure with complementary tickets to theatre, ballet and film.[202] Untroubled by illness, without a struggle for economic survival, or other big challenges, her time was spent in 'continuous glorious technicolour'.[203] However, she was self-critical about wasting time and opportunities by dithering, and suffered days 'black with bitter regrets for everything I had said and done the day before'. Admitting that she still had the capacity to agonise over unimportant things, as she grew older each mistake became magnified. Being Minnie Pallister though, she shared the worst of them with everyone.[204]

At the end of November 1956, Minnie caught flu and had to cancel everything for two months. On her return, at Derville's prompting, Minnie wrote 'On Growing Old', a wonderful evocation of the advantages, as well as problems, of aging.[205] Older women, Minnie insisted, should not be patronised. Being older should not be a time of trying to look young but of 'trying to look nice in spite of not being young'. They should set their 'face like a flint' against growing into an 'old geazer' who 'toddled along', shuffling like an amiable tramp wearing old ladies' hats. The world was packed with things to do and people to help, 'Time is your most precious possession.' Her agenda for living urged listeners to 'Be happy now... Squeeze every drop of joy out of the next two hours.'[206]

The programme was a resounding success. Minnie was pleased to hear how many older women had refused to wear dowdy clothes as a result.[207] 'On Growing Old' made such an impact it was repeated on *Home for the Day*, when it was heard by the writer Rose Macaulay, then aged 75, who wrote to her sister asking if she had heard it too.[208] An exceptional number of listeners requested the script. It was included in The *BBC Woman's Hour Year Book* and rebroadcast to the Canadian edition of *Woman's Hour*.[209] Recognising Minnie's impact, Quigley, by now Chief Assistant,

Talks, suggested that Minnie might '*very* occasionally' contribute to the *Indian Summer* series on aspects of growing older, perhaps when *Woman's Hour* was off the air. Quigley added the proviso that 'Her suggestions...are always made in a wild and woolly form... [and] Like many good broadcasters she is quite a handful but the results are usually well worth the trouble.'[210] Thrilled at this new strand of work, Minnie made *Indian Summer* broadcasts in 1958 and 1959.

In contrast, Minnie's interest in 'the modern' was given an unexpected twist when, at 72, she was commissioned to write and present 'Minnie Pallister's Guide to Modern England'. Over four monthly episodes she would visit places and situations where listeners would least expect her, and comment on current phenomena, such as 'Rock and Roll' and young people drinking and dancing.[211] To avoid this new venture shocking 'my women', Minnie thought it advisable to explain in the first programme that she was not suggesting that they should sample such places themselves.[212] The novel nature of the enterprise is clear from BBC files. Derville's suggestion that the series start by sending Minnie to the Blackpool illuminations and funfair earned the riposte, probably from Scott-Moncrieff, 'Our imagination in this series is unbounded but as our budget isn't Blackpool or anywhere too remote physically was [to] be out.' Quigley added that while she thought the general idea of the series was very good, it would be better to focus on phenomena rather than places particularly a place 'so alien as Blackpool'. Minnie would have felt quite at home in Blackpool, but those comments reveal how the class and cultural gap between the BBC and some of its audience in the 1950s limited the Corporation's horizons. In the event, they visited the nearer, less expensive and presumably less alien resort of Southend.[213]

At 9 pm on Thursday 29 August, Derville took Minnie from Broadcasting House to a dark and crowded West End coffee bar, where she observed how people just sat, hardly speaking, and mostly looking sad or bored. There she drank one of the 'cokes' she had heard so much about, finding it refreshing. After the Stork Club in the West End, then the hangout of people like John Profumo and Peter Sellers,[214] Minnie went to a pub in the East End where the noise was overwhelming, and to a dog race (with associated betting). The evening included a 'most mysterious' skiffle cellar in a crypt, full of young people 'quietly listening to funny noises', and an enormous underground jazz club that had rhythm and vitality. In contrast the noisy but sedate Hammersmith Palais de Danse seemed something of an anti-climax. Minnie sensed most people were following a familiar routine and concluded that young people who went to dance halls, pubs, coffee bars and cellars had a gloomy sense of resignation and just wanted somewhere to sit. The real challenge for her was in not getting to bed until 4 am but she reported having such a wonderful time she feared 'I shall... end up as one of the lost!'[215]

The first programme having been received very enthusiastically, Minnie argued that her series should include the bad as well as the good of society. Alongside symbols of post-war progress, including council evening classes, secondary modern schools and new towns, Minnie proposed visiting church missions doing night work with young people and looking at racism in Bexhill, and visiting a hostel in Manchester to examine race issues there.[216]

In the second programme Minnie launched a sustained feminist assault on the 1950s cultural phenomena of the commodification of beauty, beauty pageants and fashion, condemning their impact on women. The broadcast built on all she had learned in the four decades since the end of the Great War about women's issues and the imbalance in gender relationships, alongside her calls for equality. It was a concentrated feminist critique of 1950s consumer culture as it affected women. Fashion was a 'huge conspiracy' to get women to aspire to false ways of being as part of a consumer society. Glossy magazines and romantic fiction fed images of unattainable aspirations to promote women's consumption of goods. It was the essence of Minnie Pallister and merits close consideration.

Minnie recognised that beauty, and being attractive to men, had mattered to women from time immemorial. Suggesting that 'men are only too easily attracted to women', she proposed 'Some kind of make up which put(s) [sic] men off, would seem more relevant.' For Minnie the glamourisation of sex was out of place in an era when, far from ministering to men's desires, women should be demanding equality in every sphere, and claim to be persons in their own right, rather than being someone's wife, daughter or mother. Beauty contests featuring women 'parading round a ring to be judged on points, as if they were bullocks in an agricultural show' were degrading. The Brighton beauty contest she viewed as depressing, 'sordid... revolting, vulgar and disgusting'. A woman's body, Minnie concluded, should be her own affair.[217]

Minnie considered fashion a means to get women to keep buying new clothes based on 'endless pictures' in glossy magazines of women who were 'twelve feet high and twelve inches wide'. Representing *Woman's Hour* at Harrods's fashion show, she was given VIP status, in great comfort on a settee in the front row. If the fashion house had expected a sympathetic hearing, they would have been disappointed. Pointing out the difference between clothes and fashion, she rejected the artificially constructed 'ideal' body image; instead of admiring 'young goddesses with no hips' glide by, Minnie called for 'a Dress Show for ...ordinary comfortable women with busts and hips', adding the world was crying out for designers to make clothes 'in lovely materials and beautiful colours for ordinary people, at ordinary prices'.[218]

Perhaps surprisingly, Minnie took a more positive view of her visit to the Elizabeth Arden beauty salon, where its 'young priests and priestesses' pampered her and other women 'of all sorts and sizes' equally. While she was not sure whether the beauty treatment made her look any better, she felt better and her morale was boosted. It was, she concluded, a worthwhile rare luxury for women.[219]

While Minnie still did not describe herself as a feminist, it is interesting to consider her views against the critiques of attitudes of the 1950s offered by later feminists. Elizabeth Wilson writes that the creation of a conservative consensus around women was orchestrated to reassure and domesticate.[220] Minnie rejected that 1950s consensus. Shira Tarrant says 'this silent generation of feminists were careful observers of their times'.[221] Observant Minnie may have been, silent she was not. Minnie's actions challenge the assumption by some later feminists that 'feminism in the 1950s "was bound by femininity in such a manner that we as feminists today do not easily recognise its activities as *feminist*"'.[222] Minnie was not limited by the boundaries of femininity. In contrast to Barbara Caine's suggestion that 1950s feminism was 'cautious and moderate' and accepted 'the post-war emphasis on marriage, motherhood, and the pursuit of family life',[223] Minnie rejected the notion that women had achieved the goals to which they aspired. More than a decade later this became a rallying call of modern feminism.

1970s and 1980s feminists emphasised discontinuities and differences between themselves and previous feminist activity. However, Minnie's 1950s activities provide a bridge to the Women's Liberation Movement. Her withering condemnation of beauty pageants anticipated by twenty-three years the disruption of the 1970 Miss World by feminist activists and she would have welcomed their preparedness to rebel. Hers was a feminism that those later activists would have recognised and embraced.[224] In providing that continuity of thought and action, Minnie is important in filling a gap in the knowledge of 1950s feminism.

It has been suggested that no coherent feminist analysis emerged in Britain in the 1950s.[225] Although Minnie did not present her views in a single elaborated statement, threads of her feminist thought on the position of women in society form a critique that she developed over the decades from the Great War to the 1950s. Minnie's arguments are echoed in the writings of second generation feminists and have stood the test of time. In 1980, Elizabeth Wilson wrote of how women are a key component in the consumer society and women's magazines have a consumer-oriented formula aimed at women. Rosalind Coward in her 1984 book *Female Desire* shows how pleasure for women is created and managed as part of a consumerist society and is crucial to its social structure. Thus male privilege is sustained and women oppressed.[226] Coward's theme of women's domestic work being undervalued was one that Minnie consistently highlighted from the interwar period, along with the issue of economic dependency within a marriage.[227] Wilson suggests that 1950s feminists did not challenge the sexual division of labour.[228] Minnie did. Minnie may not have used the word 'subordination', but as early as 1924 in *The Orange Box* she used 'oppression', and often described and analysed it.

There is a need to be careful about generalising about feminist attitudes at any particular time. Individuals' attitudes changed over time to reflect circumstances.[229] Wilson argues that each generation had to rediscover for themselves the sources of women's oppression. Yet Minnie and a number of her contemporaries had an awareness of the importance of women's history. Since 1918 she had used earlier women's experiences to inform and educate. As Wilson says of Ray Strachey, Winifred Holtby and Virginia Woolf, Minnie drew on previous events and ideas, providing continuities from previous generations of women through history, economics and literature.[230] In her attitudes and actions, Minnie was a forerunner of Wilson's generation of the women's movement. Had they known about her, they would have hailed Minnie as a forebear.

Minnie was not a lone voice. Evelyn Sharp and others continued to endorse views that were similar to Minnie's.[231] Tarrant suggests, however, that in the 1950s such voices mainly belonged to academics, rather than activists, whose feminist theories were largely confined to university institutions.[232] Wilson states that, in the 1950s, feminists often felt isolated as there was no movement against women's oppression.[233] If she experienced a sense of isolation, Minnie did not indicate it. Neither did she waver in her efforts to rally others to the cause.

Perhaps the nearest the subsequent generation came to recognising Minnie's contribution was an acknowledgement on the 40th anniversary of *Woman's Hour* in 1986, when Coward looked back over the life of the programme for *The Listener*. When Coward argued that *Woman's Hour* throughout the 1950s had been more radical than its popular image of presenting 'entertainment' and looking at 'the light and amusing side of life' might suggest, it was to Minnie 'who hardly embodied the ideals of the conservative and home-loving wife' to whom she pointed as proof.[234] It is good that such an acknowledgement was made. Coward was, perhaps, though, unaware of how much more could have been said.

One of the factors in the origins of the late 1960s women's liberation movement and women's individual routes to feminism was the relationship between mother and daughter in the home.[235] The 1959 words of Antoinette Fortune about the impact of Minnie's *Woman's Hour* broadcasts therefore bear repeating:

> Listening to her you realised the influence these programmes must have, the gentle insistent formation of the opinions and outlook of thousands of 'ordinary' women, who in their turn will be the chief formative influence in their own homes.

There were, though, more than three million women, rather than thousands, who heard Minnie each time on the radio. It is now impossible to assess the long-term impact Minnie's feminist (or pacifist) messages had, programme after programme, year after year, as she drip-fed her values and beliefs into the consciousness of her listeners, some of whom were frustrated with their traditional, domestically bound lifestyle. Did they listen and then discuss these issues with their daughters at the dinner table? It seems unlikely that no perceptions were challenged, no attitudes shaped, no minds changed, no images radically subverted.

It would be rewarding to hear a conversation between 1950s Minnie and 1980s Coward on where their ideas diverged. One was in women's relation to food. Minnie saw it as a personal issue whereas Coward saw food as a kind of servitude whereby women were made to feel guilty about enjoying food. Would Minnie have agreed that a woman's relationship with food was 'tied to positions of power and subordination' in a 'sexually divided and hierarchical society'?[236] I suspect she would have quickly come around to seeing food in a way she recognised with fashion and beauty. Another difference would have been around sex. While the evidence suggests that the young Minnie had found a sense of sexual liberation, she dealt with it as a personal matter rather than as a political one to be discussed openly and argued for. It was in that area that boundaries had shifted and ideas moved most in the intervening decades. If this was the one feminist issue which marked her as a woman of her time, in most others she was a trailblazer.

While preparatory work was underway for her 'Modern Britain' programme on beauty and fashion, Minnie was approached by R. E. Keen of the Talks Department about a new magazine programme, *The World of Books* on Network III, a new radio channel starting that month. She had badly missed reviewing books since her regular work with *John O'London* had ended and had long craved the opportunity to review books on-air. Now, after years of waiting, her chance came. However, it did not go well. Keen thought her script included too many books and suggested she drop Colin MacInnes's *City of Spades*, which dealt with black and youth subcultures in London, and a book by Brittain – presumably *Testament of Experience* published that year – as her books were less well known than Minnie assumed. It is a shame that Minnie did not review *Testament of Experience* for we could have learned her views on Brittain's Second World War experience, and pacifist exclusion, much of which Minnie had experienced, but on which she was largely silent.

Keen added that Minnie should assume a higher 'standard of appreciation' of listeners who 'take the trouble to tune in to a

333

special programme'. He also said that the personal way she dealt with the books came between the listener and the book. The years of having to make everything personal for *Woman's Hour* was not easily unlearned. Her second draft script showed little improvement. For her third script Minnie suggested focusing on 'two intrepid women', but Keen concluded that, in spite of her enthusiasm and effort, her third talk was not the 'kind of thing at which we are aiming'.[237]

Distressed that she had been sacked without proper opportunity to demur, Minnie went to see Quigley, who took the matter up on her behalf. However, Quigley was sufficiently circumspect that the *World of Books* staff did not feel obliged to formally respond.[238] For Minnie it was an important opportunity missed.

The final episode of the 'Modern Britain' series planned to look at the highly topical issue of mental health, the handicapped and old age homes in the context of the welfare state. However, it was cancelled when, in early December, Minnie became very ill with Asian flu which lasted a fortnight. Under doctor's care, she cancelled all engagements, including two radio broadcasts.[239] Determined not to miss the 1957 Christmas Eve special edition of *Woman's Hour*, featuring the programme's top contributors, she struggled through but BBC staff were so concerned at her condition they did not schedule January broadcasts.[240] A second bout of flu left her bedbound and gave Minnie 'excruciating muscular pains all over'. She lapsed into deep despair.[241] Her first serious illness for twenty years was a salutary reminder that her health should not be taken for granted. Her February broadcast, 'Illness and Stillness' reflected on her two months of being laid low.[242] By April, now on iron tablets, Minnie pronounced herself 'full of vim and vigour'.[243]

Minnie's last pacifist event before her illness had been a conference at Manchester Free Trade Hall, with Pastor Niemoller. Niemoller, a German Lutheran Church Leader, had initially enthusiastically supported Hitler, but he opposed the Nazification of the Protestant Churches, and was held in a concentration camp from 1938 to 1945. After the war he became an outspoken pacifist and anti-war activist and wrote the poem 'First they came for the Communists'. In the evening, Niemoller and Minnie held an improvised public discussion on their personal relationships with hell.[244]

During Minnie's two-month absence, the pacifist movement was transformed by the founding of the Campaign for Nuclear Disarmament (CND) against the H-bomb. Seen as the greatest moral challenge since the Great War,[245] 'The Bomb' moved public opinion, and pacifists found themselves nearer the mainstream.[246] Many of Minnie's friends and comrades, including Brockway from NCF days and Britten and Tippett of the PPU, became founder members, as did Flora Robson. Russell became its Honorary President.[247] The threat posed to the human race by nuclear weapons provided a burst of energy to the pacifist movement, and 5,000 people attended CND's first public meeting at Central Hall, Westminster on 17 February 1958.[248]

Though pacifism was more than just opposition to nuclear weapons, the PPU welcomed the new unilateralist movement and supported the first London to Aldermaston march organised over Easter that year.[249] Two weeks after Aldermaston, a PPU march through the West End of London was followed by a public meeting. There Minnie, Donald Soper, former President of the Methodist Conference, with whom she appeared regularly, and Niemoller, who had also spoken at Aldermaston, talked on Total Peace.[250] At the subsequent PPU AGM, where the call was for the pacifist movement to 'rise to the challenge presented by the nuclear threat to humanity', Minnie, the veteran pacifist, seconded the resolution moved by John Wight, a young Quaker and representative of a new generation becoming involved in the pacifist movement, that called on Britain to renounce all war and for unilateral disarmament of all weapons including nuclear ones.[251] It marked a handing on of the generations, with those who had opposed the First World War when they were young now passing the baton to those who were growing up after the Second World War.

As the public mood changed, Minnie raised the nuclear issue directly with the BBC. While she had previously included pacifist messages in her scripts, she now told the BBC that the development of the bomb was a new and important issue to be discussed and she wanted to say something on the Hydrogen Bomb.[252] Scott-Moncrieff's reply is not on file, but Minnie's proposal would have been opposed by all in Broadcasting House. No broadcast was made.

At the Labour Party's national conference in September, Minnie joined four MPs, including Brockway, on the platform at the

Fellowship's packed fringe meeting.[253] She had argued that Labour's 1955 general election defeat was not due to the Party's socialism, but more likely to its sacrificing its basic principles: 'When has a party ever gained by being untrue to itself?' Now, in 1958, a year after Aneurin Bevan had confounded his left-wing supporters by imploring the conference not to send him, as Shadow Foreign Secretary, 'naked into the conference chamber', Minnie found it increasingly difficult to sympathise with Labour Party politics: 'I can't follow the minds of the L P, I live in the past!'[254]

Minnie spoke on CND platforms and at countless PPU meetings, residential schools and conferences on subjects like 'Peace in the Atomic Age'. After Stuart Morris and representatives of other British peace organisations met Khrushchev, Minnie chaired his talk on 'My Visit to Russia'. At her last national PPU conference, she looked back over fifty years and wondered whether she might have achieved more serving other causes, but concluded that 'in attacking the root evil of war, she was rendering the greatest service she could'.[255]

When Gladys retired, the arrangement of having a flat with her work, which had existed since 1933, also ended. Although the sisters had time to prepare, the prospect of losing their home was emotionally and organisationally hard.[256] In boxes were her half-finished autobiography, hundreds of book reviews and articles, and copies of her chatty wartime letters, which she said would have made a complete wartime diary. On surveying the hundreds of pages of 'plans for a new world, my thoughts on religion, on war and peace, on politics[,] on education, on human behaviour,' Minnie was *'staggered'* at her own industry while adding tongue-in-cheek 'I must have fancied myself tremendously as a preacher and philosopher.'[257]

The timing of their move could not have been worse. After twenty-five years of guaranteed tenure, Minnie felt she was having to face the facts of life. The 1957 Rent Act had given landlords the power to evict tenants; they wanted a three-year lease which, for the sisters, would have been ruinous. With market rents for flats high, the summer spent searching was fruitless and a source of great worry.[258] The sisters also now needed something bigger to accommodate Julia. She had lived alone after her husband's death but was struggling badly. For six weeks in the spring, 73-year-old Minnie had gone to WGC, getting in coal and doing chores for the eldest sister, whom she adored, but Julia could no longer manage on her own. Eventually the sisters had to settle for three rooms in a house in Cranfield Road that was less than ideal. Minnie did not have a bedroom of her own, having to live in the bed-sitting room. Without a garden, when the seed catalogues arrived, she was very melancholic. The move also entailed leaving the Old Town of Bexhill, which Minnie dearly liked.[259]

Against her doctor's advice to ease her schedule, in January 1959, while unwell, Minnie travelled north to undertake three meetings.[260] Her hazy recollection of speaking to a luncheon club faded to practically no memory of the Friends Meeting House in Walsall. She assumed she must have spoken at a WI in Cheshire before she collapsed. A doctor diagnosed pneumonia and she was taken by ambulance in the middle of the night, in excruciating pain, to a Manchester hospital where she stayed for twenty-seven days.[261]

After the worst was over Minnie began observing her surroundings and a *Woman's Hour* script, 'Ward 8B', resulted. This was her first time in a large ward of twenty-six beds and, although 'rather glum', her admiration grew for the patient way in which staff did dull, routine jobs 'which keep the world going on'. As the X-rays 'stubbornly refused to show a clear lung', doctors were loath to release Minnie, but in late February she was allowed to stay locally at the house of pacifist friends, who nursed her for a further month. First bedbound, then housebound for weeks, followed by long convalescence, she was prohibited from doing anything physically or mentally strenuous.[262] Unable even to go to the cinema, she resorted to things her conscience would not normally allow. In spite of her earlier assaults on women's glossy magazines, she found she enjoyed 'swimming in the[ir] warm perfumed sea'. 'Twopence Coloured', a script written as she recuperated, explored 'that strange never never land of glow and glamour and fantasy'.[263] While she appreciated 'that strange country' of colour and romance, full of 'gorgeous men, handsome, rich and charming...thick as blackberries, lying around to be picked up for the asking', with relief she looked forward to being back in circulation once more, trying to be intelligent about world affairs.[264]

Of her hundred-plus *Woman's Hour* programmes, the only surviving recording of Minnie's voice is this light-hearted critique of women's magazines. By then her voice is heavy with 1950s strangulated BBC pronunciation. It is impossible to imagine how much her voice had changed for the radio compared with how she had sounded when railing against the war in 1917 or supporting the miners in 1926.

Not allowed to take long journeys, or undertake public meetings, she cancelled her long tour of Devon and deferred broadcasting until April. In spite of her doctor's warning, although her voice was still not strong, Minnie started to speak again in public in early May.[265] The stay in hospital reminded her of lost years of health, and she worried about the prospect of infirmity. To Derville she confided, 'I suppose I must resign myself to sinking into old age – with a shawl on & TV. My Lord!! But not quite yet.' When Minnie proposed that she do a talk on religion, she suggested attending various churches over the summer, acknowledging the interest they provided for 'thousands of retired and lonely women'. Then this 75-year-old, without irony, referred to the 'old ladies (and Bexhill is full of them)' whom she saw 'toddling off to the parish church'.[266] In 1959, the sisters moved to a neglected bungalow with a large garden on De La Warr Road. Throughout the summer, while plumbers, carpenters and painters worked on it, night after night Minnie toiled up the hill to take tea to the gardener who transformed it.[267] By September, Minnie had a den with a bay window overlooking the sea, her own bedroom and a garden.[268]

Minnie's final *Woman's Hour* producer was Wyn Knowles, who had just joined the programme. As they only worked together for six months, Minnie had little opportunity to develop the rapport she had enjoyed with Quigley, Scott-Moncrieff and Derville. Knowles went on to become a formidable editor of *Woman's Hour* in the 1970s when the programme was transformed by women's liberation. Describing herself as an 'equal rights woman', rather than a feminist because it was such a difficult word, Knowles 'trod a fine line in making the programme appeal equally to women anxious to embrace liberation, equal pay and equal opportunities, and those others...who were happy to remain housewives'. She transformed it from a 'cosy, rehearsed' programme into a controversial one.[269] She was a kindred spirit. Knowles suggested Minnie go to three modern musicals about the seedy side of life – *West Side Story*, *A Crooked Mile* and *Irma La Douce*.[270] Minnie found *West Side Story* 'touching – and beautifully done'. *The Crooked Mile* was almost gentle in comparison, and *Irma La Douce*, based in a brothel and advertised as 'The sauciest play ever to pass the censor', was 'transcendentally well done'. Minnie left the theatre, though, reflecting that while plays on sordid subjects might be realistic they were not all that true to life.[271]

In January Minnie was 'iced up' and not venturing far. She told Knowles she was slowing down and not allowed to do a lot of meetings. That meant speaking to a young wives club in Dulwich, temperance women in Coventry, church rallies in Bournemouth and Ashford, and an educational event in Pevensey. In London she saw the Italian Exhibition and the 'runaway stellar hit' *Roar Like a Dove*.[272]

Minnie remained an agitator. Her homily on race at the time of the Notting Hill riots was excised by a BBC editorial pen.[273] Her practice of seeking to insert pacifist messages into all broadcasting opportunities continued. She expressed her niggling doubt that armistice day at the Cenotaph was a way of soothing the collective conscience while allowing people to forget that 'we have yet to redeem our promise to the fallen that their sacrifice should end war.'[274] With geo-political symmetry, she undertook her last known CND meeting in Bournemouth in November 1959.[275]

One of her final broadcasts, 'No-one is Unimportant', transmitted two months before she died, was a concentrated lesson in Minnie Pallister. A comment in her 'Modern Musicals' review – that a woman described as a 'sex kitten' filled Minnie with 'a sort of blind flaming rage' – had been excised from the script. Three months later, Minnie objected to it once more saying it gave her a 'sick loathing'. This time it was not cut.[276] Arguing that people bore individual responsibility, she said, 'we have to make up our minds about things we think good or evil' because 'if individuals have high standards, they create an atmosphere'. While people thought they could not influence national and international events, Minnie held up examples of women achieving small changes by protesting or writing letters. She added, 'we underestimate the immense strength of disapproval', arguing that if a million women wrote to the newspaper saying they would cancel their order if they ever see a phrase used again, it would have an influence.[277] Broadening the assault, Minnie referred to the 'quiet people [who] faithfully collect subscriptions, give out pamphlets, getting little encouragement' and kept plodding away at their causes to sustain their struggling societies. She contrasted them with 'the whole set up of giveaways, easy money, glamorised gambling, strip tease, leering louts who make horrid noise', and said women needed to raise their voices in complaint.[278] In a lovely pun, she had said that someone who wanted to get more out of life than they put in was suffering from 'soul erosion'.[279] Now Minnie ventured that 'every person counts' and making 'a child, a person, a Race or a Nation feel small, to humiliate, belittle them, is the unforgiveable sin'.[280] This lesson in decency drew 'an enormous response' from listeners and left Scott-Moncrieff, as editor, 'particularly pleased'. One shop, profiled anonymously by Minnie, changed its brochure advertisements as a result of the objections it received.[281] Knowles learned what her predecessors had come to understand – that Minnie could be a formidable broadcaster.

In early March, Minnie pointedly used Princess Margaret's recent engagement to suggest a talk on 'decoration in society'. In contrast to the 'lavish beauty of nature', she argued, it was 'a moot point where love of colour and form degenerate into vanity and waste'.[282] While Minnie enjoyed pageantry, her disquiet at the conspicuous indulgence around parts of the Royal Family pitted her, once again, against the most sacrosanct of British institutions.

However, the script was never written. A fortnight later, Gladys wrote to say Minnie was very ill with influenza and bronchitis, so could not carry out her March broadcast. Minnie deteriorated, was hospitalised in Bexhill, but did not respond to treatment and died on 26 March 1960, aged 75.[283] As she had hoped, she avoided the 'horror of fizzling out', instead going out 'with a bang'.[284]

Marjorie Anderson started the next *Woman's Hour* by paying tribute to Minnie. A letter read out from a Chelmsford listener said she was sure she spoke for thousands in mourning 'a shining light of sanity and reason in the darkness of this world, and to stand for all that is meant by true values, in an age that appears to have forgotten them...Here is one at least, who will always be a better person, for having listened to her...'[285] Fittingly, Anderson recognised her work with the PPU – without mentioning the angst it had caused the BBC. At the funeral the address was given by Stuart Morris before the cremation took place at Hastings.

A year after Minnie's death, *Woman's Hour* paid an anniversary tribute featuring guest speakers on different aspects of her life. In 1964, based on listener requests, *Woman's Hour* broadcast 'A Voice That is Still: Echoes of Minnie Pallister'. Then, in 1969, a BBC record, *Voices from Woman's Hour Past and Present* was compiled based on listener selections and, nearly a decade after her death, Minnie's 'Twopence Coloured' was chosen for the album, a testimony to her enduring popularity. Since then memories of who she was, what she did, and why she did it have faded. It is time to recapture and recount her remarkable life again. She remains a woman for our times.

---

[1] Dora Russell, *The Tamarisk Tree, Vol 3*, Virago, 1985, p. 113.

[2] *Bexhill Observer*, 6 & 20 July 1946; *Hastings & St Leonards Observer*, 1 June 1946; Pallister to Bradney, 15 November 1946, BBC/WAC/RCONTI Pallister (Talks 3b); Beaumont, 'Citizens...', p. 422.

[3] Morrison, *Stuart Morris*, pp. 10–11.

[4] *Peace News*, 16 November 1945; Matthew Frank, 'The New Morality–Victor Gollancz, "Save Europe Now" and the German Refugee Crisis, 1945–46', *Twentieth Century British History*, Vol 17 No 2, 2006, pp. 230–56. For competing campaigning priorities during late 1945 see minutes of PPU National Council, Executive, Public Action and Immediate Issues Committees.

[5] Deleted comment in draft version of Morris, 'The Flowers...'; *Barnoldswick & Earby Times*, 1 & 8 February 1946; *Burnley Express*, 2 Feb 1946.

[6] *Bury Free Press*, 29 March 1946; *Peace News*, 3 May & 21 June 1946.

[7] Brittain, *Testament of Experience*, p. 416.

[8] PPU AGM minutes, 20 April 1947.

[9] PPU National Council, 17–18 May 1947.

[10] National Council Special Meeting, 28 June 1947.

[11] PPU National Council, 13–14 December 1947; Immediate Issues Committee, 30 December 1947.

[12] Pallister to Quigley, 'Wed', nd, [but between July and September 1945], BBC/WAC/RCONTI Pallister (Talks 3b).

[13] When she expressed interest in taking part in a new series called 'The World and His Wife', she had to settle for an appointment a month later. Pallister to Molony, 6, 12 & 14 December 1945 & 26 February 1946, Molony to Pallister, 10 December 1945, BBC/WAC/RCONTI Pallister (Talks 3b).

[14] James to Pallister, 22 March 1946; internal memo James to Campbell, 22 March 1946. BBC/WAC/RCONTI Pallister (Talks 3b) (Emphasis in original).

[15] eg Barker to Pallister, 14 March 1946 & Pallister to Dear Sir, 20 October 1946, BBC/WAC/RCONTI Pallister (Talks 3b).

[16] Pallister to Benzie, 26 October 1945, BBC/WAC/RCONTI Pallister (Talks 3b).

[17] *John O'London*, 19 April 1946.

[18] Nicholas, *Echo*, p. 139.

[19] Comment of current presenter, Emma Barnett, *Guardian*, 10 October 2016.

[20] Sally Feldman, 'Twin Peaks' in ed. Caroline Mitchell, *Women and Radio*, Routledge, 2000, pp. 66–7.

[21] Talks Booking Requisition form, 14 November 1946; Pallister to Bradney, 15 November; Bradney to Pallister, 18 November; Derville to Pallister, 29 November 1946, BBC/WAC/RCONTI Pallister (Talks 3b).

[22] 'Request Week'.

[23] Pallister to Scott-Moncrieff, Euston Station, nd, but early October 1956; See also Pallister to Quigley 9 August [1939], BBC/WAC/RCONTI Pallister (Talks 8 & 1).

[24] Pallister to Bradney, 15 November & 2 December 1946, BBC/WAC/RCONTI Pallister (Talks 3b); 'Professional Women in the Eighteenth Century', *WH*, 1 April 1947, including script deletions.

[25] 'Exhibition of the Society of Women Artists', *WH*, 15 January 1947. Pallister to Derville, 28 December 1946, BBC/WAC/RCONTI Pallister (Talks 3b).

[26] Pallister to Derville, nd, but early February 1947, BBC/WAC/RCONTI Pallister (Talks 4).

[27] Pallister to Derville, 14 March 1947. Also 27 April, 16 May & 'Friday night', nd, but late April/early May 1947; Pallister to Quigley, 8 January 1951, BBC/WAC/RCONTI Pallister (Talks 4 & 5).

[28] Derville to Pallister, 3 April 1947 & handwritten note on Bradney to Collins, 2 May 1947, BBC/WAC/RCONTI Pallister (Talks 4); 'The Royal Academy Exhibition', *WH*, 5 May 1947.

[29] Derville to Boswell, 19 May 1947, BBC/WAC/RCONTI Pallister (Talks 4).

[30] Scannell and Cardiff, p. 161.

[31] See Derville to Pallister, 22 May 1947, BBC/WAC/RCONTI Pallister (Talks 4).

[32] Pallister to Derville, 10 October 1947, BBC/WAC/RCONTI Pallister (Talks 4).

[33] Derville to Pallister, 17 October 1947, Pallister to Derville, Wednesday, nd, [but November 1947]; Derville to MP, undated, handwritten draft, BBC/WAC/RCONTI Pallister (Talks 4).

[34] Pallister to Dear Sir, 29 March 1948, BBC/WAC/RCONTI Pallister (Talks 4).

[35] Pallister to Dear Sir, 16 May 1948, BBC/WAC/RCONTI Pallister (Talks 4).

[36] Derville to Pallister, 22 May 1948, BBC/WAC/RCONTI Pallister (Talks 4). Minnie's BBC files are empty from late May 1948 until August 1950.

[37] Pallister to Derville, 31 March [1947], BBC/WAC/RCONTI Pallister (Talks 4).

[38] *Everybody's Weekly*, 7 August 1948.

[39] Pallister to KBG, 29 September & 11 October 1948, GP/1/2/ 347 (i) & (ii).

[40] Pallister to Quigley, 11 July [1952], BBC/WAC/RCONTI Pallister (Talks 5).

[41] Pallister to Malcolm Bruce Glasier, 15 Jun 1950, GP/1/2/ 530.

[42] Letters to Malcolm Bruce Glasier from Miriam Lord, Bradford, August–September 1950 & part letter, nd, Pallister for Capt & Mrs Glasier, GP/1/2/ 618 7 & 8; GP 1/2/618 (7). Glen Cottage opened as a youth hostel in 1958.

[43] 'I Knew Her: Katharine Bruce Glasier', *WH*, 31 March 1953.

[44] Pallister to Quigley, 9 August 1950, BBC/WAC/RCONTI Pallister (Talks 4).

[45] *BBC Staff List*, 15 April 1950; Information from Kate Murphy; Kristin Skoog and Alexander Badenoch, 'Networking Women: The International Association of Women in Radio and Television (IAWRT)', in Jamie Medhurst, Sian Nicholas and Tom O'Malley, *Broadcasting in the UK and US in the 1950s: Historical Perspectives*, Cambridge Scholars, 2016, p. 194.

[46] Quigley to Pallister, 14 August 1950, Pallister to Quigley, 15 & 17 August 1950, BBC/WAC/RCONTI Pallister (Talks 4).

[47] Quigley to Pallister, 21 & 25 September 1950, Pallister to Quigley, 24 September 1950, BBC/WAC/RCONTI Pallister (Talks 4).

[48] *The Book of Woman's Hour*, Ariel Productions, 1953, pp. 212–3.

[49] Note scribbled on Pallister to Quigley, 17 August 1950, BBC/WAC/RCONTI Pallister (Talks 4).

[50] 'I've Been Thinking About Spring', *WH*, 27 April 1953.

[51] 'I've Been Thinking About Spring'.

[52] This is due to an absence of extant correspondence with friends for most of 1945 to 1950.

[53] *John O'London*, 3 September 1948; Pallister to Quigley, 1 & 21 October 1950, BBC/WAC/RCONTI Pallister (Talks 4); 'Diary', *WH*, 11 April 1951.

[54] See Donavon, 'Quigley...'.

[55] Pallister to Quigley, 20 August 1950 & Quigley to Pallister, 8 September 1950, BBC/WAC/RCONTI Pallister (Talks 4).

[56] Pallister to Quigley, 9 October 1950 & 26 January 1951, Quigley to Pallister, 20 November & 12 December 1950, 5 February & 13 April 1951; Talks Booking Requisition form, 30 August 1950, BBC/WAC/RCONTI Pallister (Talks 4 & 5).

[57] Pallister to Quigley, 21 November 1950, BBC/WAC/RCONTI Pallister (Talks 4).

[58] Pallister to Quigley, 26 January 1951, BBC/WAC/RCONTI Pallister (Talks 5).

[59] Pallister to Quigley, 3 October & 21 November 1950, 18 March 1951, Quigley to Pallister, 20 November 1950 & 5 February 1951, BBC/WAC/RCONTI Pallister (Talks 4 & 5).

[60] Pallister to Quigley, 25 February 1951, BBC/WAC/RCONTI Pallister (Talks 5).

[61] Quigley to Pallister, 4 April 1951, Pallister to Quigley, 6 & 18 April 1951, BBC/WAC/RCONTI Pallister (Talks 5).

[62] Quigley to Pallister, 23 November 1953, BBC/WAC/RCONTI Pallister (Talks 6).

[63] *Radio Times*, 13 July 1951. The winner was Antonia Ridge, a writer. She wrote the English lyrics to 'The Happy Wanderer' and scripted and read plays for *Children's Hour*.

[64] See Quigley–Pallister correspondence for August–September 1952; Quigley to Pallister, 19 August 1954, 24 March 1955 & Pallister to Quigley, 21 July [1953], BBC/WAC/RCONTI Pallister (Talks 5, 6 & 7).

[65] She could also ham it up. 'As One Nitwit to Another', is a brilliant example of trading on her inadequacies that even seventy years later makes you laugh out loud. ('As One Nitwit to Another', *WH*, 11 October 1950.)

[66] Pallister to Quigley, 30 Nov[ember 1953], BBC/WAC/RCONTI Pallister (Talks 6).

[67] Pallister to Quigley, 10 February [1955], BBC/WAC/RCONTI Pallister (Talks 7).

[68] See 'Minnie Pallister Speaks', *WH*, 4 January 1953 & Pallister to Quigley, 26 January & 20 February 1953, BBC/WAC/RCONTI Pallister (Talks 6).

[69] Antoinette Fortune, 'Television and Radio: Mainly for Women', quoted in *The Furrow*, Vol. 10 No. 10, October 1959, pp. 659–663.

[70] Pallister to Quigley, 9 October 1950, BBC/WAC/RCONTI Pallister (Talks 4).

[71] Pallister to Quigley, 9 August 1950, BBC/WAC/RCONTI Pallister (Talks 4).

[72] Pallister to Moore, 5 May 1951, BBC/WAC/RCONTI Pallister (Talks 5).

[73] Pallister to Quigley, 14 & 16 September 1952, BBC/WAC/RCONTI Pallister (Talks 5); 'Anniversaries', *WH*, 10 October 1952.

[74] 'Minnie Pallister Talking', *WH*, 21 September 1954; see also Pallister to Ferguson, 27 May [1954], BBC/WAC/RCONTI Pallister (Talks 6). The range of organisations with which Minnie worked was phenomenal. They included a Woman's Bright Club in Yorkshire; a woman's 'Efficiency Club' in Lincoln that promoted cooperation among business and professional women, (the name of which terrified her); a Woman's Civic Group in Worthing; the wives of the Round Table; the Wellingborough soroptimists, an organisation that promoted women's

and girls' opportunities through voluntary service, internationalism and peace, and a Mothers' Union in Swindon, though as a non-mother who was not a member of the Church of England she did wonder what she was doing there.

[75] Pallister to Scott-Moncrieff, 8 September 1957, BBC/WAC/RCONTI Pallister (Talks 8); *PPU Journal*, March 1948.

[76] *Peace News*, 1 April 1949; Brittain, *Testament of Experience*, p. 453.

[77] *Peace News*, 5 May 1950; *PPU Journal*, June 1950 & April 1951.

[78] PPU National Council, 2–3 June 1951 & 7–8 June 1952; PPU Executive Committee, 2 April, 2 July, 2 August 1952 & 4 February 1953.

[79] *Peace News*, 28 October & 11 November 1949.

[80] *Peace News*, 11 November 1949; *PPU Journal*, November & December 1949.

[81] *Coventry Evening Telegraph*, 1 March 1948.

[82] *Peace News*, 27 February & 12 March 1948.

[83] *Bulletin*, Labour Peace Fellowship, July–August 1947, Box JX 1908, TUC Library.

[84] *Peace News*, 11 November 1949. Perhaps this explains why, in 1948, two years before her death, Katharine Bruce Glasier rejoined the ILP. (*Socialist Leader*, 24 June 1950.)

[85] *Hastings and St Leonards Observer*, 18 February 1950; *Sussex Agricultural Express*, 24 February 1950.

[86] *Western Times*, 17 & 25 March 1950; *Peace News*, 31 March & 7 April 1950.

[87] *Peace News*, 14 & 28 July & 24 November 1950; Pallister to John E. Morgan, 14 December 1950, uncatalogued South Wales Coalfield Collection, Swansea University.

[88] *Peace News*, 9 & 16 February 1951.

[89] PPU Executive Committee, 31 August 1950.

[90] PPU National Council, 2 & 3 June 1951.

[91] Attachment, Pallister to Quigley, 28 July 1950, BBC/WAC/RCONTI Pallister (Talks 4); 'Request Week'.

[92] His dilapidated house had no electricity and the roof leaked so badly that a sluice was set up to drain the water straight through the window. ('Diary', 2 February 1951.)

[93] PPU AGM minutes, 22–23 April 1951.

[94] 'Diary', 2 February 1951.

[95] Pallister to Quigley, 26 January 1951, BBC/WAC/RCONTI Pallister (Talks 5); 'Diary', 5 March 1951.

[96] *South Wales Evening Post*, 2 April 1951; 'Diary', 11 April 1951 & 1 September 1952.

[97] 'Diary', WH, 13 June 1951.

[98] See, for example, Minnie Pallister to John E. Morgan, 14 December 1950.

[99] 'Diary', 22 October 1951.

[100] Quigley to Pallister, 26 September & 1 October 1951, Pallister to Quigley, 2 October 1951, BBC/WAC/RCONTI Pallister (Talks 5).

[101] Editor, Woman's Hour to CT, 8 October 1951; Quigley to Pallister, 8 October 1951, Pallister to Quigley, 15 November 1951, BBC/WAC/RCONTI Pallister (Talks 5).

[102] *Eastbourne Gazette*, 27 October 1951.

[103] 'Christmas Debate WASTE', notes, nd but early December 1951, BBC/WAC/RCONTI Pallister (Talks 5).

BROADCASTER

[104] Quigley to Wyatt, 8 November 1951, Wyatt to Pallister, 14 & 30 November 1951, Pallister to Wyatt, nd, received 3 December 1951, Pallister to Quigley, 21 December 1951 & Minnie's notes on Christmas Debate, nd, BBC/WAC/RCONTI Pallister (Talks 5); 'Christmas as a Racket', *WH*, 14 December 1951.

[105] She argued against a return to the days when food was cheap, when people were bribed to buy through advertising and free samples, and customers were always right. Minnie stated that this was achieved at the cost of low farmers' wages in Britain and 'great poverty and misery' of workers overseas and concluded, 'We don't want cheap food at the cost of other peoples' suffering.' People should be prepared to pay more for what they needed; eating food in season was cheaper and healthier. Priority should be given to necessities not luxuries. Minnie suggested that women's organisations should invite retailers to speak and challenge them, especially on over-pricing and quality. Her objection to unnecessary wrapping on products as a waste of resources was another example of her prescience. Pallister to Quigley, 8, 10 & 11 January 1952 with 'What Can I Do' attachment, BBC/WAC/RCONTI Pallister (Talks 5).

[106] 'Minnie Pallister Talks About Poetry', *WH*, 19 December 1950.

[107] 'Diary', 1 December 1952; 'Minnie Pallister Talks About Poetry', *WH*, 19 December 1950.

[108] Pallister to Quigley, 21 November & 29 December [1950], BBC/WAC/RCONTI Pallister (Talks 4).

[109] Quigley to Pallister, 17 & 28 March 1952; Talks Booking Requisition form, 9 June 1952, BBC/WAC/RCONTI Pallister (Talks 5); *Radio Times*, 20 June 1952, p. 42.

[110] Quigley to Pallister, 9 July, Pallister to Quigley, 11 & 16 July [1952], BBC/WAC/RCONTI Pallister (Talks 5).

[111] Pallister to Quigley, 11 & 13 July, 9, 18, 21 & 23 August 1952, BBC/WAC/RCONTI Pallister (Talks 5). (Emphasis in original.)

[112] Editor, Woman's Hour to Talks Booking Manager, 15 December 1952, BBC/WAC/RCONTI Pallister (Talks 5).

[113] Quigley to Pallister, 15 September 1953, Pallister to Brittain, nd [Sept 1953], BBC/WAC/RCONTI Pallister (Talks 6).

[114] Quigley to Pallister, 22 January 1953, BBC/WAC/RCONTI Pallister (Talks 6).

[115] *Man and Metal*, July & August 1941.

[116] 'Diary', *WH*, 1 December 1952.

[117] 'Diary', *WH*, 3 November 1952.

[118] Accused of being weak at a bazaar opening, she offered a timid defence that mince pies were not really food but 'a sort of religious rite'. ('Diary', *WH*, 1 December 1952.) She yearned for the fruit puddings of her youth 'before we knew it was a crime to eat'. ('Twopence Coloured', *WH*, 12 May 1959.) See also Pallister to Sylvia Rathbone, 1 August 1958, Marjorie Anderson & Nancy Price, 'The Flowers That Minnie Pallister Planted', *WH*, 27 March 1961.

[119] *PPU Journal*, December 1946.

[120] 'Illness and Stillness', *WH*, 10 February 1958 & 'How Happy I Could Be With Either', *WH*, 8 June 1959.

[121] Pallister to Quigley, 1 July 1951, BBC/WAC/RCONTI Pallister (Talks 5); 'Diary', *WH*, 27 November 1951.

[122] Pallister to Quigley, 1 July 1951, and unidentified handwritten note at bottom of Pallister to Quigley, 4 July [1951], Pallister to Paterson, 2 June [1952], BBC/WAC/RCONTI Pallister (Talks 5).

[123] Cliff Michelmore, Jean Metcalfe, *Two-Way Story: An Autobiography*, Chivers, 1988, pp. 75 & 79.

MINNIE PALLISTER: THE VOICE OF A REBEL

[124] 'Rough outline of activities for 1953 and subjects they suggest', nd, BBC/WAC/RCONTI Pallister (Talks 6); 'I've Been Thinking...About Families', 13 February 1953.

[125] 'I've Been Thinking', *WH*, 12 January 1953.

[126] On Communism, she started with Communion, 'a lovely word', before attacking the Communist Party of Great Britain for its links to the Russian dictatorship, saying it bore little resemblance to the original ideal. ('I've Been Thinking About...Words', *WH*, 26 May 1953.)

[127] eg Pallister to Derville, 'In tram', Tues, nd; Pallister to Scott-Moncrieff, 'Bexhill Station', Tues, nd, 'Victoria Station, Wed', nd, 'Euston Station, Thurs', nd, but all September or early October 1956, BBC/WAC/RCONTI Pallister (Talks 8).

[128] Pallister to Quigley, 21 August 1951, BBC/WAC/RCONTI Pallister (Talks 5).

[129] Quigley to Pallister, 30 September & Pallister to Quigley, 7 Oct [1953], BBC/WAC/RCONTI Pallister (Talks 6).

[130] 'Minnie Pallister Talking', *WH*, 1 June 1955.

[131] 'Diary', 2 February 1951; *Methodist Recorder*, 28 February 1957.

[132] 'Autumn Journeys', *WH*, 27 October 1958.

[133] 'Something Old Something New', *WH*, 17 May 1954; 'Minnie Pallister Speaking', 24 November 1954.

[134] The church had been destroyed during the war, and was now seeking a 'distinctive mission' to parallel its physical reconstruction. Minnie's talk was part of the church's 'The Word of the Woman' lecture series. A week earlier Brittain had spoken on 'Women's Public Responsibilities'. ('Minnie Pallister Talking', 5 September 1955; *Time and Tide*, 2 July 1955.)

[135] 'Minnie Pallister Talking', 7 November 1955; 'Diary', 23 April 1956; 'The Joys of Pottering', *Indian Summer*, 26 August 1959.

[136] *Peace News*, 18 May 1956.

[137] Pallister to Scott-Moncrieff, 4 March [1957], BBC/WAC/RCONTI Pallister (Talks 8).

[138] *Peace News*, 11 September 1953.

[139] *Peace News*, 20 March & 3 April 1953.

[140] The last BBC/MI5 liaison officer worked in the unit from 1987 and was based in Broadcasting House. He read the files held there before being instructed to destroy them in 1992. He concluded that, during the 1950s, 'things' happened in the BBC that were on an 'unofficial' and 'need to know' basis, without any record being kept. (Michael Hodder to author, 17 May 2020.)

[141] *BBC Staff List*, January 1953.

[142] General Secretary's Report, PPU, 1960. As recently as January 1952 Minnie had made clear her commitment to social justice and international peace, broadcasting that whatever time and money she could spare was used to fund such issues. ('I've Been Thinking', 12 January 1953.)

[143] Editor, Woman's Hour to CT Home Sound, 2 March 1953, but incorrectly dated; presumably should be 2 April 1953, BBC/WAC/RCONTI Pallister (Talks 6).

[144] Brittain, *Testament of Experience*, p. 438.

[145] They included the London Peace Council '*definitely* Left Wing' – by implication Communist – 'better left alone' and the National Peace Council '*non*-communist coordinating body...always safe'. Minnie recommended Stuart Morris as someone who 'can *always* give accurate information', and gave his phone number. ('Re Peace Movements', nd, but probably November/December 1952, BBC/WAC/RCONTI Pallister (Talks 5). Emphases in original.)

[146] When the PPU raised German rearmament, the hydrogen bomb or Suez with the Director General, the BBC made no issue of Minnie being a long-term member of the PPU National Council or subsequently its sponsor. (Morris to DG, 2 July 1954, 10 March 1955 & 10 August 1956, BBC/WAC/R34/513 Policy Peace Pledge Union 1941–1956.) In March 1955, when the front-page headline of *Peace News* read 'Minnie Pallister popular Woman's Hour broadcaster writes...' there were no repercussions. Even when Minnie started writing monthly articles in *Peace News* that carried the byline 'Popular Broadcaster on the BBC's "Woman's Hour" programme and a member of the Peace Pledge Union Executive Committee', explicitly linking her involvement with both organisations, the matter was not raised. (*Peace News*, 18 March 1955 & *Peace News*, 3 March 1956.)

[147] Minnie had vigorously argued at its 1952 AGM that the PPU should retain its distance from the Soviet-inspired World Peace Council, and by extension its British associate, the British Peace Committee. (*Peace News*, 2 May 1952.)

[148] Hodder to author 17 May 2020.

[149] *Peace News*, 3 July 1953; *Where the Labour Peace Fellowship Stands on Foreign Policy*, Autumn 1954.

[150] *Peace News*, 7 April 1955.

[151] 'Diary', 7 December 1953.

[152] Pallister to Quigley, 1 February 1954, BBC/WAC/RCONTI Pallister (Talks 6).

[153] Pallister to Quigley, 29 January & 18 February 1954, BBC/WAC/RCONTI Pallister (Talks 6).

[154] 'Minnie Pallister Speaking', 8 March 1954, 'Minnie Pallister Talking', 21 September 1954 (Emphasis in original).

[155] 'Minnie Pallister Speaking', 21 April 1954.

[156] 'How Happy I Could Be With Either', *WH*, 8 June 1959, 'I've Been Thinking About Spring', 27 April 1953.

[157] 'Minnie Pallister Speaking', 24 November 1954.

[158] Pallister to Quigley, 31 March 1954, BBC/WAC/RCONTI Pallister (Talks 6).

[159] Pallister to Keen, 11 April 1954, BBC/WAC/RCONTI Pallister (Talks 6).

[160] Quigley to Pallister, 4 May 1954, BBC/WAC/RCONTI Pallister (Talks 6).

[161] Quigley to Pallister, 27 May 1954 & 'Outline of Proposed Talk on Political Woman in Week' on 'Woman Takes a Look at the 20th Century', attached to letter Pallister to Quigley, 27 May 1954, BBC/WAC/RCONTI Pallister (Talks 6).

[162] Quigley to Pallister, 28 May, Pallister to Scott-Moncrieff, 8 June, Scott-Moncrieff to Pallister, 14 June & Pallister to Quigley, 'Rochester, Wed', nd, [but June 1954], BBC/WAC/RCONTI Pallister (Talks 6).

[163] 'Memories 1900–1910', *WH*, 21 June 1954. Minnie had an unerring knack of transgressing BBC norms, even when she was blameless. After she did a Christmas programme on Stepney Family Services, J. C. Thornton, the Assistant Controller, Talks (Sound) complained that it seemed to be more like a Sunday evening appeal for funds than a *Woman's Hour* programme. Apparently the *Woman's Hour* team had failed to consult over what could be seen as a 'veiled appeal'. Quigley replied, misleadingly, that they had not realised Minnie was dedicating herself to the visit and that the script had arrived late. Moreover Quigley said she had told Minnie she had not liked the talk at all and she should return to the Diary format. However, the idea had been subject to dialogue throughout the autumn, and Quigley had considered it good. For a second time, Minnie was blamed for errors in judgement of BBC staff. Assistant Controller, Talks (Sound) to Editor, Woman's Hour, 12 December & Editor, Woman's Hour to Assistant Controller, Talk (Sound), 16 December 1955, BBC/WAC/RCONTI Pallister (Talks 7).

[164] Pallister to Derville, Thurs?, nd & Derville to Pallister, 23 May 1955, BBC/WAC/RCONTI Pallister (Talks 7).

[165] 'My Utopia', *WH*, 26 January 1955.

[166] *Peace News*, 31 October 1958. A talk of the same title to Lincoln Co-operative Society and PPU branches would have been free of such editorial limitations and more outspoken. (Lincoln Co-operative Society, Notice of Quarterly Meeting and Half Yearly Report and Balance Sheet, for period ended 28 March 1953 http://archive.lincolnshire.coop/1950/1953_-_Directors'_Report.pdf accessed 22 May 2016.)

[167] Quigley to Pallister, 1 & 8 August 1955 & Derville to Pallister, 5 September 1956, BBC/WAC/RCONTI Pallister (Talks 7 & 8).

[168] Pallister to Derville, 6 March, Editor to Derville, 12 March 1956, BBC/WAC/RCONTI Pallister (Talks 8).

[169] Pallister to Leslie Smith, 1 June, Maria Hickman to Pallister, 21 July, Pallister to Fuller, 19 August 1955; Talks Booking Requisition, 11 August 1955, BBC/WAC/RCONTI Pallister (Talks 7).

[170] Those she ruled out of the 40-minute programme are just as interesting are those she included. Attlee was rejected because he might just make a party-political speech; Ramsay MacDonald's children Malcolm and Ishbel were not right for this programme; Flora Robson talking on Welwyn Garden City was possible; Thorndike was thought to still be in Australia. (Pallister to Quigley, 1 & 14 December 1955, BBC/WAC/RCONTI Pallister (Talks 7).)

[171] *Radio Times*, 20 January 1956.

[172] This section has benefited from Elizabeth Wilson, *Only Halfway to Paradise, Women in Postwar Britain 1945–1968*, Tavistock, 1980, pp. 12–3.

[173] Pallister to Quigley, 2 August 1953, BBC/WAC/RCONTI Pallister (Talks 6).

[174] Tippett interview, *WH*, 8 February 1955.

[175] Tippett to Dearest Niouta, 12 January 1956, quoted in Thomas Schuttenhelm ed, *Selected Letters of Michael Tippett*, faber & faber, 2005, pp. 386–7.

[176] Pallister to Derville, 16 January 1956, BBC/WAC/RCONTI Pallister (Talks 8).

[177] During the broadcast Minnie played Overture to the *Die Meistersinger*, dedicated to Ivor and Jen Thomas for Ivor's love of Wagner.

[178] 'Minnie Pallister's Day', *WH*, 25 January 1956; Quigley to Pallister, 26 January 1956; Talks Booking Requisition, 18 January 1956, BBC/WAC/RCONTI Pallister (Talks 8).

[179] *Guardian*, 10 April 2014.

[180] I am hugely grateful to Dave Hatherall for introducing me to John Dowling and providing the lead to Spike Milligan and the Goons.
http://www.thegoonshow.org.uk/page13.html accessed 5 May 2016
http://mumbyatthemovies.blogspot.co.uk/2015/07/the-goon-show-guide-meet-main-characters.html accessed 21 May 2016 and
http://www.thegoonshow.net/characters.asp _accessed 9 May 2016
http://broom02.revolvy.com/main/index.php?s=Henry%20Crun%20and%20Minnie%20Bannister&item_type=topic accessed 10 June 2016.

[181] Dowling attended Milligan's riotous army battery reunions in the Pavilion, and was at the 1973 reunion when Eamonn Andrews surprised Milligan with an episode of *This Is Your Life*, marked by Peter Sellers arriving wearing a canary-yellow German coalscuttle helmet.

[182] Dave Hatherall, email to author, 3 May 2016, with information provided by John Dowling, 2 May 2016; meeting with Dave Hatherall and John Dowling, 18 July 2016.

[183] The episode was first broadcast on 12 October 1954.

[184] Sellers and Milligan played the roles of 'Henry and Min'. Milligan pinched the skin on his neck and wobbled it about to give Min her quavering voice.

[185] Morris, 'Flowers...'.

[186] *Peace News*, 3 March 1956.

[187] *Peace News*, 28 September 1956.

[188] 'A Puritan Takes Stock'.

[189] 'Minnie Pallister Talking', *WH*, 3 October 1955.

[190] *Peace News*, 26 March 1954. As well as profoundly political, 1950s PPU AGMs were major cultural events. Pacifists including Peter Pears, Sir Lewis Casson and Clifford Evans, an actor and Conscientious Objector from Senghenydd, joined sponsors in performing, while Clifford Curzon played piano solos. (*Peace News*, 23 March & 27 April 1956.)

[191] *Peace News*, 14 January 1955; 'Minnie Pallister's Diary', 2 March 1955.

[192] *Peace News*, 13 July 1956; Pallister to Dear Fellow Member, May 1957.

[193] These included speaking at a Standing Joint Pacifist Committee event in Caxton House following a march to Trafalgar Square, serving on an International Relations panel with the prominent pacifist and journalist Ritchie Calder, and joining Raymond Williams, who lived in nearby Hastings, on a local Brains Trust. (*Peace News*, 25 May, 29 June, 17 August & 14 September 1956, & 21 June 1957.)

[194] *Peace News*, 11 June 1954.

[195] 'Diary', 1 December 1952; 'Meanderings', 6 November 1956.

[196] 'That's Me – That Was', *WH*, 22 April 1958; Pallister to Scott-Moncrieff, 18 April [1958], BBC/WAC/RCONTI Pallister (Talks 9).

[197] *The White Ribbon*, December 1956, p. 128.

[198] *Is Your Drinking Really Necessary? The Second Agnes E Slack Saunders lecture*, NBWTAU, (nd). In the late 1930s, she challenged *Man and Metal* readers on gambling and had written a leaflet 'Where's the Harm' for the campaigning National Anti-Gambling League (*Man and Metal*, March 1937; 'Where's the Harm', 1938(?), listed in fragment of document held in Gambling 1937–51 folder, Mass Observation.) http://www.massobservation.amdigital.co.uk/Documents/Images/TopicCollection-86/7183?searchId=f1f21825-b04a-4902-bb85-c0974f42ec47#Sections (accessed 9 May 2016).

[199] *Is Your Drinking...?*

[200] 'Meanderings – No 2', 14 December 1956.

[201] Pallister to Scott-Moncrieff, 29 July & nd but late July/early August 1958; Scott-Moncrieff to Pallister, 22 July 1958; Scott-Moncrieff to Derville, 6 August 1958; Conference Invitation for Caux, BBC/WAC/RCONTI Pallister (Talks 9).

[202] Pallister to Quigley, handwritten note, nd [January 1953], BBC/WAC/RCONTI Pallister (Talks 6).

[203] 'Minnie Pallister Talking', 12 December 1955.

[204] 'Minnie Pallister Talking', 3 October 1955. She arrived at Sutton for a Townswomen's Guild meeting without the address where she was due to speak. When she was not met at the station, she panicked, rang 999 and was put through to Scotland Yard and was rebuked for inappropriately using an emergency number. She arrived over an hour late. Rather than concealing the episode, as most would, she told everybody about it on-air ('Minnie Pallister Talking', 7 November 1955).

[205] Pallister to Derville, 2 December [1956] & Pallister to Walker, 31 January 1957, BBC/WAC/RCONTI Pallister (Talks 8 & 9).

[206] 'On Growing Old', *WH*, 1 February 1957. (Emphasis in original.)

[207] Listeners wrote of how they had thrown an old hat on the fire and gone out to buy a new one. One 85-year-old refused to wear the 'old lady's hat' offered by her daughter as 'she hadn't come to that yet'.

[208] 'Meanderings', 29 March 1957, including deletions from script; Derville to Pallister, 13 February 1957; 'Dearest Jeannie', 3 March 1957, Rose Macaulay, *Letters to a Sister*, Bloomsbury Reader, 2013. (Footnote no. 144 says this was probably a broadcast talk by Minnie in 'Home for the Day' on 3 March 1957.)

[209] Joanna Scott-Moncrieff, Foreword, eds Joanna Scott-Moncrieff and Madge Hart, *The BBC Woman's Hour Book*, The World's Work, 1957, pp. 9–10 & 121–6; Talks Booking Requisition 23 August 1957, BBC/WAC/RCONTI Pallister (Talks 8).

[210] Quigley to Miss Walters, 6 May 1957, Pallister to Scott-Moncrieff, Wed, nd, [but May 1957], BBC/WAC/RCONTI Pallister (Talks 8). (Emphasis in original.)

[211] Scott-Moncrieff to Pallister, 26 July 1957, BBC/WAC/RCONTI Pallister (Talks 8).

[212] Pallister to Scott-Moncrieff, 11 & 25 August 1957, BBC/WAC/RCONTI Pallister (Talks 8); The Minnie Pallister Guide to Modern Britain – 1, *WH*, 16 September 1957.

[213] Derville to 1. Editor, Woman's Hour; 2. Chief Assistant; 3. Producer, with handwritten replies, Programme Form Talks, 30 July 1957 & Derville to Editor, Woman's Hour, 9 August 1957, BBC/WAC/RCONTI Pallister (Talks 8).

[214] Wikipedia, accessed 14 January 2019.

[215] Derville to Pallister, 26 August, Pallister to Derville, 30 August, Pallister to Scott-Moncrieff, 1 September 1957, BBC/WAC/RCONTI Pallister (Talks 8); 'The Minnie Pallister Guide to Modern Britain', 16 September 1957.

[216] Derville to Pallister, 17 September & Pallister to Scott-Moncrieff, 1 September & 20 October 1957, BBC/WAC/RCONTI Pallister (Talks 8).

[217] 'No-one is Unimportant', *WH*, 27 January 1960; Deleted section of script, 'Modern Musicals'.

[218] Derville's Secretary to Pallister, 2 September 1957, BBC/WAC/RCONTI Pallister (Talks 8); 'The Minnie Pallister Guide to Modern England – 2', 14 October 1957.

[219] Pallister to Boswell, 16 October & Derville to Pallister, 16 August 1957, BBC/WAC/RCONTI Pallister (Talks 8); 'The Minnie Pallister Guide to Modern England – 2', 14 October 1957.

[220] Wilson, *Halfway*..., pp. 1–3.

[221] Shira Tarrant, *When Sex Became Gender*, Routledge, 2006, p. 2.

[222] See Birmingham Feminist History Group, 'Feminism as Femininity in the Nineteen Fifties', *Feminist Review*, No 3, 1979, pp. 48–65 & Erin Amann Holliday-Karre, 'Bad Gurley Feminism: The Myth of Post-War Domesticity', *Journal of Feminist Scholarship*, Vol 16, Issue 16, Spring/Fall 2019, pp. 39–52.

[223] Barbara Caine, *English Feminism 1780–1980*, OUP, 1997, pp. 224 & 255.

[224] Caine, pp. 222 & 223.

[225] Caine, p. 226–7.

[226] Wilson, *Halfway*..., p. 37; Rosalind Coward, *Female Desire, Women's Sexuality Today*, Paladin, 1984; See also Rosalind Coward, 'Female Desire and Sexual identity', Myriam Diaz-Diocartez and Iris M. Zavala, *Women, Feminist Identity and Society in the 1980s*, John Benjamin, 1985.

[227] Coward, *Female Desire*, pp. 71 & 130.

[228] Wilson, *Halfway*..., p. 181.

[229] I owe this point to Angela V. John.

[230] Wilson, *Halfway*, p. 195.

[231] See e.g. Angela V. John, *Evelyn Sharp. Rebel Woman, 1869–1955*, MUP, 2009. Chapter 9.

[232] Tarrant, pp. 2 & 213–5.

[233] Wilson, *Halfway...*, p. 186.

[234] *The Listener*, 23 October 1986.

[235] Sue Bruley, '"It didn't just come out of nowhere, did it?" the origins of the women's liberation movement in 1960s Britain', *Oral History*, Spring 2017, Vol 45 No 1, pp. 67–78.

[236] Coward, *Female Desire*, pp.103 & 106.

[237] Correspondence between Keen and Pallister, September to November 1957; Pallister to Scott-Moncrieff, 8 September 1957, BBC/WAC/RCONTI Pallister (Talks 8).

[238] Quigley to Newby, Chief Assistant, Talks, 11 November 1957, BBC/WAC/RCONTI Pallister (Talks 8).

[239] Pallister to Scott-Moncrieff, 20 October, 'Sunday' & 'Thurs in bed', nd but December 1957 & Pallister to Miss Hart, 12 December 1957, BBC/WAC/RCONTI Pallister (Talks 8).

[240] Scott-Moncrieff to Pallister, 24 October, 12 November & 31 December 1957 & Pallister to Scott-Moncrieff, Sunday, nd but December 1957, BBC/WAC/RCONTI Pallister (Talks 8).

[241] Talks Booking Requisition, 7 January 1958; Pallister to Scott-Moncrieff, 11 January 1958, Pallister to Derville, 11 January 1958, BBC/WAC/RCONTI Pallister (Talks 9).

[242] Pallister to Scott-Moncrieff, 4 February 1958, BBC/WAC/RCONTI Pallister (Talks 9); 'Illness and Stillness'.

[243] 'That's Me – That Was', *WH*, 22 April 1958.

[244] *Manchester Guardian*, 16 & 20 November 1957; *Peace News*, 11 April 1958.

[245] Marwick, *Allen...*, p. 20.

[246] *Peace News*, 3 & 31 January 1958.

[247] *Peace News*, 18 April 1958.

[248] *Peace News*, 25 April 1958; John Hostettler, *Dissenters, Radicals, Heretics and Blasphemers*, Waterside, 2012, p. 239.

[249] *Peace News*, 25 April 1958.

[250] Alex Comfort, fellow PPU sponsor and accomplished scientist, later made famous by his book *The Joy of Sex*, also spoke. (*Peace News*, 18 April 1958; *Irish Times*, 16 May 1958.)

[251] *Peace News*, 25 April 1958.

[252] Pallister to Scott-Moncrieff, 18 April [1958], BBC/WAC/RCONTI Pallister (Talks 9).

[253] *Peace News*, 18 July & 3 October 1958.

[254] *Peace News*, 7 October 1955; Pallister to Sybil Rathbone, 29 July 1958, RP XVB.2.255.

[255] *Peace News*, 4 July & 14 November 1958, 20 November 1959; Morris, 'The Flowers...'.

[256] Pallister to Quigley, 13 May [1958], BBC/WAC/RCONTI Pallister (Talks 9).

[257] 'Minnie Pallister Talking', 3 October 1955. (Emphasis in original.)

[258] Pallister to Scott-Moncrieff, 12 July 1958 & Pallister to Derville, 14 August 1958, BBC/WAC/RCONTI Pallister (Talks 9); 'The Toad Under the Harrow', *WH*, 22 September 1958; Pallister to Sybil Rathbone, 1 August 1958, RO XUB.2.256.

[259] 'My Very Own', 6 July 1959, (including deleted sections of script).

[260] 'Autumn Journeys'.

[261] Pallister to Derville, nd, BBC/WAC/RCONTI Pallister (Talks 10); 'Ward 8b', *WH*, 6 April 1959.

[262] 'Ward 8B'; Pallister to Derville, card date stamp 22 February 1959, BBC/WAC/RCONTI Pallister (Talks 10).

[263] Pallister to Derville, 14 April 1959, BBC/WAC/RCONTI Pallister (Talks 10).

[264] 'Twopence Coloured'.

[265] Pallister to Derville, nd but probably early March 1959 & Pallister to Walters 10 & 18 May 1959, BBC/WAC/RCONTI Pallister (Talks 10); Marjorie Claisen, 'The Flowers That Minnie Pallister Planted'.

[266] Pallister to Derville, card date stamp 22 February [1959] & nd; Pallister to Scott-Moncrieff, 20 April 1959, BBC/WAC/RCONTI Pallister (Talks 10).

[267] Pallister to Derville, 20 August 1959, BBC/WAC/RCONTI Pallister (Talks 10).

[268] 'The Flowers That Minnie Pallister Planted'; Pallister to Walters, 18 May 1959, BBC/WAC/RCONTI Pallister (Talks 10); 'How Happy I Could Be With Either', *WH*, 8 June 1959; 'My Very Own', *WH*, 6 July 1959; 'Autumn Thoughts'.

[269] Obituary, *The Scotsman*, 2 August 2010 https://www.scotsman.com/news/obituaries/obituary-wyn-knowles-1-819665, retrieved 11 February 2019; Dennis Barker, 'Wyn Knowles obituary', *Guardian*, 23 July 2010, https://www.theguardian.com/media/2010/jul/23/wyn-knowles-obituary, retrieved 11 February 2019.

[270] Knowles to Pallister, 23 September 1959, BBC/WAC/RCONTI Pallister (Talks 10).

[271] Pallister to Knowles, 24 October [1959], BBC/WAC/RCONTI Pallister (Talks 10); 'Modern Musicals', *WH*, 28 October 1959.

[272] Pallister to Knowles, 5, 12, 13 January & 25 February 1960 & Pallister to Scott-Moncrieff, 2 March 1960, BBC/WAC/RCONTI Pallister (Talks 10).

[273] 'The Toad...'.

[274] 'Winter Thoughts', *WH*, 1 December 1958.

[275] *Peace News*, 20 November 1959.

[276] Deleted section of script, 'Modern Musicals'; 'No-one is Unimportant', *WH*, 27 January 1960.

[277] 'No-one is Unimportant'.

[278] 'No-one is Unimportant'.

[279] 'Diary', 27 November 1951.

[280] 'No-one is Unimportant'.

[281] Knowles to Pallister, 3 February & Pallister to Knowles, 15 February 1960, BBC/WAC/RCONTI Pallister (Talks 10).

[282] Pallister to Scott-Moncrieff, 2 March 1960, BBC/WAC/RCONTI Pallister (Talks 10).

[283] Gladys Pallister to Knowles, 15 & 17 March 1960, BBC/WAC/RCONTI Pallister (Talks 10).

[284] Pallister to Scott-Moncrieff, 1 January 1958, BBC/WAC/RCONTI Pallister (Talks 9).

[285] *WH*, 29 March 1960.

ACKNOWLEDGEMENTS

Over seven years I have accrued debts so large that these thanks feel inadequate. Friends have been generous in their support. Ryland Wallace, Neil Evans, and Helen Thomas gave me their own papers related to Minnie Pallister and Aled Eirug shared Great War references. Ginny Blakey helped with the Pallister sisters' genealogy and John and Trudy Horton (née Pallister) provided the rest of the family tree. Elin Jones took me to meet her cousin Kitty, who had worked in the same school as Minnie. Vivienne Williams shared her family's links with Minnie in Brynmawr. Rachael Singleton and Peter Forsaith facilitated access to aspects of the Methodist world. Margaret Makepeace and Huw Bowen uncovered the Higmans' Indian connections. Hans Sienz translated parts of *Der Rote Geiger* about Eduard Soermus. Pallavi Podapati tracked down a source in Princeton that might otherwise have remained beyond reach. John Laurie sent a digitised article from Auckland. Roy Williams took me around Welwyn Garden City and Dawn showed us Minnie's former home. Dave Hatherell and John Dowling introduced me to Bexhill after pure coincidence had led to John revealing the Spike Milligan connection, for which I still thank my lucky stars. Thanks also to Jane Milligan for an enjoyable morning discussing Minnie and Spike and sharing his photo albums.

Drs Abboud Alhallak, Mardge Cohen, Bindu Desai and Gordi Schiff helped me understand the nature of Minnie's illness. June Hannam shared her knowledge of labour and socialist women, Lisa Regan of Winifred Holtby, Martin Ceadel of the pacifist movement, Kate Murphy the BBC, and I had enjoyable exchanges with the late Jo Vellacott. Elizabeth Crawford provided a photo of Minnie. Hywel Francis, to whom this book is dedicated, provided leads on Bill Cove and Aberavon, the constituency that Hywel represented in Parliament. He did not live to read this book – I wish so much that he had.

In tracking down the Schwarb family, Alf Dubbs and Esther Gilbert put me in touch with Abra Cohen of the Joint Distribution Committee in New York who obtained the family's ship passenger listings and Hans' petition for US naturalisation, which allowed me to locate the whereabouts of his descendants. Meeting Stephanie, Hans' granddaughter, in Chicago in 2016, was one of the pleasures of writing this book. It was a delight to be told they had made 'more progress unlocking the details behind my family's escape from Nazi Germany in one week than we'd made in 70 years!' Esther Gilbert always provided a generous welcome, access to papers and important leads, putting me in contact with Sandra Wellington, the granddaughter of Robert Smallbones, the British Consul General in Frankfurt. In August 2016 Esther, Sandra, Stephanie, and I took part in an intercontinental exchange that was historic in its own right.

I owe a huge debt of gratitude to Louise Miskell who arranged my honorary research fellowship in Swansea University History Department that has made this book possible. The South Wales Miners' Library has been my second home since 1977. To those generations of friends who comprise the current and previous staff, thank you. Many of the books I read there while researching Minnie were from the collection of the late Ursula Masson. Ursula died before I started this project – in many ways this should have been her book. An equal debt of gratitude is held to Louise North of the BBC Written Archive. Lynette Cawthra and Lindsey Cole in the Working Class Movement Library and Darren Treadwell in the Labour Studies Archive at the People's History Museum provided brilliant working environments, as did the Co-operative Archive. Other essential destinations included the libraries of Friends House, the TUC and the Peace Pledge Union. To work in the Wiener Library on holocaust materials is both a rewarding and disconcerting experience. I am grateful for the efficiency and scope of the National Archives, British Library and the National Library of Wales. County Archives and History Centres, public libraries and university archives have all been unfailingly helpful. One – McMaster – stands out for its stunning level of support.

Joe Street, Peter Wakelin and Chris Williams provided helpful feedback and read sections of the text. Andrew Green was the first person to read the complete text. Throughout this whole enterprise, Andrew and Carys Evans have shared Minnie's life while offering me an unwavering embrace. Aled Jones, Duncan Green and Catherine Matheson, Carolyn Miller, John Bevan, Frances Barnes and Alan Wiggins, and Sarah Jackson and Fred Ponsonby provided warmth and welcome when I was undertaking research trips. Fred

ACKNOWLEDGEMENTS

also talked of his great-grandfather, Arthur, a friend and comrade of Minnie's, as well as putting me in contact with others.

Angela John has provided so much support and friendship, including reading and commenting on the complete text that she has felt like a sister in this struggle. I have also been fortunate to have Dai Smith as Parthian's series editor. His stimulating challenge opened my eyes on how Minnie should be delivered to the world. Richard Davies of Parthian is the sort of publisher you hope for, and Dai and Rich deserve great credit for taking on the biography of a previously largely unknown person. Gina Rathbone brought professional diligence and an acute eye to the copyediting and it was a pleasure to work with her. I am very grateful to Gillian Lonergan for undertaking the indexing. Angela, Dai and myself, and many of those thanked above, are of that unique collective experience that is Llafur since the 1970s. For the decades of solidarity and comradeship in what Hywel described as the biggest Welsh Labour History Society in the world, I can only say thank you.

Quotations from Bertrand Russell are reproduced by permission of McMaster University; Clifford Allen diaries by Esther Gilbert; J. S. Middleton by the Labour History Archive of the People's History Museum; Ramsay MacDonald by his granddaughter; Vera Brittain by The Literary Executors of the Vera Brittain Will Trust (1970); Ness Edwards by Baroness Llin Golding; Jessie Stephen by the Working Class Movement Library; Norman Angell by Ball State University; the Milner papers by the Warden and Scholars of New College Oxford; Charles Philips Trevelyan by Newcastle University Special Collections; Antoinette Fortune by St Patrick's College; Len Jeffries by the South Wales Miners' Library and Catherine Marshall by Cumbria Archives Centre. Thanks also to the Churchill Archives Centre, Cambridge, Liverpool University and the London School of Economics in relation to the papers of Bernard Langdon Davies, Fenner Brockway and Kathryn Bruce Glasier, and to White Ribbon for agreeing access to their pamphlet 'Is Your Drinking Really Necessary?'

PHOTOS

Cover photo courtesy of Elizabeth Crawford.

Minnie Pallister with Mary Macdonald Taylor courtesy of Vivienne Williams.

Minnie Pallister in 1918 courtesy of the Working Class Movement Library.

Janet Quigley courtesy of the BBC.

1926 ILP delegation to the Labour Party conference courtesy of the Working Class Movement Library.

Old Town Bexhill courtesy of Bexhill Museum.

1958 Friends House meeting courtesy of the Peace Pledge Union.

Minnie Pallister at a BBC microphone courtesy of the *Methodist Recorder*.

INDEX

1898 miners' lockout 16, 17
1912 miners' strike 21–2
1917 Club 122, 123, 238
1921 miners' lockout 90, 100, 105, 109, 230 fn27
1922 general election 107–8
1924 Labour Government 29–30 fn56, 129, 130, 132, 135
1926 General Strike & miners' lockout 90, 144–146, 148, 149, 150
1929 Labour Government 29–30 fn56, 65 fn22, 101, 175–6, 178, 185–6, 196 fn88
1945–51 Labour Government 25, 30 fn57, 101, 144, 284, 297, 302–3, 304, 309–10, 312

A

Aachen 133, 252
Aberaman 53
Aberavon 58, 64 fn20, 78, 92–109, 110, 137, 170, 174–5, 176, 178, 217–218, 234 fn116, 242, 273
Aberdare 17, 18, 29–30 fns56 & 60, 50, 71, 72, 78, 88, 90
Abergavenny 13, 24, 39, 61, 63
Abertillery 12, 16, 20, 26, 30 fn72, 41, 42, 51, 58, 61, 64 fn4, 90, 111 fn4, 215, 230 fn27
Ablett, Noah 17, 20, 29–20 fn56, 57
Adams, Mary 237, 238, 258, 260–1
Afan Sentinel 102–3
Afan Valley 95, 100
agony aunt 2, 208–209, 223, 231 fns38, 39 & 41, 306–7, 313
air raid precautions 242, 257, 264, 282, 283
alcohol 15, 27, 133, 225, 315, 326, 328
Aldermaston 335
Allen, Clifford 34, 37, 40, 43–6, 48, 49, 52, 60, 67 fn68, 69 fn123, 82–84, 99, 109–110, 113 fn61, 120, 121, 122, 125, 128, 129, 132, 139, 142, 186, 198 fn153
Anderson, Marjorie 340
Anderson, W. C. 35, 60 fn123, 79, 122
Andrews, Elizabeth 18, 30 fn60, 76, 85–88, 94–5, 101, 111, 114 fn77
Angell, Norman 4, 38, 172, 181, 186, 187, 198 fn153, 212, 213–214, 216, 221–2
Anglican Church 26–7, 107, 242, 274, 343–4 fn74
animal cruelty 144, 206
Annesley, Lady 169
appeasement 241, 243–4, 251, 254, 255–6, 262–3, 269
art 9, 10, 79, 219, 220, 234 fn118, 299, 300, 301–302
ASLEF 88
Association of Girls' Clubs 210, 231–2 fns50 & 51
Astor, Nancy 279, 281
Atherall, Lydia 14, 39, 102, 112 fn33
Attlee, Christopher 312
Attlee, Clement 130, 261, 304, 312, 348fn170
Attlee, Mrs 304
austerity 300, 312
Australian women 154 fn82, 217, 302

B

Banner H. S. 258–9, 260
'Bannister, Minnie' 1, 324–325
Barclay, John 241–2, 259
Bargoed 55, 61, 84
Barker, George 71, 111 fn4, 215
Barnes, George 275, 276, 277, 280, 281, 293 fn274
Barton, Mrs 155 fn120, 190
Battle of Britain 262, 265, 270
Baxter, Richard 241, 263
Beauchamp, Joan 43
Belden, Arthur 274, 295 fn310
Bentham, Ethel 172
Besant, Annie 142
Bevan, Aneurin 3–4, 17, 30 fn57, 336
Beveridge Report 278
Bevin, Ernest 192, 309–310
Bexhill-on-Sea 173, 204–206, 210, 213–4, 216, 219, 225, 232 fn74, 239, 241–2, 248, 249, 250, 251, 253, 257, 259, 263, 264–7, 274, 278, 280, 281, 282–3, 310, 324, 325, 329, 337, 338, 340
Binder, Pearl 315
birth control 81, 82, 138, 147, 155 fn124, 189
Blackie 216, 217, 226
Blackwood, W. 166
Blaenavon 52
Blaina 10, 12, 21, 39, 42, 215, 233 fn87
Blatchford, Robert 311
blitz 267, 270
Bloomfield, Paul 301

357

bombing, opposing RAF 274, 275, 278, 293 fn254, 295 fn310, 323
Bombing Restriction Committee 274, 293 fn254
Bondfield, Margaret 61, 97, 100, 116 fn132, 120, 129, 136, 137, 139, 140, 142, 143, 155 fn120, 156 fn133, 177, 196 fn88, 283
Bonham Carter, Lady Violet 69 fn114, 279–80, 281
Bookman 135, 189, 203, 216, 219, 222, 320
Booth, General 10
Booth, Meyrick 172
Bournemouth 106, 124–132, 133, 135–136, 137, 147, 149, 161, 164, 167, 168, 169, 173, 176, 179, 240, 261, 271, 277, 284, 339
Bradford 129–30, 190, 304, 317
Brailsford, Henry Noel 121–122, 142, 143, 148, 169
Brecon 59, 63
Brennan, Capt. 125, 157 fn169
British Broadcasting Corporation (BBC) Minnie Pallister:
  BBC Bournemouth 133, 154 fn95
  first political broadcast 133
  approach to broadcasting 239, 245, 306–8
  broadcasting 3, 237–240, 242–246, 248, 249, 252–3, 255–6, 257–8, 265–6, 271–2, 275–7, 279–80, 281, 298–302, 303–308, 312–7, 318–9, 320–2, 326–30, 332–4, 335, 338–41, 347 fn163
  broadcasting prowess 239, 252, 257–8, 280, 303, 305–8, 316, 322–3, 327–8, 339–40, 350 fn207
  challenging boundaries 238, 281, 299, 308, 316, 321
  BBC concerns 237, 276–7, 279–280, 281, 283, 301–2, 316, 318–319, 321–322, 327, 335
  MI5 monitoring (see surveillance by authorities)
  broadcasting bans 1, 2, 265–266, 270, 271–2, 275, 281, 291 fn198, 301–302
  wartime broadcasting 253, 255–8, 268, 274–277
  programmes:
  Mostly for Women 275
  Woman's Page 279, 280, 281, 283, 284, 295 fn309
  Woman's Hour 1, 2, 299–302, 303, 305–308, 314–315, 315–316, 321–323, 330, 332–333, 334, 337–338, 340–341
  Indian Summer 327–8

'Minnie Pallister's Life Story' (1952) 1, 314
  guest editor (1956) 322–3, 348 fn170
'Minnie Pallister's Guide to Modern England' (1957) 328–30, 333, 334
British People's Party 260
British Union of Fascists 259, 260, 262
Briton Ferry 36, 58, 64 fn20, 70 fn147, 91, 92, 93, 98, 99, 102, 111 fn3, 143, 178
Brittain, Vera 4, 142, 171, 188, 189–90, 219, 221, 244, 258, 262–3, 270, 271, 297, 309, 310, 314–5, 325, 333, 336, 346 fn134
Britten, Benjamin 310, 325, 335
Brockway, Fenner 34, 43, 52, 60, 106, 109, 120, 121, 130, 139, 143, 148, 163, 190, 191 240, 335, 336
Brown, E. T. 166
Brown, Herbert Runham 44, 211
Browne, Stella 81
Brynmawr 10, 12–15, 16, 20, 21, 22, 23, 33, 37, 38–9, 40, 41, 42, 44, 47, 49, 51, 57, 58, 59, 61, 65–6 fn41, 67 fn99, 74, 78, 81, 88, 93, 102, 173, 205–6, 215, 314, 327
Bulletin for Women Socialists 138
Burgess, Guy 243, 244, 284 fn42
Burroughs, Dorothy 202

C
Cabbage for a Year 161–162, 189, 215–216, 219, 237, 238–9
Caerphilly 65 fn22, 68 fn95, 101–2, 108
Caine, Barbara 330
Cambrian Combine dispute 17, 18, 22, 69 fn115
Crusade for a People's Peace 297
Campaign for Nuclear Disarmament 335, 336, 339
Canary Islands 150
Candle in the Pumpkin 141
Cardiff 10, 11, 39, 52, 53, 71, 78, 97, 108, 110, 237, 253, 283
Carpenter, Edward 80–81
'Casey' (Hampson, Walter) 21, 31 fn76, 106
Catchpool, Gwen 323
Catholic Church 182, 274
Champney's 188, 190, 203–4, 319–320
chapel 11, 12, 13, 14, 18, 20, 26, 27, 34, 36, 58, 61, 94, 95, 183, 184, 246 (see also Methodism and religion)
Christianity Calling 274, 278, 283, 293 fn254, 310
Churchill, Winston 130, 174, 243, 245, 261, 301, 312
cinema (see film)

INDEX

Clarion and *New Clarion* 170, 191–192
Cleghorn, Isabel 15
Clifford, Lady Anne 226
clothes and appearance 80, 123, 140, 181, 189, 202, 208, 209, 216–7, 245, 299, 311, 320, 327, 329–30, 331, 333
Clydeside 34, 62, 88, 121, 143, 168
coal nationalisation 74, 76, 84, 90, 93, 94, 100, 284
Collins, Bill 64 fn4, 253
communism/communist 60, 96, 99, 130, 139, 219, 229, 303, 309–310, 314, 318–9, 334, 346 fns126 & 145
Communist Party of Great Britain 89, 91, 96, 101, 102, 110, 137, 140, 144, 154 fn111, 228, 230 fn27, 271, 282, 286 fn42, 303, 314
conscientious objection 37, 38, 40, 41, 50, 51, 54, 56, 58, 60, 65 fn22, 84, 89, 101, 102, 292 fn228, 297–298, 349 fn190
conscription 36, 38, 40, 42, 50, 53, 54, 61, 68 fn99, 78, 88, 137, 185, 244, 264, 274–5, 297, 298
consumer culture 312, 313, 316, 320, 329–31
Cook, A. J. 53, 57, 62, 68–9 fn111, 90, 146, 149, 173
contraception (see birth control)
co-operative movement 13, 41, 52, 57, 101, 103, 170, 179, 184, 190, 220, 240, 242, 268, 277, 311, 348 fn166
Cove, W. G. 'Bill' 123, 136, 152 fn36, 174–175, 178, 195 fn78, 242, 278
Coward, Rosalind 331-3
Cox, Lucy (Middleton) 120, 151 fn10, 176–177, 254, 284
Croft, Henry 135
Crooks, Will 16, 96
Cuthbert, Jenny 81
Cwmtillery 12
Czechoslovakia 243, 251, 254, 259

D

Daily Herald 2, 131, 135, 136–137, 165–6, 170, 182, 201–203, 206, 208–209, 210, 213, 215, 216, 217, 219, 221, 223, 227, 233 fn96, 242, 248, 253, 266, 271, 273
Daily Mirror 208, 209, 219, 224, 302
Dalton, Hugh 146, 149, 292–3 fn238
dancing 14, 15, 265, 324, 328, 329
Davies, Henry 50, 109
Davies, Rose 18, 30 fn60
Davies, Willie 14, 39, 206
De La Warr Pavilion 249, 264–265
Defence of the Realm Act 36, 53, 54, 88, 283

Derville, Anthony 300, 301–302, 308, 321, 322, 327, 328, 338
Dollan, Pat 139, 148, 150
domestic issues/work including drudgery 9, 14, 26, 61, 75, 76, 77, 78, 80, 87, 116 fn124, 122–3, 132, 143, 180, 205, 207, 208, 209, 245, 272, 278, 299, 307, 323, 331, 333
domestic service 9, 25, 132, 207–208, 220–1, 323
Dowling, John 324, 348 fn181
drama (see theatre)
Dubery, Harry 24
Dunbar, John 201, 202
Dunkirk 262, 270

E

Ebbw Vale 14, 16, 20, 21, 30 fn57, 39, 62
Edmunds, Jimmy 108
Edwards, Ness 51, 68 fn95,
eisteddfod 20, 24, 59, 192, 215
Elton, Lord 227
Equal Citizens 210
ethical trade and consumption 272–3, 274, 313, 345 fn105
Eunice Fleet 50
Exposition Internationale des Arts et Techniques dans la Vie Moderne 226

F

family allowances 61, 63, 70 fn150, 74, 137–138, 142, 143, 144, 146, 147, 148, 150, 155 fn124, 172, 173–174, 190, 257, 272, 273, 284
fascism 205, 207, 210–1, 212, 219, 224, 225, 240–241, 251, 254, 259, 260, 281–2 (see also Nazism)
fashion (see clothes and appearance)
Faversham 149, 164, 176
Feldman, Sally 299
feminism 1, 18, 19, 103–104, 107, 138, 140, 241, 273, 329–333 (see also references to 'gender', 'sexual politics' & 'women')
Festival of Britain 312
film (including cinema) 14, 15, 104, 122, 183, 240, 244, 257, 267, 268, 270–1, 273, 281, 305, 307, 311, 327, 337
fire-watching 257, 267, 270, 274–275, 315
Fitzwater Wray, W. ('Kuklos') 124, 191–2, 199 fn190
food 41, 48, 57, 61, 132, 135, 139, 142, 143, 192, 203, 249, 254, 266–7, 268, 272–3, 278, 345 fn105
Foot, Michael 3, 4
Foreign Affairs 93, 95, 96, 221
Fortune, Antoinette 307, 332

359

France, visits to 139–140, 226–227
Frankfurt 223–4, 246–8, 249, 250, 354

G

Galsworthy, John 144, 249
gambling 18, 27, 326, 328, 339, 349 fn198
Gardener's Frenzy 202, 203, 226
gardens and gardening 9, 122, 180, 181, 183–184, 192, 202–203, 205, 225, 235 fn148, 237, 245, 265,–266–267, 305, 311, 337, 338
Gee, Capt. Robert 97, 101
gender, advocating women's rights 2, 10, 25–6, 27, 61, 63, 72, 74, 75–6, 78, 86, 87, 91, 103–4, 131, 138, 172, 217, 219, 272, 275–6, 299, 304–5, 329
gender inequalities, addressing 2, 25–6, 60, 61–2, 72, 74–7, 78, 80, 87, 103–4, 104–5, 126, 131, 134, 135, 138, 170–1, 189, 203, 207–8, 209, 210, 244, 245, 272, 279, 281, 283–4, 298–99, 300–1, 302, 308, 325, 329, 331, 338
gender relations 2, 24, 72, 74, 75, 80, 92, 103–105, 126, 131, 141, 147, 164, 181–2, 189, 245, 281
gendered analysis of socialism 26, 27, 62, 74–77, 86, 87, 92, 104, 111, 131
gendered differences to fascism and war 241, 243, 244, 254, 256, 259–60, 263
Germany 27, 59, 77, 133, 173, 204, 219, 223, 224, 226, 240, 245–6, 248, 250, 251, 252, 253, 263, 273, 274, 275, 281–2, 295 fn310
Germany, visits to 133, 223–224, 246–247, 250
General Strike 1926 144, 145, 146, 218
Gill, Ted 16, 24, 26, 36–37, 64 fn4, 173
Glasgow 23, 34, 61, 88
Glasier, John Bruce 72
Glasier, Katharine Bruce 16, 18–19, 25, 27, 61, 101, 102, 120, 121, 125, 131, 139, 140, 145, 146, 151 fn3, 155 fn120, 161–162, 163–164, 165, 167, 174, 187, 191, 203, 204, 212, 244, 303, 314, 344 fn84
Gloucester 74, 126
Glyncorrwg 184
Gollancz, Victor 227, 229, 297
Goon Show 1, 324–325, 348 fns180, 181, 183 & 349 fn184
Gould, Barbara Ayrton 240
Grayson, Victor 16
Green, John 237
Greene, Richard 270

Greenwood, Arthur 177, 192, 196 fn86, 261, 304
Grenfell, Joyce 307
Grieve, Christopher 20
Griffiths, Jim 17, 18, 30 fn57
Griffiths, Trevor 3
Guildhouse 141–2, 260

H

Hamilton, Molly 40, 65–6 fn41, 96–97, 116 fn131, 121–122, 140, 141, 175, 177, 187, 191, 237–238, 258, 269, 271, 292–3 fn238
Hampson, Walter (see 'Casey')
Hands off Russia Campaign 79, 88
Hardie, Keir 1, 17, 22, 29–30 fn56, 34, 35, 41, 52, 58, 72
Hastings 206, 219, 239, 249, 253, 256, 310, 340, 349 fn193
Hartshorn, Vernon 17, 26, 29–30 fn56
Hatherall, Lydia (see Atherall, Lydia)
Haverfordwest 9, 10
Heaven for Twopence 184, 187, 190
Henderson, Arthur 63, 78, 79, 89, 96, 146, 192
Higman, Bertram (brother-in-law) 12
Hiroshima, 297
Hodges, Frank 20, 30 fn72
Hoffman, P. C. 132, 154 fn84
Holman, May 217
Holtby, Winifred 188–190, 221, 222, 244, 331
Hookey, Annie 167, 277
Hookey, Bill 161
Horner, Arthur 53, 54, 57, 62, 68–9 fn111, 69 fn125, 90
Horrabin, Winifred 183
Howard, Ebenezer 122
Hughes, Agnes 50
Hughes, Emrys 50, 51, 84, 89, 101, 107, 108, 109
Hunter, Ernest 107
Huxley, Aldous 325

I

Illustrated London News 128
Independent Labour Party (ILP)
    Aberdare 17, 18, 29–30 fn56, 30 fn60, 71, 72, 78, 90 Blaenavon 52 Briton Ferry 64 fn20, 91, 92, 98, 99, 102, 111 fn3, 143, 178 Brynmawr 22, 38–9, 51 Cardiff 71 Merthyr 16–17, 35, 71,72, 91 Newport 21, 23, 34, 37, 40, 70 fn147 Rhondda 17, 18, 77, 90 Swansea 71 Gorton 107 Gloucester 125 Oldham 131
    North Wales 73, 92
    South Wales 16–18, 20, 21, 22, 36, 62, 68 fn105, 71, 79–80, 89–91, 111 fn2

INDEX

Wales 71–73, 89, 92, 96, 109–110, 145, 178, 302
  early development 16–17
  pre-WWI culture 18–9, 20–1
  women's involvement 18, 23–4, 72, 75, 137–8, 143, 147
  suffrage 22, 24, 25, 27, 32, 41
ILP teachers 21, 50, 101
  relations with miners 17, 100, 144–7
  national conferences 22, 34, 40, 99, 105, 132, 143, 204
  opposition to First World War 21, 33–34, 36–37, 38, 39, 40, 58, 59, 62, 64 fn4, 94
  Russian revolutions 1917 55–7, 60
  post WWI unpopularity 79–80, 84, 88, 89
  relationship with Labour Party 22, 33, 62–63, 78, 84–5, 89, 108, 121, 132, 148, 191, 204, 211, 228
  miners' lockout 1921 100
  communism 88, 89, 91, 96, 99, 110
  changing nature 121, 142
  internal tensions 121–2, 142, 178, 190
  NAC 60, 120, 132–3, 137, 143–144, 147, 148, 179
  Socialism in Our Time 142–143, 144, 146, 148
  summer schools 125, 132, 139, 146, 178, 228, 305
  General Strike and miners' lockout 1926 144–146
  criticism of 1929 Labour Government 178
  disaffiliation from Labour Party 190–1, 204, 209
  'South Wales and the ILP', BBC broadcast 302
industrial unionism 17, 23, 29–30 fn56, 84, 90, 91, 100
iron and steel 13, 71, 144, 149, 220
invasion threat, 1940 261–5, 267, 274

J
Jackson, Margaret 308
James, Edward 41
James, Godfrey 298
Jews, persecution of 20, 224, 240, 246–8, 249–50, 253, 260 (see also 'Pallister, Minnie helping Jewish refugees')
Jewson, Dorothy 129, 136, 137, 138, 139, 140, 143, 155 fn120, 136 fns120 & 133, 174
Jolly George 91
John Bull 180, 202
John O'London's Weekly 202, 277, 299, 302, 320, 333

Johnson, Francis 150, 172, 190, 199 fn178
Jones, Morgan 36, 50, 51, 56, 65 fn22, 84, 89–90, 91, 101–102, 105, 108, 109, 173
Jowett, Fred 34, 52, 69 fn123, 79, 108, 121, 129, 133, 142
Judd, Margaret 15, 24–5, 59

K
Kallin, Anna 323
Keen, R. E. 333–334
Kenfig Hill 77
Kirkwood, David 85, 88, 150
Knowles, Wyn 338–9, 340
Korean War 305, 310
'Kristallnacht' (see Jews, persecution of)
Kyle, Miss 46
'Kuklos' (see Fitzwater Wray)

L
Labour & Socialist International 139
Labour Book Service 271
Labour Leader 34–35, 61, 84, 101, 103, 104, 105, 106, 121–2, 131, 152 fn36
Labour Pacifist/Peace Fellowship 310, 319
Labour Party 16, 22, 27, 30 fn60, 33, 35, 62–63, 72, 75, 78, 80, 84–85, 86, 87, 88, 89, 90, 91, 92–108, 110, 111, 111 fn2, 121, 123, 124, 127, 129, 132, 137, 139, 140, 144, 147–148, 149–50, 156 fn131, 167, 170, 172, 173, 174, 175, 176, 177, 186, 190, 191, 201, 204, 211, 214, 220, 228, 237, 240, 242, 261, 268, 271, 278, 284, 304, 309–10, 318, 319, 335–336
Labour Representation Committee 16
'Labour Women' 87
Lady Windsor colliery lodge 76
Langdon-Davies, Bernard 123, 185, 198 fn146, 290 fn164
Lansbury, George 22, 34, 69 fn123, 100, 108, 130, 136–7, 149, 169, 173, 201, 206, 261
Lawrence, Susan 128–9, 136, 140
League of Nations 187, 211, 224
League of Nations Union 212, 213, 232 fn75, 242
Lee, Jennie 1, 151 fns3 & 10, 165, 175, 178
Leeds Convention (Council of Workers and Soldiers Delegates) 56
Leicester 93
Leslie, J. R. 132
Ley, Reg 41
Lib-Lab politics 17, 22
Lief, Stanley 188

Lindsay, Lionel, Capt, Chief Constable, 54, 58
Littlefield, Joan 104–105
Llais Llafur 26, 64 fn4, 201
Llanelli 30 fn57, 84
Llanelli Star 73
Llanthony 39, 186
Lloyd George, David 88, 89, 154 fn76, 241
Londonderry, Lady 40, 65 fn40
Lutyens, Lady 100

M

MacDiarmid, Hugh (see Grieve, Christopher)
MacDonald, Malcolm 102, 348 fn170
MacDonald, Margaret 40, 65 fn37, 102, 124
MacDonald, Ramsay
 opposition to war 33, 38–9, 52, 54, 93–94
 resignation as Labour Party chair 33
 relationship with Ivor Thomas 39, 92, 108, 186, 187–8, 227
 relationship with Minnie Pallister 5, 38–40, 43, 49, 65 fns37 & 40, 65–6 fn41, 97, 98, 120, 122, 157 fn156, 165, 166, 168–70, 176, 186–188, 198 fn146, 205, 216, 217–9, 223–4, 226, 227
 relationships with women 40, 65 fn40, 65–6 fn41, 96–7, 116 fn131, 141
 hostility over war 38, 39, 52, 62, 93, 97, 98, 99, 101
 Russian revolution 55
 Henderson and the war 78
 Aberavon 92–108, 137, 174–5, 217–8, 226
 Woolwich 96–8
 resisting ILP innovations 121–2, 142
 1924 Labour Government 129, 135
 support for Minnie Pallister 161–169, 170, 180, 184, 198 fn146, 205
 1929 Labour Government 175–6, 178, 185–6
 National Government 185–8, 198 fn153
 ostracised 186–8
 support from Minnie Pallister 186–8
 Lord President 218
 death and assessment 227
MacInnes, Colin 333
Mackenzie, Millicent 11
MacNeill Weir, L. 227

Maconachie, Sir Richard 275, 276, 277, 293 fn274
Mainwaring, W. H. 52, 54, 69 fn115, 112 fn26
Malleson, Lady Constance (Colette O'Neil) 44–6, 49, 83, 169
Malleson, Miles 49, 153 fn48
Man and Metal 220, 221, 224, 242, 248, 253, 266, 267, 272, 273, 349 fn198
Mann, Tom 54, 57, 91
marriage 11, 43, 47, 48, 49, 61, 80, 105, 127, 131, 134, 139, 140, 171, 189, 194 fn59, 207, 208, 209, 272, 300, 330, 331
marriage bar 281, 300
Marseille 139–40
Marshall, Catherine 42–5, 51, 52, 60, 107
Marston, Maurice 134
Mass Observation 241
Maxton, James 133, 143, 169, 178
McMillan, Margaret 221, 304, 311
McMillan, Rachel 221, 283
menopause 209, 299
Merthyr Tydfil 3, 13, 16, 17, 22, 24, 29–30 fn56, 35, 52, 53, 65 fn37, 70 fn147, 71, 72, 76, 77, 79, 80, 88, 91, 108, 152 fn36
Metcalfe, Jean 315–316
Methodist 9, 10, 11, 12, 14, 27, 34, 39, 78, 179, 309, 317, 326, 335 (see also chapel and religion)
Methuen 202, 226
Middleton, Jim 121, 170, 172, 175, 176
Middleton Murry, John 191, 269
Midgley, Wilson 172–173, 277, 320
Milligan, Terrence ('Spike') 1, 264–265, 323–325, 348 fn181, 349 fn184
Milne, A. A. 261, 269, 292 fn228
Miners' Federation of Great Britain 30 fn72, 105, 146, 149
Ministry of Information 258–260, 262, 269, 270, 271
Mitford, Diana 205
Montefiore, Dora 206, 230 fn27
Moral Rearmament 251, 263, 269, 327
Morel, E. D. 38, 129
Morrell, Ottoline 45, 46, 47, 48
Morris, Stuart 120, 255, 318, 322, 336, 340, 346 fn145
Morris, William 10, 36, 79
Morrison, Herbert 136, 149, 192, 278
Mort, D. L. 111 fn3, 178, 234 fn116
Mosley, Cynthia, 'Cimmie' 139, 158 fn192, 168–169, 175, 205
Mosley, Oswald 139, 146, 150, 168, 173, 205
mothers 61, 63, 70 fn150, 75, 131, 139, 155, 171, 172, 175, 180,

INDEX

207, 208, 209, 220, 253-4, 272, 278, 307, 311, 320, 329, 330, 332, 343-4 fn74
Mountain Ash 27, 62, 84
Mrs Smith of Wigan 114 fn65, 141, 228
Munich agreement 243, 248
Munnings, Sir Alfred 301
music 9, 10, 11, 14, 15, 20-21, 24, 59, 79, 107, 124, 163, 219, 229, 248-9, 250, 255, 264-5, 306, 310, 312, 324, 338, 348 fn177, 349 fn190

N

Nagasaki 297
Nantyglo 10, 12, 21, 57, 166, 215, 233 fn87
National Book League 311
National Conference of Labour Women 133, 137, 174, 240
National Council Against Conscription/National Council of Civil Liberties 36, 41, 52
National Council of Women 210, 301, 305
National Federation of Women Teachers 15, 25
National Government 186, 197 fn153
National Health Service 180, 251, 284, 297
National Union of Journalists 170
National Union of Railwaymen 88, 100
National Union of Teachers 15, 174
National Union of Women's Suffrage Societies 22
Nazism 1, 2, 204, 210, 223-224, 240, 241, 243, 246-251, 254, 259, 260, 262, 263, 264, 268, 270, 273, 281-2, 309, 318, 334 (see also fascism)
Neath 76, 78
Neighbour, Rev George 27, 60, 71, 84
Nevinson, Henry 144, 169
New Era Union 20, 30 fn69, 230 fn27
News Chronicle 202
New Leader 121-122, 125, 126, 131, 133, 135, 136, 138, 143, 147, 148, 163, 164, 165, 166, 169, 170, 176, 177, 178, 183, 185, 186, 189, 190, 191, 202, 206, 211, 216, 222, 227, 238, 294 fn266
Newport 21, 23, 34, 37, 40, 64 fn20, 70 fn147, 71
Nicholas, Rev T. E., 'Niclas y Glais' 78
Nicholson, John 130
Nicholson, Otto 130
Niemoller, Pastor 334, 335
No Conscription Fellowship 36, 37-38, 40, 41, 42-44, 50-54, 56, 58, 59, 60, 66 fn45, 67 fn88, 82, 90, 106, 107, 110, 179, 211, 240, 263, 318, 335

No More War journal 133, 211-214, 222, 225, 233 fn78, 261
No More War Movement 105-106, 120, 124, 163, 179, 199 fn171, 210, 211, 212, 214, 233 fn78, 241, 254
non-conformity (see chapel)
Nottingham 105, 136, 146-7, 279
Northcliffe, Lord 106
Now for Socialism campaign 110, 119-120, 124
nuclear weapons 297, 310, 319, 321, 335-6, 347 fn146,

O

Odham's Press 201, 219
Ogilvie, Sir Frederick 266
O'Neil, Colette (Lady Constance Malleson) 44, 46, 49, 83, 169
Onions, Alf 100-101
Open Door Council 210, 284
Orange Box: thoughts of a socialist propagandist 109, 134-135, 136, 141, 166, 331
Orwell, George 4, 19, 141, 227-229, 319
Over 30s Association 210, 239, 240, 285 fn18

P

pacifism 34, 37, 41, 57-59, 106, 179, 210-214, 224, 225, 240-242, 245, 251, 254-255, 259, 261, 262-263, 266, 269, 271, 274, 275, 283, 317-319, 325-326, 334, 335, 339, 346 fn145, 349 fn193
Pallister, Gladys (sister) 9, 11, 12, 15, 58, 69 fn125, 102, 161, 164, 172, 177, 185, 192, 204, 235 fn145, 241-2, 253, 264, 285-6 fn36, 336-337, 340
Pallister, Julia (sister) 9, 10, 11, 12, 14, 57, 300, 336-337
Pallister, Minnie 305
   childhood and schooling 9-11
   university 11
   engagement to marriage 11
   teachers and teaching 10, 11, 12, 13, 14, 15, 21, 41, 44, 50, 59, 62
   life in industrial South Wales 1, 12, 13-14
   political awakening 14, 15, 16-19
   religious faith (see Methodism, chapel and religion)
   notions of sin 18, 340 (see also, alcohol, gambling, smoking, dancing)
   insecurities 2, 3, 16, 104, 222-3, 245, 299-300, 306-7, 308, 316-7
   suffrage 24-26, 27

women's emancipation 10, 18, 25, 26
ILP Monmouthshire Federation 24, 26, 27, 41, 110
opposition to the First World War 34–35, 36, 37, 38, 41, 42, 58–9
NCF London office 42–9
independent woman 38, 48–9, 81–3, 245
NCF Wales Secretary 50–54, 60
hostility over opposition to war 38–9, 50, 52, 58, 59, 62, 88, 97, 98
Russian revolutions 1917 54–57, 60
police surveillance 1, 53–54, 58, 62
father's death 57
Wales ILP organiser 71–81, 86–7, 92
South Wales ILP Divisional Council 26, 73, 92, 96, 109–110
Aberavon agent 92–108
mentoring by Ivor Thomas 94–5, 96, 99
difficult relations with some women 85–8, 94–95, 140–1, 171–172, 221–2, 279–80
opposition to communism 96, 101, 140, 228, 229, 303, 314, 319, 346 fns126 & 145
Woolwich by-election 96–98
1922 general election 107–8
national propagandist 119–20, 127, 131, 136
Bournemouth Parliamentary candidate 106, 124–129, 130, 131, 132, 133, 135–6, 137, 147, 149
speaking prowess 20, 34–36, 73, 91, 105, 119–20, 127, 133, 141–2, 239
humour 73, 75, 105, 108, 119–120, 126–7, 179, 216, 238–9, 265, 325
ILP NAC 60, 120, 132–3, 137, 143–144, 147, 148
Labour Party NEC 148–9
General Strike & miners' lockout 145–147, 150
Faversham constituency 149, 164, 176
ill health 2, 125, 131, 145, 147, 148, 149–150, 161–169, 170, 175, 176–177, 180–181, 188, 203–4, 215–6, 218–9, 222–3, 225–226, 235 fn148, 237–9, 248, 315, 319, 320, 327, 334, 337–338, 340
support during illness 161–169, 170, 172, 177, 180, 184, 185, 190, 191, 201

lost Parliamentary career 176–7, 206, 304
mother's death 172
financial difficulties 172, 177, 185, 190, 191, 192, 201, 203–204, 314, 327
journalism 2, 4, 35, 104, 106, 130–1, 169–173, 175–6, 180, 183–4, 189, 190–2, 201–2, 206–9, 216–8, 219, 221, 248, 272, 273, 277, 336
Bexhill life (see Bexhill-on-Sea)
peace not war (see No More War, pacifism, Peace Pledge Union and *Peace News*)
broadcaster (see BBC)
helping Jewish refugees 1, 223–224, 246–248, 249
dubious links 259–260, 290 fn164
absolute pacifist 262–4, 265, 269–70
under surveillance 258–61, 270, 318, 319
on the frontline 264–5, 266–8, 282–3
the home front 253–4, 257, 264, 266–7, 278
opposing RAF bombing strategy 274, 275, 278, 293 fn254
return to public speaking 273–274
BBC rehabilitation 275
celebrity (see BBC)
pacifist agitator 282, 297–298, 309–10, 317–8, 325–6
food, relationship with 9, 14–15, 46–7, 48, 224, 228, 315, 319, 320, 333, 345 fns105 & 118
hectic lifestyle 311, 317, 320, 339
depression 161, 164, 206, 223, 306, 311, 317, 327
aging 327–328, 338
death and tributes 340
books:
Orange Box: thoughts of a socialist propagandist (1924) 109, 134–135, 136, 141, 166, 331
Rain On The Corn (1928) 165–6, 184
Heaven for Twopence (1931) 184, 187, 190
Gardener's Frenzy (1933) 202, 203, 226
Cabbage for a Year (1934) 161–162, 189, 215–216, 219, 237, 238–9
pamphlets 1924–6:
Socialism for Women 131, 147, 153 fn82, 172
Socialism, Equality and Happiness 141

INDEX

The Candle in The Pumpkin: Why Be Afraid Of Bogies? 141
Mrs Smith of Wigan 114 fn65, 141, 228
Pallister, Rev William (father) 9, 10, 12, 57, 161
Pallister, Rose (mother) 9, 12, 58, 161, 167, 172
pamphlets 114 fn65, 131, 134, 141, 147, 154 fn82, 172, 217
Pankhurst, Sylvia 41–42, 53, 54, 57, 58, 60, 116 fn124
Paris 140, 226–7
Parsons, Leonard 134
Paton, John 120, 132, 146, 148, 151 fn14
Peace News 225, 250, 260, 262, 268–9, 271, 317–8, 326, 347 fn146
Peace Pledge Union 188, 214, 225, 241–242, 250, 251, 254–255, 256, 259–262, 263, 264, 265, 268–269, 270, 271, 282, 283, 297–298, 309, 310–11, 315, 318, 322, 325, 326, 335, 336, 340, 341 fn4, 347 fns146 & 147, 348 fn166, 349 fn190
People's Weekly 170, 184
Phillips, Marion 140
Picasso 226
Pioneer 35, 71, 72, 73–4, 76–7, 78, 79, 84, 92, 96, 97, 103
pithead baths 75, 76, 112 fn20
Plummer, Leslie 185
poetry 153 fn48, 252–3, 292 fn228, 313–314
Ponsonby, Arthur 38, 55, 108, 269
Port Talbot 70 fn147, 99, 104–5, 278, 317
Porthcawl 65–6 fn41, 93, 97, 98, 101, 102, 104, 122, 215
Portsmouth South 125, 151 fn13
post-war reconstruction 256, 257, 268, 271, 274, 275, 276, 278, 281, 283–4, 295 fn309
Priestley, J. B. 268, 294 fn274

Q
Quakers (see Society of Friends)
Quigley, Janet 237–238, 239, 240, 243, 244–245, 249, 250, 252, 253, 255, 257, 265, 266, 267, 271–272, 275–7, 279–80, 281, 282–283, 284, 286 fn53, 295 fn310, 298, 303, 304–305, 312, 314, 315, 316, 318–9, 320–321, 322, 323, 327–328, 334, 338, 347 fn163

R
racism 240, 329, 339, 340
Ragg, Murray 271
Rain On The Corn 165–6, 184

Rathbone, Eleanor 61, 138, 142, 155 fn124, 254
rationing 253, 257, 264, 272–3, 278, 307, 315
rearmament 221, 241, 242, 250, 292 fn219, 310, 319, 347 fn146
refugees 247–250, 313
religion 9–10, 11, 14, 26–7, 34–35, 39, 47, 95, 163, 175–176, 182, 183, 245, 251, 274, 309, 314, 336, 338 (see also chapel and Methodism)
Reynolds, Reggie 211, 212
Rhondda 17, 18, 22, 53, 54, 62, 69 fn115, 77, 87, 90, 100, 112 fn26, 152 fn36, 174
Rhondda, Lady 171, 194–5 fn59, 221–222
Rhondda Socialist Society 53, 57, 112 fn26
Riddell, Lord 202
Robson, Flora 124, 319–20, 335, 348 fn170
Rosenberg, Rose 177, 218
Routledge and Keegan Paul 271
Rowe, Will 212, 233 fn78
Rowntree, Seebohm 10
Royal Academy 299, 301, 302
Royal Albert Hall 136, 326
Royal Antediluvian Order of Buffaloes 91
royal family 129–130, 219, 226, 340
Royden, Maude 107, 122, 141–2, 156 fn147, 260, 263, 269, 290 fn164
Russell, Alys 48
Russell, Bertrand 5, 37, 42, 43, 44, 45–49, 52, 60, 65 fn41, 66 fn68, 69 fn123, 82–83, 113 fn59, 152 fn48, 212, 227, 261, 269, 335
Russell, Dora 81–82, 140
Russia 54–57, 60, 79, 84, 85, 88–89, 91, 95–96, 101, 106, 110, 119, 137, 204, 206, 219, 228, 243, 257, 273, 274, 275, 281, 303, 309, 310, 336, 346 fn126
Russian revolutions, 1917 54–7, 60, 79, 122, 137

S
Sankey Coal Commission 30 fn60, 85
Savage, Henry 172
Save Europe Now campaign 297
Seaham Harbour constituency 174
Scarfe, Joan 323
Schwarb family 223–224, 246–248, 249–250, 302
Scott-Moncrieff, Joanna, 321, 328, 338, 340
Second International 88, 89
sexual politics 77, 80–3, 103–4, 131, 329–30, 333, 339
Sharp, Evelyn 332

Shaw, George Bernard 10, 178
shop workers 116 fn132, 132, 149, 232 fn51
shortages 41, 57, 61, 267, 273, 278
Smillie, Bob 68 fn99, 105, 136
smoking 225, 315, 326
Snowden, Ethel 41, 60, 61, 66 fn45, 68 fn 99, 120, 122
Snowden, Philip 22, 34, 41, 66 fn45, 68 fn99, 69 fn123, 78, 79, 85, 99, 108, 129, 130, 185
Spectator 180
socialism 1, 3, 16–19, 21, 22, 23, 24–7, 33, 39, 41, 42, 51, 52, 56, 57, 60, 61, 62, 63, 72–81, 85–92, 101–2, 106, 109–11, 112 fn26, 119–20, 121, 122–3, 124, 126–7, 129, 130, 131, 132, 134, 135, 137, 138, 139–40, 141, 142–3, 144, 145, 146, 147, 148, 154 fn76, 156 fn146, 163, 169, 172, 174, 176, 178, 180, 186, 189, 190–1, 192, 195 fn78, 197 fn234, 202, 217, 220, 228, 240, 242, 284, 294 fn266, 299, 308, 325, 336
    ethical 18–19, 125, 191
    gendered analysis of 26, 27, 62, 74–77, 86, 87, 92, 104, 111, 131
    male definitions of 26, 27
Socialism, Equality and Happiness 141
Socialism for Women 131, 147, 153 fn82, 172
Socialism in Our Time 142–143, 144, 145, 146, 148, 174
Socialist Labour Party 30 fn67, 90, 91
Socialist Review 143
'Socialist Women' 87, 92, 103
Society of Friends (Quakers) 131, 173, 211, 215, 323, 335
Society of Women Artists 300
Soermus, Eduard and Virginia 79, 112 fn34
soldiers and ex-servicemen 58, 59, 73, 84, 102, 103, 108, 114 fn84, 127, 135, 141, 253, 257, 262, 264, 270, 289 fn130
Soper, Donald 335
South Wales 10, 12, 13, 15, 16, 17, 18, 20, 21, 22, 23, 24, 26, 33, 35, 36, 38, 39, 42, 46, 49, 51, 52, 55, 56, 60, 61, 62, 67 fn88, 71, 72, 75, 76, 79, 80, 81, 84, 87, 89, 95, 100, 105, 111, 111fn2, 119, 145, 161,173, 215, 220, 226, 237, 312
South Wales Regional Survey Committee, Ministry of Health 76
South Wales Miners' Federation 16–17, 23, 26, 29–30 fn56, 36, 71, 84, 88, 100, 101

South Wales Socialist Society 90, 91, 112 fn26
Southampton 12, 33, 288 fn104
Spanish Civil War 223, 224–5, 226, 228, 240
spinsters 189, 207, 239–240, 324
Spring, Howard 227
Stanton, C. B. 17, 29–30 fn56, 52, 78
Stephen, Jessie 95–6, 116 fn124, 119, 120, 125, 140, 147, 151 fns3 & 13
Stevenson, W. H. (Will) 201
Strachey, Ray, 122, 170–171, 331
suffrage 22, 24–5, 27, 33, 41–2, 61, 195, 207, 222, 252
surveillance by authorities 1, 53–54, 62, 237, 238, 258–61, 265, 284 fn5, 318, 319, 346 fn140
Swansea 56, 58, 71, 85, 87, 108, 253, 311
Swansea Valley 58, 64 fn4
Swanwick, Helena 51, 52, 60, 107, 124, 140, 156 fn133, 254, 263, 290 fn164
syndication 203, 216–217, 233 fn96, 248, 327

T
Tadgell, H. R. 213
Tarrant, Shira 330, 332
Taskers school 10
teachers and teaching 10, 11, 12, 13, 14, 15, 17, 21, 25, 41, 44, 50, 59, 62, 101, 174
temperance 15, 27, 133, 225, 315, 326, 328
Temple, Ann 208, 231 fns38 & 39
Third International 88, 96, 99, 155 fn111
The Miners' Next Step 17, 29–30 fn56, 53, 69 fn115
theatre 15, 124, 179, 192, 219, 249, 268, 282, 305, 315, 327, 338–9
Thomas, Howard 299
Thomas, Ivor 36, 39, 51–52, 60, 64 fn20, 92, 94, 95, 96, 98, 99, 108, 109, 111 fn3, 164, 165, 172, 174, 177, 178, 185, 186, 187–8, 227, 242, 253, 348 fn177
Thomas, J. H. 52
Thorndike, Sybil 142, 254, 263, 269, 311, 326, 348 fn170
Tidey, Mrs 205, 323
Time and Tide 171, 221–222
tinplate workers 64 fn20, 220, 234 fn118
Tippett, Michael 282, 311, 323, 326, 335, 344 fn92
Tobias, Lily 50
Tonypandy 22, 53, 54
Townswomen's Guild 210, 297, 305, 349 fn204

366

INDEX

trades (& labour) councils 30 fn60, 38, 52, 55, 56, 71, 72, 232 fn74
Trades Union Congress 126, 137, 144–7, 167, 201, 217, 252, 271, 292–3 fn238, 309
Tredegar 3, 17, 20
Trevelyan, Charles 38, 65 fn41, 108
Triple Alliance 100
Tromans, Noah 84

U

Union of Democratic Control 36, 38, 51, 129
United Nations Association 325
United States of America 47, 188, 216, 247, 250, 302, 310
University College of South Wales & Monmouthshire 11
Unofficial Reform Committee 17, 29–30 fn56, 53, 54, 84, 112 fn26, 174
Unpublished Story, film 270–1
using the vote 78–79, 93, 97–98, 101, 105, 108, 170, 175, 207, 217, 219, 221, 252, 274

V

Vaughan, W. H. 102, 108
vegetarian 19, 27, 80, 123, 124, 192, 225, 228, 235 fn145, 316
Versailles treaty 89, 100, 129, 133, 224, 241, 259, 283

W

Wake, Egerton 99
Wales 1, 3, 5, 9, 34, 63, 72, 75, 78, 80, 92, 109, 110, 111, 124, 149, 156 fn146, 215, 217, 242
Walker, Melvina 42
Wallhead, Dick 68 fn99, 69 fn123, 85, 99, 108, 120, 121, 123, 133, 150, 152 fn36
War Resister's International 212
Ward, Mrs Humphrey 10
Wattsville 58
Webb, Beatrice 37, 283
Webb, Sidney 126, 130
Wellington, R. E. L. 318, 319
Wellock, Wilfred 179, 212
Welsh language 13, 14
Welwyn Garden City 122–124, 152 fn31, 161, 167, 168, 169, 172, 173, 175, 179, 184, 185, 188, 192, 205, 228, 300, 336, 348 fn170
Westminster by-election 130
Whatley, Monica 188, 199 fn171
Wheatley, John 129, 132, 133, 146
Wiener Library 354
Wigan 114 fn65, 141, 227–229
Wilkinson, Ellen 1, 27, 132, 136, 140–141, 142, 146, 147, 148, 149, 150, 151 fn10, 156 fn136, 169, 174, 177, 183, 254, 274, 304
Williams, David 85, 108, 111 fn3
Williams, Francis (Frank) 271
Williams, W. E. (Bill) 258, 259
Williams-Ellis, Clough 179
Wilson, Elizabeth 330, 331
Wilton, Alan 128
Winstone, James (Jim) 17, 23, 24, 26, 29–30 fn56, 52, 54, 55, 64 fn4, 68 fn106, 71, 80
women and girls, conditions of 1, 14, 17, 122–3, 61–2, 84, 103, 131, 132, 134–135, 143, 146, 147, 164, 170–1, 180, 181, 192, 203, 207, 209, 210, 220, 221, 231 fn51, 239, 242, 245, 255, 266, 272, 281, 284, 299, 300, 301 (see also 'feminism', 'gender' & 'sexual politics')
women, exclusion from South Wales labour movement 17
women's organising and organisations 3, 26, 51, 41–2, 51–2, 57, 60–1, 63, 72, 73–7, 78, 85–8, 90, 93, 95, 96–8, 101, 103–5, 108–9, 126, 134, 137, 138, 141, 143, 147, 155 fn124, 171, 206–9, 209–210, 216–217, 220, 273–4, 184, 297, 298, 301, 302, 308, 313, 317, 326, 339, 343 fn74, 345 fn105
women's rights, advocating 2, 10, 25–6, 27, 61, 63, 72, 74, 75–6, 78, 86, 87, 91, 103–4, 131, 138, 172, 217, 219, 272, 275–6, 299, 304–5, 329
women, war and peace 33, 36, 37, 40–1, 41–2, 50–1, 52, 57, 58, 60–2, 63, 72–3, 87, 93, 97–8, 107, 179, 206, 207, 217, 221, 225, 240–2, 243–4, 247, 251, 252, 254, 255, 256, 259, 260, 262, 263, 266, 269, 271, 272, 274, 275, 295 fn309, 298, 299, 305, 309, 326
and post-war reconstruction 257, 271, 272, 274, 278
Women and the New World 271, 317
Women for Westminster 210, 279, 284
Women's Co-operative Guild 17, 101, 155 fn120, 179, 190, 242, 311
Women's Freedom League 22, 24, 25, 126–127, 199 fn171, 206, 210
Women's Institute 2, 210, 273–274, 297, 305, 308, 311, 316, 322, 337
Women's International League 51–52, 107, 124, 254, 256
Women's International League for Peace and Freedom 298, 326
Women's Labour League 17, 102, 116 fn132
Women's Liberation Movement 2, 331, 332

367

women's magazines 103, 252, 276, 299, 329, 330, 331, 337
Women's Peace Campaign 256, 269
Women's Peace Crusade 61
Women's Social and Political Union 22, 116 fn124
Women's Socialist International 139–140
Women's Trades Union conference 147
Woolf, Leonard 122
Woolf, Virginia 122, 331
Woolwich by-election 96–98, 99, 101, 109, 176

Workers' Educational Association 275, 305, 311
Workers' Suffrage Federation 41, 42, 57, 60, 116 fn124
Wyatt, Honor 313

Y
Ynyshir 56, 62
Ystradgynlais 79

Z
Zinoviev 136, 141, 165

Modern Wales by Parthian Books

The Modern Wales Series, edited by Dai Smith and supported by the Rhys Davies Trust, was launched in 2017. The Series offers an extensive list of biography, memoir, history and politics which reflect and analyse the development of Wales as a modernised society into contemporary times. It engages widely across places and people, encompasses imagery and the construction of iconography, dissects historiography and recounts plain stories, all in order to elucidate the kaleidoscopic pattern which has shaped and changed the complex culture and society of Wales and the Welsh.

The inaugural titles in the Series were *To Hear the Skylark's Song*, a haunting memoir of growing up in Aberfan by Huw Lewis, and Joe England's panoramic *Merthyr: The Crucible of Modern Wales*. The impressive list has continued with Angela John's *Rocking the Boat*, essays on Welsh women who pioneered the universal fight for equality and Daryl Leeworthy's landmark overview *Labour Country*, on the struggle through radical action and social democratic politics to ground Wales in the civics of common ownership. Myths and misapprehension, whether naïve or calculated, have been ruthlessly filleted in Martin Johnes' startling *Wales: England's Colony?* and a clutch of biographical studies will reintroduce us to the once seminal, now neglected, figures of Cyril Lakin, Minnie Pallister and Gwyn Thomas, whilst Meic Stehens' *Rhys Davies: A Writer's Life* and Dai *Smith's Raymond Williams: A Warrior's Tale* form part of an associated back catalogue from Parthian.

the RHYS DAVIES TRUST

PARTHIAN

MODERN WALES

WALES: ENGLAND'S COLONY?

Martin Johnes

From the very beginnings of Wales, its people have defined themselves against their large neighbour. This book tells the fascinating story of an uneasy and unequal relationship between two nations living side-by-side.

PB / £8.99
978-1-912681-41-9

RHYS DAVIES: A WRITER'S LIFE

Meic Stephens

Rhys Davies (1901-78) was among the most dedicated, prolific and accomplished of Welsh prose writers. This is his first full biography.

'This is a delightful book, which is itself a social history in its own right, and funny.'
– The Spectator

PB / £11.99
978-1-912109-96-8

MERTHYR, THE CRUCIBLE OF MODERN WALES

Joe England

Merthyr Tydfil was the town where the future of a country was forged: a thriving, struggling surge of people, industry, democracy and ideas. This book assesses an epic history of Merthyr from 1760 to 1912 through the focus of a fresh and thoroughly convincing perspective.

PB / £18.99
978-1-913640-05-7

TO HEAR THE SKYLARK'S SONG
Huw Lewis

To Hear the Skylark's Song is a memoir about how Aberfan survived and eventually thrived after the terrible disaster of the 21st of October 1966.

'A thoughtful and passionate memoir, moving and respectful.'
– Tessa Hadley

PB / £8.99
978-1-912109-72-2

ROCKING THE BOAT
Angela V. John

This insightful and revealing collection of essays focuses on seven Welsh women who, in a range of imaginative ways, resisted the status quo in Wales, England and beyond during the nineteenth and twentieth centuries.

PB / £11.99
978-1-912681-44-0

TURNING THE TIDE
Angela V. John

This rich biography tells the remarkable tale of Margaret Haig Thomas (1883-1958) who became the second Viscountess Rhondda. She was a Welsh suffragette, held important posts during the First World War and survived the sinking of the *Lusitania*.

PB / £17.99
978-1-909844-72-8

BRENDA CHAMBERLAIN, ARTIST & WRITER
Jill Piercy

The first full-length biography of Brenda Chamberlain chronicles the life of an artist and writer whose work was strongly affected by the places she lived, most famously Bardsey Island and the Greek island of Hydra.

PB / £11.99
978-1-912681-06-8

PARTHIAN

MODERN WALES

SMOOTH OPERATOR
Geoff Andrews

Cyril Lakin was the epitome of a smooth operator. From a humble background in Barry, Cyril Lakin studied at Oxford, survived the first world war, and went on to become a Fleet Street editor, radio presenter and war-time member of parliament. As literary editor of both the *Daily Telegraph* and the *Sunday Times*, Lakin was at the centre of a vibrant and radical generation of writers, poets and critics.

Geoff Andrews brings a fresh perspective to the life and times of a fascinating man who was involved in the national story at a time of great change for the United Kingdom and Wales.

HB / £20
978-1-913640-18-7

BETWEEN WORLDS: A QUEER BOY FROM THE VALLEYS
Jeffrey Weeks

A man's own story from the Rhondda. Jeffrey Weeks was born in the Rhondda in 1945, of mining stock. As he grew up he increasingly felt an outsider in the intensely community-minded valleys, a feeling intensified as he became aware of his gayness. Escape came through education. He left for London, to university, and to realise his sexuality. He has been described as the 'most significant British intellectual working on sexuality to emerge from the radical sexual movements of the 1970s'.

HB / £20
978-1-912681-88-4